WOMEN KNOW EVERYTHING!

3,241 Quips, Quotes, & Brilliant Remarks

by Karen Weekes

QUIRK BOOKS
PHILADELPHIA

Library of Congress Cataloging in Publication Number: 2010935935

ISBN 978-1-59474-506-5

Printed in China

Typeset in Bulmer

Cover designed by Jenny Kraemer
Interior designed by Bryn Ashburn
Cover photo by Superstock/Everett Collection
Production management by John J. McGurk

10 9 8 7 6 5 4 3

Quirk Books
215 Church Street
Philadelphia, PA 19106
www.quirkbooks.com

FOR
BARB MORTIMER
1960–2006

My much-loved and much-missed friend

INTRODUCTION

My time spent working on this project has been incredibly enjoyable because of the company I've kept: days spent with Dorothy Parker, Jeanette Winterson, Margaret Atwood, Maya Angelou, and Katharine Hepburn. Each evening I would find myself newly inspired by their wisdom and wit.

Even better, though, was the discovery of women whose accomplishments I'd heard little to nothing of, despite my background in, and years of teaching, women's studies. Hedy Lamarr's invention of "frequency hopping" (a key element in wireless communication technology), Grace Murray Hopper's revolutionizing of computer programming, Wangari Maathai's Nobel Peace Prize for her environmental sustainability work in Kenya, and Aung San Suu Kyi's undaunted nonviolent resistance and wrongful imprisonment made me proud to be a woman and determined that this book would give voices not only to literary and entertainment figures but to activists, politicians, and aviators; athletes, educators, and scientists.

So it is my hope that this entire book will be a true "introduction" for its readers—that you will be intrigued by these women, will seek out more of their writings and learn more about their lives, will appreciate the brains accompanying beauty, and will have many laughs and new insights along the way. In short, that you will enjoy reading and quoting from this book as much as I have enjoyed compiling it.

Many thanks to my editor at Quirk Books, Jason Rekulak, for his patience and good humor, and kudos to Bryn Ashburn for all of her work on the book's design. Also thanks to Danielle Fitzpatrick and Joe Benhabib for their assistance, and to all my friends and family for not gagging me after I said, "That reminds me of a great quote. . . ." for the millionth time. But mostly thanks go to all the wise, wonderful women whose words appear here: Thank you not just for thinking them, but for saying them, writing them, sharing them, and for inspiring new generations of women to do the same.

A

"ABILITY"

I have learnt that I am me, that I can do the things that, as one might put it, me can do, but I cannot do the things that me would like to do.

–AGATHA CHRISTIE (1890–1976) • ENGLISH MYSTERY WRITER

Everyone has inside of him a piece of good news. The good news is that you don't know how great you can be! How much you can love! What you can accomplish! And what your potential is!

–ANNE FRANK (1929–1945) • GERMAN-JEWISH DIARIST

Whatever women do they must do twice as well as men to be thought half as good. Luckily, this is not difficult.

–CHARLOTTE WHITTON (1896–1975) • CANADIAN POLITICIAN AND JOURNALIST

Ability is sexless.

–CHRISTABEL PANKHURST (1880–1958)
ENGLISH SUFFRAGETTE

Because I am a woman, I must make unusual efforts to succeed. If I fail, no one will say, "She doesn't have what it takes." They will say, "Women don't have what it takes."

–CLARE BOOTHE LUCE (1903–1987) • AMERICAN PLAYWRIGHT, JOURNALIST, AND POLITICIAN

It is not my ability, but my response to God's ability, that counts.

–CORRIE TEN BOOM (1892–1983) • DUTCH EVANGELIST AND HOLOCAUST SURVIVOR

Just watch, all of you men. I'll show you what a woman can do. . . . I'll go across the country, I'll race to the Moon. . . . I'll never look back.

–EDNA GARDNER WHYTE (1902–1991)
PIONEERING AMERICAN AIR RACER, FLIGHT INSTRUCTOR, AND ENTREPRENEUR

Every person is responsible for all the good within the scope of his abilities, and for no more, and none can tell whose sphere is the largest.

–GAIL HAMILTON (MARY ABIGAIL DODGE) (1833-1896)
AMERICAN WRITER AND HUMORIST

•

Ability hits the mark where presumption overshoots and diffidence falls short.

–GOLDA MEIR (1898-1978)
RUSSIAN-BORN FIRST FEMALE PRIME MINISTER OF ISRAEL

•

I seldom think about my limitations, and they never make me sad. Perhaps there is just a touch of yearning at times; but it is vague, like a breeze among flowers.

–HELEN KELLER (1880-1968) • AMERICAN WRITER AND ACTIVIST

•

A sobering thought: What if, at this very moment, I am living up to my full potential?

–JANE WAGNER (1935-)
AMERICAN PLAYWRIGHT AND COMEDY WRITER

•

I know I have the ability to do so much more than just stand in front of the camera the rest of my life.

–JENNIE GARTH (1972-) • AMERICAN ACTOR

•

When I see the elaborate study and ingenuity displayed by women in the pursuit of trifles, I feel no doubt of their capacity for the most Herculean undertakings.

–JULIA WARD HOWE (1819-1910) • AMERICAN POET AND PHILANTHROPIST

•

Ability is of little account without opportunity.

–LUCILLE BALL (1911-1989) • AMERICAN COMIC ACTOR

Knowing what you cannot do is more important than knowing what you can do. In fact, that's good taste.

–LUCILLE BALL (1911–1989) • AMERICAN COMIC ACTOR

You have to have confidence in your ability, and then be tough enough to follow through.

–ROSALYNN CARTER (1927–) • FIRST LADY OF THE UNITED STATES

"ABORTION"

See Reproductive Rights

"ACTING"

Acting is not about dressing up. Acting is about stripping bare. The whole essence of learning lines is to forget them so you can make them sound like you thought of them that instant.

–GLENDA JACKSON (1936–) • ENGLISH ACTOR AND POLITICIAN

It's amazing. All you have to do is to look like crap on film and everyone thinks you're a brilliant actress.

–HELEN MIRREN (1945–) • ENGLISH STAGE, TELEVISION, AND MOVIE ACTOR

It is not whether you really cry. It's whether the audience thinks you are crying.

–INGRID BERGMAN (1915–1982) • SWEDISH ACTOR

My husband was actually very keen that I would become a Bond girl.

–JUDI DENCH (1934–) • ENGLISH STAGE AND FILM ACTOR

I was born at the age of 12 on an MGM lot.

–JUDY GARLAND (1922–1969) • AMERICAN ACTOR AND SINGER

Acting is the most minor of gifts. After all, Shirley Temple could do it when she was four.

—KATHARINE HEPBURN (1907–2003) • AMERICAN ACTOR

•

Hollywood is a place where they'll pay you a thousand dollars for a kiss and fifty cents for your soul.

—MARILYN MONROE (1926–1962) • AMERICAN ACTOR AND SEX SYMBOL

•

People find out I'm an actress and I see that "whore" look flicker across their eyes.

—RACHEL WEISZ (1971–) • ENGLISH ACTOR

•

There are two kinds of directors in the theater. Those who think they are God and those who are certain of it.

—RHETTA HUGHES • 20TH/21ST-CENTURY AMERICAN R&B SINGER AND ACTOR

•

"*ACTION*"

•

The most effective way to do it, is to do it.

—AMELIA EARHART (1897–1937)
PIONEERING AMERICAN AVIATOR; FIRST PERSON TO FLY SOLO ACROSS PACIFIC

•

Now I say that with cruelty and oppression it is everybody's business to interfere when they see it.

—ANNA SEWELL (1820–1878) • ENGLISH WRITER

•

How wonderful it is that nobody need wait a single moment before starting to improve the world.

—ANNE FRANK (1929–1945)
GERMAN-JEWISH DIARIST

It is vain to say human beings ought to be satisfied with tranquillity: They must have action; and they will make it if they cannot find it.

–CHARLOTTE BRONTË (1816-1855) • ENGLISH WRITER

In a world where there is so much to be done, I felt strongly impressed that there must be something for me to do.

–DOROTHEA DIX (1802-1887)
AMERICAN SOCIAL REFORMER AND MENTAL HEALTH ACTIVIST

Just put on your makeup and get out there and do it.

–EMMA BUNTON (1976-) • ENGLISH SINGER

You cannot contribute anything to the ideal condition of mind and heart known as Brotherhood, however much you preach, posture, or agree, unless you live it.

–FAITH BALDWIN (1893-1978) • AMERICAN WRITER

The biggest sin is sitting on your ass.

–FLORYNCE KENNEDY (1916-2000)
AFRICAN-AMERICAN LAWYER AND ACTIVIST

I am only one, but still I am one. I cannot do everything, but still I can do something. I will not refuse to do the something I can do.

–HELEN KELLER (1880-1968) • AMERICAN WRITER AND ACTIVIST

The important thing is that when you come to understand something you act on it, no matter how small that act is. Eventually it will take you where you need to go.

–SISTER HELEN PREJEAN (1939-)
AMERICAN ROMAN CATHOLIC NUN AND ACTIVIST

It is difficult to steer a parked car, so get moving.

–HENRIETTA MEARS (1890–1963) • AMERICAN BIBLE TEACHER

•

Action is the antidote to despair.

–JOAN BAEZ (1941–)
AMERICAN FOLK SINGER AND ACTIVIST

•

I believe that worrying about the problems plaguing our planet without taking steps to confront them is absolutely irrelevant. The only thing that changes this world is taking action.

–JODY WILLIAMS (1950–)
AMERICAN NOBEL PEACE PRIZE RECIPIENT AND ACTIVIST

•

Opportunity is like a hair on a bald-headed man; it only comes around once and you have to grab it while it's there.

–JOYCELYN ELDERS (1933–) • FIRST AFRICAN-AMERICAN U.S. SURGEON GENERAL

•

Just trying to do something—just being there, showing up—is how we get braver. Self-esteem is about doing.

–JOY BROWNE • 20TH/21ST-CENTURY AMERICAN RADIO PSYCHOLOGIST

•

If you talk enough, you don't feel you have to do anything.

–LINDA GRACE UPDIKE
20TH-CENTURY AMERICAN, MOTHER OF WRITER JOHN UPDIKE

•

You can't build a reputation on what you intend to do.

–LIZ SMITH (1923–) • AMERICAN GOSSIP COLUMNIST

•

It's more important to know where you are going than to get there quickly. Do not mistake activity for achievement.

–MABEL NEWCOMER • 20TH-CENTURY AMERICAN ECONOMIST

There is a vitality, a life force, an energy, a quickening, that is translated through you into action, and because there is only one of you in all time, this expression is unique. And if you block it, it will never exist through any other medium and will be lost.

–MARTHA GRAHAM (1894–1991) • AMERICAN DANCER AND CHOREOGRAPHER

•

Never retract, never explain, never apologize—
get the thing done and let them howl.

–NELLIE MCCLUNG (1873–1951)
CANADIAN JOURNALIST AND SUFFRAGIST

•

Our work as citizens is a lot like housework: It never ends. We can either wring our hands in despair or use them to roll up our shirtsleeves and try to find new ways to make a difference.

–PAT SCHROEDER (1940–) • AMERICAN POLITICIAN

•

Those who do not move do not notice their chains.

–ROSA LUXEMBURG (1870–1919)
GERMAN MARXIST POLITICAL THEORIST AND REVOLUTIONARY

•

When people made up their minds that they wanted to be free and took action, then there was a change.

–ROSA PARKS (1913–2005) • AFRICAN-AMERICAN CIVIL RIGHTS ACTIVIST

•

It is a common delusion that you can make
things better by talking about them.

–ROSE MACAULAY (1881–1958)
ENGLISH NOVELIST AND ESSAYIST

•

The secret of getting ahead is getting started.

–SALLY BERGER
20TH/21ST-CENTURY AMERICAN VIDEO, FILM, AND NEW MEDIA CURATOR

Don't even make a list. Do everything right now.

–SIGOURNEY WEAVER (1949–) • AMERICAN ACTOR

•

Sisters, I a'n't clear what you'd be after. Ef women want any rights more'n dey's got, why don't dey jes take 'em, an' not be talkin' about it?

–SOJOURNER TRUTH (1797–1883) • AFRICAN-AMERICAN ABOLITIONIST

•

Do not wait for leaders; do it alone, person to person.

–MOTHER TERESA (1910–1997)
ALBANIAN CATHOLIC NUN; WINNER OF NOBEL PEACE PRIZE

•

"ACTIVISM"

•

Activism is my rent for living on this planet.

–ALICE WALKER (1944–)
AFRICAN-AMERICAN WRITER AND POET

•

We all participate in weaving the social fabric; we should therefore all participate in patching the fabric when it develops holes.

–ANNE C. WEISBERG • 20TH/21ST-CENTURY AMERICAN ATTORNEY

•

It takes six simpletons and one zealot to start a movement.

–ANZIA YEZIERSKA (1881–1970) • POLISH-AMERICAN WRITER

•

We have to support our small heroes. (Of these we have many. Many.) We have to fight specific wars in specific ways. Who knows, perhaps that's what the twenty-first century has in store for us. The dismantling of the Big. Big bombs, big dams, big ideologies, big heroes, big mistakes. Perhaps it will be the century of the small.

–ARUNDHATI ROY (1961–) • INDIAN WRITER AND ACTIVIST

[America] is the greatest country under the sun but we must not let our love of country, our patriotic loyalty, cause us to abate one whit in our protest against wrong and injustice.

—MADAME C. J. WALKER (1867–1919)
AFRICAN-AMERICAN ENTREPRENEUR AND PHILANTHROPIST

•

The belief that we are defending the highest good of the mothers of our race and the ultimate welfare of society makes every sacrifice seem trivial, every duty a pleasure. The pressing need spurs us on, the certainty of victory gives us daily inspiration.

—CARRIE CHAPMAN CATT (1859–1947) • AMERICAN SUFFRAGIST AND JOURNALIST

•

Individual advances turn into social change when enough of them happen.

—ELIZABETH JANEWAY (1913–2005)
AMERICAN WRITER AND CRITIC

•

The struggle is eternal. The tribe increases. Somebody else carries on.

—ELLA J. BAKER (1903–1986) • AFRICAN-AMERICAN CIVIL RIGHTS ACTIVIST

•

I have never been especially impressed by the heroics of people who are convinced they are about to change the world. I am more awed by those who struggle to make one small difference after another.

—ELLEN GOODMAN (1941–) • AMERICAN JOURNALIST

•

One cannot be too extreme in dealing with social ills; the extreme thing is generally the true thing.

—EMMA GOLDMAN (1869–1940) • RUSSIAN ANARCHIST AND FEMINIST

You have to make more noise than anybody else, you have to make yourself more obtrusive than anybody else, you have to fill all the papers more than anybody else, in fact you have to be there all the time and see that they do not snow you under, if you are really going to get your reform realized.

–EMMELINE PANKHURST (1858–1928) • ENGLISH SUFFRAGIST AND FEMINIST

•

The demonstrations are always early in the morning, at six o'clock. It's wonderful, because I'm not doing anything at six anyway, so why not demonstrate? . . . When you've written to your president, to your congressman, to your senator, and nothing, nothing has come of it, you take to the streets.

–ERICA BOUZA • 20TH/21ST-CENTURY AMERICAN PACIFIST

•

There is one thing you have got to learn about our movement. Three people are better than no people.

–FANNIE LOU HAMER (1917–1977) • AFRICAN-AMERICAN CIVIL RIGHTS ACTIVIST

•

Don't agonize, organize.

–FLORYNCE KENNEDY (1916–2000)
AFRICAN-AMERICAN LAWYER AND ACTIVIST

•

Ours is the old, old story of every uprising race or class or order. The work of elevation must be wrought by ourselves or not at all.

–FRANCES POWER COBBE (1822–1904)
ENGLISH RELIGIOUS PHILOSOPHER AND SOCIAL ACTIVIST

•

Under conditions of tyranny it is far easier to act than to think.

–HANNAH ARENDT (1906–1975)
GERMAN-BORN POLITICAL PHILOSOPHER AND HISTORIAN

•

I never ran my train off the track, and I never lost a passenger.

–HARRIET TUBMAN (1820–1913) • AFRICAN-AMERICAN ABOLITIONIST

I believe that words are easy. I believe the truth is told in the actions we take. And I believe that if enough ordinary people back up our desire for a better world with action, I believe we can, in fact, accomplish absolutely extraordinary things.

–JODY WILLIAMS (1950–)
AMERICAN NOBEL PEACE PRIZE RECIPIENT AND ACTIVIST

•

The question is not "can you make a difference?" You already do make a difference. It's just a matter of what kind of difference you want to make, during your life on this planet.

–JULIA BUTTERFLY HILL (1974–) • AMERICAN ENVIRONMENTAL ACTIVIST

•

Around the time my mother taught me how to tie my shoes, she also taught me how to protest. Her rules were simple: Look respectable, act respectable, and don't give the opposition any ammunition. Together we buttoned those top buttons and combed our hair for peace, civil rights, the ERA. You name it, we marched for it. In sensible shoes.

–JULIA KING • 20TH/21ST-CENTURY AMERICAN RADIO COMMENTATOR AND ACTIVIST

•

A disturber of the peace, am I? Yes indeed, of my own peace. Do you call this disturbing the peace? . . . Instead of spending my time in frivolous amusements, I have visited the plague-infested and carried out the dead.

–KATHERINE ZELL (CA. 1497–1562) • GERMAN HYMNIST, REFORMER, AND WRITER

•

If we can't turn the world around we can at least bolster the victims.

–LIZ CARPENTER (1920–) • AMERICAN WRITER AND FEMINIST

•

Never doubt that a small number of dedicated people can change the world; indeed it is the only thing that ever has.

–MARGARET MEAD (1901–1978) • AMERICAN CULTURAL ANTHROPOLOGIST

All of us [are] driven by a simple belief that the world as it is just won't do—that we have an obligation to fight for the world as it should be.

–MICHELLE OBAMA (1964-)
AFRICAN-AMERICAN FIRST LADY OF THE UNITED STATES

•

My address is like my shoes. It travels with me.
I abide where there is a fight against wrong.

–MOTHER JONES (1837-1930)
AMERICAN LABOR AND COMMUNITY ORGANIZER AND ACTIVIST

•

I cannot say to a person who suffers injustice, "Wait." Perhaps you can. I can't. And having decided that I cannot urge caution, I must stand with him.

–SANDRA "CASEY" CASON (1939-) • AMERICAN POLITICAL ACTIVIST

•

A single decision by the chairman of Royal Dutch/Shell has a greater impact on the health of the planet than all the coffee-ground-composting, organic-cotton-wearing ecofreaks gathering in Washington, D.C., for Earth Day festivities this weekend.

–SHARON BEGLEY • 20TH/21ST-CENTURY AMERICAN SCIENCE JOURNALIST AND EDITOR

•

The beauty of life is to fight in a difficult situation.

–SHIRIN EBADI (1947-)
IRANIAN LAWYER AND HUMAN RIGHTS ACTIVIST; FIRST FEMALE MUSLIM WINNER OF THE NOBEL PEACE PRIZE

•

And no doubt it is more comfortable to submit to a bland enslavement than to work for liberation: The dead, for that matter, are better adapted to the earth than are the living.

–SIMONE DE BEAUVOIR (1908-1986) • FRENCH WRITER AND PHILOSOPHER

•

"Organize, agitate, educate," must be our war cry.

–SUSAN B. ANTHONY (1820-1906)
AMERICAN SUFFRAGIST AND NEWSPAPER PUBLISHER

What we have is because someone stood up before. What our seventh generation will have is a consequence of our actions today.

–WINONA LADUKE (1959–) • NATIVE AMERICAN ACTIVIST, ENVIRONMENTALIST, AND WRITER

UNITY IN

During my years of being close to people engaged in changing the world, I have seen fear turn into courage. Sorrow into joy. Funerals into celebrations. Because whatever the consequences, people, standing side by side, have expressed who they really are, and that ultimately they believe in the love of the world and each other enough to be that.

–ALICE WALKER (1944–) • AFRICAN-AMERICAN WRITER AND POET

I know we're termites. But if all the termites got together, the house would fall down.

–FLORYNCE KENNEDY (1916–2000)
AFRICAN-AMERICAN LAWYER AND ACTIVIST

Divide and conquer—that's what they try to do to any group trying to make social change. I call it D&C. Black people are supposed to turn against Puerto Ricans. Women are supposed to turn against their mothers and mothers-in-law. We're all supposed to compete with each other for the favors of the ruling class.

–FLORYNCE KENNEDY (1916–2000) • AFRICAN-AMERICAN LAWYER AND ACTIVIST

A movement is only composed of people moving. To feel its warmth and motion around us is the end as well as the means.

–GLORIA STEINEM (1934–) • AMERICAN FEMINIST, COFOUNDER OF *MS.* MAGAZINE

So often we think we have got to make a difference and be a big dog. Let us just try to be little fleas biting. Enough fleas biting strategically can make a very big dog very uncomfortable.

–MARIAN WRIGHT EDELMAN (1939–)
AFRICAN-AMERICAN FOUNDER OF THE CHILDREN'S DEFENSE FUND

"ADULTERY"

It is better to be unfaithful than to be faithful without wanting to be.

–BRIGITTE BARDOT (1934–) • FRENCH ACTOR AND ANIMAL RIGHTS ACTIVIST

I don't sleep with happily married men.

–BRITT EKLAND (1942–) • SWEDISH ACTOR

Infidelity—cheating—is the easiest, stupidest, dumbest thing you can do.

–JOY BROWNE • 20TH/21ST-CENTURY AMERICAN RADIO PSYCHOLOGIST

When you were six you thought *mistress* meant to put your shoes on the wrong feet. Now you are older and know it can mean many things, but essentially it means to put your shoes on the wrong feet.

–LORRIE MOORE (1957–) • AMERICAN WRITER

How many husbands have I had? You mean apart from my own?

–ZSA ZSA GABOR (1917–) • HUNGARIAN-AMERICAN ACTOR AND SOCIALITE

"ADVERTISING"

There are no models, in the mainstream media, suggesting that anything less than middle-class affluence might be an honorable and dignified condition, nor is there any reason why corporate advertisers should promote such a subversive possibility.

–BARBARA EHRENREICH (1941–) • AMERICAN ESSAYIST AND SOCIAL CRITIC

In general my children refuse to eat anything that hasn't danced on television.

–ERMA BOMBECK (1927–1996) • AMERICAN HUMORIST

Most women's magazines simply try to mold women into bigger and better consumers.

–GLORIA STEINEM (1934–)
AMERICAN FEMINIST AND COFOUNDER OF *MS.* MAGAZINE

•

[Advertising] legitimizes the idealized, stereotyped roles of woman as temptress, wife, mother, and sex object, and portrays women as less intelligent and more dependent than men. . . . It makes women believe that their own lives, talents, and interests ought to be secondary to the needs of their husbands and families, and that they are almost totally defined by these relationships.

–LUCY KOMISAR (1942–) • AMERICAN JOURNALIST

•

"ADVICE"

•

Advice is what we ask for when we already know the answer but wish we didn't.

–ERICA JONG (1942–) • AMERICAN WRITER

•

Never ask anyone if you should do something, if ultimately you are afraid to do it. You'll save yourself a lot of trouble.

–LAURA SCHLESSINGER (1947–) • AMERICAN CULTURAL COMMENTATOR

•

As time passes we all get better at blazing a trail through the thicket of advice.

–MARGOT BENNETT (1912–1980) • SCOTTISH-BORN WRITER

•

GIVING OF

I, who fall short in managing my own affairs, can see just how it would profit my neighbor if I managed his.

–ANNE ELLIS (1875–1938) • AMERICAN PIONEER

The true secret of giving advice is, after you have honestly given it, to be perfectly indifferent whether it is taken or not, and never persist in trying to set people right.

–HANNAH WHITALL SMITH (1832–1911)
AMERICAN EVANGELIST, WRITER, AND REFORMER,
COFOUNDER OF THE WOMAN'S CHRISTIAN TEMPERANCE UNION

•

As long as any adult thinks that he, like the parents and teachers of old, can become introspective, invoking his own youth to understand the youth before him, he is lost.

–MARGARET MEAD (1901–1978) • AMERICAN CULTURAL ANTHROPOLOGIST

•

"*AGE*"

See also Youth

•

I've always believed in the adage that the secret of eternal youth is arrested development.

–ALICE ROOSEVELT LONGWORTH (1884–1980)
AMERICAN; DAUGHTER OF PRESIDENT THEODORE ROOSEVELT

•

A woman may develop wrinkles and cellulite, lose her waistline, her bustline, her ability to bear a child, even her sense of humor, but none of that implies a loss of her sexuality, her femininity.

–BARBARA GORDON (1935–) • AMERICAN PRODUCER

•

It is sad to grow old but nice to ripen.

–BRIGITTE BARDOT (1934–)
FRENCH ACTOR AND ANIMAL RIGHTS ACTIVIST

The years that a woman subtracts from her age are not lost. They are added to other women's.

–DIANE DE POITIERS (1499-1566) • FRENCH COURTESAN

•

In the last 100 years, the average age of a Nobel Prize winner is 65 years old. Why should they deny us the ability to flourish and accomplish things because we're older people?

–DORIS ROBERTS (1930-) • AMERICAN ACTOR

•

I'm not interested in age. People who tell me their age are silly. You're as old as you feel.

–ELIZABETH ARDEN (1878-1966)
CANADIAN-BORN COSMETICS ENTREPRENEUR

•

A woman's always younger than a man at equal years.

–ELIZABETH BARRETT BROWNING (1806-1861) • ENGLISH POET

•

There is a certain age when a woman must be beautiful to be loved, and then there comes a time when she must be loved to be beautiful.

–FRANÇOISE SAGAN (1935-2004) • FRENCH NOVELIST AND PLAYWRIGHT

•

Nature gives you the face you have at 20; it is up to you to merit the face you have at 50.

–GABRIELLE "COCO" CHANEL (1883-1971)
FRENCH FASHION DESIGNER

•

We are always the same age inside.

–GERTRUDE STEIN (1874-1946) • AMERICAN POET

Women grow radical with age. One day an army of gray-haired women may quietly take over the earth.

–GLORIA STEINEM (1934-)
AMERICAN FEMINIST AND COFOUNDER OF *MS.* MAGAZINE

•

Old age is like a plane flying through a storm. Once you're aboard, there's nothing you can do.

–GOLDA MEIR (1898-1978) • RUSSIAN-BORN FIRST FEMALE PRIME MINISTER OF ISRAEL

•

The hardest years in life are those between 10 and 70. [Said at age 73]

–HELEN HAYES (1900-1993) • AMERICAN ACTOR

•

Age does not protect you from love. But love, to some extent, protects you from age.

–JEANNE MOREAU (1928-) • FRENCH ACTOR

•

Aging gracefully is supposed to mean trying not to hide time passing and just looking a wreck. Don't worry girls, look like a wreck, that's the way it goes.

–JEANNE MOREAU (1928-) • FRENCH ACTOR

•

The three ages of man: youth, middle age, and "my word you do look well."

–JUNE WHITFIELD (1925-) • ENGLISH COMEDIC ACTOR

•

Sure, I'm for helping the elderly. I'm going to be old myself someday. [Said at age 85]

–LILLIAN CARTER (1898-1983) • AMERICAN, MOTHER OF U.S. PRESIDENT JIMMY CARTER

•

The age I'm at now, you go from being a young girl to suddenly you blossom into a woman. You ripen, you know? And then you start to rot.

–LIV TYLER (1977-) • AMERICAN ACTOR

Being 65 . . . became a crossroads. We said we have nothing to lose, so we can raise hell.

–MAGGIE KUHN (1905–1995)
AMERICAN ACTIVIST AND FOUNDER OF THE GRAY PANTHERS

•

There are no old people nowadays; they are either "wonderful for their age" or dead.

–MARY PETTIBONE POOLE • 20TH-CENTURY AMERICAN WRITER

•

I don't know how you feel about old age, but in my case I didn't even see it coming. It hit me in the rear.

–PHYLLIS DILLER (1917–) • AMERICAN COMEDIAN

•

You know you're old if they have discontinued your blood type.

–PHYLLIS DILLER (1917–) • AMERICAN COMEDIAN

•

I will age ungracefully until I become an old woman in a small garden, doing whatever the hell I want.

–ROBIN CHOTZINOFF • 20TH/21ST-CENTURY AMERICAN WRITER

•

When you are 50, you're neither young nor old; you're just uninteresting. When you are 60, and still dancing, you become something of a curiosity. And boy! If you hit 70, and can still get a foot off the ground, you're phenomenal!

–RUTH ST. DENIS (1879–1968) • AMERICAN MODERN DANCE PIONEER

•

As long as you can see each day as a chance for something new to happen, something you never experienced before, you will stay young.

–SADIE DELANY (1889–1999) • AFRICAN-AMERICAN EDUCATOR AND MEMOIRIST

•

In our dreams, we are always young.

–SADIE DELANY (1889–1999)
AFRICAN-AMERICAN EDUCATOR AND MEMOIRIST

From birth to age 18, a girl needs good parents. From 18 to 35, she needs good looks. From 35 to 55 she needs a good personality. And from 55 on, she needs cash.

–SOPHIE TUCKER (1884-1966) • RUSSIAN-BORN SINGER AND COMEDIAN

ACTING

You know, my hair is very upsetting to people, but it's upsetting on purpose. It is important to look old so that the young will not be afraid of dying. People don't like old women. We don't honor age in our society, and we certainly don't honor it in Hollywood.

–TYNE DALY (1946-) • AMERICAN STAGE AND SCREEN ACTOR

You know, when I first went into the movies Lionel Barrymore played my grandfather. Later he played my father, and finally he played my husband. If he had lived I'm sure I would have played his mother. That's the way it is in Hollywood. The men get younger and the women get older.

–LILLIAN GISH (1893-1993) • AMERICAN ACTOR

There are only three ages for women in Hollywood—Babe, District Attorney, and Driving Miss Daisy.

–GOLDIE HAWN (1945-) • AMERICAN ACTOR

No amount of skill on the part of the actress can make up for the loss of youth.

–ELLEN TERRY (1847-1928) • ENGLISH STAGE ACTOR

DEFEATING

The secret to staying young is to live honestly, eat slowly, and lie about your age.

–LUCILLE BALL (1911-1989) • AMERICAN COMIC ACTOR

There is a fountain of youth: It is your mind, your talents, the creativity you bring to your life and the lives of the people you love. When you learn to tap this source, you will truly have defeated age.

–SOPHIA LOREN (1934–) • ITALIAN ACTOR

MIDDLE AGE

She was a handsome woman of 45 and would remain so for many years.

–ANITA BROOKNER (1928–) • ENGLISH WRITER AND ART HISTORIAN

After 40, a woman has to choose between losing her figure or her face. My advice is to keep your face, and stay sitting down.

–BARBARA CARTLAND (1901–2000) • ENGLISH WRITER

The really frightening thing about middle age is the knowledge that you'll grow out of it.

–DORIS DAY (1924–)
AMERICAN SINGER, ACTOR, AND ANIMAL RIGHTS ACTIVIST

And then, not expecting it, you become middle-aged and anonymous. No one notices you. You achieve a wonderful freedom.

–DORIS LESSING (1919–) • ENGLISH WRITER

One of the many things nobody ever tells you about middle age is that it's such a nice change from being young.

–DOROTHY CANFIELD FISHER (1879–1958)
AMERICAN EDUCATIONAL REFORMER, SOCIAL ACTIVIST, AND WRITER

This is what 40 looks like. We've been lying so long, who would know?

–GLORIA STEINEM (1934–) • AMERICAN FEMINIST AND COFOUNDER OF *MS.* MAGAZINE

When you're 50, you start thinking about things you haven't thought about before. I used to think getting old was about vanity, but actually it's about losing people you love. Getting wrinkles is trivial.

—JOYCE CAROL OATES (1938–) • AMERICAN WRITER

A woman, till five and thirty, is only looked upon as a raw girl, and can possibly make no noise in the world till about 40.

—LADY MARY WORTLEY MONTAGU (1689–1762) • ENGLISH POET, EPISTOLARY WRITER, AND SMALLPOX VACCINE ADVOCATE

I'm a full woman at 50—full of knowledge, full of love, full of compassion.

—PATTI LABELLE (1944–) • AFRICAN-AMERICAN R&B AND SOUL SINGER

"*ALCOHOL*"

Liquor is such a nice substitute for facing adult life.

—DOROTHY B. HUGHES (1904–1993) • AMERICAN CRIME WRITER

One more drink and I'll be under the host.

—DOROTHY PARKER (1893–1967)
AMERICAN WRITER AND CRITIC

You can't drown your troubles . . . because troubles can swim.

—MARGARET MILLAR (1915–1994) • CANADIAN MYSTERY WRITER

Alcohol is a good preservative for everything but brains.

—MARY PETTIBONE POOLE • 20TH-CENTURY AMERICAN WRITER

The chief reason for drinking is the desire to behave in a certain way, and to be able to blame it on alcohol.

–MIGNON MCLAUGHLIN (1913–1983)
AMERICAN JOURNALIST AND WRITER

One reason I don't drink is that I want to know when I am having a good time.

–LADY NANCY ASTOR (1879–1964)
FIRST FEMALE TO TAKE A SEAT IN BRITISH HOUSE OF COMMONS

ALCOHOLISM

There are plenty of alcoholics who can be magnificent when drunk: It does not make them any less alcoholic.

–INGRID BENGIS (1944–) • AMERICAN-BORN RUSSIAN WRITER

Alcoholism isn't a spectator sport. Eventually the whole family gets to play.

–JOYCE REBETA-BURDITT (1938–) • AMERICAN WRITER

Your medicine is your poison is your medicine is your poison and there is no end but madness.

–LILLIAN ROTH (1910–1980) • AMERICAN ACTOR

I was court-ordered to Alcoholics Anonymous on television. Pretty much blows the hell out of the second A, wouldn't you say?

–PAULA POUNDSTONE (1959–) • AMERICAN COMEDIAN

I'm the child of an alcoholic. I know about promises.

–SANDRA SCOPPETTONE (1936–)
AMERICAN WRITER OF MYSTERIES AND YOUNG ADULT BOOKS

"AMBITION"

My passions were all gathered together like fingers that made a fist. Drive is considered aggression today; I knew it then as purpose.

–BETTE DAVIS (1908–1989) • AMERICAN ACTOR

I'm ambitious. But if I weren't as talented as I am ambitious, I would be a gross monstrosity.

–MADONNA (1958–) • AMERICAN POP SINGER AND ACTOR

There are no persons capable of stooping so low as those who desire to rise in the world.

–LADY MARGUERITE BLESSINGTON (1789–1849)
IRISH-BORN ENGLISH WRITER AND LITERARY SALON HOST

We should see dreaming as one of our responsibilities, rather than an alternative to one.

–MARY ENGELBREIT
20TH/21ST-CENTURY AMERICAN ARTIST, GRAPHIC DESIGNER, AND ENTREPRENEUR

Ambition, if it feeds at all, does so on the ambition of others.

–SUSAN SONTAG (1933–2004) • AMERICAN ESSAYIST, NOVELIST, INTELLECTUAL, AND ACTIVIST

Ambition, old as mankind—the immemorial weakness of the strong.

–VITA SACKVILLE-WEST (1892–1962) • ENGLISH POET AND WRITER

Mama exhorted her children at every opportunity to "jump at de sun." We might not land on the sun, but at least we would get off the ground.

–ZORA NEALE HURSTON (1891–1960) • AFRICAN-AMERICAN FOLKLORIST AND WRITER

"ANGER"

Anger is its own excuse and its own reward.

—ANNE RIVERS SIDDONS (1928–) • AMERICAN WRITER

Anger is loaded with information and energy.

—AUDRE LORDE (1934–1992)
AFRICAN-AMERICAN FEMINIST WRITER AND ACTIVIST

As you get older, though, you realize there are fire extinguishers. You do have an ability to control the flames.

—CHAKA KHAN (1953–) • AMERICAN SINGER

Anger makes dull men witty, but it keeps them poor.

—QUEEN ELIZABETH I (1533–1603) • QUEEN OF ENGLAND

Many of our problems with anger occur when we choose between having a relationship and having a self.

—HARRIET LERNER • 20TH/21ST-CENTURY AMERICAN CLINICAL PSYCHOLOGIST

In anger, you look ten years older.

—HEDDA HOPPER (1885–1966)
AMERICAN GOSSIP COLUMNIST

Anger makes us all stupid.

—JOHANNA SPYRI (1827–1901)
SWISS WRITER

I am angry nearly every day of my life, but I have learned not to show it; and I still try to hope not to feel it, though it may take me another 40 years to do it.

—LOUISA MAY ALCOTT (1832–1888) • AMERICAN WRITER

Bitterness is like cancer. It eats upon the host.
But anger is like fire. It burns it all clean.

–MAYA ANGELOU (1928-)
AFRICAN-AMERICAN POET, MEMOIRIST, AND CIVIL RIGHTS ACTIVIST

•

Anger is like milk, it should not be kept too long.

–PHYLLIS BOTTOME (1884-1963) • ENGLISH WRITER

•

Their anger dug out for itself a deep channel, so
that future angers might more easily follow.

–RADCLYFFE HALL (1880-1943) • ENGLISH WRITER AND POET

•

"ANIMALS"

See also Birds, Cats, Dogs, Horses

•

I've always thought a hotel ought to offer optional small animals. I mean a cat to sleep on your bed at night, or a dog of some kind to act pleased when you come in.

–ANNE TYLER (1941-) • AMERICAN WRITER

•

The animals of the world exist for their own reasons. They were not made for humans any more than black people were made for white, or women created for men.

–ALICE WALKER (1944-) • AFRICAN-AMERICAN WRITER AND POET

•

Some of my best leading men have been dogs and horses.

–ELIZABETH TAYLOR (1932-) • ENGLISH-BORN AMERICAN ACTOR

When it comes to having a central nervous system, and the ability to feel pain, hunger, and thirst, a rat is a pig is a dog is a boy.

–INGRID NEWKIRK (1949-)
ENGLISH ANIMAL RIGHTS ACTIVIST, WRITER, AND PRESIDENT OF PEOPLE FOR THE ETHICAL TREATMENT OF ANIMALS (PETA)

HUNTING

I ask people why they have deer heads on their walls. They always say because it's such a beautiful animal. There you go. I think my mother is attractive, but I have photographs of her.

–ELLEN DEGENERES (1958-) • AMERICAN COMEDIAN AND TELEVISION HOST

We cannot have peace among men whose hearts find delight in killing any living creature.

–RACHEL CARSON (1907-1964)
AMERICAN ZOOLOGIST AND MARINE BIOLOGIST

PETS

Our perfect companions never have fewer than four feet.

–COLETTE (1873-1954) • FRENCH WRITER

In my day, we didn't have dogs or cats. All I had was Silver Beauty, my beloved paper clip.

–JENNIFER HART • 20TH/21ST-CENTURY AMERICAN COMEDIAN

I was constantly coming home with stray dogs, cats, and even horses. Sometimes they weren't strays, but I felt that their owners were neglecting them.

–JULIETTE GORDON LOW (1860-1927) • AMERICAN, FOUNDER OF GIRL SCOUTS OF THE USA

It's difficult to understand why people don't realize that pets are gifts to mankind.

–LINDA BLAIR (1959-) • AMERICAN ACTOR

You enter into a certain amount of madness when you marry a person with pets.

—NORA EPHRON (1941–) • AMERICAN FILM DIRECTOR, PRODUCER, SCREENWRITER, AND NOVELIST

"APATHY"

The accomplice to the crime of corruption is frequently our own indifference.

—BESS MYERSON (1924–)
AMERICAN BEAUTY QUEEN, CONSUMER ADVOCATE, AND POLITICIAN

The sad truth is that most evil is done by people who never make up their minds to be either good or evil.

—HANNAH ARENDT (1906–1975) • GERMAN-BORN POLITICAL PHILOSOPHER AND HISTORIAN

Science may have found a cure for most evils, but it has found no remedy for the worst of them all—the apathy of human beings.

—HELEN KELLER (1880–1968) • AMERICAN WRITER AND ACTIVIST

I think if we had a greater focus on the bigger picture, instead of being locked in our cubicles, in front of our computer screen, in front of television or movie screen or the rave or the band, that we might consider the larger picture of what's happening personally in our lives and globally.

—LYDIA LUNCH (1959–) • AMERICAN SINGER, WRITER, AND ACTOR

The main dangers in this life are the people who want to change everything . . . or nothing.

—LADY NANCY ASTOR (1879–1964)
FIRST FEMALE TO TAKE A SEAT IN BRITISH HOUSE OF COMMONS

"APPEARANCE"

See also Beauty

We can lie in the language of dress or try to tell the truth;
but unless we are naked and bald, it is impossible to be silent.

–ALISON LURIE (1926–) • AMERICAN WRITER

I'm getting a wrinkle above my eyebrow because I just
can't stop lifting it, and I love that you know.

–ANGELINA JOLIE (1975–) • AMERICAN ACTOR

My passport photo is one of the most remarkable photographs I have
ever seen—no retouching, no shadows, no flattery—just stark me.

–ANNE MORROW LINDBERGH (1906–2001) • AMERICAN WRITER AND PIONEERING AVIATOR

I began wearing hats as a young lawyer because it helped
me to establish my professional identity. Before that, whenever
I was at a meeting, someone would ask me to get coffee.

–BELLA ABZUG (1920–1998) • AMERICAN FEMINIST AND POLITICIAN

I put on my silly face and do what they expect me to do.
I didn't even comb my hair today. Interview vérité.

–CASS ELLIOT ("MAMA" CASS) (1941–1974) • AMERICAN SINGER

So a fulfilled woman sometimes looks beautiful, and sometimes doesn't look
so beautiful, but you don't have to worry about that because it's all in a day.

–CHARLOTTE RAMPLING (1946–) • ENGLISH ACTOR

I think that the longer I look good, the better gay men feel.

–CHER (1946–) • AMERICAN SINGER, ACTOR, AND POP ICON

My grandma was like, "Oh Christina, you look like a whore!"
I explained that's the idea.

–CHRISTINA AGUILERA (1980–) • AMERICAN POP SINGER AND SONGWRITER

It matters more what's in a woman's face than what's on it.

–CLAUDETTE COLBERT (1903-1996) • FRENCH-AMERICAN ACTOR

After a certain number of years, our faces become our biographies.

–CYNTHIA OZICK (1928-) • AMERICAN NOVELIST, ESSAYIST, AND POET

I hope people realize that there is a brain underneath
the hair and a heart underneath the boobs.

–DOLLY PARTON (1946-) • AMERICAN COUNTRY SINGER AND ENTERTAINER

Men look at themselves in mirrors. Women look for themselves.

–ELISSA MELAMED • 20TH-CENTURY WRITER AND PSYCHOTHERAPIST

Any girl can be glamorous. All you have to do is stand still and look stupid.

–HEDY LAMARR (1913-2000) • AUSTRIAN-BORN ACTOR AND INVENTOR

I never go out unless I look like Joan Crawford the movie
star. If you want to see the girl next door, go next door.

–JOAN CRAWFORD (1905-1977) • AMERICAN ACTOR

There's more to life than cheekbones.

–KATE WINSLET (1975-) • ENGLISH ACTOR

I could announce one morning that the world was going to blow
up in three hours, and people would be calling in about my hair!

–KATIE COURIC (1957-) • AMERICAN NEWS ANCHOR AND TELEVISION HOST

I'm just trying to change the world, one sequin at a time.

–LADY GAGA (1986-) • AMERICAN POP SINGER AND CELEBRITY

Ugly. Is irrelevant. It is an immeasurable insult to a woman, and then supposedly the worst crime you can commit as a woman.

–MARGARET CHO (1968–) • KOREAN-AMERICAN COMEDIAN AND ACTOR

When a man meets catastrophe on the road, he looks in his purse, but a woman looks in her mirror.

–MARGARET TURNBULL
20TH-CENTURY ENGLISH-BORN AMERICAN WRITER AND DRAMATIST

Nobody objects to a woman being a good writer or sculptor or geneticist if at the same time she manages to be a good wife, good mother, good looking, good tempered, well groomed, and unaggressive.

–MARYA MANNES (1904–1990) • AMERICAN COLUMNIST AND CRITIC

When a man gets up to speak, people listen then look. When a woman gets up, people look; then if they like what they see, they listen.

–PAULINE FREDERICK (1883–1938) • AMERICAN ACTOR

I'd have to say that, in general, models take themselves too seriously. Basically, they are genetic freaks who spend a couple of hours in hair and makeup.

–REBECCA ROMIJN (1972–) • AMERICAN MODEL AND ACTOR

They used to shoot [Shirley Temple] through gauze. You should shoot me through linoleum.

–TALULLAH BANKHEAD (1902–1968) • AMERICAN ACTOR

"ARCHITECTURE"

[On the shanties of the homeless in New York City:] The architecture of despair.

–MARGARET MORTON • 20TH/21ST-CENTURY AMERICAN PHOTOGRAPHER

Architecture is frozen music.

—MADAME DE STAËL (1766–1817)
SWISS-BORN FRENCH WRITER AND SOCIETY FIGURE

•

Architecture is the printing press of all ages, and gives a history of the state of the society in which it was erected.

—LADY SYDNEY MORGAN (1781–1859) • IRISH-BORN ENGLISH NOVELIST AND MEMOIRIST

•

"ART"

•

Deliver me from writers who say the way they live doesn't matter. I'm not sure a bad person can write a good book. If art doesn't make us better, then what on earth is it for?

—ALICE WALKER (1944–) • AFRICAN-AMERICAN WRITER AND POET

•

It is the function of art to renew our perception. What we are familiar with we cease to see. The writer shakes up the familiar scene, and, as if by magic, we see a new meaning in it.

—ANAÏS NIN (1903–1977) • FRENCH WRITER AND DIARIST

•

The camera is an instrument that teaches people how to see without a camera.

—DOROTHEA LANGE (1895–1965) • AMERICAN DOCUMENTARY PHOTOGRAPHER

•

Art is the tangible evidence of the human spirit.

—DORY GRADE • 20TH/21ST-CENTURY AMERICAN ARTIST

•

I don't understand art for art's sake. Art is the guts of the people.

—ELMA LEWIS (1921–2004)
AFRICAN-AMERICAN ARTIST, EDUCATOR, AND FOUNDER OF
NATIONAL CENTER OF AFRO-AMERICAN ARTISTS

Art must take reality by surprise.

–FRANÇOISE SAGAN (1935–2004)
FRENCH NOVELIST AND PLAYWRIGHT

•

The arts are the rainforests of society. They produce the oxygen of freedom, and they are the early warning system when freedom is in danger.

–JUNE WAYNE (1918–) • AMERICAN ARTIST

•

The artist must possess the courageous soul that dares and defies.

–KATE CHOPIN (1850–1904) • AMERICAN WRITER

•

I think most of the people involved in any art always secretly wonder whether they are really there because they're good—or because they're lucky.

–KATHARINE HEPBURN (1907–2003) • AMERICAN ACTOR

•

Art knows no prejucide, art knows no boundaries, art really doesn't have judgment in its purest form.

–K.D. LANG (1961–) • CANADIAN SINGER AND SONGWRITER

•

Forgiveness lives alone and far off down the road, but bitterness and art are close, gossipy neighbors, sharing the same clothesline, hanging out their things, getting their laundry confused.

–LORRIE MOORE (1957–) • AMERICAN WRITER

•

An artist can show things that other people are terrified of expressing.

–LOUISE BOURGEOIS (1911–) • FRENCH ARTIST AND SCULPTOR

•

Great artists are people who find ways to be themselves in their art. Any sort of pretension induces mediocrity in art and life alike.

–MARGOT FONTEYN (1919–1991) • ENGLISH BALLET DANCER

Image is an international language.

–MARJANE SATRAPI (1969–)
IRANIAN GRAPHIC NOVELIST

•

We [unfortunately] see achievement as purposeful and monolithic, like the sculpting of a massive tree trunk that has first to be brought from the forest and then shaped by long labor to assert the artist's vision, rather than something crafted from odds and ends, like a patchwork quilt, and lovingly used to warm different nights and bodies.

–MARY CATHERINE BATESON (1939–) • AMERICAN WRITER AND CULTURAL ANTHROPOLOGIST

•

Good art is art that allows you to enter it from a variety of angles and to emerge with a variety of views.

–MARY SCHMICH • 20TH/21ST-CENTURY AMERICAN COLUMNIST

•

Any authentic work of art must start an argument between the artist and his audience.

–REBECCA WEST (1892–1983) • ANGLO-IRISH FEMINIST AND WRITER

•

[People] should fear art, should fear film, should fear theater. This is where ideas happen. This is where somebody goes into a dark room and starts to watch something and their perspective can be completely questioned. The very seeds of activism are empathy and imagination.

–SUSAN SARANDON (1946–) • AMERICAN ACTOR AND POLITICAL ACTIVIST

•

What was any art but an effort to make a sheath, a mold in which to imprison for a moment the shining, elusive element which is life itself.

–WILLA CATHER (1873–1947) • AMERICAN WRITER

•

Anyone who says you can't see a thought simply doesn't know art.

–WYNETKA ANN REYNOLDS • 20TH/21ST-CENTURY AMERICAN UNIVERSITY PRESIDENT

"ATTITUDE"

If you can't change your fate, change your attitude.

–AMY TAN (1952–) • ASIAN-AMERICAN WRITER

We don't see things as they are. We see them as we are.

–ANAÏS NIN (1903–1977) • FRENCH WRITER AND DIARIST

I have my litany of frustrations, as everyone does, but ultimately I try to be hopeful because I don't see any decent alternative. I want to believe we can turn things around. It would be cynical to give up on life and turn our backs on the kids: Cynicism is irresponsible. And having hope is a much more healthy way to live.

–BARBARA KINGSOLVER (1955–) • AMERICAN WRITER

Both optimists and pessimists contribute to our society. The optimist invents the airplane and the pessimist the parachute.

–GLADYS BRONWYN STERN (1890–1973) • ENGLISH WRITER

Life's a bitch . . . and then you change your attitude.

–JENNIFER UNLIMITED (JENNIFER YANE) (1946–)
AMERICAN INSPIRATIONAL ARTIST AND WRITER

I discovered I always have choices, and sometimes it's only a choice of attitude.

–JUDITH M. KNOWLTON • 20TH/21ST-CENTURY SELF-HELP WRITER

Could we change our attitude, we should not only see life differently, but life itself would be different.

–KATHERINE MANSFIELD (1888–1923) • NEW ZEALAND WRITER

I've learned from experience that the greater part of our happiness or misery depends on our dispositions and not on our circumstances.

–MARTHA WASHINGTON (1731-1802) • FIRST LADY OF THE UNITED STATES

If you have a vagina and an attitude in this town, then that's a lethal combination.

–SHARON STONE (1958-) • AMERICAN ACTOR AND PRODUCER

We have been taught to believe that negative equals realistic and positive equals unrealistic.

–SUSAN JEFFERS • 20TH/21ST-CENTURY AMERICAN WRITER

OPTIMISM

Set your sights high, the higher the better. Expect the most wonderful things to happen, not in the future but right now. Realize that nothing is too good. Allow absolutely nothing to hamper you or hold you up in any way.

–EILEEN CADDY (1917-)
ENGLISH SPIRITUAL WRITER AND COFOUNDER OF THE FINDHORN FOUNDATION

My deepest impulses are optimistic; an attitude that seems to me as spiritually necessary and proper as it is intellectually suspect.

–ELLEN WILLIS
20TH/21ST-CENTURY AMERICAN POLITICAL ESSAYIST AND JOURNALISM PROFESSOR

Keep your face to the sunshine, and you cannot see the shadow.

–HELEN KELLER (1880-1968) • AMERICAN WRITER AND ACTIVIST

I would rather stay positive and get 60 percent good results than stay negative and get 100 percent bad results.

–JOYCE MEYER • 20TH/21ST-CENTURY AMERICAN SPIRITUAL LEADER AND WRITER

I make the most of all that comes and the least of all that goes.

–SARA TEASDALE (1884–1933) • AMERICAN LYRICAL POET

•

"AWARDS"

•

The greatest award given to me was by the firemen and policemen at Ground Zero. They said, we've been here looking for our friends, and we'd go home at night, turn on the television, and you were there, making us laugh.

–DORIS ROBERTS (1930–) • AMERICAN ACTOR

•

Would that there were an award for people who come to understand the concept of enough. Good enough. Successful enough. Thin enough. Rich enough. Socially responsible enough. When you have self-respect, you have enough.

–GAIL SHEEHY (1937–) • AMERICAN SOCIAL CRITIC

•

You have no idea how many men I've had to sleep with to win this.

–KIM CATTRALL (1956–) • ANGLO-CANADIAN ACTOR

•

[On receiving the 1963 Nobel Prize in Physics:] Winning the prize wasn't half as exciting as doing the work itself.

–MARIA GOEPPERT MAYER (1906–1972) • GERMAN PHYSICIST

•

OSCARS

All that glitters is probably spray-on brass.

–MERYL STREEP (1949–) • AMERICAN ACTOR

•

Some people can be so goofy, especially the ones that say, "I'd like to thank our Lord Jesus up above!" I'm like, "For the love of God, keep your mouth shut. That's why the world is so fucked up, because God is focusing solely on your career!"

–SCARLETT JOHANSSON (1984–) • AMERICAN ACTOR

B

"BABIES"

Now the thing about having a baby—and I can't be the first person to have noticed this—is that thereafter you have it.

–JEAN KERR (1923–2003) • AMERICAN PLAYWRIGHT AND HUMORIST

If you want a baby, have a new one. Don't baby the old one.

–JESSAMYN WEST (1902–1984) • AMERICAN WRITER

I adopted a baby. I wanted a highway, but it was a lot of red tape.

–MARGARET SMITH • 20TH/21ST-CENTURY AMERICAN COMEDIAN

"BEAUTY"

See also Appearance

Beauty is only skin deep, but ugly goes clean to the bone.

–DOROTHY PARKER (1893–1967) • AMERICAN WRITER AND CRITIC

The beautiful seems right by force of beauty, and the feeble wrong because of weakness.

–ELIZABETH BARRETT BROWNING (1806–1861) • ENGLISH POET

I feel like a defective model, like I came off the assembly line flat-out fucked and my parents should have taken me back for repairs before the warranty ran out. But that was so long ago.

–ELIZABETH WURTZEL (1967–) • AMERICAN WRITER

I'm tired of all this nonsense about beauty being only skin deep. That's deep enough. What do you want—an adorable pancreas?

–JEAN KERR (1923–2003) • AMERICAN PLAYWRIGHT AND HUMORIST

Plain women know more about men than beautiful ones do. But beautiful women don't need to know about men. It's the men who have to know about beautiful women.

—KATHARINE HEPBURN (1907-2003) • AMERICAN ACTOR

•

If truth is beauty, how come no one has their hair done in a library?

—LILY TOMLIN (1939-) • AMERICAN COMEDIAN AND ACTOR

•

It was God who made me so beautiful. If I weren't, then I'd be a teacher.

—LINDA EVANGELISTA (1965-) • CANADIAN SUPERMODEL

•

Taught from infancy that beauty is woman's sceptre, the mind shapes itself to the body, and roaming round its gilt cage, only seeks to adorn its prison.

—MARY WOLLSTONECRAFT (1759-1797) • ENGLISH WRITER

•

Men really prefer reasonably attractive women; they go after the sensational ones to impress other men.

—MIGNON MCLAUGHLIN (1913-1983) • AMERICAN JOURNALIST AND WRITER

•

Whatever you may look like, marry a man your own age—as your beauty fades, so will his eyesight.

—PHYLLIS DILLER (1917-) • AMERICAN COMEDIAN

•

What is beautiful is good, and who is good will soon also be beautiful.

—SAPPHO (CA. 630 BCE) • ANCIENT GREEK LYRIC POET

•

INNER BEAUTY

I was sweaty, and my hair was matted and all over the place. And I was happy and hot and accomplishing a lot and running around, and I could feel my heart beating, and I felt beautiful.

—ANGELINA JOLIE (1975-) • AMERICAN ACTOR

Despite the message of self-doubt and inadequacy hammered home by the beauty industry, the truth is simple: If you feel gorgeous, you'll look gorgeous.

—ANITA RODDICK (1942–) • ENGLISH ACTIVIST AND ENTREPRENEUR, FOUNDER OF THE BODY SHOP

•

When I lay my head on the pillow at night I can say I was a decent person today. That's when I feel beautiful.

—DREW BARRYMORE (1975–) • AMERICAN ACTOR AND PRODUCER

•

Beauty can't amuse you, but brainwork—reading, writing, thinking—can.

—HELEN GURLEY BROWN (1922–) • AMERICAN EDITOR AND WRITER

•

Character contributes to beauty. It fortifies a woman as her youth fades. A mode of conduct, a standard of courage, discipline, fortitude, and integrity can do a great deal to make a woman beautiful.

—JACQUELINE BISSET (1944–) • ENGLISH ACTOR

•

I am so beautiful, sometimes people weep when they see me. And it has nothing to do with what I look like really, it is just that I gave myself the power to say that I am beautiful, and if I could do that, maybe there is hope for them too. And the great divide between the beautiful and the ugly will cease to be. Because we are all what we choose.

—MARGARET CHO (1968–) • KOREAN-AMERICAN COMEDIAN AND ACTOR

•

"BEHAVIOR"

•

You've got to have something to eat and a little love in your life before you can hold still for any damn body's sermon on how to behave.

—BILLIE HOLIDAY (1915–1959) • AFRICAN-AMERICAN JAZZ SINGER

•

When a woman behaves like a man, why doesn't she behave like a nice man?

—EDITH EVANS (1888–1976) • ENGLISH STAGE AND FILM ACTOR

She must not swing her arms as though they were dangling ropes; she must not switch herself this way and that; she must not shout; and she must not, while wearing her bridal veil, smoke a cigarette.

—EMILY POST (1873-1960) • AMERICAN ETIQUETTE EXPERT

Good girls go to heaven; bad girls go everywhere.

—HELEN GURLEY BROWN (1922-) • AMERICAN EDITOR AND WRITER

When a woman starts out in the world on a mission, secular or religious, she should leave her feminine charms at home.

—JANE GREY SWISSHELM (1815-1884)
AMERICAN NEWSPAPERWOMAN, ABOLITIONIST, AND FEMINIST ACTIVIST

We are born charming, fresh, and spontaneous and must be civilized before we are fit to participate in society.

—JUDITH "MISS MANNERS" MARTIN (1938-)
AMERICAN ETIQUETTE EXPERT

Charm is the ability to make someone else think that both of you are pretty wonderful.

—KATHLEEN WINSOR (1919-2003) • AMERICAN WRITER

Well-behaved women rarely make history.

—LAUREL THATCHER ULRICH (1938-)
AMERICAN HISTORIAN OF EARLY AMERICA AND WOMEN'S HISTORY

Why is it that men can be bastards and women must wear pearls and smile?

—LYNN HECHT SCHAFRAN
20TH/21ST-CENTURY AMERICAN ATTORNEY AND EXPERT ON GENDER DISCRIMINATION LAW

Until you lose your reputation, you never realize
what a burden it was or what freedom really is.

–MARGARET MITCHELL (1900-1949) • AMERICAN WRITER

No matter what your fight, don't be ladylike! God Almighty made
women and the Rockefeller gang of thieves made the ladies.

–MOTHER JONES (1837-1930)
AMERICAN LABOR AND COMMUNITY ORGANIZER AND ACTIVIST

"Easy" is an adjective used to describe a woman
who has the sexual morals of a man.

–NANCY LINN-DESMOND • 20TH/21ST-CENTURY AMERICAN WRITER

Being powerful is like being a lady. If you
have to tell people you are, you aren't.

–MARGARET THATCHER (1925-)
FIRST FEMALE BRITISH PRIME MINISTER

"*BIRDS*"

For most bird-watchers, the coming of the warblers
has the same effect as catnip on a cat.

–ARLINE THOMAS • 20TH/21ST-CENTURY AMERICAN NATURALIST

The sound of birds stops the noise in my mind.

–CARLY SIMON (1945-) • AMERICAN SINGER-SONGWRITER

I hope you love birds, too. It is economical. It saves going to Heaven.

–EMILY DICKINSON (1830-1886) • AMERICAN POET

The wild geese were passing over. . . . There was an infinite cold passion in their flight, like the passion of the universe, a proud mystery never to be solved.

—MARTHA OSTENSO (1900–1963) • NORWEGIAN-BORN WRITER

•

A bird doesn't sing because it has an answer, it sings because it has a song.

—MAYA ANGELOU (1928–) • AFRICAN-AMERICAN POET, MEMOIRIST, AND CIVIL RIGHTS ACTIVIST

•

Over increasingly large areas of the United States, spring now comes unheralded by the return of the birds, and the early mornings are strangely silent where once they were filled with the beauty of bird song.

—RACHEL CARSON (1907–1964) • AMERICAN ZOOLOGIST AND MARINE BIOLOGIST

•

Did St. Francis preach to the birds? Whatever for? If he really liked birds he would have done better to preach to the cats.

—REBECCA WEST (1892–1983) • ANGLO-IRISH FEMINIST AND WRITER

•

"BITCH"

•

When a man gives his opinion he's a man. When a woman gives her opinion she's a bitch.

—BETTE DAVIS (1908–1989) • AMERICAN ACTOR

•

Bitches are aggressive, assertive, domineering, overbearing, strong-minded, spiteful, hostile, direct, blunt, candid, obnoxious, thick-skinned, hard-headed, vicious, dogmatic, competent, competitive, pushy, loud-mouthed, independent, stubborn, demanding, manipulative, egotistic, driven, achieving, overwhelming, threatening, scary, ambitious, tough, brassy, masculine, boisterous, and turbulent. Among other things.

—JOREEN (JO FREEMAN) (1945–) • AMERICAN FEMINIST AND WRITER

I'm tough, ambitious, and I know exactly what I want.
If that makes me a bitch, okay.

—MADONNA (1958–) • AMERICAN POP SINGER AND ACTOR

"BODY"

See also Breasts

We must claim our bodies as our own to love and honor in their infinite shapes and sizes. Fat, thin, soft, hard, puckered, smooth, our bodies are our homes.

—ABRA FORTUNE CHERNIK • 20TH/21ST-CENTURY AMERICAN FEMINIST ESSAYIST

I know of no woman—virgin, mother, lesbian, married, celibate—whether she earns her keep as a housewife, a cocktail waitress, or a scanner of brain waves—for whom the body is not a fundamental problem: its clouded meanings, its fertility, its desire, its so-called frigidity, its bloody speech, its silences, its changes and mutilations, its rapes and ripenings.

—ADRIENNE RICH (1929–) • AMERICAN POET, THEORIST, AND FEMINIST

I see my body as an instrument, rather than an ornament.

—ALANIS MORISSETTE (1974–) • CANADIAN SINGER AND SONGWRITER

As long as you smile, have sparkly eyes and stick your shoulders back, nobody's going to notice your bum or your waist or your feet, for that matter.

—CAT DEELEY (1976–) • ENGLISH MODEL AND TV HOST

We have to have faith in ourselves. I have never met a woman who, deep down in her core, really believes she has great legs. And if she suspects that she might have great legs, then she's convinced that she has a shrill voice and no neck.

—CYNTHIA HEIMEL • 20TH/21ST-CENTURY AMERICAN WRITER

God made a very obvious choice when he made me voluptuous; why would I go against what he decided for me? My limbs work, so I'm not going to complain about the way my body is shaped.

–DREW BARRYMORE (1975–) • AMERICAN ACTOR AND PRODUCER

I know I have the body of a weak and feeble woman, but I have the heart and stomach of a king, and of a king of England, too.

–QUEEN ELIZABETH I (1533–1603) • QUEEN OF ENGLAND

Emotion always has its roots in the unconscious and manifests itself in the body.

–IRENE CLAREMONT DE CASTILLEJO
20TH/21ST-CENTURY JUNGIAN PSYCHOLOGIST

We have these earthly bodies. We don't know what they want. Half the time, we pretend they are under our mental thumb, but that is the illusion of the healthy and protected. Of sedate lovers. . . . For the body has emotions it conceives and carries through without concern for anyone or anything else.

–LOUISE ERDRICH (1954–) • NATIVE AMERICAN WRITER AND POET

The basic female body comes with the following accessories: garter belt, panti-girdle, crinoline, camisole, bustle, brassiere, stomacher, chemise, virgin zone, spike heels, nose ring, veil, kid gloves, fishnet stockings, fichu, bandeau, Merry Widow, weepers, chokers, barrettes, bangles, beads, lorgnette, feather boa, basic black, compact, Lycra stretch one-piece with modesty panel, designer peignoir, flannel nightie, lace teddy, bed, head.

–MARGARET ATWOOD (1939–) • CANADIAN POET, WRITER, CRITIC, AND ACTIVIST

Flesh goes on pleasuring us, and humiliating us, right to the end.

–MIGNON MCLAUGHLIN (1913–1983) • AMERICAN JOURNALIST AND WRITER

We've learned that . . . the bodies we inhabit and the lives those bodies carry on need not be perfect to have value.

–NANCY MAIRS (1943–) • AMERICAN WRITER

I have a brain and a uterus, and I use both.

–PAT SCHROEDER (1940–) • AMERICAN POLITICIAN

Our bodies are at once the receiving and transmitting stations for life itself. It is the highest wisdom to recognize this fact and train our bodies to render them sensitive and responsive to nature, art, and religion.

–RUTH ST. DENIS (1879–1968) • AMERICAN MODERN DANCE PIONEER

I think the quality of sexiness comes from within. It is something that is in you or it isn't and it really doesn't have much to do with breasts or thighs or the pout of your lips.

–SOPHIA LOREN (1934–) • ITALIAN ACTOR

AGING

You start out happy that you have no hips or boobs. All of a sudden you get them, and it feels sloppy. Then just when you start liking them, they start drooping.

–CINDY CRAWFORD (1966–) • AMERICAN SUPERMODEL

I am beautiful as I am. I am the shape that was gifted. My breasts are no longer perky and upright like when I was a teenager. My hips are wider than that of a fashion model's. For this I am glad, for these are the signs of a life lived.

–CINDY OLSEN • 20TH/21ST-CENTURY AMERICAN ADVOCATE OF TOPFREEDOM

BUTT

My bottom is so big it's got its own gravitational field.

–CAROL VORDERMAN (1960–) • ENGLISH TV PERSONALITY

All I can say is, if they show my butt in a movie, it better be a wide shot.

–JENNIFER LOPEZ (1969–) • AMERICAN ACTOR, DANCER, AND POP/LATIN SINGER

CURVES

The most popular image of the female despite the exigencies of the clothing trade is all boobs and buttocks, a hallucinating sequence of parabolae and bulges.

–GERMAINE GREER (1939–) • AUSTRALIAN-BORN WRITER AND SOCIAL CRITIC

Curve: the loveliest distance between two points.

–MAE WEST (1893–1980)
AMERICAN ACTOR, WRITER, AND SEX SYMBOL

I can't wait for the time when curves will be back in style and little fat bellies will be sexy again.

–SHAKIRA (1977–) • COLOMBIAN POP SINGER AND SONGWRITER

HIPS

The hip is the most erotic and neglected body part. Kiss the hip bone with your lips.

–KAREN MCDOUGAL (1971–) • AMERICAN MODEL

LEGS

There are two reasons why I'm in show business, and I'm standing on both of them.

–BETTY GRABLE (1916–1973)
AMERICAN ACTOR, SINGER, DANCER, AND PIN-UP GIRL

The average man is more interested in a woman who is interested in him than he is in a woman—any woman—with beautiful legs.

–MARLENE DIETRICH (1901–1992) • GERMAN-BORN ACTOR AND SINGER

A woman is as young as her knees.

–MARY QUANT (1934–) • ENGLISH FASHION DESIGNER

•

THIGHS

I have flabby thighs, but fortunately my stomach covers them.

–JOAN RIVERS (1933–) • AMERICAN COMEDIAN AND TELEVISION HOST

•

"BREASTS"

•

What's so beautiful about breasts is their uniqueness. I don't understand the obsession with fakeness. It's a very odd thing, isn't it, to prefer fake and big to small and unique or just beautiful and real.

–ANNE HECHE (1969–) • AMERICAN ACTOR

•

[Kentucky is] where the people are real and so are the breasts.

–ASHLEY JUDD (1968–) • AMERICAN ACTOR

•

My breasts are so versatile now—I can wear them down, up, or side by side.

–CYBILL SHEPHERD (1950–) • AMERICAN ACTOR, SINGER, AND FASHION MODEL

•

I have got little feet because nothing grows in the shade.

–DOLLY PARTON (1946–) • AMERICAN COUNTRY SINGER AND ENTERTAINER

•

The truest cliché about Hollywood is that women have boobs and that everybody wants to see them.

–HALLE BERRY (1966–) • AFRICAN-AMERICAN ACTOR AND BEAUTY QUEEN

•

There are three reasons for breastfeeding: The milk is always at the right temperature; it comes in attractive containers; and the cat can't get it.

–IRENA CHALMERS • 20TH/21ST-CENTURY AMERICAN CULINARY WRITER AND LECTURER

Who ever thought up the word "mammogram?" Every time I hear it, I think I'm supposed to put my breast in an envelope and send it to someone.

–JAN KING

20TH/21ST-CENTURY AMERICAN WRITER, HUMORIST, AND BREAST CANCER SURVIVOR

•

Christians can have big tits, too.

–JANE RUSSELL (1921-)

AMERICAN ACTOR AND SEX SYMBOL

•

My breasts have a career of their own. Theirs is going better.

–JENNIFER LOVE HEWITT (1979-) • AMERICAN ACTOR

•

Next time, Janet, use the left boob. The right boob is bad luck.

–LIL' KIM (1974-) • AFRICAN-AMERICAN RAPPER

•

In my films my breasts are definitely computer animated, because I don't have any. They spend most of the money in the film's budget just making my breasts. That's why producers never like me.

–MILLA JOVOVICH (1975-)

UKRAINIAN-BORN AMERICAN ACTOR, MODEL, AND FASHION DESIGNER

•

I was about 12 years old when I started getting boobs. I never tried to hide them because I started to realize the power I had with them.

–NATASHA HENSTRIDGE (1974-) • CANADIAN MODEL AND ACTOR

•

In junior high a boy poured water down my shirt and yelled, "Now maybe they'll grow."

–PAMELA ANDERSON (1967-)

CANADIAN-AMERICAN MODEL AND ACTOR

My mother-in-law had a pain beneath her left breast. Turned out to be a trick knee.

–PHYLLIS DILLER (1917–) • AMERICAN COMEDIAN

•

I need my nipples squeezed before every show. It gets me pumped to go onstage. My assistant Jackie has it down to a fine art.

–PINK (1979–) • AMERICAN POP SINGER AND SONGWRITER

•

[On her breasts:] I'm proud of my girls. They're my charms, my feminine wiles.

–SCARLETT JOHANSSON (1984–) • AMERICAN ACTOR

•

It's hard to be naked and not be upstaged by your nipples.

–SUSAN SARANDON (1946–) • AMERICAN ACTOR AND POLITICAL ACTIVIST

•

If God had intended for breasts to be seen, He wouldn't have created large woolen pullovers.

–TRACEY ULLMAN (1959–)
ENGLISH COMEDIAN, ACTOR, SINGER, AND SCREENWRITER

•

"BROTHERS"

See Family

C

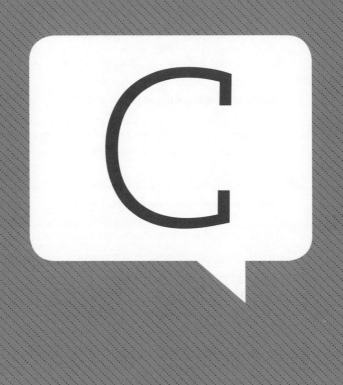

"CARS"

See also Driving

A car is just a moving, giant handbag! You never have actually to carry groceries, or dry cleaning, or anything! You can have five pairs of shoes with you at all times!

–CYNTHIA HEIMEL • 20TH/21ST-CENTURY AMERICAN WRITER

My boyfriend, like a lot of men, takes great pride in his car. Honey, his car is detailed, waxed, and vacuumed weekly. On the other hand, my car looks like a really big purse.

–DIANE NICHOLS • 20TH/21ST-CENTURY AMERICAN COMEDIAN

Every time I go to a mechanic, they look at me like I'm stupid, "It's a gasket, honey." I know what a gasket is; it's $150. But a "gasket, honey" is $200.

–EMILY LEVINE • 20TH/21ST-CENTURY AMERICAN COMEDIAN

Never have more children than you have car windows.

–ERMA BOMBECK (1927–1996) • AMERICAN HUMORIST

America will hardly need to ponder a mystery that has troubled men for millennia: What is the purpose of life? For us, the answer will be clear, established and for all practical purposes indisputable: The purpose of life is to produce and consume automobiles.

–JANE JACOBS (1916–2006) • AMERICAN-BORN CANADIAN WRITER AND ACTIVIST

My boyfriend keeps telling me I've got to own things. So, first I bought this car. And then he told me I oughta get a house. Why a house? Well, you gotta have a place to park the car.

–JULIA ROBERTS (1967–) • AMERICAN ACTOR

Is it sufficient that you have learned to drive the car, or shall we look and see what is under the hood? Most people go through life without ever knowing.

–JUNE SINGER (1899-2004) • AMERICAN JUNGIAN PSYCHOLOGIST

A car is useless in New York, essential everywhere else. The same with good manners.

–MIGNON MCLAUGHLIN (1913-1983
AMERICAN JOURNALIST AND WRITER

What I like, or one of the things I like, about motoring is the sense it gives one of lighting accidentally, like a voyager who touches another planet with the tip of his toe, upon scenes which would have gone on, have always gone on, will go on, unrecorded, save for this chance glimpse. Then it seems to me I am allowed to see the heart of the world uncovered for a moment.

–VIRGINIA WOOLF (1882-1941) • ENGLISH NOVELIST, ESSAYIST, AND CRITIC

My license plate says PMS. Nobody cuts me off.

–WENDY LIEBMAN (1961-) • AMERICAN COMEDIAN

Divorced men are more likely to meet their car payments than their child support obligations.

–SUSAN FALUDI (1959-) • AMERICAN JOURNALIST, WRITER, AND FEMINIST

"CATS"

Cats think about three things: food, sex, and nothing.

–ADAIR LARA • 20TH/21ST-CENTURY AMERICAN COLUMNIST AND MEMOIRIST

A catless writer is almost inconceivable. It's a perverse taste, really, since it would be easier to write with a herd of buffalo in the room than even one cat; they make nests in the notes and bite the end of the pen and walk on the typewriter keys.

–BARBARA HOLLAND • 20TH/21ST-CENTURY AMERICAN WRITER

By and large, people who enjoy teaching animals to roll over will find themselves happier with a dog.

–BARBARA HOLLAND • 20TH/21ST CENTURY AMERICAN WRITER

After scolding one's cat one looks into its face and is seized by the ugly suspicion that it understood every word. And has filed it for reference.

–CHARLOTTE GRAY (1948–) • ENGLISH-BORN CANADIAN JOURNALIST AND HISTORIAN

My cat does not talk as respectfully to me as I do to her.

–COLETTE (1873–1954) • FRENCH WRITER

There are no ordinary cats.

–COLETTE (1873–1954) • FRENCH WRITER

Nobody keeps a cat. They condescend to live with you is all.

–DELL SHANNON (ELIZABETH LININGTON) (1921–1988) • AMERICAN WRITER

If a fish is the movement of water embodied, given shape, then cat is a diagram and pattern of subtle air.

–DORIS LESSING (1919–) • ENGLISH WRITER

Oh cat, I'd say, or pray: Be-*oooo*tiful cat! Delicious cat! Exquisite cat! Satiny cat! Cat like a soft owl, cat with paws like moths, jeweled cat, miraculous cat! Cat, cat, cat, cat.

–DORIS LESSING (1919–) • ENGLISH WRITER

If I die before my cat, I want a little of my ashes put in his food so I can live inside him.

–DREW BARRYMORE (1975–) • AMERICAN ACTOR AND PRODUCER

•

That cat is in love with me, but to say that it's "mutual" doesn't begin to describe *anything*. I'm totally irrational about her. She and I are a *scandal*.

–HELEN GURLEY BROWN • AMERICAN EDITOR AND WRITER

•

Your cat will never threaten your popularity by barking at three in the morning. He won't attack the mailman or eat the drapes, although he may climb the drapes to see how the room looks from the ceiling.

–HELEN POWERS • 20TH-CENTURY AMERICAN WRITER

•

You cannot look at a sleeping cat and feel tense.

–JANE PAULEY (1950–)
AMERICAN TV NEWS ANCHOR AND JOURNALIST

•

A dog, I have always said, is prose; a cat is a poem.

–JEAN BURDEN
20TH/21ST-CENTURY AMERICAN POET, ESSAYIST, AND EDITOR

•

Dogs come when they're called. Cats take a message and get back to you.

–MARY BLY • 20TH/21ST-CENTURY AMERICAN PROFESSOR AND WRITER

•

Some people say that cats are sneaky, evil, and cruel. True, and they have many other fine qualities as well.

–MISSY DIZICK • 20TH/21ST-CENTURY AMERICAN WRITER AND ARTIST

•

Cats can work out mathematically the exact place to sit that will cause most inconvenience.

–PAM BROWN • 20TH-CENTURY AUSTRALIAN POET

The problem with cats is that they get the same exact look whether they see a moth or an ax-murderer.

–PAULA POUNDSTONE (1959–) • AMERICAN COMEDIAN

•

Cats sleep fat and walk thin.

–ROSALIE MOORE (1910–) • AMERICAN POET

•

"CENSORSHIP"

•

Censorship, like charity, should begin at home; but unlike charity, it should end there.

–CLARE BOOTHE LUCE (1903–1987)
AMERICAN PLAYWRIGHT, JOURNALIST, AND POLITICIAN

•

One cannot and must not try to erase the past merely because it does not fit the present.

–GOLDA MEIR (1898–1978)
RUSSIAN-BORN FIRST FEMALE PRIME MINISTER OF ISRAEL

•

If librarianship is the connecting of people to ideas—and I believe that is the truest definition of what we do—it is crucial to remember that we must keep and make available not just good ideas and noble ideas, but bad ideas, silly ideas, and yes, even dangerous or wicked ideas.

–GRACEANNE A. DECANDIDO
20TH/21ST-CENTURY AMERICAN BOOK CRITIC, EDITOR, AND LECTURER

•

. . . nothing that could be censored can be so bad in its effects, in the long run, as censorship itself.

–KATHARINE WHITEHORN (1926–)
ENGLISH JOURNALIST, WRITER, AND COLUMNIST

I believe in censorship. I made a fortune out of it.

–MAE WEST (1893–1980) • AMERICAN ACTOR, WRITER, AND SEX SYMBOL

I am thankful for all the complaining I hear about our government because it means we have freedom of speech.

–NANCIE J. CARMODY • 20TH/21ST-CENTURY WRITER

God forbid that any book should be banned.
The practice is as indefensible as infanticide.

–REBECCA WEST (1892–1983)
ANGLO-IRISH FEMINIST AND WRITER

I disapprove of what you say, but will defend to the death your right to say it.

–S. G. TALLENTYRE (EVELYN BEATRICE HALL) (1868–1919) • ENGLISH BIOGRAPHER

"CHALLENGE"

Never interrupt someone doing what you said couldn't be done.

–AMELIA EARHART (1897–1937)
PIONEERING AMERICAN AVIATOR; FIRST PERSON TO FLY SOLO ACROSS PACIFIC

I want to do it because I want to do it. Women must try to do things as men have tried. When they fail, their failure must be but a challenge to others.

–AMELIA EARHART (1897–1937)
PIONEERING AMERICAN AVIATOR; FIRST PERSON TO FLY SOLO ACROSS PACIFIC

If you want to touch the other shore badly enough,
barring an impossible situation, you will.

–DIANA NYAD (1949–) • AMERICAN LONG-DISTANCE SWIMMER

I was annoyed from the start by the attitude of doubt by the spectators that I would never really make the flight. This attitude made me more determined than ever to succeed.

–HARRIET QUIMBY (1875-1912)
AMERICAN, FIRST WOMAN TO FLY ACROSS THE ENGLISH CHANNEL

•

I am not afraid of storms for I am learning how to sail my ship.

–LOUISA MAY ALCOTT (1832-1888) • AMERICAN WRITER

•

When people say, "It can't be done," or "You don't have what it takes," it makes the task all the more interesting.

–LYNN HILL (1961-) • AMERICAN ROCK CLIMBER

•

Don't assume a door is closed; push on it. Do not assume if it was closed yesterday that it is closed today.

–MARIAN WRIGHT EDELMAN (1939-)
AFRICAN-AMERICAN FOUNDER OF THE CHILDREN'S DEFENSE FUND

•

I never see what has been done; I only see what remains to be done.

–MARIE CURIE (1867-1934)
POLISH-FRENCH CHEMIST AND RADIOLOGY PIONEER; FIRST TWO-TIME NOBEL LAUREATE

•

If I see a door comin' my way, I'm knockin' it down. And if I can't knock down the door, I'm sliding through the window.

–ROSIE PEREZ (1964-) • AMERICAN ACTOR

•

"CHANGE"

•

The moment of change is the only poem.

–ADRIENNE RICH (1929-)
AMERICAN POET, THEORIST, AND FEMINIST

People want progress, but they don't want change.

–EVA BURROWS (1929–)
AUSTRALIAN; LEADER OF SALVATION ARMY

Clinging to the past is the problem. Embracing change is the solution.

–GLORIA STEINEM (1934–) • AMERICAN FEMINIST AND COFOUNDER OF *MS.* MAGAZINE

Humans are allergic to change. They love to say, "We've always done it this way." I try to fight that. That's why I have a clock on my wall that runs counter-clockwise.

–GRACE MURRAY HOPPER (1906–1992)
PIONEERING COMPUTER SCIENTIST AND U.S. NAVY REAR ADMIRAL

Going back after a long time will make you mad, because the people you left behind do not like to think of you as changed, will treat you as they always did, accuse you of being indifferent, when you are only different.

–JEANETTE WINTERSON (1959–) • ENGLISH WRITER

Life changes in the instant. You sit down to dinner and life as you know it ends.

–JOAN DIDION (1934–) • AMERICAN WRITER

We are taught you must blame your father, your sisters, your brothers, the school, the teachers—but never blame yourself. It's never your fault. But it's always your fault, because if you wanted to change you're the one who has got to change.

–KATHARINE HEPBURN (1907–2003) • AMERICAN ACTOR

The need for change bulldozed a road down the center of my mind.

–MAYA ANGELOU (1928–)
AFRICAN-AMERICAN POET, MEMOIRIST, AND CIVIL RIGHTS ACTIVIST

"CHILDBIRTH"

Having a baby is like suddenly getting the world's worst roommate, like having Janis Joplin with a bad hangover and PMS come to stay with you.

–ANNE LAMOTT (1954–) • AMERICAN NOVELIST AND MEMOIRIST

If God were a woman, She would have installed one of those turkey thermometers in our belly buttons. When we were done, the thermometer pops up, the doctor reaches for the zipper conveniently located beneath our bikini lines, and out comes a smiling, fully diapered baby.

–CANDICE BERGEN (1946–) • AMERICAN ACTOR

Giving birth is like taking your lower lip and forcing it over your head.

–CAROL BURNETT (1933–) • AMERICAN COMEDIAN

Hard labor: a redundancy, like "working mother."

–JOYCE ARMOR • 20TH/21ST-CENTURY AMERICAN WRITER

If men had to have babies they would only ever have one each.

–PRINCESS DIANA (1961–1997)
PRINCESS OF WALES, FIRST WIFE OF CHARLES, PRINCE OF WALES

I think of birth as the search for a larger apartment.

–RITA MAE BROWN (1944–) • AMERICAN WRITER AND ACTIVIST

I realize why women die in childbirth—it's preferable.

–SHERRY GLASER
20TH/21ST-CENTURY AMERICAN FEMINIST PLAYWRIGHT,
PERFORMANCE ARTIST, AND ACTIVIST

"CHILDREN"

Who would ever think that so much went on in the soul of a young girl?

–ANNE FRANK (1929–1945) • GERMAN-JEWISH DIARIST

The hearts of small children are delicate organs. A cruel beginning in the world can twist them into curious shapes.

–CARSON MCCULLERS (1917–1967)
AMERICAN NOVELIST AND PLAYWRIGHT

Many things can wait. Children cannot. Today their bones are being formed, their blood is being made, their senses are being developed. To them we cannot say "tomorrow." Their name is today.

–GABRIELA MISTRAL (LUCILA GODOY ALCAYAGA) (1899–1957)
NOBEL PRIZE–WINNING CHILEAN POET

One hour with a child is like a ten-mile run.

–JOAN BENOIT SAMUELSON (1957–)
AMERICAN MARATHON RUNNER AND GOLD-MEDAL OLYMPIAN

To heir is human.

–MARCELENE COX
20TH-CENTURY AMERICAN WRITER

Children in a family are like flowers in a bouquet; there's always one determined to face in an opposite direction from the way the arranger desires.

–MARCELENE COX
20TH-CENTURY AMERICAN WRITER

To nourish children and raise them against
odds is in any time, any place, more valuable than
to fix bolts in cars or design nuclear weapons.

–MARILYN FRENCH (1929-2009)
AMERICAN WRITER AND FEMINIST

•

A child is fed with milk and praise.

–MARY LAMB (1764-1847) • ENGLISH WRITER

•

I love children: especially when they cry,
for then someone takes them away.

–NANCY MITFORD (1904-1973)
ENGLISH NOVELIST AND BIOGRAPHER

•

One of the things I've discovered in general about raising kids is that
they really don't give a damn if you walked five miles to school.

–PATTY DUKE (1946-) • AMERICAN ACTOR

•

If I had influence with the good fairy who is supposed to
preside over the christening of all children, I should ask
that her gift to each child in the world be a sense of wonder
so indestructible that it would last throughout life.

–RACHEL CARSON (1907-1964)
AMERICAN ZOOLOGIST AND MARINE BIOLOGIST

•

Few things are more rewarding than a child's
open, uncalculating devotion.

–VERA BRITTAIN (1893-1970)
ENGLISH WRITER, PACIFIST, AND FEMINIST

"CHOCOLATE"

After eating chocolate you feel godlike, as though you can conquer enemies, lead armies, entice lovers.

—EMILY LUCHETTI
20TH/21ST-CENTURY AMERICAN PASTRY CHEF AND COOKBOOK WRITER

Chocolate . . . is not something you can take or leave, something you like only moderately. You don't like chocolate. You don't even love chocolate. Chocolate is something you have an affair with.

—GENEEN ROTH (1951–) • AMERICAN CONSULTANT ON EATING AND HEALING

It's not that chocolates are a substitute for love. Love is a substitute for chocolate. Chocolate is, let's face it, far more reliable than a man.

—MIRANDA INGRAM • 20TH/21ST-CENTURY ENGLISH JOURNALIST

The taste of chocolate is a sensual pleasure in itself, existing in the same world as sex. . . . For myself, I can enjoy the wicked pleasure of chocolate . . . entirely by myself. Furtiveness makes it better.

—RUTH WESTHEIMER (1928–) • GERMAN-BORN SEX THERAPIST AND MEDIA PERSONALITY

There is a simple memory aid that you can use to determine whether it is the correct time to order chocolate dishes: Any month whose name contains the letter A, E, or U is the proper time for chocolate.

—SANDRA BOYNTON (1953–) • AMERICAN WRITER AND ILLUSTRATOR

"CHOICES"

If you choose to do something, then you shouldn't say it's a sacrifice, because nobody forced you to do it.

–AUNG SAN SUU KYI (1945–) • BURMESE OPPOSITION LEADER AND NOBEL LAUREATE

Choose well: Your choice is brief and yet endless.

–ELLA WINTER (1898–1980)
AUSTRALIAN-BORN ENGLISH JOURNALIST

The point is less what we choose than that we have the power to make a choice.

–GLORIA STEINEM (1934–) • AMERICAN FEMINIST AND COFOUNDER OF *MS.* MAGAZINE

Was there ever in anyone's life span a point free in time, devoid of memory, a night when choice was any more than the sum of all the choices gone before?

–JOAN DIDION (1934–) • AMERICAN WRITER

The will is never free—it is always attached to an object, a purpose. It is simply the engine in the car—it can't steer.

–JOYCE CARY (1888–1957) • IRISH WRITER AND ARTIST

It is the ability to choose which makes us human.

–MADELEINE L'ENGLE (1918–) • AMERICAN WRITER

Standing in the middle of the road is very dangerous; you get knocked down by traffic from both sides.

–MARGARET THATCHER (1925–) • FIRST FEMALE BRITISH PRIME MINISTER

As simple as it sounds, we all must try to be the best person we can: by making the best choices, by making the most of the talents we've been given.

–MARY LOU RETTON (1968–) • AMERICAN GYMNAST

"CHRISTMAS"

See Holidays

"CLOTHES"

See also Fashion

I dress for women and I undress for men.

–ANGIE DICKINSON (1931–) • AMERICAN ACTOR

Clothes can suggest, persuade, connote, insinuate, or indeed lie, and apply subtle pressure while their wearer is speaking frankly and straightforwardly of other matters.

–ANNE HOLLANDER • 20TH/21ST-CENTURY AMERICAN ART HISTORIAN

I'm not dissing them or anything, but people like Britney or Beyoncé have wardrobe people. I have a suitcase. I'm a bit lower maintenance.

–AVRIL LAVIGNE (1984–) • CANADIAN SINGER-SONGWRITER

A little bad taste is like a nice dash of paprika.

–DOROTHY PARKER (1893–1967)
AMERICAN WRITER AND CRITIC

If the trousers do not attract you, so much the worse: For the moment I do not want to attract you. I want to enjoy myself as a human being.

–DOROTHY SAYERS (1893–1957) • ENGLISH WRITER AND TRANSLATOR

Put even the plainest woman into a beautiful dress and unconsciously she will try to live up to it.

–LADY DUFF-GORDON (LUCILE CHRISTIANA SUTHERLAND) (1863–1935)
ENGLISH-BORN CANADIAN FASHION DESIGNER AND *TITANIC* SURVIVOR

Women dress alike all over the world: They dress to be annoying to other women.

–ELSA SCHIAPARELLI (1890–1973) • ITALIAN FASHION DESIGNER

A dress makes no sense unless it inspires men to want to take it off you.

–FRANÇOISE SAGAN (1935–2004) • FRENCH NOVELIST AND PLAYWRIGHT

Adornment is never anything except a reflection of the heart.

–GABRIELLE "COCO" CHANEL (1883–1971) • FRENCH FASHION DESIGNER

I wear my sort of clothes to save me the trouble of deciding which clothes to wear.

–KATHARINE HEPBURN (1907–2003) • AMERICAN ACTOR

Friendship is not possible between two women, one of whom is very well dressed.

–LAURIE COLWIN (1944–1992) • AMERICAN NOVELIST AND FOOD WRITER

A woman's dress should be like a barbed-wire fence: serving its purpose without obstructing the view.

–SOPHIA LOREN (1934–) • ITALIAN ACTOR

FUR

Cruelty is one fashion statement we can all do without.

–RUE MCCLANAHAN (1934–)
AMERICAN ACTOR AND ANIMAL-RIGHTS ADVOCATE

MEN'S

If men can run the world, why can't they stop wearing neckties? How intelligent is it to start the day by tying a little noose around your neck?

–LINDA ELLERBEE (1944–) • AMERICAN TELEVISION ANCHOR, WRITER, AND PRODUCER

AND POLITICS

You don't have to signal a social conscience by looking like a frump. Lace knickers won't hasten the holocaust, you can ban the bomb in a feather boa just as well as without, and a mild interest in the length of hemlines doesn't necessarily disqualify you from reading *Das Kapital* and agreeing with every word.

–ELIZABETH BIBESCO (1897-1945) • ENGLISH WRITER

I'll do anything to pass the ERA [Equal Rights Amendment], even if it means wearing babydoll nightgowns and padded bras, if that will make people less afraid.

–JOAN HACKETT (1934-1983) • AMERICAN ACTOR

"COFFEE"

Making coffee has become the great compromise of the decade. It's the only thing "real" men do that doesn't seem to threaten their masculinity. To women, it's on the same domestic entry level as putting the spring back into the toilet-tissue holder or taking a chicken out of the freezer to thaw.

–ERMA BOMBECK (1927-1996) • AMERICAN HUMORIST

Once you wake up and smell the coffee, it's hard to go back to sleep.

–FRAN DRESCHER (1957-) • AMERICAN ACTOR

For a writer, it's more essential than food.

–JOAN FRANK • 20TH/21ST-CENTURY AMERICAN ESSAYIST AND WRITER

Almost all my middle-aged and elderly acquaintances, including me, feel about 25, unless we haven't had our coffee, in which case we feel 107.

–MARTHA BECK • 20TH/21ST-CENTURY AMERICAN THERAPIST, LIFE COACH, AND WRITER

Behind every successful woman . . . is a substantial amount of coffee.

—STEPHANIE PIRO • 20TH/21ST-CENTURY AMERICAN CARTOONIST

•

"COLLEGE"

•

I learned three important things in college—to use a library, to memorize quickly and visually, to drop asleep at any time given a horizontal surface and 15 minutes.

—AGNES DE MILLE (1905–1993) • AMERICAN DANCER AND CHOREOGRAPHER

•

Don't ever dare to take your college as a matter of course—because, like democracy and freedom, many people you'll never know have broken their hearts to get it for you.

—ALICE DUER MILLER (1874–1942) • AMERICAN WRITER AND SUFFRAGIST

•

A liberal arts education is supposed to provide you with a value system, a standard, a set of ideas, not a job.

—CAROLINE BIRD (1915–) • AMERICAN JOURNALIST AND SOCIAL CRITIC

•

Professors complain about students who arrive at college with strong convictions but not enough knowledge to argue persuasively for their beliefs. . . . Having opinions without knowledge is not of much value; not knowing the difference between them is a positive indicator of ignorance.

—DIANE RAVITCH (1938–) • AMERICAN EDUCATIONAL POLICY ANALYST

•

In the university they don't tell you that the greater part of the law is learning to tolerate fools.

—DORIS LESSING (1919–) • ENGLISH WRITER

College isn't the place to go for ideas.

–HELEN KELLER (1880-1968)
AMERICAN WRITER AND ACTIVIST

"COMMUNICATION"

See also Language

It is well within the order of things that man should listen when his mate sings; but the true male never yet walked who liked to listen when his mate talked.

–ANNA WICKHAM (1884-1947) • ENGLISH POET

Good communication is as stimulating as black coffee, and just as hard to sleep after.

–ANNE MORROW LINDBERGH (1906-2001)
AMERICAN WRITER AND PIONEERING AVIATOR

They say that women talk too much. If you have worked in Congress you know that the filibuster was invented by men.

–CLARE BOOTHE LUCE (1903-1987) • AMERICAN PLAYWRIGHT, JOURNALIST, AND POLITICIAN

Each person's life is lived as a series of conversations.

–DEBORAH TANNEN (1945-) • AMERICAN WRITER AND SOCIOLINGUIST

Polite conversation is rarely either.

–FRAN LEBOWITZ (1950-) • AMERICAN HUMORIST

The first woman I approached tried to tell me she wasn't interested. I pretended that my deafness prevented me from hearing her refusals.

–JULIETTE GORDON LOW (1860-1927) • AMERICAN, FOUNDER OF GIRL SCOUTS OF USA

What a lot we lost when we stopped writing letters. You can't reread a phone call.

–LIZ CARPENTER (1920–) • AMERICAN WRITER AND FEMINIST

Eating without conversation is only stoking.

–MARCELENE COX • 20TH-CENTURY AMERICAN WRITER

Most conversations are simply monologues delivered in the presence of witnesses.

–MARGARET MILLAR (1915–1994) • CANADIAN MYSTERY WRITER

Maturity is knowing to say what to whom and when. Sometimes saying stuff is not a very good idea. You want to make yourself feel a little bit lighter, so you take your shit and you put it on somebody else's back. Well, that's extremely egotistic. One should know also how to hold things back and assume his or her own responsibility.

–MARJANE SATRAPI (1969–) • IRANIAN GRAPHIC NOVELIST

The ruder lecturers are, and the louder their voices, the more converts they make to their opinions.

–WINIFRED HOLTBY (1898–1935) • ENGLISH NOVELIST AND JOURNALIST

ARGUING

Fighting is essentially a masculine idea; a woman's weapon is her tongue.

–HERMIONE GINGOLD (1897–1987) • ENGLISH ACTOR

LISTENING

It takes a disciplined person to listen to convictions which are different from their own.

–DOROTHY FULDHEIM (1893–1989)
FIRST WOMAN TO ANCHOR AMERICAN TELEVISION NEWS PROGRAM

I'll not listen to reason. Reason always means what someone else has got to say.

–ELIZABETH GASKELL (1810-1865) • ENGLISH WRITER

Listening, not imitation, may be the sincerest form of flattery.

–JOYCE BROTHERS (1928-) • AMERICAN PSYCHOLOGIST AND COLUMNIST

A good listener is not someone with nothing to say. A good listener is a good talker with a sore throat.

–KATHARINE WHITEHORN (1926-)
ENGLISH JOURNALIST, WRITER, AND COLUMNIST

Don't talk over me, don't argue with me, just listen.

–LAURA SCHLESSINGER (1947-) • AMERICAN CULTURAL COMMENTATOR

No one really listens to anyone else, and if you try it for a while you'll see why.

–MIGNON MCLAUGHLIN (1913-1983)
AMERICAN JOURNALIST AND WRITER

SILENCE

The real art of conversation is not only to say the right thing in the right place but to leave unsaid the wrong thing at the tempting moment.

–LADY DOROTHY NEVILL (1826-1913) • ENGLISH WRITER AND SOCIETY FIGURE

Blessed is the man who, having nothing to say, abstains from giving us worthy evidence of the fact.

–GEORGE ELIOT (MARY ANN EVANS) (1819-1880) • ENGLISH WRITER

I like people who refuse to speak until they are ready to speak.

–LILLIAN HELLMAN (1905-1984) • AMERICAN PLAYWRIGHT

"COMPUTERS"

See also Technology

The New York Hilton is laid out with a competence that would make a computer blush.

–ADA LOUISE HUXTABLE • 20TH/21ST-CENTURY AMERICAN ARCHITECTURE CRITIC

No one ever said on their deathbed, "Gee, I wish I had spent more time alone with my computer."

–DANIELLE BERRY (1949–1998)
AMERICAN COMPUTER PROGRAMMER AND GAME DESIGNER

We build our computer [systems] the way we build our cities: over time, without a plan, on top of ruins.

–ELLEN ULLMAN • 20TH/21ST-CENTURY AMERICAN COMPUTER PROGRAMMER AND WRITER

Few influential people involved with the Internet claim that it is a good in and of itself. It is a powerful tool for solving social problems, just as it is a tool for making money, finding lost relatives, receiving medical advice, or, come to that, trading instructions for making bombs.

–ESTHER DYSON (1951–) • AMERICAN EXPERT IN DIGITAL MEDIA AND NEW TECHNOLOGIES

It was not so very long ago that people thought that semiconductors were part-time orchestra leaders and microchips were very small snack foods.

–GERALDINE FERRARO (1935–) • AMERICAN POLITICIAN AND NOMINEE FOR U.S. VICE PRESIDENT

To me programming is more than an important practical art. It is also a gigantic undertaking in the foundations of knowledge.

–GRACE MURRAY HOPPER (1906–1992)
PIONEERING COMPUTER SCIENTIST AND U.S. NAVY REAR ADMIRAL

They have computers, and they may have other weapons of mass destruction.

–JANET RENO (1938-) • FIRST FEMALE ATTORNEY GENERAL OF THE UNITED STATES

You're much more interesting when you're online—all of us are.

–JOY BROWNE • 20TH/21ST-CENTURY AMERICAN RADIO PSYCHOLOGIST

How would a car function if it were designed like a computer? Occasionally, executing a maneuver would cause your car to stop and fail, and you would have to re-install the engine, and the airbag system would say, "Are you sure?" before going off.

–KATIE HAFNER • 20TH/21ST-CENTURY AMERICAN JOURNALIST

What do people mean when they say the computer went down on them?

–MARILYN PITTMAN • 20TH/21ST-CENTURY AMERICAN COMEDIAN

I appreciate the sentiment that I am a popular woman in computer gaming circles; but I prefer being thought of as a computer game designer rather than a woman computer game designer. I don't put myself into gender mode when designing a game.

–ROBERTA WILLIAMS (1953-) • AMERICAN COMPUTER GAME DESIGNER

The mind can store an estimated one hundred trillion bits of information—compared with which a computer's mere billions are virtually amnesiac.

–SHARON BEGLEY • 20TH/21ST-CENTURY AMERICAN SCIENCE JOURNALIST AND EDITOR

"CONFIDENCE"

We gain power in our refusal to accept less than we deserve.

–AMBER HOLLIBAUGH

20TH/21ST-CENTURY AMERICAN FILMMAKER AND GLBT ACTIVIST

The Babe is here. Who's coming in second?

–BABE DIDRIKSON ZAHARIAS (1914–1956)
AMERICAN GOLFER

Success breeds confidence.

–BERYL MARKHAM (1902–1986)
ENGLISH-BORN KENYAN PILOT AND WRITER

I was thought to be "stuck up." I wasn't. I was just sure of myself. This is and always has been an unforgivable quality to the unsure.

–BETTE DAVIS (1908–1989) • AMERICAN ACTOR

I shall stay the way I am because I do not give a damn.

–DOROTHY PARKER (1893–1967) • AMERICAN WRITER AND CRITIC

Where so many hours have been spent in convincing myself that I am right, is there not some reason to fear I may be wrong?

–JANE AUSTEN (1775–1817) • ENGLISH WRITER

Women who are confident of their abilities are more likely to succeed than those who lack confidence, even though the latter may be much more competent and talented and industrious.

–JOYCE BROTHERS (1928–) • AMERICAN PSYCHOLOGIST AND COLUMNIST

You have the power. You are the magic wand.

–LAURA SCHLESSINGER (1947–)
AMERICAN CULTURAL COMMENTATOR

If you think you can, you're right; and if you think you can't, you're right.

–MARY KAY ASH (1918–2001) • AMERICAN COSMETICS ENTREPRENEUR

"CONFLICT"

Even when you think people are wrong, it is easy to tell when they are right. When they are right about something you are trying very hard to hide from others and yourself, you know they are right because you want to kill them.

–CANDICE BERGEN (1946–) • AMERICAN ACTOR

I do not love strife, because I have always found that in the end each remains of the same opinion.

–CATHERINE THE GREAT (1729–1796) • RUSSIAN EMPRESS

To handle yourself, use your head; to handle others, use your heart.

–ELEANOR ROOSEVELT (1884–1962) • AMERICAN POLITICAL LEADER AND FIRST LADY

The children worked on each other like two indestructible pieces of sandpaper.

–ELIZABETH BOWEN (1899–1973) • ANGLO-IRISH WRITER

Conflict begins at the moment of birth.

–JEAN BAKER MILLER (1927–2006) • AMERICAN PSYCHIATRIST

There can be no reconciliation where there is no open warfare. There must be a battle, a brave, boisterous battle, with pennants waving and cannon roaring, before there can be peaceful treaties and enthusiastic shaking of hands.

–MARY ELIZABETH BRADDON (1837–1915) • ENGLISH WRITER

You can't take sides when you know the earth is round.

–PATRICIA SUN

20TH/21ST-CENTURY AMERICAN PHILOSOPHER, ETHICIST, AND LEADER

It's truly a blessing to have total freaking idiots as your enemy.

–RACHEL MADDOW (1973–) • AMERICAN POLITICAL COMMENTATOR

"CONFORMITY"

What a sense of superiority it gives one to escape reading some book which everyone else is reading.

–ALICE JAMES (1848-1892) • AMERICAN DIARIST

It's very easy to be unconventional in a conventional manner.

–AUDRE LORDE (1934-1992) • AFRICAN-AMERICAN FEMINIST WRITER AND ACTIVIST

In order to be irreplaceable one must always be different.

–GABRIELLE "COCO" CHANEL (1883-1971) • FRENCH FASHION DESIGNER

Sane people did what their neighbors did, so that if any lunatics were at large, one might know and avoid them.

–GEORGE ELIOT (MARY ANN EVANS) (1819-1880) • ENGLISH WRITER

Normal is not something to aspire to, it's something to get away from.

–JODIE FOSTER (1962-) • AMERICAN ACTOR, DIRECTOR, AND PRODUCER

If you obey all the rules you miss all the fun.

–KATHARINE HEPBURN (1907-2003) • AMERICAN ACTOR

People in America, of course, live in all sorts of fashions, because they are foreigners, or unlucky, or depraved, or without ambition; people live like that, but Americans live in white detached houses with green shutters. Rigidly, blindly, the dream takes precedence.

–MARGARET MEAD (1901-1978) • AMERICAN CULTURAL ANTHROPOLOGIST

I once complained to my father that I didn't seem to be able to do things the same way other people did. Dad's advice? "Margo, don't be a sheep. People hate sheep. They eat sheep."

–MARGO KAUFMAN (1954-2000) • AMERICAN SCREENWRITER

Every society honors its live conformists and its dead troublemakers.

–MIGNON MCLAUGHLIN (1913-1983) • AMERICAN JOURNALIST AND WRITER

The reward for conformity is everyone likes you but yourself.

–RITA MAE BROWN (1944-) • AMERICAN WRITER AND ACTIVIST

"CONSCIENCE"

A guilty conscience is the mother of invention.

–CAROLYN WELLS (1869-1942) • AMERICAN WRITER

When will our consciences grow so tender that we will act to prevent human misery rather than avenge it?

–ELEANOR ROOSEVELT (1884-1962) • AMERICAN POLITICAL LEADER AND FIRST LADY

The one thing that doesn't abide by majority rule is a person's conscience.

–HARPER LEE (1926-) • AMERICAN WRITER

That's what a conscience is made of, scar tissue. . . . Little strips and pieces of remorse sewn together year by year until they formed a distinct pattern, a design for living.

–MARGARET MILLAR (1915-1994) • CANADIAN WRITER

While conscience is our friend, all is at peace; however once it is offended, farewell to a tranquil mind.

–LADY MARY WORTLEY MONTAGU (1689-1762)
ENGLISH POET, EPISTOLARY WRITER, AND SMALLPOX VACCINE ADVOCATE

•

The needle of our conscience is as good a compass as any.

–RUTH WOLFF (1932-) • AMERICAN WRITER

•

"CONSERVATION"

•

We have these earthquakes and other natural disasters because people are poisoning their Mother the Earth, they are poisoning her bloodstreams and cutting off her hair. They're not following the laws about caring for the Earth.

–JANET MCCLOUD (1934-2003) • NATIVE AMERICAN ACTIVIST AND ORATOR

•

People think I'm some kind of hippie. I don't even recycle.

–JEWEL (1974-) • AMERICAN SINGER-SONGWRITER

•

As consumers in the global marketplace, the collective power of our seemingly small actions is staggeringly large. Most of us, directly or indirectly, consume our own body weight in the natural resources of the Earth every day. We are literally stealing from the future to pay for our lifestyles today. What kind of planetary portfolio are we leaving behind for those who come after us?

–JULIA BUTTERFLY HILL (1974-) • AMERICAN ENVIRONMENTAL ACTIVIST

The notion of saving the planet has nothing to do with intellectual honesty or science. The fact is that the planet was here long before us and will be here long after us. The planet is running fine. What people are talking about is saving themselves and saving their cash flow.

–LYNN MARGULIS (1938-)
AMERICAN MICROBIOLOGIST AND CODEVELOPER OF THE GAIA HYPOTHESIS

•

We won't have a society if we destroy the environment.

–MARGARET MEAD (1901-1978)
AMERICAN CULTURAL ANTHROPOLOGIST

•

In an age when man has forgotten his origins and is blind even to his most essential needs for survival, water along with other resources has become the victim of his indifference.

–RACHEL CARSON (1907-1964) • AMERICAN ZOOLOGIST AND MARINE BIOLOGIST

•

The human race is challenged more than ever before to demonstrate our mastery—not over nature but of ourselves.

–RACHEL CARSON (1907-1964) • AMERICAN ZOOLOGIST AND MARINE BIOLOGIST

•

Environmentalists have long been fond of saying that the sun is the only safe nuclear reactor, situated as it is some 93 million miles away.

–STEPHANIE MILLS • 20TH/21ST-CENTURY AMERICAN WRITER, EDITOR, AND ECOLOGICAL ACTIVIST

•

The challenge is to . . . give back to our children a world of beauty and wonder.

–WANGARI MAATHAI (1940-)
KENYAN ENVIRONMENTALIST, FOUNDER OF THE GREEN BELT MOVEMENT
AND WINNER OF THE NOBEL PEACE PRIZE

"CONTRACEPTION"

See Reproductive Rights

"COOKING"

See also Food

There are people who claim to be instinctive cooks, who never follow recipes or weigh anything at all. All I can say is they're not very fussy about what they eat. For me, cooking is an exact art and not some casual game.

–DELIA SMITH (1941–) • ENGLISH CHEF AND COOKBOOK WRITER

A good cook is like a sorceress who dispenses happiness.

–ELSA SCHIAPARELLI (1890–1973) • ITALIAN FASHION DESIGNER

To the old saying that man built the house but woman made of it a "home" might be added the modern supplement that woman accepted cooking as a chore but man has made of it a recreation.

–EMILY POST (1873–1960) • AMERICAN ETIQUETTE EXPERT

When it comes to cooking, five years ago I felt guilty "just adding water." Now I want to bang the tube against the countertop and have a five-course meal pop out. If it comes with plastic silverware and a plate that self-destructs, all the better.

–ERMA BOMBECK (1927–1996) • AMERICAN HUMORIST

When men reach their sixties and retire, they go to pieces. Women go right on cooking.

–GAIL SHEEHY (1937–) • AMERICAN SOCIAL CRITIC

Cooking is like love. It should be entered into with abandon or not at all.

–HARRIET VAN HORNE (1920–) • AMERICAN COLUMNIST AND CRITIC

•

Non-cooks think it's silly to invest two hours' work in two minutes' enjoyment; but if cooking is evanescent, so is the ballet.

–JULIA CHILD (1912–2004) • AMERICAN CHEF AND TELEVISION PERSONALITY

•

I was 32 when I started cooking; up until then, I just ate.

–JULIA CHILD (1912–2004) • AMERICAN CHEF AND TELEVISION PERSONALITY

•

Cooking is actually quite aggressive and controlling and sometimes, yes, there is an element of force-feeding going on.

–NIGELLA LAWSON (1960–) • ENGLISH JOURNALIST, CHEF, AND TELEVISION PERSONALITY

•

AVOIDING

I prefer Hostess fruit pies to pop-up toaster tarts because they don't require as much cooking.

–CARRIE P. SNOW • 20TH/21ST-CENTURY AMERICAN COMEDIAN

•

I don't even butter my bread. I consider that cooking.

–KATHERINE CEBRIAN

20TH-CENTURY AMERICAN SOCIALITE, WRITER, AND ARTIST

•

My mother was a good recreational cook, but what she basically believed about cooking was that if you worked hard and prospered, someone else would do it for you.

–NORA EPHRON (1941–)

AMERICAN FILM DIRECTOR, PRODUCER, SCREENWRITER, AND NOVELIST

•

The worst mistake of a woman is to go to the kitchen, because then she never gets out of there.

–SHAKIRA (1977–) • COLOMBIAN POP SINGER AND SONGWRITER

“COOPERATION”

Alone we can do so little; together we can do so much.

–HELEN KELLER (1880-1968) • AMERICAN WRITER AND ACTIVIST

The one hand trying to wash itself is a pitiful spectacle, but when one hand washes the other, power is increased, and it becomes a force to be reckoned with.

–MAYA ANGELOU (1928-) • AFRICAN AMERICAN POET, MEMOIRIST, AND CIVIL RIGHTS ACTIVIST

Until all of us have made it, none of us have made it.

–ROSEMARY BROWN (1930-2003) • JAMAICAN-BORN CANADIAN POLITICIAN

Cooperation is the thorough conviction that nobody can get there unless everybody gets there.

–VIRGINIA BURDEN TOWER • 20TH-CENTURY AMERICAN WRITER

When you collaborate with other people, you tend to regard your own individual contribution as the most important.

–YANG JIANG (1911-) • CHINESE WRITER AND TRANSLATOR

“COURAGE”

Courage is not the towering oak that sees storms come and go; it is the fragile blossom that opens in the snow.

–ALICE M. SWAIM (1911-1996) • WRITER AND POET

Courage is the price that life exacts for granting peace.

–AMELIA EARHART (1897-1937)

PIONEERING AMERICAN AVIATOR; FIRST PERSON TO FLY SOLO ACROSS PACIFIC

Life shrinks or expands in proportion to one's courage.

—ANAÏS NIN • FRENCH WRITER AND DIARIST

But there are no new ideas waiting in the wings to save us as women, as humans. There are only old and forgotten ones, new combinations, extrapolations, and recognitions from within ourselves, along with the renewed courage to try them out.

—AUDRE LORDE (1934–1992) • AFRICAN-AMERICAN FEMINIST WRITER AND ACTIVIST

If there's one thing you've got to hold on to, it's the courage to fight!

—BESSIE DELANY (1891–1995) • AFRICAN-AMERICAN DENTIST AND MEMOIRIST

Courage is the ladder on which all other virtues mount.

—CLARE BOOTHE LUCE (1903–1987)
AMERICAN PLAYWRIGHT, JOURNALIST, AND POLITICIAN

The bravest thing you can do when you are not brave is to profess courage and act accordingly.

—CORRA HARRIS (1869–1935) • AMERICAN WRITER

Courage is fear that has said its prayers.

—DOROTHY BERNARD (1890–1955)
SOUTH AFRICAN-BORN EARLY FILM STAR

As for keeping the attack dogs from nibbling away your courage? My theory, after decades in this business, is that you only give a few people the right to make you feel rotten. You have a handful of chits to give out, penuriously, to those you trust and respect. You don't give them to just anyone with an e-mail address and an epithet.

—ELLEN GOODMAN (1941–) • AMERICAN JOURNALIST

The uplift of a fearless heart will help us over barriers. No one ever overcomes difficulties by going at them in a hesitant, doubtful way.

–LAURA INGALLS WILDER (1867–1957) • AMERICAN PIONEER AND WRITER

The right way is not always the popular and easy way. Standing for right when it is unpopular is a true test of moral character.

–MARGARET CHASE SMITH (1897–1995) • AMERICAN CONGRESSWOMAN

Courage doesn't always roar. Sometimes courage is the quiet voice at the end of the day saying, "I will try again tomorrow."

–MARY ANNE RADMACHER • 20TH/21ST-CENTURY AMERICAN WRITER AND ARTIST

True champions aren't always the ones that win, but those with the most guts.

–MIA HAMM (1972–) • AMERICAN SOCCER PLAYER

Even cowards can endure hardship; only the brave can endure suspense.

MIGNON MCLAUGHLIN (1913–1983) • AMERICAN JOURNALIST AND WRITER

"CREATIVITY"

Helped are those who create anything at all, for they shall relive the thrill of their own conception, and realize a partnership in the creation of the Universe that keeps them responsible and cheerful.

–ALICE WALKER (1944–) • AFRICAN-AMERICAN WRITER AND POET

I believe that true identity is found in creative activity springing from within. It is found when one loses oneself.

–ANNE MORROW LINDBERGH (1906–2001) • AMERICAN WRITER AND PIONEERING AVIATOR

There is a microscopically thin line between being brilliantly creative and acting like the most gigantic idiot on Earth.

–CYNTHIA HEIMEL • 20TH/21ST-CENTURY AMERICAN WRITER

●

Very few people possess true artistic ability. It is therefore both unseemly and unproductive to irritate the situation by making an effort. If you have a burning, restless urge to write or paint, simply eat something sweet and the feeling will pass.

–FRAN LEBOWITZ (1950–) • AMERICAN HUMORIST

●

The things we fear most in organizations—fluctuations, disturbances, imbalances—are the primary sources of creativity.

–MARGARET J. WHEATLEY
20TH/21ST-CENTURY AMERICAN ORGANIZATIONAL EXPERT AND MANAGEMENT CONSULTANT

●

Creativity comes from trust. Trust your instincts.
And never hope more than you work.

–RITA MAE BROWN (1944–) • AMERICAN WRITER AND ACTIVIST

●

You start by copying other people's paintings or music or whatever. You get all of those skills before you branch out. Really creative people have a fantastic ability to copy things and then combine them in new ways. And whether we're talking about genes or memes, recombination is the real heart of creativity.

–SUSAN BLACKMORE (1951–)
ENGLISH FREELANCE WRITER, LECTURER, AND BROADCASTER

"CRIME"

Crime seems to change character when it crosses a bridge or a tunnel. In the city, crime is taken as emblematic of class and race. In the suburbs, though, it's intimate and psychological—resistant to generalization, a mystery of the individual soul.

—BARBARA EHRENREICH (1941-) • AMERICAN ESSAYIST AND SOCIAL CRITIC

One crime is everything; two nothing.

—DOROTHÉE DELUZY (1747-1830) • FRENCH ACTOR

Lawlessness is a self-perpetuating, ever-expanding habit.

—DOROTHY THOMPSON (1894-1961)
AMERICAN JOURNALIST AND RADIO COMMENTATOR

Crime is naught but misdirected energy. So long as every institution of today, economic, political, social, and moral, conspires to misdirect human energy into wrong channels; so long as most people are out of place doing the things they hate to do, living a life they loathe to live, crime will be inevitable, and all the laws on the statutes can only increase, but never do away with, crime.

—EMMA GOLDMAN (1869-1940) • RUSSIAN ANARCHIST AND FEMINIST

Where all are guilty, no one is; confessions of collective guilt are the best possible safeguard against the discovery of culprits, and the very magnitude of the crime the best excuse for doing nothing.

—HANNAH ARENDT (1906-1975) • GERMAN-BORN POLITICAL PHILOSOPHER AND HISTORIAN

"Crimes of passion"—that phrase drives me crazy. A man murdering his girlfriend is not a crime of passion. Premature ejaculation, that's a crime of passion.

—HELLURA LYLE • 20TH/21ST-CENTURY AMERICAN COMEDIAN

White criminals commit the biggest crimes. A brother might rob a bank. A white man will rob a pension fund. The brother is going to get ten to fifteen years because he had a gun. The white guy will get a congressional hearing because he had a job and a nice suit.

—WANDA SYKES • 20TH/21ST-CENTURY AFRICAN-AMERICAN COMEDIAN AND ACTOR

"CRYING"

I often want to cry. That is the only advantage women have over men—at least they can cry.

—JEAN RHYS (1890–1979) • CARIBBEAN WRITER

Certainly tears are given to us to use. Like all good gifts, they should be used properly.

—LORETTA YOUNG (1913–2000) • AMERICAN ACTOR

Rich tears! What power lies in those falling drops.

—MARY DELARIVIÈRE MANLEY (1663–1724)
ENGLISH NOVELIST AND PLAYWRIGHT

Women are never landlocked: They're always mere minutes away from the briny deep of tears.

—MIGNON MCLAUGHLIN (1913–1983)
AMERICAN JOURNALIST AND WRITER

Time engraves our faces with all the tears we have not shed.

—NATALIE CLIFFORD BARNEY (1876–1972)
AMERICAN POET, MEMOIRIST, AND SOCIAL REBEL

I didn't know why I was going to cry, but I knew that if anybody spoke to me or looked at me too closely the tears would fly out of my eyes and the sobs would fly out of my throat, and I'd cry for a week. I could feel the tears brimming and sloshing in me like water in a glass that is unsteady and too full.

–SYLVIA PLATH (1932–1963) • AMERICAN POET AND PROSE WRITER

"CULTURE"

Placing on writers the responsibility to represent a culture is an onerous burden.

–AMY TAN (1952–) • ASIAN-AMERICAN WRITER

A people's literature is the great textbook for real knowledge of them. The writings of the day show the quality of the people as no historical reconstruction can.

–EDITH HAMILTON (1867–1963) • AMERICAN EDUCATOR, TRANSLATOR, AND CLASSICS SCHOLAR

American culture is torn between our long romance with violence and our terror of the devastation wrought by war and crime and environmental havoc.

–KATHERINE DUNN • 20TH/21ST-CENTURY AMERICAN NOVELIST, JOURNALIST, AND POET

In fact, Western culture has spent decades drawing lines and boxes around interconnected phenomena. We've chunked the world into pieces rather than explored its webby nature.

–MARGARET J. WHEATLEY
20TH/21ST-CENTURY AMERICAN ORGANIZATIONAL EXPERT AND MANAGEMENT CONSULTANT

Why is terrorism so much more in evidence now than before? The kind of society we are going to be living in more and more tends to make isolates of us all. This means obviously an impoverished cultural life, narrow horizons, the sense of meaninglessness, futility—in short, an apathetic culture.

–MARY DOUGLAS (1921–) • ENGLISH ANTHROPOLOGIST

Culture is what your butcher would have if he were a surgeon.

—MARY PETTIBONE POOLE • 20TH-CENTURY AMERICAN WRITER

•

The trilogy composed of politics, religion, and sex is the most sensitive of all issues in any society.

—NAWAL EL SAADAWI (1931–)
EGYPTIAN PSYCHIATRIST, FEMINIST WRITER, ACTIVIST

•

Culture is both an intellectual phenomenon and a moral one.

—RAISA GORBACHEV (1932–1999)
RUSSIAN POLITICAL FIGURE, SOCIOLOGIST, AND WIFE OF SOVIET LEADER MIKHAIL GORBACHEV

•

Ours is a culture based on excess, on overproduction; the result is a steady loss of sharpness in our sensory experience. All the conditions of modern life—its material plenitude, its sheer crowdedness—conjoin to dull our sensory faculties.

—SUSAN SONTAG (1933–2004)
AMERICAN ESSAYIST, NOVELIST, INTELLECTUAL, AND ACTIVIST

•

"*CURIOSITY*"

•

It is inconceivable that anything should be existing. It is not inconceivable that a lot of people should also be existing who are not interested in the fact that they exist. But it is certainly very odd.

—CELIA GREEN (1935–) • ENGLISH PHILOSOPHER AND PSYCHOLOGIST

•

The cure for boredom is curiosity. There is no cure for curiosity.

—DOROTHY PARKER (1893–1967) • AMERICAN WRITER AND CRITIC

One thing life has taught me: If you are interested, you never have to look for new interests. They come to you. When you are genuinely interested in one thing, it will always lead to something else.

–ELEANOR ROOSEVELT (1884–1962) • AMERICAN POLITICAL LEADER AND FIRST LADY

I think, at a child's birth, if a mother could ask a fairy godmother to endow it with the most useful gift, that gift would be curiosity.

–ELEANOR ROOSEVELT (1884–1962) • AMERICAN POLITICAL LEADER AND FIRST LADY

A stale mind is the devil's breadbox.

–MARY BLY

20TH/21ST-CENTURY AMERICAN PROFESSOR AND WRITER

D

"DANCE"

To dance is to be out of yourself. Larger, more beautiful, more powerful. This is power; it is glory on earth, and it is yours for the taking.

–AGNES DE MILLE (1905–1993) • AMERICAN DANCER AND CHOREOGRAPHER

Master technique and then forget about it and be natural.

–ANNA PAVLOVA (1881–1931) • RUSSIAN BALLERINA

If I cannot dance, I want no part in your revolution.

–EMMA GOLDMAN (1869–1940) • RUSSIAN ANARCHIST AND FEMINIST

Remember, Ginger Rogers did everything Fred Astaire did, but backward and in high heels.

–FAITH WHITTLESEY (1939–)
LAWYER, POLITICIAN, AND AMERICAN AMBASSADOR

Classical dancing is like being a mother: If you've never done it, you can't imagine how hard it is.

–HARRIET CAVALLI
20TH/21ST-CENTURY AMERICAN PIANIST, DANCER, AND WRITER

Dancing: The Highest Intelligence in the Freest Body.

–ISADORA DUNCAN (1877–1927) • AMERICAN MODERN DANCER

To be fond of dancing was a certain step towards falling in love.

–JANE AUSTEN (1775–1817) • ENGLISH WRITER

I improvised, crazed by the music. . . . Even my teeth and eyes burned with fever. Each time I leaped I seemed to touch the sky, and when I regained earth it seemed to be mine alone.

–JOSEPHINE BAKER (1906–1975)
NATIVE AMERICAN/AFRICAN-AMERICAN DANCER, SINGER, AND ACTOR

•

Every dancer lives on the threshold of chucking it.

–JUDITH JAMISON (1943–)
AFRICAN-AMERICAN MODERN DANCER AND CHOREOGRAPHER

•

Bleeding feet will bond us.

–LIZA MINELLI (1946–)
AMERICAN ACTOR, DANCER, AND SINGER

•

La danse, c'est le mouvement, et le mouvement, c'est la vie.
(Dance is movement, and movement is life.)

–LUDMILLA CHIRIAEFF (1924–1996)
CANADIAN BALLET DANCER, CHOREOGRAPHER, AND DIRECTOR

•

Dancing is just discovery, discovery, discovery.

–MARTHA GRAHAM (1894–1991)
AMERICAN DANCER AND CHOREOGRAPHER

•

Movement never lies. It is a barometer telling the state of the soul's weather.

–MARTHA GRAHAM (1894–1991) • AMERICAN DANCER AND CHOREOGRAPHER

•

The dance is a poem of which each movement is a word.

–MATA HARI (1876–1917)
DUTCH DANCER EXECUTED FOR ALLEGED ESPIONAGE IN WORLD WAR I

Everything in the universe has rhythm. Everything dances.

–MAYA ANGELOU (1928-)
AFRICAN-AMERICAN POET, MEMOIRIST, AND CIVIL RIGHTS ACTIVIST

•

Learning to walk sets you free. Learning to dance gives you the greatest freedom of all: to express with your whole self the person you are.

–MELISSA HAYDEN (1923-) • CANADIAN DANCER

•

Even the ears must dance.

–NATALIA MAKAROVA (1940-)
RUSSIAN BALLET DANCER

•

I have performed for thousands when they found me exotic, the vogue, daring, but I have danced, at any given time, for about ten people. . . . They were the ones that left the theater forever different from the way they were when they came in. All of my long, long life, I have danced for those ten.

–RUTH ST. DENIS (1879-1968) • AMERICAN MODERN DANCE PIONEER

•

There's a hunger for learning, and I think that dancers are wonderful in their ability to turn 'round and say, "every day is a learning day."

–SIOBHAN DAVIES (1950-) • ENGLISH DANCER AND CHOREOGRAPHER

•

Technical perfection is insufficient. It is an orphan without the true soul of the dancer.

–SYLVIE GUILLEM (1965-) • FRENCH BALLET DANCER

•

Dancing is like bank robbery; it takes split-second timing.

–TWYLA THARP (1941-) • AMERICAN DANCER AND CHOREOGRAPHER

•

There are shortcuts to happiness, and dancing is one of them.

–VICKI BAUM (1888-1960) • AUSTRIAN WRITER

BALLET

Ballet technique is arbitrary and very difficult.
It never becomes easy—it becomes possible.

—AGNES DE MILLE (1905–1993)
AMERICAN DANCER AND CHOREOGRAPHER

•

Toe dancing is a dandy attention getter, second only to screaming.

—AGNES DE MILLE (1905–1993) • AMERICAN DANCER AND CHOREOGRAPHER

•

CHOREOGRAPHY

The choreographic process is exhausting. It happens on one's feet after hours of work, and the energy required is roughly the equivalent of writing a novel and winning a tennis match simultaneously.

—AGNES DE MILLE (1905–1993) • AMERICAN DANCER AND CHOREOGRAPHER

•

"DATING"

•

On a plane you can pick up more and better people than on any other public conveyance since the stagecoach.

—ANITA LOOS (1889–1981) • AMERICAN SCREENWRITER, NOVELIST, AND ESSAYIST

•

I'm like an expensive menu . . . you can look but you can't afford.

—ANNA KOURNIKOVA (1981–) • RUSSIAN TENNIS PLAYER AND MODEL

•

Why get married and make one man miserable when I can stay single and make thousands miserable?

—CARRIE P. SNOW • 20TH/21ST-CENTURY AMERICAN COMEDIAN

•

A girl can wait for the right man to come along but, in the meantime, that doesn't mean she can't have a wonderful time with all the wrong ones.

—CHER (1946–) • AMERICAN SINGER, ACTOR, AND POP ICON

One does not have to sleep with, or even touch, someone who has paid for your meal. All those obligations are hereby rendered null and void, and any man who doesn't think so needs a quick jab in the kidney.

–CYNTHIA HEIMEL • 20TH/21ST-CENTURY AMERICAN WRITER

•

A man on a date wonders if he'll get lucky. The woman already knows.

–MONICA PIPER • 20TH/21ST-CENTURY AMERICAN COMEDIAN AND WRITER

•

Computer dating is fine, if you're a computer.

–RITA MAE BROWN (1944–)
AMERICAN WRITER AND ACTIVIST

•

I was on a date recently, and the guy took me horseback riding. That was kind of fun, until we ran out of quarters.

–SUSIE LOUCKS • 20TH/21ST-CENTURY AMERICAN ACTOR

•

"DEATH"

•

I postpone death by living, by suffering, by error, by risking, by giving, by losing.

–ANAÏS NIN (1903–1977)
FRENCH WRITER AND DIARIST

•

There's something about death that is comforting. The thought that you could die tomorrow frees you to appreciate your life now.

–ANGELINA JOLIE (1975–) • AMERICAN ACTOR

•

It's so unfair that we should die, just because we are born.

–ANNA MAGNANI (1918–1973) • ITALIAN ACTOR

[On being told that her death was rumored:] With the newspaper strike on, I wouldn't consider dying.

–BETTE DAVIS (1908–1989) • AMERICAN ACTOR

•

That would be a good thing for them to cut on my tombstone: Wherever she went, including here, it was against her better judgment.

–DOROTHY PARKER (1893–1967) • AMERICAN WRITER AND CRITIC

I don't fear death because I don't fear anything I don't understand. When I start to think about it, I order a massage and it goes away.

–HEDY LAMARR (1913–2000) • AUSTRIAN-BORN ACTOR AND INVENTOR

•

I could not count the times during the average day when something would come up that I needed to tell him. . . . This impulse did not end with his death. What ended was the possibility of response.

–JOAN DIDION (1934–) • AMERICAN WRITER

•

I welcome death. In death there are no interviews.

–KATHARINE HEPBURN (1907–2003) • AMERICAN ACTOR

•

I still miss those I loved who are no longer with me, but I find I am grateful for having loved them. The gratitude has finally conquered the loss.

–RITA MAE BROWN (1944–) • AMERICAN WRITER AND ACTIVIST

•

I tell myself that God gave my children many gifts—spirit, beauty, intelligence, the capacity to make friends and to inspire respect. There was only one gift he held back—length of life.

–ROSE KENNEDY (1890–1995)

AMERICAN; MOTHER OF PRESIDENT JOHN F. KENNEDY

For those who live neither with religious consolations about death nor with a sense of death (or of anything else) as natural, death is the obscene mystery, the ultimate affront, the thing that cannot be controlled. It can only be denied.

–SUSAN SONTAG (1933–2004)
AMERICAN ESSAYIST, NOVELIST, INTELLECTUAL, AND ACTIVIST

•

Death is a tangible reminder that life is too short to not do what you love.

–TAMMY CRAVIT • 20TH/21ST-CENTURY AMERICAN JOURNALIST AND WRITER

•

EUTHANASIA

The time is approaching when we shall consider it abhorrent to our civilization to allow a human being to die in prolonged agony which we should mercifully end in any other creature.

–CHARLOTTE PERKINS GILMAN (1860–1935) • AMERICAN WRITER AND SOCIAL CRITIC

•

Euthanasia is a long, smooth-sounding word, and it conceals its danger as long, smooth words do, but the danger is there, nevertheless.

–PEARL S. BUCK (1892–1973)
FIRST FEMALE AMERICAN WINNER OF THE NOBEL PRIZE IN LITERATURE

•

Euthanasia . . . is simply to be able to die with dignity at a moment when life is devoid of it.

–MARYA MANNES (1904–1990) • AMERICAN COLUMNIST AND CRITIC

PENALTY

As one whose husband and mother-in-law have died the victims of murder and assassination, I stand firmly and unequivocally opposed to the death penalty for those convicted of capital offenses. An evil deed is not redeemed by an evil deed of retaliation. Justice is never advanced in the taking of a human life. Morality is never upheld by legalized murder.

–CORETTA SCOTT KING (1927–2006)
AFRICAN-AMERICAN CIVIL RIGHTS ACTIVIST AND WIDOW OF DR. MARTIN LUTHER KING JR.

•

The people doin' the thinkin' and the people doin' the murderin' are two separate sets of people.

–SISTER HELEN PREJEAN (1939–)
AMERICAN ROMAN CATHOLIC NUN AND ANTI-DEATH-PENALTY ACTIVIST

•

"*DEPRESSION*"

•

Sadness is more or less like a head cold—with patience, it passes. Depression is like cancer.

–BARBARA KINGSOLVER (1955–) • AMERICAN WRITER

•

Depression is a very sensible reaction to just about everything we live in now.

–CHRYSTOS (1946–) • NATIVE AMERICAN ARTIST, POET, AND ACTIVIST

•

Studies show that 80 percent of the population suffers from depression, and the other 20 percent of you cause it.

–DANA EAGLE • 20TH/21ST-CENTURY AMERICAN COMEDIAN

•

Noble deeds and hot baths are the best cures for depression.

–DODIE SMITH (1896–1990) • ENGLISH NOVELIST AND PLAYWRIGHT

When women are depressed, they eat or go shopping. Men invade another country. It's a whole different way of thinking.

—ELAYNE BOOSLER (1952–) • AMERICAN COMEDIAN

I cannot remember the time when I have not longed for death. . . . For years and years I used to watch for death as no sick man ever watched for the morning.

—FLORENCE NIGHTINGALE (1820–1910)
ENGLISH NURSE AND MEDICAL REFORMER

There is this difference between depression and sorrow—sorrowful, you are in great trouble because something matters so much; depressed, you are miserable because nothing really matters.

—J. E. BUCKROSE (ANNIE EDITH JAMESON) (1868–1931) • ENGLISH WRITER

Poor me. There's nothing so sweet as wallowing in it is there? Wallowing is sex for depressives.

—JEANETTE WINTERSON (1959–) • ENGLISH WRITER

It is one of the secrets of Nature in its mood of mockery that fine weather lays heavier weight on the mind and hearts of the depressed and the inwardly tormented than does a really bad day with dark rain sniveling continuously and sympathetically from a dirty sky.

—MURIEL SPARK (1918–2006) • SCOTTISH-BORN ENGLISH WRITER

Depression sits on my chest like a sumo wrestler.

—SANDRA SCOPPETTONE (1936–) • AMERICAN WRITER

"DESIRE"

Our visions begin with our desires.

–AUDRE LORDE (1934–1992)
AFRICAN-AMERICAN FEMINIST WRITER AND ACTIVIST

How helpless we are, like netted birds, when we are caught by desire!

–BELVA PLAIN (1919–) • AMERICAN WRITER

Nobody speaks the truth when there is something they must have.

–ELIZABETH BOWEN (1899–1973) • ANGLO-IRISH WRITER

When we start deceiving ourselves into thinking not that we want something or need something, not that it is a pragmatic necessity for us to have it, but that it is a moral imperative that we have it, then is when we join the fashionable madmen, and then is when the thin whine of hysteria is heard across the land, and then is when we are in bad trouble.

–JOAN DIDION (1934–) • AMERICAN WRITER

One must desire something, to be alive; perhaps absolute satisfaction is only another name for Death.

–MARGARET DELAND (1857–1945) • AMERICAN WRITER AND POET

Desire can blind us to the hazards of our enterprises.

–MARIE DE FRANCE (1155–1190) • FRENCH POET

Nothing's far when one wants to get there.

–QUEEN MARIE OF RUMANIA (1875–1938)
BORN PRINCESS MARIE OF EDINBURGH; MEMBER OF THE BRITISH ROYAL FAMILY

Desire is in men a hunger, in women only an appetite.

–MIGNON MCLAUGHLIN (1913-1983)
AMERICAN JOURNALIST AND WRITER

•

If the medieval alchemists had ever discovered a way to distill the essence of need in their retorts, they would have found a substance potent enough to turn smoke into pure gold.

–PAM DURBAN (1947-) • AMERICAN WRITER

•

If neurotic is wanting two mutually exclusive things at one and the same time, then I'm neurotic as hell. I'll be flying back and forth between one mutually exclusive thing and another for the rest of my days.

–SYLVIA PLATH (1932-1963) • AMERICAN POET AND PROSE WRITER

•

This is my ultimate fantasy: watching QVC with a credit card while making love and eating at the same time.

–YASMINE BLEETH (1968-) • AMERICAN ACTOR

•

"DIARIES/JOURNALS"

•

My diary seems to keep me whole.

–ANAÏS NIN (1903-1977)
FRENCH WRITER AND DIARIST

•

It seems to me that the problem with diaries, and the reason that most of them are so boring, is that every day we vacillate between examining our hangnails and speculating on cosmic order.

–ANN BEATTIE (1947-) • AMERICAN WRITER

Journal writing is a voyage to the interior.

–CHRISTINA BALDWIN

20TH/21ST-CENTURY AMERICAN RETREAT LEADER ON SPIRITUALITY AND PERSONAL WRITING

•

My notebook does not help me think, but it eases my crabbed heart.

–FLORIDA SCOTT-MAXWELL (1883–1979) • AMERICAN SUFFRAGIST AND PSYCHOLOGIST

•

What is a diary as a rule? A document useful to the person who keeps it. Dull to the contemporary who reads it and invaluable to the student, centuries afterward, who treasures it.

–HELEN TERRY (1956–) • ENGLISH SINGER

•

It's not a bad idea to get in the habit of writing down one's thoughts. It saves one having to bother anyone with them.

–ISABEL COLEGATE (1931–) • ENGLISH WRITER

•

When I first began this diary I said I would give a record of my inner life. I begin to wonder if I have said anything about my inner life. What if I have no inner life?

–JANET FRAME (1924–2004) • NEW ZEALAND WRITER

•

People who keep journals have life twice.

–JESSAMYN WEST (1902–1984) • AMERICAN WRITER

•

Keep a diary, and someday it'll keep you.

–MAE WEST (1893–1980)

AMERICAN ACTOR, WRITER, AND SEX SYMBOL

•

I think this journal will be disadvantageous for me, for I spend my time now like a spider spinning my own entrails.

–MARY BOYKIN CHESNUT (1823–1886) • AMERICAN DIARIST

That all my dreams might not prove empty, I have been writing this useless account—though I doubt it will long survive me.

–LADY NIJO (1258–1307) • JAPANESE POET AND DIARIST

Keep a grateful journal. Every night, list five things that you are grateful for. What it will begin to do is change your perspective of your day and your life.

–OPRAH WINFREY (1954–) • AFRICAN-AMERICAN TELEVISION HOST AND MAGAZINE PUBLISHER

It makes me laugh to read over this diary. It's so full of contradictions, and one would think I was such an unhappy woman. Yet is there a happier woman than I?

–SOPHIE TOLSTOY (1844–1919) • RUSSIAN DIARIST

Only good girls keep diaries. Bad girls don't have time.

–TALLULAH BANKHEAD (1902–1968) • AMERICAN ACTOR

A journal is a leap of faith. You write without knowing what the next day's entry will be—or when the last.

–VIOLET WEINGARTEN (1915–1976) • AMERICAN WRITER

"DIETING"

See also Food, Weight

I've been on a constant diet for the last two decades. I've lost a total of 789 pounds. By all accounts, I should be hanging from a charm bracelet.

–ERMA BOMBECK (1927–1996) • AMERICAN HUMORIST

The first thing I did when I made the decision to kill myself was to stop dieting. Let them dig a wider hole.

–GRACE PARENT (1940–) • AMERICAN WRITER

If you have formed the habit of checking on every new diet that comes along, you will find that, mercifully, they all blur together, leaving you with only one definite piece of information: French-fried potatoes are out.

–JEAN KERR (1923–2003) • AMERICAN PLAYWRIGHT AND HUMORIST

•

The only time to eat diet food is while you're waiting for the steak to cook.

–JULIA CHILD (1912–2004) • AMERICAN CHEF AND TELEVISION PERSONALITY

•

If one doesn't have a character like Abraham Lincoln or Joan of Arc, a diet simply disintegrates into eating exactly what you want to eat, but with a bad conscience.

–MARIA AUGUSTA TRAPP (1905–1987)
AUSTRIAN-BORN SINGER, WRITER, AND MATRIARCH OF THE TRAPP FAMILY SINGERS

•

[On her weight loss:] I've learned not to put things in my mouth that are bad for me.

–MONICA LEWINSKY (1973–)
AMERICAN WOMAN MADE FAMOUS BY HER AFFAIR WITH PRESIDENT BILL CLINTON

•

I never diet. I smoke. I drink now and then. I never work out. I work very hard, and I am worth every cent.

–NAOMI CAMPBELL (1970–) • ENGLISH MODEL

•

I've been on a diet for two weeks, and all I've lost is two weeks.

–TOTIE FIELDS (1930–1978) • AMERICAN COMEDIAN

•

"DIVERSITY"

See also Identity, Race/Racism

Differences challenge assumptions.

—ANNE WILSON SCHAEF (1934–)
AMERICAN PSYCHOTHERAPIST AND ACTIVIST

•

Variety is the soul of pleasure.

—APHRA BEHN (1640–1689)
ENGLISH PLAYWRIGHT, POET, NOVELIST, AND SPY

•

Few are the giants of the soul who actually feel that the human race is their family circle.

—FREYA STARK (1893–1993) • FRENCH-BORN ENGLISH TRAVEL WRITER

•

What we have to do . . . is to find a way to celebrate our diversity and debate our differences without fracturing our communities.

—HILLARY RODHAM CLINTON (1947–) • AMERICAN POLITICIAN AND FIRST LADY

•

Mankind will endure when the world appreciates the logic of diversity.

—INDIRA GANDHI (1917–1984) • PRIME MINISTER OF INDIA

•

As a child I sought perfection and so denied myself the claim to any identity. As an adult I accept that a bicultural upbringing is a rich but imperfect thing.

—JHUMPA LAHIRI (1967–) • INDIAN-AMERICAN WRITER

•

Militant Islam may be the beginning of the end for multiculturalism, the live-and-let-live philosophy that asks, Why can't we all enjoy our differences? Ethnic food and world music are all very well, but fatwas and amputations and suicide bombings just don't put a smile on the day.

—KATHA POLLITT (1949–) • AMERICAN FEMINIST WRITER AND CULTURAL CRITIC

Diversity is the most basic principle of creation. No two snowflakes, blades of grass, or people are alike.

—LYNN MARIA LAITALA (1947–) • AMERICAN WRITER

Fear of difference is fear of life itself.

—M. P. FOLLETT (1868–1933) • AMERICAN SOCIOLOGIST

What people often mean by getting rid of conflict is getting rid of diversity, and it is of the utmost importance that these should not be considered the same.

—M. P. FOLLETT (1868–1933) • AMERICAN SOCIOLOGIST

When Jesus Christ asked little children to come to him, he didn't say only rich children, or white children, or children with two-parent families, or children who didn't have a mental or physical handicap. He said, "Let all children come unto me."

—MARIAN WRIGHT EDELMAN (1939–)
AFRICAN-AMERICAN FOUNDER OF THE CHILDREN'S DEFENSE FUND

Insight, I believe, refers to the depth of understanding that comes by setting experiences, yours and mine, familiar and exotic, new and old, side by side, learning by letting them speak to one another.

—MARY CATHERINE BATESON (1939–) • AMERICAN WRITER AND CULTURAL ANTHROPOLOGIST

We all should know that diversity makes for a rich tapestry, and we must understand that all the threads of the tapestry are equal in value no matter what their color.

—MAYA ANGELOU (1928–) • AFRICAN-AMERICAN POET, MEMOIRIST, AND CIVIL RIGHTS ACTIVIST

Living more lives than one, knowing people of all classes, all shades of opinion, monarchists, republicans, socialists, anarchists, has had a salutary effect on my mind. If every year of my life, every month of the year, I had lived with reformers and crusaders, I should be, by this time, a fanatic. As it is I have had such varied things to do, I have had so many different contacts, that I am not even very much of a crank.

—RHETA CHILDE DORR (1868–1948) • AMERICAN JOURNALIST AND SUFFRAGIST

"DIVORCE"

A divorcée is a woman who got married so she didn't have to work, but now works so she doesn't have to get married.

—ANNA MAGNANI (1918–1973) • ITALIAN ACTOR

If divorce has increased by one thousand percent, don't blame the women's movement. Blame the obsolete sex roles on which our marriages were based.

—BETTY FRIEDAN (1921–2006)
AMERICAN FEMINIST, WRITER, AND COFOUNDER OF NATIONAL ORGANIZATION FOR WOMEN

So many persons think divorce a panacea for every ill, who find out, when they try it, that the remedy is worse than the disease.

—DOROTHEA DIX (1802–1887) • AMERICAN SOCIAL REFORMER AND MENTAL HEALTH ACTIVIST

It serves me right for putting all my eggs in one bastard.

—DOROTHY PARKER (1893–1967) • AMERICAN WRITER AND CRITIC

I've given my memoirs far more thought than any of my marriages. You can't divorce a book.

—GLORIA SWANSON (1899–1983) • AMERICAN SILENT FILM STAR

When two people decide to get a divorce, it isn't a sign that they "don't understand" one another, but a sign that they have, at last, begun to.

–HELEN ROWLAND (1875–1950) • AMERICAN JOURNALIST AND HUMORIST

•

Divorce is only less painful than the need for divorce.

–JANE O'REILLY • 20TH/21ST-CENTURY AMERICAN WRITER AND MEMOIRIST

•

Divorce is like being hit by a Mack truck. If you live through it, you start looking very carefully to the right and to the left.

–JEAN KERR (1923–2003) • AMERICAN PLAYWRIGHT AND HUMORIST

•

The divorced person is like a man with a black patch over one eye: He looks rather dashing but the fact is that he has been through a maiming experience.

–JO COUDERT (1923–) • AMERICAN WRITER

•

Trust your husband, adore your husband, and get as much as you can in your own name.

–JOAN RIVERS (1933–) • AMERICAN COMEDIAN AND TELEVISION HOST

•

She did not want any more ties with this house, she was going to leave it, and she was not going back to her husband's family either. She would have no more bonds that smothered her in love and hatred. She knew now why she had run away to marriage, and she was not going to stay in any place, with anyone, that threatened to forbid her making her own discoveries, that said "No" to her.

–KATHERINE ANNE PORTER (1890–1980) • AMERICAN WRITER

•

In Hollywood, an equitable divorce settlement means each party getting fifty percent of the publicity.

–LAUREN BACALL (1924–) • AMERICAN MODEL AND ACTOR

A divorce is like an amputation—you survive, but there's less of you.

—MARGARET ATWOOD (1939–) • CANADIAN POET, WRITER, CRITIC, AND ACTIVIST

Divorce is the psychological equivalent of a triple coronary bypass. After such a monumental assault on the heart, it takes years to amend all the habits and attitudes that led up to it.

—MARY KAY BLAKELY (1948–) • AMERICAN JOURNALIST

I doubt if there is one married person on Earth who can be objective about divorce. It is always a threat, admittedly or not, and such a dire threat that it is almost a dirty word.

—NORA JOHNSON • 20TH/21ST-CENTURY AMERICAN ESSAYIST, NOVELIST, AND SCREENWRITER

I find to my astonishment that an unhappy marriage goes on being unhappy when it is over.

—REBECCA WEST (1892–1983) • ANGLO-IRISH FEMINIST AND WRITER

I'm not upset about my divorce. I'm only upset that I'm not a widow.

—ROSEANNE BARR (1952–) • AMERICAN COMEDIAN

[On the British Royal Divorce (Charles and Diana):] She is such a sad soul. It is good that it is over. Nobody was happy anyhow. I know I should preach family love and unity, but in their case. . . .

—MOTHER TERESA (1910–1997) • ALBANIAN CATHOLIC NUN; WINNER OF NOBEL PEACE PRIZE

My mother always said don't marry for money, divorce for money.

—WENDY LIEBMAN (1961–) • AMERICAN COMEDIAN

Getting divorced just because you don't love a man is almost as silly as getting married just because you do.

—ZSA ZSA GABOR (1917–)
HUNGARIAN-AMERICAN ACTOR AND SOCIALITE

"DOCTORS"

One has a greater sense of degradation after an interview with a doctor than from any human experience.

—ALICE JAMES (1848–1892) • AMERICAN DIARIST

You can argue with a theologian or a politician, but doctors are sacrosanct. They know; you do not.

—BRENDA UELAND (1891–1985) • AMERICAN WRITER

I had never gone to a doctor in my adult life, feeling instinctively that doctors meant either cutting or, just as bad, diet.

—CARSON MCCULLERS (1917–1967) • AMERICAN NOVELIST AND PLAYWRIGHT

Some people think that doctors and nurses can put scrambled eggs back into the shell.

—DOROTHY CANFIELD FISHER (1879–1958)
AMERICAN EDUCATIONAL REFORMER, SOCIAL ACTIVIST, AND WRITER

Doctors always think anybody doing something they aren't is a quack; also they think all patients are idiots.

—FLANNERY O'CONNOR (1925–1964) • AMERICAN WRITER

Instead of wishing to see more doctors made by women joining what there are, I wish to see as few doctors, either male or female, as possible. For, mark you, the women have made no improvement—they have only tried to be "men" and they have only succeeded in being third-rate men.

—FLORENCE NIGHTINGALE (1820–1910) • ENGLISH NURSE AND MEDICAL REFORMER

. . . his little black bag like a small sample cut from the shadow of death.

—HELEN HUDSON (1920–) • AMERICAN WRITER

A physician can sometimes parry the scythe of death, but has no power over the sand in the hourglass.

—HESTER LYNCH PIOZZI (1741–1821) • ENGLISH DIARIST

He will persist in laboring under the delusion that patients want common sense instead of magic.

—RAE FOLEY (ELINORE DENNISTON) (1900–1978) • AMERICAN WRITER

You know doctors. For every one thing they tell you, there are two things hidden under the tongue.

—ROSE CHERNIN (1903–1995) • RUSSIAN-BORN AMERICAN LEFT-WING ACTIVIST

The real trouble with the doctor image in America is that it has been grayed by the image of the doctor-as-businessman, the doctor-as-bureaucrat, the doctor-as-medical-robot, and the doctor-as-terrified-victim-of-malpractice-suits.

—SHANA ALEXANDER (1925–2005) • AMERICAN JOURNALIST AND COLUMNIST

GYNECOLOGISTS

A male gynecologist is like an auto mechanic who has never owned a car.

—CARRIE P. SNOW • 20TH/21ST-CENTURY AMERICAN COMEDIAN

I got a postcard from my gynecologist. It said, "Did you know it's time for your annual checkup?" No, but now my mailman does.

—CATHY LADMAN • 20TH/21ST-CENTURY AMERICAN COMEDIAN AND ACTOR

"DOGS"

A puppy is but a dog, plus high spirits, and minus common sense.

—AGNES REPPLIER (1855–1950) • AMERICAN ESSAYIST

Dogs' lives are too short. Their only fault, really.

–AGNES SLIGH TURNBULL (1888-1982)
AMERICAN WRITER

•

There is no such thing as a difficult dog, only an inexperienced owner.

–BARBARA WOODHOUSE (1910-1988) • IRISH-BORN ENGLISH DOG TRAINER

•

Dogs act exactly the way we would act if we had no shame.

–CYNTHIA HEIMEL • 20TH/21ST-CENTURY AMERICAN WRITER

•

Dogs are a habit, I think.

–ELIZABETH BOWEN (1899-1973)
ANGLO-IRISH WRITER

•

You ask of my companions. Hills, sir, and the sundown, and a dog as large as myself that my father bought me. They are better than human beings, because they know but do not tell.

–EMILY DICKINSON (1830-1886) • AMERICAN POET

•

We long for an affection altogether ignorant of our faults. Heaven has accorded this to us in the uncritical canine attachment.

–GEORGE ELIOT (MARY ANN EVANS) (1819-1880) • ENGLISH WRITER

•

I think dogs are the most amazing creatures; they give unconditional love. For me they are the role model for being alive.

–GILDA RADNER (1946-1989) • AMERICAN COMEDIAN

•

Dog lovers are a good breed themselves.

–GLADYS TABER (1899-1980)
AMERICAN COLUMNIST AND NOVELIST

The only food he has ever stolen has been down on a coffee table. He claims that he genuinely believed it to be a table meant for dogs.

—JEAN LITTLE (1932–) • CANADIAN WRITER

•

I've heard that dogs are man's best friend. That explains where men are getting their hygiene tips.

—KELLY MAGUIRE
20TH/21ST-CENTURY AMERICAN ACTOR AND COMEDIAN

•

From the dog's point of view, his master is an elongated and abnormally cunning dog.

—MABEL LOUISE ROBINSON (1864–1962)
AMERICAN CHILDREN'S BOOK AUTHOR

•

I hate dogs. They pee in your house and get dog hair on your clothes. . . . It's like having a kid, only kids wear diapers and later on in life they learn how to say decipherable words.

—MADONNA (1958–) • AMERICAN POP SINGER AND ACTOR

•

I sometimes look into the face of my dog Stan and see wistful sadness and existential angst, when all he is actually doing is scanning the ceiling for flies.

—MERRILL MARKOE
20TH/21ST-CENTURY AMERICAN COMEDIAN AND COMEDY WRITER

•

Oh, that dog! All he does is piddle. He's nothing but a fur-covered kidney that barks.

—PHYLLIS DILLER (1917–) • AMERICAN COMEDIAN

•

The more I see of man, the more I like dogs.

—MADAME DE STAËL (1766–1817)
SWISS-BORN FRENCH WRITER AND SOCIETY FIGURE

Did you ever walk into a room and forget why you walked in? I think that is how dogs spend their lives.

–SUE MURPHY • 20TH/21ST-CENTURY AMERICAN COMEDIAN AND COMEDY WRITER

"DREAMS"

The dream was always running ahead of one. To catch up, to live for a moment in unison with it, that was the miracle.

–ANAÏS NIN (1903–1977) • FRENCH WRITER AND DIARIST

Rose-colored glasses are never made in bifocals. Nobody wants to read the small print in dreams.

–ANN LANDERS (ESTHER PAULINE FRIEDMAN) (1918–2002)
AMERICAN ADVICE COLUMNIST

Dreams are, by definition, cursed with short life spans.

–CANDICE BERGEN (1946–) • AMERICAN ACTOR

Dreams say what they mean, but they don't say it in daytime language.

–GAIL GODWIN (1937–) • AMERICAN WRITER

We cast away priceless time in dreams, born of imagination, fed upon illusion, and put to death by reality.

–JUDY GARLAND (1922–1969) • AMERICAN ACTOR AND SINGER

If growing up is the process of creating ideas and dreams about what life should be, then maturity is letting go again.

–MARY BETH DANIELSON • 20TH/21ST-CENTURY AMERICAN COLUMNIST AND JOURNALIST

If one is lucky, a solitary fantasy can totally transform one million realities.

–MAYA ANGELOU (1928–) • AFRICAN-AMERICAN POET, MEMOIRIST, AND CIVIL RIGHTS ACTIVIST

To anyone who has a dream, I say follow that dream.
You are never too old. It is never too late.

–SUSAN BOYLE (1961–) • SCOTTISH SINGER

Yet it is in our idleness, in our dreams, that the submerged truth sometimes comes to the top.

–VIRGINIA WOOLF (1882–1941) • ENGLISH NOVELIST, ESSAYIST, AND CRITIC

"DRIVING"

See also Cars

I had this dream that I was driving down the freeway and slamming into everyone, just slamming into them. From side to side to side, right to left, all the way down the freeway. Not hurting anyone, though, just knocking the phones out of their hands.

–LAURA KIGHTLINGER (1969–) • AMERICAN COMEDIAN AND WRITER

I drive with my knees. Otherwise, how can I put on my lipstick and talk on the phone?

–SHARON STONE (1958–) • AMERICAN ACTOR AND PRODUCER

The freeway is the last frontier. It is unsurpassed as a training ground for the sharpening of survival skills.

–SHEILA BALLANTYNE (1936–) • AMERICAN WRITER

For a driver to be driven by somebody else is an ordeal, for there are only three types of drivers: the too fast, the timid, and oneself.

–VIRGINIA GRAHAM (1912–1998) • AMERICAN WRITER AND TELEVISION AND RADIO PERFORMER

I am the worst driver. Let's just say I always wear clean underwear. I should drive a hearse and cut out the middle man.

–WENDY LIEBMAN (1961–) • AMERICAN COMEDIAN

"DRUGS"

Dope never helped anybody sing better or play music better or do anything better. All dope can do for you is kill you—and kill you the long, slow, hard way.

–BILLIE HOLIDAY (1915–1959) • AFRICAN-AMERICAN JAZZ SINGER

There's so much talk about the drug generation and songs about drugs. That's stupid. They aren't songs about drugs; they're about life.

–CASS ELLIOT ("MAMA" CASS) (1941–1974) • AMERICAN SINGER

Drugs are a carnival in hell.

–EDITH PIAF (1915–1963)
FRENCH SINGER

The era of pharmacology has dawned and with it the offer of the "chemical vacation," not however without the hazards of the road.

–JUDITH GROCH (1929–) • AMERICAN WRITER

Druggies don't keep their looks any longer than they keep their promises.

–LIZA CODY (1944–) • ENGLISH SUSPENSE WRITER

I love drugs, but I hate hangovers, and the hatred of the hangover wins by a landslide every time.

–MARGARET CHO (1968–) • KOREAN-AMERICAN COMEDIAN AND ACTOR

Just say no.

–NANCY REAGAN (1921–)
FIRST LADY OF THE UNITED STATES

Cocaine isn't habit forming. I should know—I've been using it for years.

–TALULLAH BANKHEAD (1902–1968) • AMERICAN ACTOR

Medication without explanation is obscene.

–TONI CADE BAMBARA (1939–1995)
AFRICAN-AMERICAN WRITER AND SOCIAL ACTIVIST

E

"EDUCATION"

See also Learning, Teaching

The carefully fostered theory that schoolwork can be made easy and enjoyable breaks down as soon as anything, however trivial, has to be learned.

–AGNES REPPLIER (1855–1950) • AMERICAN ESSAYIST

It is among the commonplaces of education that we often first cut off the living root and then try to replace its natural functions by artificial means. Thus we suppress the child's curiosity and then when he lacks a natural interest in learning he is offered special coaching for his scholastic difficulties.

–ALICE DUER MILLER (1874–1942) • AMERICAN WRITER AND SUFFRAGIST

When we escaped from Cuba, all we could carry was our education.

–ALICIA CORÓ

20TH/21ST-CENTURY CUBAN-BORN U.S. DEPARTMENT OF EDUCATION PROGRAM DIRECTOR

A good education is another name for happiness.

–ANN PLATO • 19TH-CENTURY AFRICAN-AMERICAN TEACHER AND WRITER

I am beginning to suspect all elaborate and special systems of education. They seem to me to be built up on the supposition that every child is a kind of idiot who must be taught to think.

–ANNE SULLIVAN (1866–1936) • AMERICAN EDUCATOR OF THE BLIND AND DEAF

Without comprehension, the immigrant would forever remain shut—a stranger in America. Until America can release the heart as well as train the hand of the immigrant, he would forever remain driven back upon himself, corroded by the very richness of the unused gifts within his soul.

—ANZIA YEZIERSKA (1881-1970) • POLISH-AMERICAN WRITER

•

Prejudices, it is well known, are most difficult to eradicate from the heart whose soil has never been loosened or fertilized by education; they grow there, firm as weeds among rocks.

—CHARLOTTE BRONTË (1816-1855) • ENGLISH WRITER

•

It has always seemed strange to me that in our endless discussions about education so little stress is laid on the pleasure of becoming an educated person, the enormous interest it adds to life. To be able to be caught up into the world of thought—that is to be educated.

—EDITH HAMILTON (1867-1963) • AMERICAN EDUCATOR, TRANSLATOR, AND CLASSICS SCHOLAR

•

The most violent element in society is ignorance.

—EMMA GOLDMAN (1869-1940) • RUSSIAN ANARCHIST AND FEMINIST

•

Stand firm in your refusal to remain conscious during algebra. In real life, I assure you, there is no such thing as algebra.

—FRAN LEBOWITZ (1950-) • AMERICAN HUMORIST

•

Those who trust us educate us.

—GEORGE ELIOT (MARY ANN EVANS) (1819-1880)
ENGLISH WRITER

•

The first problem for all of us, men and women, is not to learn, but to unlearn.

—GLORIA STEINEM (1934-) • AMERICAN FEMINIST AND COFOUNDER OF *MS.* MAGAZINE

The danger of mass education is precisely that it may become very entertaining indeed; there are many great authors of the past who have survived centuries of oblivion and neglect, but it is still an open question whether they will be able to survive an entertaining version of what they have to say.

—HANNAH ARENDT (1906–1975) • GERMAN-BORN POLITICAL PHILOSOPHER AND HISTORIAN

•

The highest result of education is tolerance.

—HELEN KELLER (1880–1968)
AMERICAN WRITER AND ACTIVIST

•

The educational system is regarded simultaneously as the nation's scapegoat and savior.

—JUDITH GROCH (1929–) • AMERICAN WRITER

•

If written directions alone would suffice, libraries wouldn't need to have the rest of the universities attached.

—JUDITH "MISS MANNERS" MARTIN (1938–)
AMERICAN ETIQUETTE EXPERT

•

It's not what is poured into a student, but what is planted.

—LINDA CONWAY • 20TH/21ST-CENTURY AMERICAN MEDIA SCHOLAR

•

Schooling, instead of encouraging the asking of questions, too often discourages it.

—MADELEINE L'ENGLE (1918–) • AMERICAN WRITER

•

Expecting all children the same age to learn from the same materials is like expecting all children the same age to wear the same size clothing.

—MADELINE HUNTER (1916–1994) • AMERICAN EDUCATIONAL INNOVATOR

We are now at a point where we must educate our children in what no one knew yesterday, and prepare our schools for what no one knows yet.

–MARGARET MEAD (1901–1978) • AMERICAN CULTURAL ANTHROPOLOGIST

•

Education is not something which the teacher does . . . it is a natural process which develops spontaneously in the human being.

–MARIA MONTESSORI (1870–1952)
ITALIAN EDUCATIONAL INNOVATOR, SCIENTIST, AND PHILOSOPHER

•

The task of the educator lies in seeing that the child does not confound good with immobility and evil with activity.

–MARIA MONTESSORI (1870–1952)
ITALIAN EDUCATIONAL INNOVATOR, SCIENTIST, AND PHILOSOPHER

•

Education is for improving the lives of others and for leaving your community and world better than you found it.

–MARIAN WRIGHT EDELMAN (1939–)
AFRICAN-AMERICAN FOUNDER OF THE CHILDREN'S DEFENSE FUND

•

To repeat what others have said requires education; to challenge it requires brains.

–MARY PETTIBONE POOLE • 20TH-CENTURY AMERICAN WRITER

•

My mother said I must always be intolerant of ignorance but understanding of illiteracy. That some people, unable to go to school, were more educated and more intelligent than college professors.

–MAYA ANGELOU (1928–) • AFRICAN-AMERICAN POET, MEMOIRIST, AND CIVIL RIGHTS ACTIVIST

•

Educate yourself for the coming conflicts.

–MOTHER JONES (1837–1930)
AMERICAN LABOR AND COMMUNITY ORGANIZER AND ACTIVIST

Real education should educate us out of self into something far finer; into a selflessness which links us with all humanity.

–LADY NANCY ASTOR (1879-1964)
FIRST FEMALE TO TAKE A SEAT IN BRITISH HOUSE OF COMMONS

•

If you educate a man you educate a person, but if you educate a woman you educate a family.

–RUBY MANIKAN • 20TH-CENTURY INDIAN CHURCH LEADER

•

If you are not educated—if you can't write clearly, speak articulately, think logically—you have lost control of your own life.

–SADIE DELANY (1889-1999) AFRICAN-AMERICAN EDUCATOR AND MEMOIRIST

•

The joy of learning is as indispensable in study as breathing is in running. Where it is lacking there are no real students, but only poor caricatures of apprentices who, at the end of their apprenticeship, will not even have a trade.

–SIMONE WEIL (1909-1943) • FRENCH SOCIAL PHILOSOPHER AND ACTIVIST

•

I read Shakespeare and the Bible, and I can shoot dice. That's what I call a liberal education.

–TALULLAH BANKHEAD (1902-1968) • AMERICAN ACTOR

•

The ability to think straight, some knowledge of the past, some vision of the future, some skill to do useful service, some urge to fit that service into the well-being of the community—these are the most vital things education must try to produce.

–VIRGINIA CROCHERON GILDERSLEEVE (1877-1965)
AMERICAN EDUCATOR AND COLLEGE ADMINISTRATOR

Only people who die very young learn all they
really need to know in kindergarten.

–WENDY KAMINER (1950-)
AMERICAN LAW PROFESSOR AND FEMINIST WRITER

•

I don't think anybody anywhere can talk about the future of their people or of an organization without talking about education. Whoever controls the education of our children controls our future.

–WILMA MANKILLER (1945-2010)
NATIVE AMERICAN LEADER, FIRST FEMALE PRINCIPLE CHIEF OF THE CHEROKEE NATION

•

PRACTICALITY

If you are truly serious about preparing your child for the future, don't teach him to subtract—teach him to deduct.

–FRAN LEBOWITZ (1950-) • AMERICAN HUMORIST

•

If I didn't have some kind of education, then
I wouldn't be able to count my money.

–MISSY ELLIOT (1971-)
AMERICAN SINGER, RAPPER, SONGWRITER, AND RECORD PRODUCER

•

SCHOOLS

Thank goodness I was never sent to school; it would have rubbed off some of the originality.

–BEATRIX POTTER (1866-1943) • ENGLISH WRITER AND ILLUSTRATOR

•

Good schools, like good societies and good families, celebrate and cherish diversity.

–DEBORAH MEIER (1931-)
AMERICAN EDUCATIONAL INNOVATOR, FOUNDER OF SMALL SCHOOLS MOVEMENT

If all the rich and all of the church people should send their children to the public schools they would feel bound to concentrate their money on improving these schools until they met the highest ideals.

–SUSAN B. ANTHONY (1820–1906) • AMERICAN SUFFRAGIST AND NEWSPAPER PUBLISHER

•

"EQUALITY"

•

Justice is better than chivalry if we cannot have both.

–ALICE STONE BLACKWELL (1857–1950)
AMERICAN FEMINIST AND JOURNALIST

•

[Women] must pay for everything. . . . They do get more glory than men for comparable feats. But, also, women get more notoriety when they crash.

–AMELIA EARHART (1897–1937)
PIONEERING AMERICAN AVIATOR; FIRST PERSON TO FLY SOLO ACROSS PACIFIC

•

The ceiling isn't glass; it's a very dense layer of men.

–ANNE JARDIM • 20TH/21ST-CENTURY BUSINESS WRITER

•

The education and empowerment of women throughout the world cannot fail to result in a more caring, tolerant, just, and peaceful life for all.

–AUNG SAN SUU KYI (1945–) • BURMESE OPPOSITION LEADER AND NOBEL LAUREATE

•

We are coming down from our pedestal and up from the laundry room.

–BELLA ABZUG (1920–1998) • AMERICAN FEMINIST AND POLITICIAN

•

. . . it is the right and duty of every woman to employ the power of organization and agitation in order to gain those advantages which are given to the one sex and unjustly withheld from the other.

–CATHARINE BEECHER (1800–1878) • AMERICAN EDUCATOR AND REFORMER

When you belong to a minority, you have to be better in order to have the right to be equal.

–CHRISTIANE COLLANGE (1930–) • FRENCH EDITOR AND WRITER

•

We've got a generation now who were born with semiequality. They don't know how it was before, so they think, this isn't too bad. We're working. We have our attaché cases and our three-piece suits. I get very disgusted with the younger generation of women. We had a torch to pass, and they are just sitting there. They don't realize it can be taken away. Things are going to have to get worse before they join in fighting the battle.

–ERMA BOMBECK (1927–1996) • AMERICAN HUMORIST

•

Women's chains have been forged by men, not by anatomy.

–ESTELLE RAMEY (1917–2006) • AMERICAN PROFESSOR OF BIOPHYSICS AND PHYSIOLOGY

•

We have to be careful in this era of radical feminism, not to emphasize an equality of the sexes that leads women to imitate men to prove their equality. To be equal does not mean you have to be the same.

–EVA BURROWS (1929–) • AUSTRALIAN; LEADER OF SALVATION ARMY

•

Can anyone tell me why reporters, in making mention of lady speakers, always consider it to be necessary to report, fully and firstly, the dresses worn by them? When John Jones or Senator Rouser frees his mind in public, we are left in painful ignorance of the color and fit of his pants, coat, necktie, and vest—and worse still, the shape of his boots. This seems to me a great omission.

–FANNY FERN (1752–1840) • ENGLISH WRITER

•

We've chosen the path to equality, don't let them turn us around.

–GERALDINE FERRARO (1935–)

AMERICAN POLITICIAN AND NOMINEE FOR U.S. VICE PRESIDENT

I have come to the conclusion that the modern interpretation of the Declaration of Independence is something like this: I am as good as those that think themselves better and a long sight better than those who only think themselves as good.

–GERTRUDE ATHERTON (1857–1948) • AMERICAN WRITER

•

Whether women are better than men I cannot say—but I can say they are certainly no worse.

–GOLDA MEIR (1898–1978)
RUSSIAN-BORN FIRST FEMALE PRIME MINISTER OF ISRAEL

•

You don't have to be anti-man to be pro-woman.

–JANE GALVIN LEWIS (1957–) • ENGLISH COMEDIAN AND ACTOR

•

We're half the people—we should be half the Congress.

–JEANNETTE RANKIN (1880–1973)
AMERICAN, FIRST WOMAN ELECTED TO THE U.S. HOUSE OF REPRESENTATIVES AND THE FIRST FEMALE MEMBER OF CONGRESS

•

I never realized until lately that women were supposed to be the inferior sex.

–KATHARINE HEPBURN (1907–2003) • AMERICAN ACTOR

•

In an age that boasts equality between the sexes, why do women lead a painfully laborious and depressing life?

–LI XIAOJIANG (1951–) • CHINESE PROFESSOR AND WOMEN'S STUDIES SCHOLAR

•

Learning, while at school, that the charge for the education of girls was the same as that for boys, and that, when they became teachers, women received only half as much as men for their services, the injustice of this distinction was so apparent.

–LUCRETIA MOTT (1793–1880)
AMERICAN QUAKER ABOLITIONIST, SOCIAL REFORMER, AND PROPONENT OF WOMEN'S RIGHTS

Treat everyone the same until you find out they're an idiot.

–LUCY LAWLESS (1968–) • NEW ZEALAND ACTOR AND SINGER

Genius has no sex!

–MADAME DE STAËL (1766–1817)
SWISS-BORN FRENCH WRITER AND SOCIETY FIGURE

The entire social order . . . is arrayed against a woman who wants to rise to a man's reputation.

–MADAME DE STAËL (1766–1817)
SWISS-BORN FRENCH WRITER AND SOCIETY FIGURE

One of the things about equality is not just that you be treated equally to a man, but that you treat yourself equally to the way you treat a man.

–MARLO THOMAS (1938–) • AMERICAN ACTOR

I want to see young women who come right out of school and start running for office or start moving into some positions where they will be able to shape the institutions that define our culture. And so if there are men who just don't get it, then they're just going to have to get it.

–PATRICIA IRELAND (1945–) • AMERICAN FEMINIST LEADER AND ACTIVIST

I ask no favors for my sex. . . . All I ask of our brethren is that they will take their feet from off our necks.

–SARAH MOORE GRIMKÉ (1792–1873) • AMERICAN ATTORNEY AND SOCIAL REFORMER

Men will often admit other women are oppressed, but not you.

–SHEILA ROWBOTHAM (1943–) • ENGLISH SOCIALIST FEMINIST THEORIST AND WRITER

If colored men get their rights and not colored women theirs, you see the colored men will be masters over the women, and it will be just as bad as it was before.

–SOJOURNER TRUTH (1797–1883) • AFRICAN-AMERICAN ABOLITIONIST

•

It was we, the people; not we, the white male citizens; nor yet we, the male citizens; but we, the whole people, who formed the Union. . . . Men, their rights and nothing more; women, their rights and nothing less.

–SUSAN B. ANTHONY (1820–1906)
AMERICAN SUFFRAGIST AND NEWSPAPER PUBLISHER

•

The day will come when men will recognize woman as his peer, not only at the fireside, but in councils of the nation. Then, and not until then, will there be the perfect comradeship, the ideal union between the sexes that shall result in the highest development of the race.

–SUSAN B. ANTHONY (1820–1906) • AMERICAN SUFFRAGIST AND NEWSPAPER PUBLISHER

•

All this pitting of sex against sex, of quality against quality; all this claiming of superiority and imputing of inferiority, belong to the private-school stage of human existence where there are "sides," and it is necessary for one side to beat another side, and of the utmost importance to walk up to a platform and receive from the hands of the Headmaster himself a highly ornamental pot. As people mature, they cease to believe in sides or in Headmasters or in highly ornamental pots.

–VIRGINIA WOOLF (1882–1941) • ENGLISH NOVELIST, ESSAYIST, AND CRITIC

•

EMPLOYMENT

The test for whether or not you can hold a job should not be the arrangement of your chromosomes.

–BELLA ABZUG (1920–1998) • AMERICAN FEMINIST AND POLITICIAN

Our struggle today is not to have a female Einstein get appointed as an assistant professor. It is for a woman schlemiel to get as quickly promoted as a male schlemiel.

–BELLA ABZUG (1920–1998) • AMERICAN FEMINIST AND POLITICIAN

I wanted to be the best dentist that ever lived. People said, "But she's a woman; she's colored," and I said, "Ha! Just you wait and see."

–BESSIE DELANY (1891–1995) • AFRICAN-AMERICAN DENTIST AND MEMOIRIST

As to the great mass of working girls and women, how much independence is gained if the narrowness and lack of freedom of the home is exchanged for the narrowness and lack of freedom of the sweatshop, the factory, the department store, or the office?

–EMMA GOLDMAN (1869–1940) • RUSSIAN ANARCHIST AND FEMINIST

There are very few jobs that actually require a penis or vagina. All other jobs should be open to everybody.

–FLORYNCE KENNEDY (1916–2000) • AFRICAN-AMERICAN LAWYER AND ACTIVIST

Black women are trained from childhood to become workers and expect to be financially self-supporting for most of their lives. They know they will have to work, whether they are married or single; work to them, unlike to white women, is not a liberating goal, but rather an imposed lifelong necessity.

–GERDA LERNER (1920–) • AUSTRIAN-BORN AMERICAN HISTORIAN

[On being denied a foreign affairs position because she was a woman:] I can't change my sex. But you can change your policy.

–HELEN KIRKPATRICK (1909–) • AMERICAN JOURNALIST

The last speaker alluded to this movement as being that of a few disappointed women. From the first years to which my memory stretches, I have been a disappointed woman. . . . I was disappointed when I came to seek a profession worthy an immortal being—every employment was closed to me, except those of the teacher, the seamstress, and the housekeeper. In education, in marriage, in religion, in everything, disappointment is the lot of woman. It shall be the business of my life to deepen this disappointment in every woman's heart until she bows down to it no longer.

—LUCY STONE (1818–1893) • AMERICAN SUFFRAGIST

•

There is a world-old controversy that crops up whenever women attempt to enter a new field. Is a woman fit for that work? It would seem that a woman's success in any particular field would prove her fitness for that work, without regard to theories to the contrary.

—RUTH LAW (1887–1970) • PIONEERING AMERICAN AVIATOR

•

If women can be railroad workers in Russia, why can't they fly in space?

—VALENTINA TERESHKOVA (1937–) • RUSSIAN ASTRONAUT, FIRST WOMAN IN SPACE

•

The only jobs for which no man is qualified are human incubators and wet nurse. Likewise, the only job for which no woman is or can be qualified is sperm donor.

—WILMA SCOTT HEIDE (1921–1985) • AMERICAN FEMINIST WRITER AND ACTIVIST

•

"EVIL"

•

There is evil everywhere under the sun.

—AGATHA CHRISTIE (1890–1976)
ENGLISH MYSTERY WRITER

We believe at once in evil, we only believe in good upon reflection. Is this not sad?

—DOROTHÉE DELUZY (1747–1830) • FRENCH ACTOR

Evil to some is always good to others.

—JANE AUSTEN (1775–1817) • ENGLISH WRITER

Little evil would be done in the world if evil never could be done in the name of good.

—MARIE VON EBNER-ESCHENBACH (1830–1916) • AUSTRIAN WRITER

In all men is evil sleeping; the good man is he who will not waken it, in himself or in other men.

—MARY RENAULT (1905–1983) • ENGLISH WRITER

No man chooses evil because it is evil; he only mistakes it for happiness.

—MARY WOLLSTONECRAFT (1759–1797) • ENGLISH WRITER

The lesser evil is also evil.

—NAOMI MITCHISON (1897–1999)
SCOTTISH WRITER AND POET

"*EXERCISE*"

I'm not into working out. My philosophy: No pain, no pain.

—CAROL LEIFER (1956–) • AMERICAN COMEDIAN

I really don't think I need buns of steel. I'd be happy with buns of cinnamon.

—ELLEN DEGENERES (1958–) • AMERICAN COMEDIAN AND TELEVISION HOST

Getting fit is a political act—you are taking charge of your life.

–JANE FONDA (1937-) • AMERICAN ACTOR, FITNESS CELEBRITY, AND POLITICAL ACTIVIST

I don't work out. If God wanted us to bend over he'd have put diamonds on the floor.

–JOAN RIVERS (1933-)
AMERICAN COMEDIAN AND TELEVISION HOST

Running is the greatest metaphor for life, because you get out of it what you put into it.

–OPRAH WINFREY (1954-)
AFRICAN-AMERICAN TELEVISION HOST AND MAGAZINE PUBLISHER

Exercise makes you more graceful. When you exercise you walk as if you own the street—with pride and fluidity.

–SOPHIA LOREN (1934-) • ITALIAN ACTOR

Bicycling has done more to emancipate woman than any one thing in the world. . . . It gives her a feeling of self-reliance and independence the moment she takes her seat; and away she goes, the picture of untrammelled womanhood.

–SUSAN B. ANTHONY (1820-1906)
AMERICAN SUFFRAGIST AND NEWSPAPER PUBLISHER

I concentrate on exercises from the waist down, since that is the laziest part of a woman's body.

–TINA LOUISE (1934-)
AMERICAN MODEL, SINGER, AND FILM AND TELEVISION ACTOR

"EXPERIENCE"

If we could sell our experiences for what they cost us we'd be millionaires.

–ABIGAIL VAN BUREN (PAULINE PHILLIPS) (1918-)
AMERICAN ADVICE COLUMNIST, ORIGINATOR OF COLUMN "DEAR ABBY"

Learning from experience is a faculty almost never practiced.

–BARBARA TUCHMAN (1912-1989) • AMERICAN HISTORIAN AND WRITER

A happy childhood is poor preparation for human contacts.

–COLETTE (1873-1954) • FRENCH WRITER

Everything you experience is what constitutes you as a human being, but the experience passes away and the person's left. The person is the residue.

–ILKA CHASE (1905-1978) • AMERICAN ACTOR, WRITER, AND RADIO PERSONALITY

When we think of what it is that politicizes people, it is not so much books or ideas, but experience.

–IRENE PESLIKIS (1943-2002) • AMERICAN FEMINIST ARTIST

What is it which is bought dearly, offered for nothing, and then most often refused?—Experience, old people's experience.

–ISAK DINESEN (KAREN BLIXEN) (1885-1962) • DANISH WRITER AND AUTOBIOGRAPHER

Over the airways, in movies, experiences have come to be dogmatized to certain kinds of experience at the cost of all others.

–JOSEPHINE HERBST (1892-1969) • AMERICAN WRITER AND CRITIC

Experience—a comb life gives you after you lose your hair.

–JUDITH STERN (1942-) • AMERICAN WRITER

Adventure is something you see for pleasure, or even for profit, like a gold rush or invading a country . . . but experience is what really happens to you in the long run, the truth that finally overtakes you.

–KATHERINE ANNE PORTER (1890–1980) • AMERICAN WRITER

•

Experience teaches, it is true, but she never teaches in time.

–L. E. LANDON (1802–1838) • ENGLISH WRITER AND POET

•

Experience is what you get looking for something else.

–MARY PETTIBONE POOLE • 20TH-CENTURY AMERICAN WRITER

•

Experience is a good teacher, but she sends in terrific bills.

–MINNA THOMAS ANTRIM (1856–1950) • AMERICAN WRITER

•

Good judgment comes from experience, and often experience comes from bad judgment.

–RITA MAE BROWN (1944–) • AMERICAN WRITER AND ACTIVIST

•

We can teach from our experience, but we cannot teach experience.

–SASHA AZEVEDO (1978–) • AMERICAN ACTOR, ATHLETE, AND MODEL

•

The real stuff of life was experience, in which sorrow and fear and disaster had as important a part to play as beauty and joy.

–SHEILA KAYE-SMITH (1887–1956) • ENGLISH WRITER

•

One never believes other people's experience, and one is only very gradually convinced by one's own.

–VITA SACKVILLE-WEST (1892–1962) • ENGLISH POET AND WRITER

F

"FAILURE"

People think that when something goes "wrong," it's their fault. If only they had done something differently. But sometimes things go wrong to teach you what is right.

—ALICE WALKER (1944-) • AFRICAN-AMERICAN WRITER AND POET

We learn nothing by being right.

—ELIZABETH BIBESCO (1897-1945)
ENGLISH WRITER

You must never feel that you have failed. You can always come back to something later when you have more knowledge or better equipment and try again.

—GERTRUDE ELION (1918-1999) • NOBEL PRIZE-WINNING AMERICAN BIOCHEMIST

Success and failure are greatly overrated. But failure gives you a whole lot more to talk about.

—HILDEGARD KNEF (1925-2002) • GERMAN ACTOR, SINGER, AND WRITER

Groan and forget it.

—JESSAMYN WEST (1902-1984)
AMERICAN WRITER

Show me a person who has never made a mistake and I'll show you somebody who has never achieved much.

—JOAN COLLINS (1933-) • ENGLISH ACTOR AND WRITER

The person interested in success has to learn to view failure as a healthy, inevitable part of the process of getting to the top.

—JOYCE BROTHERS (1928-) • AMERICAN PSYCHOLOGIST AND COLUMNIST

When you lose a couple of times, it makes
you realize how difficult it is to win.

–STEFFI GRAF (1969–) • GERMAN TENNIS PROFESSIONAL

Failure happens all the time. It happens every day in practice.
What makes you better is how you react to it.

–MIA HAMM (1972–) • AMERICAN SOCCER PLAYER

"FAME"

In a recent Valentine's Day posting on her fan Web site,
Britney Spears says that—oh, who cares.

–AMY POEHLER (1971–) • AMERICAN COMEDIAN AND ACTRESS

You know when there's a star, like in show business, the star
has her name in lights on the marquee! Right? And the star gets
the money because the people come to see the star, right?
Well, I'm the star, and all of you are in the chorus.

–BABE DIDRIKSON ZAHARIAS (1914–1956) • AMERICAN GOLFER

People look at us head to toe, judge us, and think we're
not human. We are. Nobody's a celebrity but God.

–BEYONCÉ KNOWLES (1981–)
AFRICAN-AMERICAN R&B SINGER AND SONGWRITER

I don't mind if my skull ends up on a shelf as long as it's got my name on it.

–DEBBIE HARRY (1945–) • AMERICAN SINGER

Some people obtain fame, others deserve it.

–DORIS LESSING (1919–) • ENGLISH WRITER

I don't buy the tabloids, but you're surrounded by it all and people tell you things they've read. I'd be sitting on a train looking over someone's shoulder and thinking: That's familiar . . . oh my God, it's me.

—FRANCESCA ANNIS (1944–) • ENGLISH ACTOR

•

All my life, I always wanted to be somebody. Now I see that I should have been more specific.

—JANE WAGNER (1935–)
AMERICAN PLAYWRIGHT AND COMEDY WRITER

•

[On being told that a store was not open to the public:] I'm not the public.

—LAUREN BACALL (1924–) • AMERICAN MODEL AND ACTOR

•

People think they will wake up one day and I'll be gone. But I'm never going away.

—MADONNA (1958–)
AMERICAN POP SINGER AND ACTOR

•

I can't think of anything less worth striving for than fame.

—ZADIE SMITH (1975–) • ENGLISH WRITER

•

"FAMILY"

See also Babies, Children, Fathers, Mothers, Parenting

•

The family—that dear octopus from whose tentacles we never quite escape, nor, in our inmost hearts, ever quite wish to.

—DODIE SMITH (1896–1990) • ENGLISH NOVELIST AND PLAYWRIGHT

In family life, love is the oil that eases friction, the cement that binds closer together, and the music that brings harmony.

–EVA BURROWS (1929-)
AUSTRALIAN; LEADER OF SALVATION ARMY

•

The peace and stability of a nation depend upon the proper relationships established in the home.

–JADE SNOW WONG (1922-2006)
ASIAN-AMERICAN CERAMICIST AND MEMOIRIST

•

Call it a clan, call it a network, call it a tribe, call it a family. Whatever you call it, whoever you are, you need one.

–JANE HOWARD (1935-1996) • AMERICAN JOURNALIST AND WRITER

•

When you look at your life, the greatest happinesses are family happinesses.

–JOYCE BROTHERS (1928-) • AMERICAN PSYCHOLOGIST AND COLUMNIST

•

Nobody has ever before asked the nuclear family to live all by itself in a box the way we do. With no relatives, no support, we've put it in an impossible situation.

–MARGARET MEAD (1901-1978)
AMERICAN CULTURAL ANTHROPOLOGIST

•

I don't visit my parents often because Delta Airlines won't wait in the yard while I run in.

–MARGARET SMITH • 20TH/21ST-CENTURY AMERICAN COMEDIAN

•

The informality of family life is a blessed condition that allows us to become our best while looking our worst.

–MARGE KENNEDY • 20TH/21ST-CENTURY AMERICAN WRITER

If you have only one smile in you, give it to the people you love. Don't be surly at home, then go out in the street and start grinning "Good morning" at total strangers.

—MAYA ANGELOU (1928-)
AFRICAN-AMERICAN POET, MEMOIRIST, AND CIVIL RIGHTS ACTIVIST

•

There's an awful lot of blood around that water is thicker than.

—MIGNON MCLAUGHLIN (1913-1983) • AMERICAN JOURNALIST AND WRITER

•

The great advantage of living in a large family is that early lesson of life's essential unfairness.

—NANCY MITFORD (1904-1973) • ENGLISH NOVELIST AND BIOGRAPHER

•

BROTHERS

Blessings on that brother of mine!

—DOROTHY WORDSWORTH (1771-1855)
ENGLISH POET AND DIARIST

•

My brothers, the dragon slayers, capable and strong.

—PATRICIA PENTON LEIMBACH (1927-)
AMERICAN WRITER

•

GRANDPARENTS

A home without a grandmother is like an egg without salt.

—FLORENCE KING (1936-) • AMERICAN WRITER

•

As I do not live in an age when rustling black skirts billow about me, and I do not carry an ebony stick to strike the floor in sharp rebuke, as this is denied me, I rap out a sentence in my note book and feel better. If a grandmother wants to put her foot down, the only safe place to do it these days is in a note book.

—FLORIDA SCOTT-MAXWELL (1883-1979) • AMERICAN SUFFRAGIST AND PSYCHOLOGIST

I'm a flower, *poa*, a flower opening and reaching for the sun.
You are the sun, grandma, you are the sun in my life.

–KITTY TSUI (1952-) • HONG KONG–BORN AMERICAN ACTOR, WRITER, AND BODYBUILDER

•

A house needs a grandma in it.

–LOUISA MAY ALCOTT (1832–1888)
AMERICAN WRITER

•

The closest friends I have made all through life have been people who grew up close to a loved and loving grandmother or grandfather.

–MARGARET MEAD (1901–1978) • AMERICAN CULTURAL ANTHROPOLOGIST

•

Grandpa . . . was ever ready to cheer and help me, ever sure that I was a remarkable specimen. He was a dear old man who asked little from life and got less.

–MILES FRANKLIN (1879–1954) • AUSTRALIAN WRITER

•

I loved their home. Everything smelled older, worn but safe;
the food aroma had baked itself into the furniture.

–SUSAN STRASBERG (1938–1999) • AMERICAN ACTOR

•

No one . . . who has not known the inestimable privilege can possibly realize what good fortune it is to grow up in a home where there are are grandparents.

–SUZANNE LA FOLLETTE (1893–1983) • AMERICAN JOURNALIST

•

SISTERS

Sisters define their rivalry in terms of competition for the gold cup of parental love. It is never perceived as a cup which runneth over, rather a finite vessel from which the more one sister drinks, the less is left for the others.

–ELIZABETH FISHEL • 20TH/21ST-CENTURY AMERICAN JOURNALIST AND WRITER

If you don't understand how a woman could both love her sister dearly and want to wring her neck at the same time, then you were probably an only child.

–LINDA SUNSHINE • 20TH/21ST-CENTURY AMERICAN WRITER AND EDITOR

Between sisters, often, the child's cry never dies down. "Never leave me," it says; "do not abandon me."

–LOUISE BERNIKOW • 20TH/21ST-CENTURY AMERICAN WRITER

There can be no situation in life in which the conversation of my dear sister will not administer some comfort to me.

–LADY MARY WORTLEY MONTAGU (1689–1762)
ENGLISH POET, EPISTOLARY WRITER, AND SMALLPOX VACCINE ADVOCATE

"FASHION"

See also Clothes

Be sure what you want and be sure about yourself. Fashion is not just beauty, it's about good attitude. You have to believe in yourself and be strong.

–ADRIANA LIMA (1981–) • BRAZILIAN MODEL

"Women's fashion" is a euphemism for fashion created by men for women.

–ANDREA DWORKIN (1946–2005) • AMERICAN RADICAL FEMINIST

I wouldn't say I invented tacky, but I definitely brought it to its present high popularity.

–BETTE MIDLER (1945–) • AMERICAN ACTOR AND SINGER

People used to complain to me all the time, "I can't even hear you sing because your clothes are so loud."

–CYNDI LAUPER (1953–) • AMERICAN SINGER

Today, fashion is really about sensuality—how a woman feels on the inside. In the eighties women used suits with exaggerated shoulders and waists to make a strong impression. Women are now more comfortable with themselves and their bodies—they no longer feel the need to hide behind their clothes.

–DONNA KARAN (1949-) • AMERICAN FASHION DESIGNER

•

Fashion can be bought. Style one must possess.

–EDNA WOOLMAN CHASE (1877-1957)
AMERICAN EDITOR AND FASHION JOURNALIST

•

There is no fashion for the old.

–GABRIELLE "COCO" CHANEL (1883-1971)
FRENCH FASHION DESIGNER

•

Fashion is made to become unfashionable.

–GABRIELLE "COCO" CHANEL (1883-1971)
FRENCH FASHION DESIGNER

•

I base most of my fashion sense on what doesn't itch.

–GILDA RADNER (1946-1989) • AMERICAN COMEDIAN

•

Fashion is an imposition, a reign on freedom.

–GOLDA MEIR (1898-1978)
RUSSIAN-BORN FIRST FEMALE PRIME MINISTER OF ISRAEL

•

No fashion has ever been created expressly for the lean purse or for the fat woman: The dressmaker's ideal is the thin millionaires.

–KATHERINE FULLERTON GEROULD (1879-1944) • AMERICAN TEACHER AND WRITER

•

Fashion should not be expected to serve in the stead of courage or character.

–LORETTA YOUNG (1913-2000) • AMERICAN ACTOR

Fashion exists for women with no taste, etiquette for people with no breeding.

–QUEEN MARIE OF RUMANIA (1875–1938)
BORN PRINCESS MARIE OF EDINBURGH; MEMBER OF THE BRITISH ROYAL FAMILY

•

Oh, never mind the fashion. When one has a style of one's own, it is always 20 times better.

–MARGARET OLIPHANT (1828–1897) • SCOTTISH WRITER

•

Fashion, as we knew it, is over; people wear now exactly what they feel like wearing.

–MARY QUANT (1934–) • ENGLISH FASHION DESIGNER

•

Although a lifelong fashion dropout, I have absorbed enough by reading *Harper's Bazaar* while waiting at the dentist's to have grasped that the purpose of fashion is to make A Statement. My own modest Statement, discerned by true cognoscenti, is, "Woman Who Wears Clothes So She Won't Be Naked."

–MOLLY IVINS (1944–2007) • AMERICAN JOURNALIST AND POLITICAL COMMENTATOR

•

Her only flair is in her nostrils.

–PAULINE KAEL (1919–2001)
AMERICAN FILM CRITIC

•

Fashion offers no greater challenge than finding what works for night without looking like you are wearing a costume.

–VERA WANG (1949–) • CHINESE-AMERICAN FASHION DESIGNER

•

Fashion is very important. It is life-enhancing and, like everything that gives pleasure, it is worth doing well.

–VIVIENNE WESTWOOD (1941–) • ENGLISH FASHION DESIGNER

"FATHERS"

I wanted him to cherish and approve of me, not as he had when I was a child, but as the woman I was, who had her own mind and had made her own choices.

–ADRIENNE RICH (1929–) • AMERICAN POET, THEORIST, AND FEMINIST

It doesn't matter who my father was. It matters who I remember he was.

–ANNE SEXTON (1928–1974) • AMERICAN POET

Why are men reluctant to become fathers? They aren't through being children.

–CINDY GARNER • 20TH-CENTURY AMERICAN ACTOR

Into the father's grave the daughter, sometimes a gray-haired woman, lays away forever the little pet names and memories which to all the rest of the world are but foolishness.

–CONSTANCE FENIMORE WOOLSON (1840–1894) • AMERICAN WRITER

How many of the people I know—sons and daughters—have intricate abstract expressionist paintings of their mothers, created out of their own emotions, attitudes, hands. And how many have only Polaroid pictures of their fathers.

–ELLEN GOODMAN (1941–) • AMERICAN JOURNALIST

All the feeling which my father could not put into words was in his hand—any dog, child, or horse would recognize the kindness of it.

–FREYA STARK (1893–1993) • FRENCH-BORN ENGLISH TRAVEL WRITER

Old as she was, she still missed her daddy sometimes.

–GLORIA NAYLOR (1950–) • AFRICAN-AMERICAN WRITER

No man is responsible for his father. That was entirely his mother's affair.

–MARGARET TURNBULL • 20TH-CENTURY ENGLISH-BORN AMERICAN WRITER AND DRAMATIST

•

A father had to work only half as hard as any mother to be considered twice as good.

–MARY KAY BLAKELY (1948-) • AMERICAN JOURNALIST

•

Down in the bottom of my childhood my father stands laughing.

–TOVE DITLEVSEN (1918–1976) • DANISH POET AND PROSE WRITER

•

"FEAR"

•

In morals what begins in fear usually ends in wickedness; in religion what begins in fear usually ends in fanaticism. Fear, either as a principle or a motive, is the beginning of all evil.

–ANNA JAMESON (1794–1860) • IRISH/ENGLISH WRITER

•

The only real prison is fear, and the only real freedom is freedom from fear.

–AUNG SAN SUU KYI (1945-) • BURMESE OPPOSITION LEADER AND NOBEL LAUREATE

•

Anything I've ever done that ultimately was worthwhile . . . initially scared me to death.

–BETTY BENDER • 20TH/21ST-CENTURY AMERICAN PROFESSOR

•

Only when we are no longer afraid do we begin to live.

–DOROTHY THOMPSON (1893–1961) • AMERICAN JOURNALIST

•

You gain strength, courage, and confidence by every experience in which you really stop to look fear in the face. You must do the thing which you think you cannot do.

–ELEANOR ROOSEVELT (1884–1962) • AMERICAN POLITICAL LEADER AND FIRST LADY

The things you fear are undefeatable not by their nature but by your approach.

–JEWEL (1974–) • AMERICAN SINGER-SONGWRITER

•

To fear is one thing. To let fear grab you by the tail and swing you around is another.

–KATHERINE PATERSON (1932–) • AMERICAN WRITER

•

The way you overcome shyness is to become so wrapped up in something you forget to be afraid.

–LADY BIRD JOHNSON (1912–) • FIRST LADY OF THE UNITED STATES

•

Nothing in life is to be feared. It is only to be understood.

–MARIE CURIE (1867–1934)
POLISH-FRENCH CHEMIST AND RADIOLOGY PIONEER; FIRST TWO-TIME NOBEL LAUREATE

•

Fear is not a good teacher. The lessons of fear are quickly forgotten.

–MARY CATHERINE BATESON (1939–) • AMERICAN WRITER AND CULTURAL ANTHROPOLOGIST

•

I have learned that even if you are terrified, it's best not to show it. Then you get credit for being fearless.

–SUSAN MOIR ALLISON (1845–1937) • AMERICAN PIONEER

•

"FEMINISM"

•

My idea of feminism is self-determination, and it's very open-ended; every woman has the right to become herself, and do whatever she needs to do.

–ANI DIFRANCO (1970–)
AMERICAN FEMINIST SINGER, GUITARIST, AND SONGWRITER

It's babe feminism—we're young, we're fun, we do what we want in bed—and it has a shorter shelf life than the feminism of sisterhood. I've been a babe, and I've been a sister. Sister lasts longer.

—ANNA QUINDLEN (1953-) • AMERICAN JOURNALIST AND WRITER

What we need is a tough new kind of feminism with no illusions. Women do not change institutions simply by assimilating into them. We need a feminism that teaches a woman to say no—not just to the date rapist or overly insistent boyfriend but, when necessary, to the military or corporate hierarchy within which she finds herself. We need a kind of feminism that aims not just to assimilate into the institutions that men have created over the centuries, but to infiltrate and subvert them.

—BARBARA EHRENREICH (1941-) • AMERICAN ESSAYIST AND SOCIAL CRITIC

One of the greatest gifts of black feminism to ourselves has been to make it a little easier simply to be black and female.

—BARBARA SMITH • 20TH/21ST-CENTURY AFRICAN-AMERICAN FEMINIST ACTIVIST

Feminist politics aims to end domination, to free us to be who we are—to live lives where we love justice, where we can live in peace. Feminism is for everybody.

—BELL HOOKS (1952-) • AFRICAN-AMERICAN ACTIVIST AND THEORIST

Scratch most feminists and underneath there is a woman who longs to be a sex object. The difference is that is not all she wants to be.

—BETTY ROLLIN (1936-) • AMERICAN NEWS CORRESPONDENT AND WRITER

Feminism is the radical notion that women are people.

—CHERIS KRAMARAE AND PAULA TREICHLER
20TH/21ST-CENTURY AMERICAN PROFESSORS OF WOMEN'S STUDIES AND COMMUNICATIONS

Feminism has fought no wars. It has killed no opponents. It has set up no concentration camps, starved no enemies, practiced no cruelties. Its battles have been for education, for the vote, for better working conditions . . . for safety on the streets . . . for child care, for social welfare. . . for rape crisis centers, women's refuges, reforms in the law. [If someone says] "Oh, I'm not a feminist," [I ask] "Why? What's your problem?"

–DALE SPENDER (1943–) • AUSTRALIAN SOCIOLINGUIST AND TECHNOLOGY THEORIST

[Addressing a group of professional military officers:] Are you a feminist? Oh . . . *wrong* question. I should have asked, "Are you a father?" When your daughter loses her job to a clearly less-qualified man, you will discover *you* are a feminist.

–ESTELLE RAMEY (1917–2006) • AMERICAN PROFESSOR OF BIOPHYSICS AND PHYSIOLOGY

In my heart, I think a woman has two choices:
Either she's a feminist or a masochist.

–GLORIA STEINEM (1934–)
AMERICAN FEMINIST AND COFOUNDER OF *MS.* MAGAZINE

[Feminism is] about women having intrinsic value as persons rather than contingent value as a means to an end for others: fetuses, children, the "family," men.

–KATHA POLLITT (1949–) • AMERICAN FEMINIST WRITER AND CULTURAL CRITIC

To me, feminism is about men and women sharing power equally. And so it necessarily transforms the world for the better for women and men. If women change, men have to change too. And we're still in the process of changing.

–KIKE ROACH • 20TH/21ST-CENTURY AFRICAN-CANADIAN LAWYER, WRITER, AND ACTIVIST

I am a feminist, and I define myself: Be yourself, because if you can get away with it, that is the ultimate feminist act.

–LIZ PHAIR (1967–) • AMERICAN SINGER-SONGWRITER AND GUITARIST

Does feminist mean large unpleasant person who'll shout at you, or someone who believes women are human beings? To me it's the latter, so I sign up.

—MARGARET ATWOOD (1939–) • CANADIAN POET, WRITER, CRITIC, AND ACTIVIST

•

I used to go on college campuses 25 years ago and announce I was a feminist, and people thought it meant I believed in free love and was available for a quick hop in the sack. . . . Now I go on college campuses and say I'm a feminist, and half of them think it means I'm a lesbian. How'd we get from there to here without passing "Go"?

—MOLLY IVINS (1944–2007) • AMERICAN JOURNALIST AND POLITICAL COMMENTATOR

•

I myself have never been able to find out precisely what feminism is: I only know that people call me a feminist whenever I express sentiments that differentiate me from a doormat or a prostitute.

—REBECCA WEST (1892–1983) • ANGLO-IRISH FEMINIST AND WRITER

•

To me, a feminist belongs in the same category as a humanist or an advocate for human rights. I don't see why someone who's a feminist should be thought of differently.

—SUZANNE VEGA (1959–) • AMERICAN SONGWRITER AND SINGER

•

Does being a feminist mean that I believe I'm as good as any man? Yes.

—YASMINE BLEETH (1968–) • AMERICAN ACTOR

•

RESISTANCE TO

Now you ask a group of young women on the college campus, "How many of you are feminists?" Very few will raise their hands, because young women don't want to be associated with it anymore because they know it means male-bashing, it means being a victim, and it means being bitter and angry.

—CHRISTINA HOFF SOMMERS • 20TH/21ST-CENTURY AMERICAN WRITER AND SOCIAL CRITIC

Feminism is a dirty word . . . because your feminists are so ugly. Every picture I saw of those women at the nuclear plants, they were not pretty. So I didn't want to be associated with feminism because I thought it would make me ugly.

–COURTNEY LOVE (1964-) • AMERICAN ROCK MUSICIAN AND ACTOR

"I'm not a feminist," some women say sternly as they march off to work where equal opportunity legislation protects them. . . . Women who say they are not feminists and act like individuals with basic human rights have just got their terminology wrong.

–KAZ COOKE • 20TH/21ST-CENTURY AUSTRALIAN WRITER AND CARTOONIST

[We could] change the word "feminist" to a word with fewer stigmas attached. But inevitably the same thing will happen to that magical word. Part of the radical connotation of feminism is not due to the word, but to the action. The act of a woman standing up for herself is radical, whether she calls herself a feminist or not.

–PAULA KAMEN (1967-) • AMERICAN FEMINIST JOURNALIST, PLAYWRIGHT, AND WRITER

"FLIRTING"

Flirtation envies Love, and Love envies Flirtation.

–CAROLYN WELLS (1869-1942) • AMERICAN WRITER

I really think it gets easier to flirt as you get older because you learn to listen to any man, employing the same charm and rapt attention you once reserved for seven-year-olds.

–HELEN GURLEY BROWN (1922-) • AMERICAN EDITOR AND WRITER

Why does a man take it for granted that a girl who flirts with him wants him to kiss her—when, nine times out of ten, she only wants him to want to kiss her?

–HELEN ROWLAND (1875–1950) • AMERICAN JOURNALIST AND HUMORIST

There are times not to flirt. When you're sick. When you're with children. When you're on the witness stand.

–JOYCE JILLSON (1946–2004) • AMERICAN ASTROLOGER

Flirtation . . . is a graceful salute to sex, a small impermanent spark between one human being and another, between a man and a woman not in need of fire.

–MARYA MANNES (1904–1990) • AMERICAN COLUMNIST AND CRITIC

Women flirt to keep their stock high, men to get somewhere.

–MARYA MANNES (1904–1990) • AMERICAN COLUMNIST AND CRITIC

"FLOWERS"

See also Gardening

The grape hyacinth is the favorite spring flower of my garden—but no! I thought a minute ago the scilla was! And what place has the violet? The flower de luce? I cannot decide, but this I know—it is some blue flower.

–ALICE MORSE EARLE (1851–1911) • AMERICAN WRITER AND ANTIQUARIAN

There came a time when the risk to remain tight in the bud was more painful than the risk it took to blossom.

–ANAÏS NIN (1903–1977) • FRENCH WRITER AND DIARIST

Forsythia is pure joy. There is not an ounce, not a glimmer of sadness of even knowledge in forsythia. Pure, undiluted, untouched joy.

–ANNE MORROW LINDBERGH (1906–2001) • AMERICAN WRITER AND PIONEERING AVIATOR

Arranging a bowl of flowers in the morning can give a sense of quiet in a crowded day—like writing a poem or saying a prayer.

—ANNE MORROW LINDBERGH (1906-2001)
AMERICAN WRITER AND PIONEERING AVIATOR

•

Does anything eat flowers? I couldn't recall having seen anything eat a flower—are they nature's privileged pets?

—ANNIE DILLARD (1945-) • AMERICAN WRITER AND POET

•

He who is born with a silver spoon in his mouth is generally considered a fortunate person, but his good fortune is small compared to that of the happy mortal who enters this world with a passion for flowers in his soul.

—CELIA THAXTER (1835-1894) • AMERICAN POET AND WRITER

•

What a desolate place would be a world without flowers. It would be a face without a smile; a feast without a welcome. Are not flowers the stars of the earth? Are not our stars the flowers of heaven?

—CLARA L. BALFOUR (1808-1878) • AMERICAN WRITER

•

Flowers grow out of dark moments.

—CORITA KENT (1918-1986)
AMERICAN ARTIST

•

Big doesn't necessarily mean better. Sunflowers aren't better than violets.

—EDNA FERBER (1885-1968) • AMERICAN WRITER

•

I knew in my heart that I wanted to know the garden intimately, to know all the flowers in each season, to be there from spring through autumn, digging, pruning, planting, feeding, rejoicing. In short, I had fallen in love.

—ELIZABETH MURRAY
20TH/21ST-CENTURY AMERICAN PHOTOGRAPHER, ARTIST, GARDENER, AND WRITER

I'd rather have roses on my table than diamonds on my neck.

–EMMA GOLDMAN (1869–1940) • RUSSIAN ANARCHIST AND FEMINIST

•

When you take a flower in your hand and really look at it, it's your world for the moment. I want to give that world to someone else. Most people in the city rush around so, they have no time to look at a flower. I want them to see it whether they want to or not.

–GEORGIA O'KEEFFE (1887–1986) • AMERICAN ARTIST

•

The flowers of late winter and early spring occupy places in our hearts well out of proportion to their size.

–GERTRUDE S. WISTER (1905–1999)
AMERICAN HORTICULTURIST AND PHILANTHROPIST

•

A rose is a rose is a rose.

–GERTRUDE STEIN (1874–1946)
AMERICAN POET

•

I smelt the violets in her hand and asked, half in words, half in signs, a question which meant "is love the sweetness of flowers?"

–HELEN KELLER (1880–1968) • AMERICAN WRITER AND ACTIVIST

•

People from a planet without flowers would think we must be mad with joy the whole time to have such things about us.

–IRIS MURDOCH (1919–1999) • IRISH-BORN ENGLISH WRITER

•

Where flowers bloom so does hope.

–LADY BIRD JOHNSON (1912–)
FIRST LADY OF THE UNITED STATES

Flowers have spoken to me more than I can tell in written words. They are the hieroglyphics of angels, loved by all men for the beauty of their character, though few can decipher even fragments of their meaning.

–LYDIA MARIA CHILD (1802–1880) • AMERICAN ACTIVIST, WRITER, AND JOURNALIST

•

Help us to be ever faithful gardeners of the spirit, who know that without darkness nothing comes to birth, and without light nothing flowers.

–MAY SARTON (1912–1995) • BELGIUM-BORN AMERICAN POET, NOVELIST, AND MEMOIRIST

•

Who would have thought it possible that a tiny little flower could occupy a person so completely that there simply wasn't room for any other thought.

–SOPHIE SCHOLL (1921–1943)
GERMAN RESISTER; CONVICTED OF TREASON AND EXECUTED BY NAZIS

•

Science, or parascience, tells us that geraniums bloom better if they are spoken to. But a kind word every now and then is really quite enough. Too much attention, like too much feeding and weeding and hoeing, inhibits and embarrasses them.

–VICTORIA GLENDINNING (1937–)
ENGLISH BIOGRAPHER, CRITIC, BROADCASTER, AND NOVELIST

•

A flowerless room is a soulless room, to my way of thinking; but even one solitary little vase of a living flower may redeem it.

–VITA SACKVILLE-WEST (1892–1962) • ENGLISH POET AND WRITER

•

GIFTS OF

Women who buy perfume and flowers for themselves because their men won't do it are called "self-basting."

–ADAIR LARA • 20TH/21ST-CENTURY AMERICAN COLUMNIST AND MEMOIRIST

•

If you want to say it with flowers, a single rose says: "I'm cheap!"

–DELTA BURKE (1956–) • AMERICAN ACTOR

A gift of flowers to a woman implies that she is as deliciously desirable as the blossoms themselves; but there may be another and hidden message, contained in the old-fashioned phrases like "shy as a violet," "clinging vine," not originaly conceived as pejoratives, that tells more of the truth—which is that flowers are also emblems of feminine submission.

—ELEANOR PERÉNYI (1918–) • AMERICAN WRITER

•

When a woman receives flowers from a man, it fills up your heart.

—NASTASSJA KINSKI (1961–) • GERMAN ACTOR

•

GROWING

To pick a flower is so much more satisfying than just observing it, or photographing it. . . . So in later years, I have grown in my garden as many flowers as possible for children to pick.

—ANNE SCOTT-JAMES • 20TH/21ST-CENTURY ENGLISH JOURNALIST AND GARDENING WRITER

•

As I work among my flowers, I find myself talking to them, reasoning and remonstrating with them, adoring them as if they were human beings. Much laughter I provoke among my friends by so doing, but that is of no consequence. We are on such good terms, my flowers and I.

—CELIA THAXTER (1835–1894) • AMERICAN POET AND WRITER

•

It will never rain roses. When we want to have more roses, we must plant more roses.

—GEORGE ELIOT (MARY ANN EVANS) (1819–1880) • ENGLISH WRITER

•

"FLYING"

•

Trouble in the air is very rare. It is hitting the ground that causes it.

—AMELIA EARHART (1897–1937)

PIONEERING AMERICAN AVIATOR; FIRST PERSON TO FLY SOLO ACROSS PACIFIC

Beware of men on airplanes. The minute a man reaches thirty thousand feet, he immediately becomes consumed by distasteful sexual fantasies which involve doing uncomfortable things in those tiny toilets.

–CYNTHIA HEIMEL • 20TH/21ST-CENTURY AMERICAN WRITER

•

Every time we hit an air pocket and the plane dropped about five hundred feet (leaving my stomach in my mouth) I vowed to give up sex, bacon, and air travel if I ever made it back to terra firma in one piece.

–ERICA JONG (1942-) • AMERICAN WRITER

•

I feel about airplanes the way I feel about diets. It seems they are wonderful things for other people to go on.

–JEAN KERR (1923-2003) • AMERICAN PLAYWRIGHT AND HUMORIST

•

The world is divided into two kind of people: normal, intelligent, sensitive people with some breadth of imagination, and people who aren't the least bit afraid of flying.

–LAYNE RIDLEY • 20TH/21ST-CENTURY WRITER

•

I go out of my way to stay off commuter planes. I have skipped conferences because I would not fly on marginal airlines.

–MARY SCHIAVO
20TH/21ST-CENTURY AMERICAN INSPECTOR GENERAL OF THE U.S. DEPARTMENT OF TRANSPORTATION

•

A plane is a bad place for an all-out sleep, but a good place to begin rest and recovery from the trip to the faraway places you've been, a decompression chamber between Here and There. Though a plane is not the ideal place really to think, reassess or reevaluate things, it is a great place to have the illusion of doing so, and often the illusion will suffice.

–SHANA ALEXANDER (1925-2005) • AMERICAN JOURNALIST AND COLUMNIST

FEMALE PILOTS

So I accept these awards on behalf of the cake bakers and all of those other women who can do some things quite as important, if not more important, than flying, as well as in the name of women flying today.

–AMELIA EARHART (1897–1937)

PIONEERING AMERICAN AVIATOR; FIRST PERSON TO FLY SOLO ACROSS THE PACIFIC

•

I decided blacks should not have to experience the difficulties I had faced, so I decided to open a flying school and teach other black women to fly.

–BESSIE COLEMAN (1892–1926)

FIRST AFRICAN-AMERICAN WOMAN TO BECOME AN AIRPLANE PILOT

•

In the early days they said I was trying to make a statement, but I was just trying to make a living.

–BONNIE TIBURZI

20TH-CENTURY AMERICAN PILOT, FIRST WOMAN HIRED BY A MAJOR AIRLINE

•

Any girl who has flown at all grows used to the prejudice of most men pilots who will trot out any number of reasons why women can't possibly be good pilots. . . . The only way to show the disbelievers, the snickering hangar pilots, is to show them.

–CORNELIA FORT (1919–1943) • AMERICAN ARMED FORCES PILOT

•

The aeroplane should open a fruitful occupation for women. I see no reason they cannot realize handsome incomes by carrying passengers between adjacent towns, from parcel delivery, taking photographs, or conducting schools of flying.

–HARRIET QUIMBY (1875–1912)

AMERICAN AVIATOR; FIRST WOMAN TO FLY ACROSS THE ENGLISH CHANNEL

There is a decided prejudice on the part of the general public against being piloted by a woman, and as great an aversion, partially because of this, by executives of those companies whose activities require employing pilots.

–LOUISE THADEN (1905–1979)
AMERICAN AVIATION PIONEER AND HOLDER OF NUMEROUS AVIATION RECORDS

"FOOD"

See also Cooking, Dieting

We are indeed much more than what we eat, but what we eat can nevertheless help us to be much more than what we are.

–ADELLE DAVIS (1904–1974) • AMERICAN PIONEER IN THE FIELD OF NUTRITION

Let things taste of what they are.

–ALICE WATERS (1944–) • AMERICAN CHEF

Good food can only come from good ingredients. Its proper price includes the cost of preserving the environment and paying fairly for the labor of the people who produce it.

–ALICE WATERS (1944–) • AMERICAN CHEF

Ever consider what dogs must think of us? I mean, here we come back from a grocery store with the most amazing haul—chicken, pork, half a cow. They must think we're the greatest hunters on earth!

–ANNE TYLER (1941–) • AMERICAN WRITER

Food is like sex: When you abstain, even the worst stuff begins to look good.

–BETH MCCOLLISTER • 20TH/21ST-CENTURY ACTOR

The odds of going to the store for a loaf of bread and coming out with only a loaf of bread are three billion to one.

–ERMA BOMBECK (1927–1996) • AMERICAN HUMORIST

•

Seize the moment. Remember all those women on the Titanic who waved off the dessert cart.

–ERMA BOMBECK (1927–1996) • AMERICAN HUMORIST

•

When I buy cookies I eat just four and throw the rest away. But first I spray them with Raid so I won't dig them out of the garbage later. Be careful, though, because that Raid really doesn't taste that bad.

–JANETTE BARBER • 20TH/21ST-CENTURY AMERICAN COMEDIAN AND WRITER

•

Always serve too much hot fudge sauce on hot fudge sundaes. It makes people overjoyed, and puts them in your debt.

–JUDITH OLNEY • 20TH/21ST-CENTURY AMERICAN COOK AND WRITER

•

If you have enough butter, anything is good.

–JULIA CHILD (1912–2004) • AMERICAN CHEF AND TELEVISION PERSONALITY

•

Why does Sea World have a seafood restaurant? I'm halfway through my fishburger and I realize, Oh my God. I could be eating a slow learner.

–LYNDA MONTGOMERY • 20TH/21ST-CENTURY AMERICAN COMEDIAN

•

Food imaginatively and lovingly prepared, and eaten in good company, warms the being.

–MARJORIE KINNAN RAWLINGS (1896–1953) • AMERICAN WRITER

•

I know that I am essentially a sort of fun-loving person who really just wants to sit around and eat pies.

–NORA EPHRON (1941–)
AMERICAN FILM DIRECTOR, PRODUCER, SCREENWRITER, AND NOVELIST

As I ramble through life, whatever be my goal, I will unfortunately always keep my eye upon the doughnut and not upon the whole.

–WENDY WASSERSTEIN (1950–2006) • AMERICAN FEMINIST PLAYWRIGHT

MEAT

There exists no politician in India daring enough to attempt to explain to the masses that cows can be eaten.

–INDIRA GANDHI (1917–1984) • PRIME MINISTER OF INDIA

If we aren't supposed to eat animals, then why are they made out of meat?

–JO BRAND (1957–) • ENGLISH COMEDIAN

"FORGIVENESS"

Forgiveness is the act of admitting we are like other people.

–CHRISTINA BALDWIN
20TH/21ST-CENTURY AMERICAN LEADER OF SPIRITUALITY AND PERSONAL WRITING RETREATS

If you haven't forgiven yourself something, how can you forgive others?

–DOLORES HUERTA (1930–) • AMERICAN LABOR LEADER AND SOCIAL ACTIVIST

You could have forgiven my committing a sin if you hadn't feared that I'd committed a pleasure as well.

–ELLEN GLASGOW (1873–1945) • AMERICAN WRITER

It's easier to ask forgiveness than it is to get permission.

–GRACE MURRAY HOPPER (1906–1992)
PIONEERING COMPUTER SCIENTIST AND REAR ADMIRAL IN THE U.S. NAVY

Forgiveness is the economy of the heart. . . . Forgiveness saves the expense of anger, the cost of hatred, the waste of spirits.

–HANNAH MORE (1745-1833)
ENGLISH PLAYWRIGHT, RELIGIOUS WRITER, AND PHILANTHROPIST

Surely it is much more generous to forgive and remember, than to forgive and forget.

–MARIA EDGEWORTH (1767-1849) • IRISH WRITER

Many people believe in turning the other cheek, especially when it is your cheek.

–ANNE ELLIS (1875-1938) • AMERICAN PIONEER

Forgiveness is a gift of high value. Yet its cost is nothing.

–BETTY SMITH (1896-1972) • AMERICAN WRITER AND DRAMATIST

It is very easy to forgive others their mistakes. It takes more grit and gumption to forgive them for having witnessed your own.

–JESSAMYN WEST (1902-1984) • AMERICAN WRITER

Once a woman has forgiven a man, she must not reheat his sins for breakfast.

–MARLENE DIETRICH (1901-1992) • GERMAN-BORN ACTOR AND SINGER

Who understands much, forgives much.

–MADAME DE STAËL (1766-1817)
SWISS-BORN FRENCH WRITER AND SOCIETY FIGURE

"FREEDOM"

We know that the road to freedom has always been stalked by death.

–ANGELA DAVIS (1944-) • AMERICAN SOCIAL JUSTICE ACTIVIST

The political core of any movement for freedom in the society has to have the political imperative to protect free speech.

–BELL HOOKS (1952-) • AFRICAN-AMERICAN ACTIVIST AND THEORIST

True emancipation begins neither at the polls nor in the courts. It begins in woman's soul.

–EMMA GOLDMAN (1869-1940) • RUSSIAN ANARCHIST AND FEMINIST

Freedom is like taking a bath: You got to keep doing it every day.

–FLORYNCE KENNEDY (1916-2000) • AFRICAN-AMERICAN LAWYER AND ACTIVIST

Being offended is the natural consequence of leaving one's home. I do not like aftershave lotion, adults who rollerskate, children who speak French, or anyone who is unduly tan. I do not, however, go around enacting legislation and putting up signs.

–FRAN LEBOWITZ (1950-) • AMERICAN HUMORIST

I don't know if a country where the people are so ignorant of reality and of history, if you can call that a free world.

–JANE FONDA (1937-) • AMERICAN ACTOR, FITNESS CELEBRITY, AND POLITICAL ACTIVIST

The secret point of money and power in America is neither the things that money can buy nor power for power's sake . . . but absolute personal freedom, mobility, privacy. It is the instinct which drove America to the Pacific, all through the nineteenth century, the desire to be able to find a restaurant open in case you want a sandwich, to be a free agent, live by one's own rules.

–JOAN DIDION (1934-) • AMERICAN WRITER

This is a nation that has lost the ability to be self-critical, and that makes a lie out of the freedoms.

–JONI MITCHELL (1943-) • CANADIAN SINGER, SONGWRITER, MUSICIAN

What is the essence of America? Finding and maintaining that perfect, delicate balance between freedom "to" and freedom "from."

–MARILYN VOS SAVANT (1946–)
AMERICAN COLUMNIST, HOLDER OF GUINNESS WORLD RECORD FOR HIGHEST IQ

•

If all men are born free, how is it that all women are born slaves?

–MARY ASTELL (1666–1731) • ENGLISH FEMINIST WRITER

•

I prefer liberty to chains of diamonds.

–LADY MARY WORTLEY MONTAGU (1689–1762)
ENGLISH POET, EPISTOLARY WRITER, AND SMALLPOX VACCINE ADVOCATE

•

The suppression of civil liberties is to many less a matter of horror than the curtailment of the freedom to profit.

–MARYA MANNES (1904–1990) • AMERICAN COLUMNIST AND CRITIC

•

In every soul, God has implanted a principle which we call love of freedom; it is impatient of oppression and pants for deliverance . . .

–PHILLIS WHEATLEY (1753?–1784) • AFRICAN-AMERICAN POET AND FREED SLAVE

•

Without general elections, without freedom of the press, freedom of speech, freedom of assembly, without the free battle of opinions, life in every public institution withers away, becomes a caricature of itself, and bureaucracy rises as the only deciding factor.

–ROSA LUXEMBURG (1870–1919) • GERMAN MARXIST POLITICAL THEORIST AND REVOLUTIONARY

•

I wish that every human life might be pure transparent freedom.

–SIMONE DE BEAUVOIR (1908–1986) • FRENCH WRITER AND PHILOSOPHER

O Liberté, que de crimes on commet en ton nom!
(Oh Liberty, what crimes are committed in thy name!)

—JEANNE-MARIE ROLAND (1754–1793)
FRENCH WRITER AND REVOLUTIONARY

•

"FRIENDSHIP"

•

What I cannot love, I overlook. Is that real friendship?

—ANAÏS NIN (1903–1977) • FRENCH WRITER AND DIARIST

•

We challenge one another to be funnier and smarter. . . .
It's the way friends make love to one another.

—ANNIE GOTTLIEB • 20TH/21ST-CENTURY AMERICAN CULTURAL CRITIC

•

Trouble is a sieve through which we sift our acquaintances.
Those too big to pass through are our friends.

—ARLENE FRANCIS (1907–2001) • AMERICAN ACTOR

•

Winning has always meant much to me, but winning
friends has meant the most.

—BABE DIDRIKSON ZAHARIAS (1914–1956) • AMERICAN GOLFER

•

If we would build on a sure foundation in friendship, we must
love friends for their sake rather than for our own.

—CHARLOTTE BRONTË (1816–1855) • ENGLISH WRITER

Oh, the comfort, the inexpressible comfort of feeling safe with a person, having neither to weigh thoughts nor measure words, but pouring them all out, just as they are, chaff and grain together, certain that a faithful hand will take and sift them, keep what is worth keeping, and with a breath of kindness blow the rest away.

–DINAH CRAIK (1826–1887) • ENGLISH POET AND WRITER

•

Many people will walk in and out of your life, but only true friends will leave footprints in your heart.

–ELEANOR ROOSEVELT (1884–1962)
AMERICAN POLITICAL LEADER AND FIRST LADY

•

The best time to make friends is before you need them.

–ETHEL BARRYMORE (1879–1959) • AMERICAN ACTOR

•

True friendship is like a rose: We don't realize its beauty until it fades.

–EVELYN LOEB • 20TH/21ST-CENTURY WRITER AND EDITOR

•

I have learned that to have a good friend is the purest of all God's gifts, for it is a love that has no exchange of payment.

–FRANCES FARMER (1914–1970) • AMERICAN ACTOR

•

Still—in a way—nobody sees a flower—really—it is so small—we haven't the time—and to see takes time, like to have a friend takes time.

–GEORGIA O'KEEFFE (1887–1986) • AMERICAN ARTIST

•

Treat your friends as you do your pictures, and place them in their best light.

–JENNIE JEROME CHURCHILL (1854–1921)
ANGLO-AMERICAN SOCIETY FIGURE, MOTHER OF WINSTON CHURCHILL

As you grow older, you'll find that you enjoy talking to strangers far more than to your friends.

–JOY WILLIAMS (1944-) • AMERICAN WRITER

•

Friendships aren't perfect and yet they are very precious. For me, not expecting perfection all in one place was a great release.

–LETTY COTTIN POGREBIN
20TH/21ST-CENTURY AMERICAN WRITER, LECTURER, AND SOCIAL JUSTICE ACTIVIST

•

True friendship is never serene.

–MARIE DE RABUTIN-CHANTAL (1626-1696)
FRENCH LETTER-WRITER

•

It is the friends you can call at 4 a.m. that matter.

–MARLENE DIETRICH (1901-1992)
GERMAN-BORN ACTOR AND SINGER

•

It is not what you give your friend, but what you are willing to give him that determines the quality of friendship.

–MARY DIXON THAYER • 20TH-CENTURY AMERICAN POET

•

This is what we can all do to nourish and strengthen one another: Listen to one another very hard, ask hard questions, too, send one another away to work again, and laugh in all the right places.

–NANCY MAIRS (1943-) • AMERICAN WRITER

•

Lots of people want to ride with you in the limo, but what you want is someone who will take the bus with you when the limo breaks down.

–OPRAH WINFREY (1954-) • AFRICAN-AMERICAN TELEVISION HOST AND MAGAZINE PUBLISHER

I think we are realizing that the relationships we have with our girlfriends are as important as the career, as important as the marriage. They are sovereign.

–REBECCA WELLS (1892-1983) • ANGLO-IRISH FEMINIST AND WRITER

My means of empowerment has always been to search out wonderful friends, people who believe in me, who help me believe in myself.

–SANDY WARSHAW • 20TH/21ST-CENTURY AMERICAN ACTIVIST

Some of my best friends are illusions. Been sustaining me for years.

–SHEILA BALLANTYNE (1936-) • AMERICAN WRITER

"FRUSTRATION"

If women are often frustrated because men do not respond to their troubles by offering matching troubles, men are often frustrated because women do.

–DEBORAH TANNEN (1945-) • AMERICAN WRITER AND SOCIOLINGUIST

My recipe for dealing with anger and frustration: Set the kitchen timer for 20 minutes, cry, rant, and rave, and at the sound of the bell, simmer down and go about business as usual.

–PHYLLIS DILLER (1917-) • AMERICAN COMEDIAN

I don't have pet peeves like some people. I have whole kennels of irritation.

–WHOOPI GOLDBERG (1955-) • AMERICAN COMEDIAN AND ACTOR

G

"GARDENING"

See also Flowers

•

The greatest gift of the garden is the restoration of the five senses.

–HANNA RION (1875–1924) • IMPRESSIONIST ARTIST

•

Weather means more when you have a garden. There's nothing like listening to a shower and thinking how it is soaking in around your green beans.

–MARCELENE COX • 20TH-CENTURY AMERICAN WRITER

•

Everything that slows us down and forces patience, everything that sets us back into the slow circles of nature, is a help. Gardening is an instrument of grace.

–MAY SARTON (1912–1995) • BELGIAN-BORN AMERICAN POET, NOVELIST, AND MEMOIRIST

•

In the garden the door is always open into the "holy"—growth, birth, death. Every flower holds the whole mystery in its short cycle, and in the garden we are never far away from death, the fertilizing, good, creative death.

–MAY SARTON (1912–1995) • BELGIAN-BORN AMERICAN POET, NOVELIST, AND MEMOIRIST

•

Our attitude toward plants is a singularly narrow one. If we see any immediate utility in a plant we foster it. If for any reason we find its presence undesirable or merely a matter of indifference, we may condemn it to destruction forthwith.

–RACHEL CARSON (1907–1964) • AMERICAN ZOOLOGIST AND MARINE BIOLOGIST

•

I appreciate the misunderstanding I have had with Nature over my perennial border. I think it is a flower garden; she thinks it is a meadow lacking grass, and tries to correct the error.

–SARA STEIN (1935–2005)

AMERICAN NATURAL GARDENING ADVOCATE, EDUCATOR, AND WRITER

"GENDER"

See also Gender Roles, Sexual Orientation

The only useful answer to the question, "Who is smarter, a man or a woman?" is, *Which* man and *which* woman?

–ESTELLE RAMEY (1917–2006)
AMERICAN PROFESSOR OF BIOPHYSICS AND PHYSIOLOGY

Many of our troubles in the world today arise from an overemphasis of the masculine, and a neglect of the feminine. This modern world is an aggressive, hyperactive, competitive, masculine world, and it needs the woman's touch as never before.

–EVA BURROWS (1929–) • AUSTRALIAN; LEADER OF SALVATION ARMY

The Rubicons which women must cross, the sex barriers which they must breach, are ultimately those that exist in their own minds.

–FREDA ADLER (1934–) • AMERICAN PROFESSOR OF CRIMINAL JUSTICE

I'm not denyin' the women are foolish: God
Almighty made 'em to match the men.

–GEORGE ELIOT (MARY ANN EVANS) (1819–1880) • ENGLISH WRITER

There is only one sex. . . . A man and a woman are so entirely the same thing that one can scarcely understand the subtle reasons for sex distinction with which our minds are filled.

–GEORGE SAND (AMANDINE-AURORE-LUCIE DUPIN, BARONNE DUDEVANT) (1804–1876)
FRENCH WRITER AND FEMINIST

There is more difference within the sexes than between them.

–IVY COMPTON-BURNETT (1884–1969) • ENGLISH WRITER

If only we could all accept that there is no difference between us where human values are concerned. Whatever sex.

–LIV ULLMAN (1938–) • NORWEGIAN ACTOR AND DIRECTOR

Yet if any human being is to reach full maturity, both the masculine and feminine sides of the personality must be brought up into consciousness.

–M. ESTHER HARDING (1888–1971) • AMERICAN JUNGIAN PSYCHOANALYST

Exclusive gender identity is not an expression of natural differences between the sexes but a suppression of natural similarities.

–MARILYN FRENCH (1929–2009) • AMERICAN WRITER AND FEMINIST

A woman's a woman until the day she dies, but a man's a man only as long as he can.

–JACKIE "MOMS" MABLEY (LORETTA MARY AIKEN) (1894–1975)
AFRICAN-AMERICAN COMEDIAN

I didn't want to be a boy, ever, but I was outraged that his height and intelligence were graces for him and gaucheries for me.

–JANE RULE (1931–) • CANADIAN WRITER

Men are taught to apologize for their weaknesses, women for their strengths.

–LOIS WYSE (1926–2007) • AMERICAN WRITER

Biology is destiny only for girls.

–ELIZABETH HARDWICK (1916–)
AMERICAN WRITER AND CRITIC

To be meek, patient, tactful, modest, honorable, brave is not to be either manly or womanly; it is to be humane.

–JANE HARRISON (1850–1928)
ENGLISH CLASSICS SCHOLAR, LINGUIST, AND FEMINIST

What is asserted by a man is an opinion; what is asserted by a woman is opinionated.

—MARYA MANNES (1904–1990)
AMERICAN COLUMNIST AND CRITIC

"GENDER ROLES"

When someone with the authority of a teacher, say, describes the world and you are not in it, there is a moment of psychic disequilibrium, as if you looked into a mirror and saw nothing. Yet you know you exist and others like you, that this is a game with mirrors. It takes some strength of soul—and not just individual strength, but collective understanding—to resist this void, this nonbeing, into which you are thrust, and to stand up, demanding to be seen and heard.

—ADRIENNE RICH (1929–) • AMERICAN POET, THEORIST, AND FEMINIST

We have a double standard, which is to say, a man can show how much he cares by being violent—see, he's jealous, he cares—a woman shows how much she cares by how much she's willing to be hurt; by how much she will take; how much she will endure; how suicidal she's prepared to be.

—ANDREA DWORKIN (1946–2005) • AMERICAN RADICAL FEMINIST

Clearly, society has a tremendous stake in insisting on a woman's natural fitness for the career of mother: The alternatives are all too expensive.

—ANN OAKLEY (1944–) • ENGLISH FEMINIST, SOCIOLOGIST, AND WRITER

And who knows? Somewhere out there in this audience may even be someone who will one day follow in my footsteps, and preside over the White House as the president's spouse. I wish him well.

—BARBARA BUSH (1925–) • FIRST LADY OF THE UNITED STATES

I refuse to believe that trading recipes is silly. Tunafish casserole is at least as real as corporate stock.

–BARBARA GRIZZUTI HARRISON (1934-2002)
ITALIAN-AMERICAN ESSAYIST AND TRAVEL WRITER

•

And when women do not need to live through their husbands and children, men will not fear the love and strength of women, nor need another's weakness to prove their own masculinity.

–BETTY FRIEDAN (1921-2006)
AMERICAN FEMINIST, WRITER, AND COFOUNDER OF NATIONAL ORGANIZATION FOR WOMEN

•

The feminine mystique has succeeded in burying millions of American women alive.

–BETTY FRIEDAN (1921-2006)
AMERICAN FEMINIST, WRITER, AND COFOUNDER OF NATIONAL ORGANIZATION FOR WOMEN

•

I live by a man's code, designed to fit a man's world, yet at the same time I never forget that a woman's first job is to choose the right shade of lipstick.

–CAROLE LOMBARD (1908-1942) • AMERICAN ACTOR

•

Now, you have to be really good at your job, thin, have great hair and be really clever. And you have to be really good at looking after your children, feeding them well, dressing them trendily. I just think, how do people do it? So the answer is that I shan't.

–DAISY DONOVAN (1975-) • ENGLISH TELEVISION PERSONALITY AND ACTOR

•

When women are supposed to be quiet, a talkative woman is a woman who talks at all.

–DALE SPENDER (1943-)
AUSTRALIAN SOCIOLINGUIST AND TECHNOLOGY THEORIST

The beaux and the babies, the servant troubles, and the social aspirations of the other girls seemed to me superficial. My work did not. I was professional. I could earn my own money, or I could be fired if I were inefficient. It was something to get your teeth into. It was living.

—EDNA WOOLMAN CHASE (1877–1957) • AMERICAN EDITOR AND FASHION JOURNALIST

•

If I had ever learned to type, I never would have made brigadier general.

—ELIZABETH HOISINGTON (1918–) • FIRST FEMALE GENERAL IN U.S. ARMED FORCES

•

I have yet to hear a man ask for advice on how to combine marriage and a career.

—GLORIA STEINEM (1934–)
AMERICAN FEMINIST AND COFOUNDER OF *MS.* MAGAZINE

•

The myth that men are the economic providers and women, mainly, are mothers and caregivers in the family has now been thoroughly refuted. This family pattern has never been the norm, except in a narrow middle-class segment.

—GRO HARLEM BRUNDTLAND (1939–)
NORWEGIAN DIPLOMAT, PHYSICIAN, AND INTERNATIONAL LEADER

•

What is sad for women of my generation is that they weren't supposed to work if they had families. What were they going to do when the children were grown? Watch the raindrops coming down the windowpane?

—JACQUELINE KENNEDY ONASSIS (1929–1994) • FIRST LADY OF THE UNITED STATES

•

From birth, women are taught, through means direct and indirect, that their value as romantic partners, as moral agents—in fact, their very femininity—can be assessed through a close reading of their household habits. While a man's home is his castle, a woman's is a moral register.

—JANET WONDRA • 20TH/21ST-CENTURY AMERICAN POET AND FILMMAKER

A successful man is one who makes more money than his wife can spend. A successful woman is one who can find such a man.

—LANA TURNER (1921–1995) • AMERICAN ACTOR

Every time we liberate a woman, we liberate a man.

—MARGARET MEAD (1901–1978)
AMERICAN CULTURAL ANTHROPOLOGIST

I can't be a rose in any man's lapel.

—MARGARET TRUDEAU (1948–)
CANADIAN WRITER AND WIFE OF PRIME MINISTER OF CANADA

I wish someone would have told me that, just because I'm a girl, I don't have to get married.

—MARLO THOMAS (1938–) • AMERICAN ACTOR

I ran away. I hurried more than if lions had chased me. Without telling him. Without telling my mother or father. There wasn't any liberty in San Francisco for ordinary women. . . . You got married, were an old maid, or went to hell. Take your pick.

—MAUD PARRISH (1878–1976) • AMERICAN TRAVELER AND WRITER

Women polish the silver and water the plants and wait to be really needed.

—MIGNON MCLAUGHLIN (1913–1983) • AMERICAN JOURNALIST AND WRITER

We still live in a world in which a significant fraction of people, including women, believe that a woman belongs and wants to belong exclusively in the home.

—ROSALYN SUSSMAN (1921–)
AMERICAN MEDICAL PHYSICIST, COWINNER OF THE NOBEL PRIZE

It is not women's fault if we are so tender. It is in the nature of the lives we live. And further, it would be a terrible catastrophe if men had to live men's lives and women's also. Which is precisely what has happened today—to women.

–SELMA JAMES (1930-)
AMERICAN WRITER, FEMINIST ACTIVIST, AND FOUNDER OF THE INTERNATIONAL WAGES FOR HOUSEWORK CAMPAIGN

•

And when I'm with men in the studio, they don't like a woman telling them what to do, no matter how famous you are.

–SHAKIRA (1977-) • COLUMBIAN POP SINGER AND SONGWRITER

•

I wanted to be a marine biologist, then I wanted to be a stewardess. Then I wanted to cut hair! But my biggest dream when I was young was to have the perfect home and the picket fence, and babies crawling around, and I'd be cooking in the kitchen.

–SHERILYN FENN (1965-) • AMERICAN ACTOR

•

The emotional, sexual, and psychological stereotyping of females begins when the doctor says, "It's a girl."

–SHIRLEY CHISHOLM (1924-2005)
EDUCATOR, WRITER, AND FIRST AFRICAN-AMERICAN WOMAN ELECTED TO U.S. CONGRESS

•

One can hardly tell women that washing up saucepans is their divine mission, [so] they are told that bringing up children is their divine mission. But the way things are in this world, bringing up children has a great deal in common with washing up saucepans.

–SIMONE DE BEAUVOIR (1908-1986) • FRENCH WRITER AND PHILOSOPHER

•

The torment that so many young women know, bound hand and foot by love and motherhood, without having forgotten their former dreams.

–SIMONE DE BEAUVOIR (1908-1986) • FRENCH WRITER AND PHILOSOPHER

My wish is to ride the tempest, tame the waves, kill the sharks. I will not resign myself to the usual lot of women who bow their heads and become concubines.

–TRIEU THI TRINH (225–248) • VIETNAMESE PEASANT WARRIOR AND REVOLUTIONARY

"GIVING"

To give without any reward, or any notice, has a special quality of its own.

–ANNE MORROW LINDBERGH (1906–2001)
AMERICAN WRITER AND PIONEERING AVIATOR

We are rich only through what we give, and poor only through what we refuse.

–ANNE-SOPHIE SWETCHINE (1782–1857) • RUSSIAN-FRENCH WRITER

Giving frees us from the familiar territory of our own needs by opening our mind to the unexplained worlds occupied by the needs of others.

–BARBARA BUSH (1925–) • FIRST LADY OF THE UNITED STATES

I don't want expensive gifts; I don't want to be bought. I have everything I want. I just want someone to be there for me, to make me feel safe and secure.

–PRINCESS DIANA (1961–1997)
PRINCESS OF WALES, FIRST WIFE OF CHARLES, PRINCE OF WALES

When we grow old, there can only be one regret—not to have given enough of ourselves.

–ELEONORA DUSE (1858–1924) • ITALIAN ACTOR

Charity always feels better to the donor than to the recipient.

–JOY BROWNE • 20TH/21ST-CENTURY AMERICAN RADIO PSYCHOLOGIST

A touch, a word, the semblance of food. With such small gifts we sustain ourselves, the receiving no more crucial than the offering.

–JOYCE REISER KORNBLATT • 20TH/21ST-CENTURY AMERICAN WRITER

•

Sharing is sometimes more demanding than giving.

–MARY CATHERINE BATESON (1939-)
AMERICAN WRITER AND CULTURAL ANTHROPOLOGIST

•

Lots of people think they're charitable if they give away their old clothes and things they don't want.

–MYRTLE REED (1874-1911) • AMERICAN POET, JOURNALIST, AND WRITER

•

Let no one come to you without leaving better and happier.

–MOTHER TERESA (1910-1997) • ALBANIAN CATHOLIC NUN; WINNER OF NOBEL PEACE PRIZE

•

"GOALS"

•

Before I was ever in my teens, I knew exactly what I wanted to be when I grew up. My goal was to be the greatest athlete that ever lived.

–BABE DIDRIKSON ZAHARIAS (1914-1956) • AMERICAN GOLFER

•

Goals are dreams with deadlines.

–DIANA SCHARF-HUNT
20TH/21ST-CENTURY AMERICAN WRITER

•

A soul without a high aim is like a ship without a rudder.

–EILEEN CADDY (1917-)
ENGLISH SPIRITUAL WRITER AND COFOUNDER OF THE FINDHORN FOUNDATION

I long to accomplish a great and noble task, but it is my chief duty to accomplish small tasks as if they were great and noble.

–HELEN KELLER (1880-1968) • AMERICAN WRITER AND ACTIVIST

•

Far away there in the sunshine are my highest aspirations. I may not reach them, but I can look up and see their beauty, believe in them, and try to follow where they lead.

–LOUISA MAY ALCOTT (1832-1888) • AMERICAN WRITER

•

I have the same goal I've had ever since I was a girl. I want to rule the world.

–MADONNA (1958-) • AMERICAN POP SINGER AND ACTOR

•

Nothing contributes so much to tranquilize the mind as a steady purpose—a point on which the soul may fix its intellectual eye.

–MARY SHELLEY (1797-1851) • ENGLISH WRITER

•

The big secret in life is that there is no big secret. Whatever your goal, you can get there if you're willing to work.

–OPRAH WINFREY (1954-)
AFRICAN-AMERICAN TELEVISION HOST AND MAGAZINE PUBLISHER

•

It is good to have an end to journey toward, but it is the journey that matters in the end.

–URSULA K. LE GUIN (1929-) • AMERICAN WRITER

•

"GOD"

See Religion

"GOSSIP"

If it's very painful for you to criticize your friends—you're safe in doing it. But if you take the slightest pleasure in it, that's the time to hold your tongue.

–ALICE DUER MILLER (1874-1942) • AMERICAN WRITER AND SUFFRAGIST

If you can't say something good about someone, sit right here by me.

–ALICE ROOSEVELT LONGWORTH (1884-1980)
AMERICAN; DAUGHTER OF PRESIDENT THEODORE ROOSEVELT

Show me someone who never gossips, and I'll show you someone who isn't interested in people.

–BARBARA WALTERS (1929-) • AMERICAN TELEVISION COMMENTATOR

Great minds discuss ideas, mediocre minds discuss events, small minds discuss personalities.

–ELEANOR ROOSEVELT (1884-1962)
AMERICAN POLITICAL LEADER AND FIRST LADY

Gossip is the opiate of the oppressed.

–ERICA JONG (1942-) • AMERICAN WRITER

A gossip is someone who talks to you about others, a bore is someone who talks to you about himself, and a brilliant conversationalist is one who talks to you about yourself.

–LISA KIRK (1925-1990) • AMERICAN ACTOR

Gossip is just news running ahead of itself in a red satin dress.

–LIZ SMITH (1923-) • AMERICAN GOSSIP COLUMNIST

A cruel story runs on wheels, and every hand oils the wheels as they run.

—OUIDA (LOUISE DE LA RAMÉE) (1839–1908) • ENGLISH WRITER

Trying to squash a rumor is like trying to unring a bell.

—SHANA ALEXANDER (1925–2005) • AMERICAN JOURNALIST AND COLUMNIST

Often the best thing about not saying anything is that it can't be repeated.

—SUZAN WIENER • 20TH/21ST-CENTURY AMERICAN POET AND WRITER

"GOVERNMENT"

The government's like a mule, it's slow and it's sure; it's slow to turn, and it's sure to turn the way you don't want it.

—ELLEN GLASGOW (1873–1945) • AMERICAN WRITER

There is something that governments care far more for than human life, and that is the security of property.

—EMMELINE PANKHURST (1858–1928) • ENGLISH SUFFRAGIST AND FEMINIST

In all modesty, we must admit that governments are not always the best doctors when it comes to diagnosing economic ailments and prescribing the right treatment.

—KIM CAMPBELL (1947–) • FIRST FEMALE PRIME MINISTER OF CANADA

The plague of government is senile delinquency.

—MIGNON MCLAUGHLIN (1913–1983)
AMERICAN JOURNALIST AND WRITER

Government is a tool, like a hammer. You can use a hammer to build with or you can use a hammer to destroy with.

—MOLLY IVINS (1944–2007) • AMERICAN JOURNALIST AND POLITICAL COMMENTATOR

Men alone are not capable of making laws for men and women.

–NELLIE MCCLUNG (1873-1951) • CANADIAN JOURNALIST AND SUFFRAGIST

•

"GRANDPARENTS"

See Family

•

"GRATITUDE"

•

We often take for granted the very things that most deserve our gratitude.

–CYNTHIA OZICK (1928-) • AMERICAN NOVELIST, ESSAYIST, AND POET

•

Silent gratitude isn't much use to anyone.

–GLADYS BRONWYN STERN (1890-1973)
ENGLISH WRITER

•

Like most people who felt they owed a debt they could never repay, she was vaguely uncomfortable in my presence.

–MARCIA MULLER • 20TH/21ST-CENTURY AMERICAN WRITER

•

For what I have received may the Lord make me truly thankful. And more truly for what I have not received.

–STORM JAMESON (1891-1986) • ENGLISH WRITER AND EDITOR

•

"GUILT"

•

Good women always think it is their fault when someone else is being offensive. Bad women never take the blame for anything.

–ANITA BROOKNER (1928-) • ENGLISH WRITER AND ART HISTORIAN

I have no creative use for guilt, yours or my own. Guilt is only another way of avoiding informed action, of buying time out of the pressing need to make clear choices, out of the approaching storm that can feed the earth as well as bend the trees.

–AUDRE LORDE (1934-1992) • AFRICAN-AMERICAN FEMINIST WRITER AND ACTIVIST

•

I cannot keep feeling guilty about that which guilt will not change.

–BARBARA A. ROBINSON (1938-) • AFRICAN-AMERICAN ENTREPRENEUR

•

Mothers, food, love, and career: the four major guilt groups.

–CATHY GUISEWITE (1950-)
AMERICAN CARTOONIST, CREATOR OF SYNDICATED COMIC "CATHY"

•

Show me a woman who doesn't feel guilty, and I'll show you a man.

–ERICA JONG (1942-) • AMERICAN WRITER

•

Guilt is the gift that keeps on giving.

–ERMA BOMBECK (1927-1996) • AMERICAN HUMORIST

•

I believe in guilt. There's not enough guilt around these days for my taste.

–JOY WILLIAMS (1944-) • AMERICAN WRITER

•

In passing, also, I would like to say that the first time Adam had a chance he laid the blame on woman.

–LADY NANCY ASTOR (1879-1964)
FIRST FEMALE TO TAKE A SEAT IN BRITISH HOUSE OF COMMONS

H

"HAIR"

I'm a big woman. I need big hair.

–ARETHA FRANKLIN (1942-)
AMERICAN SOUL, GOSPEL, AND R&B SINGER

My blackness has never been in my hair. Blackness is not a hairstyle.

–BERTHA GILKEY • 20TH/21ST-CENTURY AFRICAN-AMERICAN PUBLIC HOUSING ACTIVIST

Once you've had chemotherapy, there's no such thing as a bad-hair day.

–ELIZABETH TILBERIS (1947-1999) • ENGLISH EDITOR IN CHIEF OF *HARPER'S BAZAAR*

I'm undaunted in my quest to amuse myself by constantly changing my hair.

–HILLARY RODHAM CLINTON (1947-) • AMERICAN POLITICIAN AND FIRST LADY

Gorgeous hair is the best revenge.

–IVANA TRUMP (1949-)
CZECH-BORN FASHION MODEL AND BUSINESSWOMAN

I've discovered that how I look is not a function of anything as ephemeral as my hair.

–JUDITH LIGHT (1949-) • AMERICAN ACTOR

When a woman ceases to alter the fashion of her hair, you guess that she has passed the crisis of her experience.

–MARY AUSTIN (1868–1934) • AMERICAN WRITER

Hair brings one's self-image into focus; it is vanity's proving ground. Hair is terribly personal, a tangle of mysterious prejudices.

–SHANA ALEXANDER (1925-2005) • AMERICAN JOURNALIST AND COLUMNIST

BALDNESS

You never see a man walking down the street with a woman who has a little potbelly and a bald spot.

—ELAYNE BOOSLER (1952–) • AMERICAN COMEDIAN

•

The tenderest spot in a man's makeup is sometimes the bald spot on top of his head.

—HELEN ROWLAND (1875–1950)
AMERICAN JOURNALIST AND HUMORIST

•

BLONDES

The heck with the natural look. After all, you can't take credit for what you're born with, only for what you do yourself. Where would Marilyn Monroe be if she'd clung to the hair color God gave her? We'd have a movie called Gentlemen Prefer Mousy Brown Hair.

—ADAIR LARA • 20TH/21ST-CENTURY AMERICAN COLUMNIST AND MEMOIRIST

•

It isn't that gentlemen really prefer blondes, it's just that we look dumber.

—ANITA LOOS (1889–1981) • AMERICAN SCREENWRITER, NOVELIST, AND ESSAYIST

•

I'm not offended by all the dumb-blonde jokes because I know that I'm not dumb. I also know I'm not blonde.

—DOLLY PARTON (1946–) • AMERICAN COUNTRY SINGER AND ENTERTAINER

•

My real hair color is kind of a dark blonde. Now I just have mood hair.

—JULIA ROBERTS (1967–) • AMERICAN ACTOR

•

When you're not blonde and thin, you come up with a personality real quick.

—KATHY NAJIMY (1957–) • AMERICAN ACTOR AND COMEDIAN

•

It is possible that blondes also prefer gentlemen.

—MAMIE VAN DOREN (1931–) • AMERICAN ACTOR

My question is, why does everybody want to be blonde? The grass may always be greener, but once you hop the fence, you step in dog crap.

–MONICA POTTER (1971–) • AMERICAN ACTOR

It is great to be a blonde. With low expectations it's very easy to surprise people.

–PAMELA ANDERSON (1967–) • CANADIAN-AMERICAN FASHION MODEL AND ACTOR

I may be a dumb blonde, but I'm not that blonde.

–PATRICIA NEAL (1926–) • AMERICAN ACTOR

Once I put that [blonde] wig on, I didn't say an intelligent thing for four months. My voice went up. I walked differently. I'd ask incredibly stupid questions.

–SIGOURNEY WEAVER (1949–) • AMERICAN ACTOR

BRUNETTES

Gentlemen prefer blondes . . . but gentlemen marry brunettes.

–ANITA LOOS (1889–1981) • AMERICAN SCREENWRITER, NOVELIST, AND ESSAYIST

Violet will be a good color for hair at just about the same time that brunette becomes a good color for flowers.

–FRAN LEBOWITZ (1950–) • AMERICAN HUMORIST

I was a puke brunette.

–JENNY MCCARTHY (1972–)
AMERICAN MODEL AND ACTOR

REDHEADS

Once in his life, every man is entitled to fall madly in love with a gorgeous redhead.

–LUCILLE BALL (1911–1989) • AMERICAN COMIC ACTOR

WIGS

People always ask me how long it takes to do my hair. I don't know, I'm never there.

—DOLLY PARTON (1946-)
AMERICAN COUNTRY SINGER AND ENTERTAINER

•

UNWANTED

I refuse to think of them as chin hairs. I think of them as stray eyebrows.

—JANETTE BARBER
20TH/21ST-CENTURY AMERICAN COMEDIAN AND WRITER

•

I'm waxed clean—hairless as the day I was born. But don't say "Tia has no pubic hair." That's so clinical. Use a nice euphemism. Say "She's mowed her secret garden" or "She's cleared the way to the Promised Land." Because that's what it is, right?

—TIA CARRERE (1967-) • AMERICAN MODEL AND ACTOR

•

"HAPPINESS"

•

It is not easy to find happiness in ourselves, and it is not possible to find it elsewhere.

—AGNES REPPLIER (1855-1950) • AMERICAN ESSAYIST

•

We all live with the objective of being happy; our lives are all different and yet the same.

—ANNE FRANK (1929-1945)
GERMAN-JEWISH DIARIST

My philosophy, in essence, is the concept of man as a heroic being, with his own happiness as the moral purpose of his life, with productive achievement as his noblest activity, and reason as his only absolute.

—AYN RAND (1905-1982) • RUSSIAN-AMERICAN WRITER AND PHILOSOPHER

I would always rather be happy than dignified.

—CHARLOTTE BRONTË (1816-1855) • ENGLISH WRITER

Be happy. It is a way of being wise.

—COLETTE (1873-1954) • FRENCH WRITER

Nobody really cares if you're miserable, so you might as well be happy.

—CYNTHIA NELMS (1942-1995) • AMERICAN MUSICIAN AND SINGER

If only we'd stop trying to be happy, we'd have a pretty good time.

—EDITH WHARTON (1862-1937) • AMERICAN WRITER

Earth's crammed with heaven.

—ELIZABETH BARRETT BROWNING (1806-1861)
ENGLISH POET

Happiness must be cultivated. It is like character. It is not a thing to be safely let alone for a moment, or it will run to weeds.

—ELIZABETH STUART PHELPS (1844-1911)
AMERICAN WRITER AND SOCIAL REFORMER

The excursion is the same when you go looking for your sorrow as when you go looking for your joy.

—EUDORA WELTY (1899-2001) • AMERICAN WRITER

There can be no happiness if the things we believe in are different from the things we do.

—FREYA STARK (1893–1993)
FRENCH-BORN ENGLISH TRAVEL WRITER

•

One is happy as a result of one's own efforts, once one knows the necessary ingredients of happiness—simple tastes, a certain degree of courage, self-denial to a point, love of work, and above all, a clear conscience.

—GEORGE SAND (AMANDINE-AURORE-LUCIE DUPIN, BARONNE DUDEVANT) (1804–1876)
FRENCH WRITER AND FEMINIST

•

I do not like the idea of happiness—it is too momentary. I would say that I was always busy and interested in something—interest has more meaning than happiness.

—GEORGIA O'KEEFFE (1887–1986) • AMERICAN ARTIST

•

I don't choose to stay in the state of sadness any more than I would choose to stay in a room with the smoke alarm going off.

—GLORIA JONES (1938–) • AFRICAN-AMERICAN SINGER

•

When one door of happiness closes, another opens; but often we look so long at the closed door that we do not see the one which has opened for us.

—HELEN KELLER (1880–1968) • AMERICAN WRITER AND ACTIVIST

•

Happiness is good health and a bad memory.

—INGRID BERGMAN (1915–1982) • SWEDISH ACTOR

•

I don't think that . . . one gets a flash of happiness once, and never again; it is there within you, and it will come as certainly as death.

—ISAK DINESEN (KAREN BLIXEN) (1885–1962) • DANISH WRITER AND AUTOBIOGRAPHER

Why not seize the pleasure at once? How often is happiness destroyed by preparation, foolish preparation!

–JANE AUSTEN (1775–1817) • ENGLISH WRITER

The capacity for delight is the gift of paying attention.

–JULIA CAMERON • 20TH/21ST-CENTURY AMERICAN WRITER

If you always do what interests you, at least one person is pleased.

–KATHARINE HEPBURN (1907–2003) • AMERICAN ACTOR

I'm so happy, I can hardly spit.

–LAURA SCHLESSINGER (1947–)
AMERICAN CULTURAL COMMENTATOR

She knew there were only small joys in life—the big ones were too complicated to be joys when you got all through—and once you realized that, it took a lot of the pressure off.

–LORRIE MOORE (1957–) • AMERICAN WRITER

Happiness is a choice. You grieve, you stomp your feet, you pick yourself up and choose to be happy.

–LUCY LAWLESS (1968–) • NEW ZEALAND ACTOR AND SINGER

Often people attempt to live their lives backward: They try to have more things, or more money, in order to do more of what they want so that they will be happier. The way it actually works is the reverse. You must first be who you really are, then do what you need to do, in order to have what you want.

–MARGARET YOUNG (1900–1969) • AMERICAN SINGER

To be happy, it first takes being comfortable being in your own shoes. The rest can work up from there.

–SOPHIA BUSH (1982–) • AMERICAN ACTOR

I was something that lay under the sun and felt it, like the pumpkins, and I did not want to be anything more. I was entirely happy. Perhaps we feel like that when we die and become a part of something entire, whether it is sun and air, or goodness and knowledge. At any rate, that is happiness; to be dissolved into something complete and great. When it comes to one, it comes as naturally as sleep.

–WILLA CATHER (1873–1947) • AMERICAN WRITER

"HARASSMENT"

We need to turn the question around to look at the harasser, not the target. We need to be sure that we can go out and look anyone who is a victim of harassment in the eye and say, "You do not have to remain silent anymore."

–ANITA HILL (1956–) • AFRICAN-AMERICAN ATTORNEY AND EDUCATOR

Dear me no dears, sir.

–APHRA BEHN (1640–1689)
ENGLISH PLAYWRIGHT, POET, NOVELIST, AND SPY

All your fine officials debauch the young girls who are afraid to lose their jobs; that's as old as Washington.

–CHRISTINA STEAD (1902–1983) • AUSTRALIAN WRITER

The only women who don't believe that sexual harassment is a real problem in this country are women who have never been in the workplace.

–CYNTHIA HEIMEL • 20TH/21ST-CENTURY AMERICAN WRITER

Sexual harassment at work . . . is it a problem for the self-employed?

–VICTORIA WOOD (1953–) • ENGLISH COMEDIAN

"HATE"

You can safely assume that you've created God in your own image when it turns out that God hates all the same people you do.

–ANNE LAMOTT (1954–) • AMERICAN NOVELIST AND MEMOIRIST

Hate is too great a burden to bear. It injures the hater more than it injures the hated.

–CORETTA SCOTT KING (1927–2006)
AFRICAN-AMERICAN CIVIL RIGHTS ACTIVIST AND WIDOW OF DR. MARTIN LUTHER KING, JR.

As long as you keep a person down, some part of you has to be down there to hold him down, so it means you cannot soar as you otherwise might.

–MARIAN ANDERSON (1897–1993) • AFRICAN-AMERICAN CONTRALTO

It's a sign of your own worth sometimes if you are hated by the right people.

–MILES FRANKLIN (1879–1954) • AUSTRALIAN WRITER

They say that oppression engenders hate. They are heard on all sides crying "hate hate."

–MONIQUE WITTIG (1935–2003) • FRENCH THEORIST AND WRITER

You cannot hate other people without hating yourself.

–OPRAH WINFREY (1954–)
AFRICAN-AMERICAN TELEVISION HOST AND MAGAZINE PUBLISHER

When all that hate energy was focused on me, it was transformed into a fantastic energy. It was supporting me. If you are centered and you can transform all this energy that comes in, it will help you. If you believe it is going to kill you, it will kill you.

–YOKO ONO (1933–) • JAPANESE-BORN AMERICAN MUSICIAN, ARTIST, AND PEACE ACTIVIST

"HEALTH"

You're bound to lose your health at some point,
but you don't have to lose your dignity, too.

–BESSIE & SADIE DELANY (1891–1995; 1889–1999) • AFRICAN-AMERICAN CO-MEMOIRISTS

I recently became a Christian Scientist. It was the only health plan I could afford.

–BETSY SALKIND
20TH/21ST-CENTURY AMERICAN COMEDIAN AND CHILD ABUSE ACTIVIST

Physical activity is one of the most powerful, yet underutilized
tools for personal development, balance, and creativity.

–COLLEEN CANNON • 20TH/21ST-CENTURY AMERICAN TRIATHLETE

All sanity depends on this: that it should be a delight
to feel heat strike the skin, a delight to stand upright, knowing
the bones are moving easily under the flesh.

–DORIS LESSING (1919–) • ENGLISH WRITER

Money cannot buy health, but I'd settle for a diamond-studded wheelchair.

–DOROTHY PARKER (1893–1967) • AMERICAN WRITER AND CRITIC

Never have so many had such broad and advanced access to health
care. But never have so many been denied access to health.

–GRO HARLEM BRUNDTLAND (1939–)
NORWEGIAN DIPLOMAT, PHYSICIAN, AND INTERNATIONAL LEADER

Women in particular need to keep an eye on their physical and mental
health, because . . . we don't have a lot of time to take care of ourselves. We
need to do a better job of putting ourselves higher on our own "to do" list.

–MICHELLE OBAMA (1964–) • AFRICAN-AMERICAN FIRST LADY OF THE UNITED STATES

In medicine, as in statecraft and propaganda, words are sometimes the most powerful drugs we can use.

—SARA MURRAY JORDAN • 20TH-CENTURY AMERICAN GASTROENTEROLOGIST

CANCER

Cancer is a demonic pregnancy.

—SUSAN SONTAG (1933-2004)
AMERICAN ESSAYIST, NOVELIST, INTELLECTUAL, AND ACTIVIST

•

Cancer patients are lied to, not just because the disease is (or is thought to be) a death sentence, but because it is felt to be obscene—in the original meaning of that word: ill-omened, abominable, repugnant to the senses.

—SUSAN SONTAG (1933-2004) • AMERICAN ESSAYIST, NOVELIST, INTELLECTUAL, AND ACTIVIST

•

An individual doesn't get cancer, a family does.

—TERRY TEMPEST WILLIAMS
20TH/21ST-CENTURY AMERICAN ESSAYIST AND NATURALIST

•

DISABILITY

People used to say to my friend Mary, a quadriplegic, "You still have your mind." She would say, "I still have my body." The world tells me to divorce myself from my flesh, to live in my head. . . . I didn't want to be fleshless.

—ANNE FINGER • 20TH/21ST-CENTURY AMERICAN WRITER AND ADVOCATE FOR THE DISABLED

•

Our disabilities may impose limitations, but physical, economic, and political barriers impede us far more.

—LAURA HERSHEY
20TH/21ST-CENTURY AMERICAN DISABILITY RIGHTS ACTIVIST

•

It was ability that mattered, not disability, which is a word I'm not crazy about using.

—MARLEE MATLIN (1965-)
AMERICAN ACTOR AND DEAF RIGHTS ADVOCATE

Disability is a matter of perception. If you can do just one thing well, you're needed by someone.

–MARTINA NAVRATILOVA (1956–)
CZECH-AMERICAN TENNIS PLAYER

•

The fact is that ours is the only minority you can join involuntarily, without warning, at any time. And if you live long enough, as you're increasingly likely to do, you may well join it.

–NANCY MAIRS (1943–) • AMERICAN WRITER

•

Like children in a schoolyard, they want to know what was my accident, how much did it hurt, and what did I look like afterward. . . . I am not the only person who has encountered emotional sightseers.

–NATALIE KUSZ • 20TH/21ST-CENTURY AMERICAN MEMOIRIST

•

It is a lonely existence to be a child with a disability which no one can see or understand; you exasperate your teachers, you disappoint your parents, and worst of all you know that you are not just stupid.

–SUSAN HAMPSHIRE (1937–) • ENGLISH ACTOR

•

HOSPITALS

One of the most difficult things to contend with in a hospital is that assumption on the part of the staff that because you have lost your gall bladder you have also lost your mind.

–JEAN KERR (1923–2003) • AMERICAN PLAYWRIGHT AND HUMORIST

•

Hospitals, like airports and supermarkets, only pretend to be open nights and weekends.

–MOLLY HASKELL (1939–)
AMERICAN JOURNALIST AND FILM CRITIC

"HEART VS. HEAD"

If any part of your uncertainty is a conflict between your heart and your mind, follow your mind.

–AYN RAND (1905–1982) • RUSSIAN-AMERICAN WRITER AND PHILOSOPHER

I don't go by the rule book. I lead from the heart, not the head.

–PRINCESS DIANA (1961–1997)
PRINCESS OF WALES, FIRST WIFE OF CHARLES, PRINCE OF WALES

You don't need to make your heart and your head agree. Let your head make the decision—your heart will catch up eventually.

–LAURA SCHLESSINGER (1947–) • AMERICAN CULTURAL COMMENTATOR

The head never rules the heart, but just becomes its partner in crime.

–MIGNON MCLAUGHLIN (1913–1983) • AMERICAN JOURNALIST AND WRITER

"HISTORY"

What is not recorded is not remembered.

–BENAZIR BHUTTO (1953–)
PRIME MINISTER OF PAKISTAN; FIRST WOMAN TO LEAD A MODERN MUSLIM STATE

Women's history is the primary tool for women's emancipation.

–GERDA LERNER (1920–) • AUSTRIAN-BORN AMERICAN HISTORIAN

The main thing history can teach us is that human actions have consequences and that certain choices, once made, cannot be undone. They foreclose the possibility of making other choices and thus they determine future events.

—GERDA LERNER (1920–) • AUSTRIAN-BORN AMERICAN HISTORIAN

History is the quarrels of popes and kings, with wars or pestilences in every page; the men all so good for nothing, and hardly any women at all.

—JANE AUSTEN (1775–1817) • ENGLISH WRITER

History is a better guide than good intentions.

—JEANE KIRKPATRICK (1926–)

AMERICAN POLITICAL SCIENTIST; FIRST FEMALE U.S. AMBASSADOR TO THE UNITED NATIONS

We need to haunt the halls of history and listen anew to the ancestors' wisdom.

—MAYA ANGELOU (1928–)

AFRICAN-AMERICAN POET, MEMOIRIST, AND CIVIL RIGHTS ACTIVIST

I have noticed that as soon as you have soldiers the story is called history. Before their arrival it is called myth, folktale, legend, fairy tale, oral poetry, ethnography. After the soldiers arrive, it is called history.

—PAULA GUNN ALLEN (1939–2008) • NATIVE AMERICAN POET, LITERARY CRITIC, ACTIVIST, AND WRITER

History is the key to everything: politics, religion, even fashion.

—EVA HERZIGOVA (1973–) • CZECH MODEL AND ACTOR

History should be a hammock for swinging and a game for playing, the way cats play. Claw it, chew it, rearrange it, and at bedtime it's still a ball of string full of knots.

—JEANETTE WINTERSON (1959–) • ENGLISH WRITER

"HOLIDAYS"

CHRISTMAS

What is Christmas? It is tenderness for the past, courage for the present, hope for the future. It is a fervent wish that every cup may overflow with blessings rich and eternal, and that every path may lead to peace.

—AGNES M. PHARO • 19TH/20TH-CENTURY AMERICAN WRITER

Orphans, dead parents, lonely children at Christmas, morose spoken word recordings, everything you love about the holidays. Move the turkey over so you can fit your head in the oven.

—APRIL WINCHELL (1962–) • AMERICAN VOICE ACTOR AND RADIO HOST

Every time we love, every time we give, it's Christmas.

—DALE EVANS (1912–2001)
AMERICAN SINGER, SONGWRITER, ACTOR, AND INSPIRATIONAL WRITER

There's nothing sadder in this world than to awake Christmas morning and not be a child.

—ERMA BOMBECK (1927–1996) • AMERICAN HUMORIST

From a commercial point of view, if Christmas did not exist it would be necessary to invent it.

—KATHARINE WHITEHORN (1926–)
ENGLISH JOURNALIST, WRITER, AND COLUMNIST

Christmas is for children. But it is for grown-ups too. Even if it is a headache, a chore, and a nightmare, it is a period of necessary defrosting of chilled hidebound hearts.

—LENORA MATTINGLY WEBER (1895–1971) • AMERICAN WRITER

Do give books—religious or otherwise—for Christmas. They're never fattening, seldom sinful, and permanently personal.

–LENORE HERSHEY
20TH/21ST-CENTURY AMERICAN EDITOR IN CHIEF OF *LADIES' HOME JOURNAL*

•

Our children await Christmas presents like politicians getting election returns; there's the Uncle Fred precinct and the Aunt Ruth district still to come in.

–MARCELENE COX • 20TH-CENTURY AMERICAN WRITER

•

Christmas, children, is not a date. It is a state of mind.

–MARY ELLEN CHASE (1887-1973)
AMERICAN TEACHER, SCHOLAR, AND WRITER

•

What I don't like about office Christmas parties is looking for a job the next day.

–PHYLLIS DILLER (1917-) • AMERICAN COMEDIAN

•

Christmas is a time when everybody wants his past forgotten and his present remembered.

–PHYLLIS DILLER (1917-) • AMERICAN COMEDIAN

•

I stopped believing in Santa Claus when my mother took me to see him in a department store, and he asked for my autograph.

–SHIRLEY TEMPLE (1928-) • AMERICAN DIPLOMAT AND FORMER CHILD ACTOR

•

HALLOWEEN

A grandmother pretends she doesn't know who you are on Halloween.

–ERMA BOMBECK (1927-1996) • AMERICAN HUMORIST

Being in a band you can wear whatever you want—
it's like an excuse for Halloween every day.

—GWEN STEFANI (1969–) • AMERICAN POP/ROCK SINGER

THANKSGIVING

I have strong doubts that the first Thanksgiving even remotely resembled the "history" I was told in second grade. But considering that (when it comes to holidays) mainstream America's traditions tend to be overeating, shopping, or getting drunk, I suppose it's a miracle that the concept of giving thanks even surfaces at all.

—ELLEN ORLEANS • 20TH/21ST-CENTURY AMERICAN WRITER AND HUMORIST

For, after all, put it as we may to ourselves, we are all of us from birth to death guests at a table which we did not spread. The sun, the earth, love, friends, our very breath are parts of the banquet. . . . Shall we think of the day as a chance to come nearer to our Host, and to find out something of Him who has fed us so long?

—REBECCA HARDING DAVIS (1831–1919) • AMERICAN WRITER AND JOURNALIST

"HOME"

I have no home but me.

—ANNE TRUITT (1921–2004)
AMERICAN MINIMALIST SCULPTOR

There is probably no thrill in life to compare with that of turning the key in one's first house or apartment.

—BELLE LIVINGSTONE (1875–1957)
AMERICAN WRITER AND ADVENTURER

One's own surroundings mean so much to one when one is feeling miserable.

–EDITH SITWELL (1887-1964) • ENGLISH POET AND CRITIC

I had to leave home so I could find myself, find my own intrinsic nature buried under the personality that had been imposed on me.

–GLORIA ANZALDÚA (1942-2004) • CHICANA FEMINIST AND CULTURAL THEORIST

Home wasn't built in a day.

–JANE ACE (1900-1974)
AMERICAN RADIO PERSONALITY

Ah! There is nothing like staying at home, for real comfort.

–JANE AUSTEN (1775-1817) • ENGLISH WRITER

There are homes you run from, and homes you run to.

–LAURA CUNNINGHAM (1947-) • AMERICAN WRITER

You can never go home again, but the truth is you can never leave home, so it's all right.

–MAYA ANGELOU (1928-)
AFRICAN-AMERICAN POET, MEMOIRIST, AND CIVIL RIGHTS ACTIVIST

"HOPE"

Hope begins in the dark, the stubborn hope that if you just show up and try to do the right thing, the dawn will come.

–ANNE LAMOTT (1954-) • AMERICAN NOVELIST AND MEMOIRIST

Another world is not only possible, she is on her way. On a quiet day, I can hear her breathing.

–ARUNDHATI ROY (1961-) • INDIAN WRITER AND ACTIVIST

Hope costs nothing.

—COLETTE (1873–1954)
FRENCH WRITER

The road that is built in hope is more pleasant to the traveler than the road built in despair, even though they both lead to the same destination.

—MARIAN ZIMMER BRADLEY (1930–1999) • AMERICAN WRITER

Take hope from the heart of man and you make him a beast of prey.

—OUIDA (LOUISE DE LA RAMÉE) (1839–1908) • ENGLISH WRITER

To eat bread without hope is still slowly to starve to death.

—PEARL S. BUCK (1892–1973)
FIRST FEMALE AMERICAN WINNER OF THE NOBEL PRIZE IN LITERATURE

"HORSES"

They are more beautiful than anything in the world—kinetic sculptures, perfect form in motion.

—KATE MILLETT (1934–) • AMERICAN FEMINIST WRITER AND ACTIVIST

I still subscribe to the minority view that all horses are offensive weapons and not to be trusted a yard.

—M. M. KAYE (1908–2004) • INDIAN-BORN ENGLISH WRITER

When Allah created the horse, he said to the wind, "I will that a creature proceed from thee. Condense thyself." And the wind condensed itself, and the result was the horse.

—MARGUERITE HENRY (1902–1997) • AMERICAN WRITER

A horse is the projection of people's dreams about themselves—strong, powerful, beautiful—and it has the capability of giving us escape from our mundane existence.

—PAM BROWN • 20TH-CENTURY AUSTRALIAN POET

"HOUSEWORK"

There are days when housework seems the only outlet.

—ADRIENNE RICH (1929–) • AMERICAN POET, THEORIST, AND FEMINIST

Most women work one shift at the office or factory and a "second shift" at home.

—ARLIE HOCHSCHILD (1940–) • AMERICAN SOCIOLOGIST

The labor of women in the house, certainly, enables men to produce more wealth than they otherwise could; and in this way women are economic factors in society. But so are horses.

—CHARLOTTE PERKINS GILMAN (1860–1935) • AMERICAN WRITER AND SOCIAL CRITIC

My husband and I have figured out a really good system about the housework: Neither one of us does it.

—DOTTIE ARCHIBALD • 20TH/21ST-CENTURY AMERICAN COMEDIAN

The works of women are symbolical. We sew, sew, prick our fingers, dull our sight, producing what? A pair of slippers, sir, to put on when you're weary—or a stool to stumble over and vex you . . . or else at best, a cushion, where you lean and sleep, and dream of something we are not, but would be for your sake. Alas, alas! This hurts most, this . . . that, after all, we are paid the worth of our work, perhaps.

—ELIZABETH BARRETT BROWNING (1806–1861) • ENGLISH POET

My theory on housework is, if the item doesn't multiply, smell, catch fire, or block the refrigerator door, let it be. No one else cares. Why should you?

–ERMA BOMBECK (1927–1996) • AMERICAN HUMORIST

•

I think housework is the reason most women go to the office.

–HELOISE CRUSE (1919–1977)

AMERICAN HOUSEKEEPING COLUMNIST, ORIGINATOR OF "HINTS FROM HELOISE"

•

Sometimes I like to think about cleaning. Please do not confuse thinking with doing, though. . . . it is, ultimately, a chore, a repetitive activity that bears within it the seeds of its own undoing.

–JANET WONDRA • 20TH/21ST-CENTURY AMERICAN POET AND FILMMAKER

•

What do we have after a lifetime of cleaning? Strong shoulders, lungs sandpapered by corrosive chemicals, and a house still not quite up to par. I would like to see, all in one place . . . the dust and grime I have removed over the years from all my residences.

–JANET WONDRA • 20TH/21ST-CENTURY AMERICAN POET AND FILMMAKER

•

When it comes to housework the one thing no book of household management can ever tell you is how to begin. Or maybe I mean why.

–KATHARINE WHITEHORN (1926–) • ENGLISH JOURNALIST, WRITER, AND COLUMNIST

•

No laborer in the world is expected to work for room, board, and love—except the housewife.

–LETTY COTTIN POGREBIN

20TH/21ST-CENTURY AMERICAN WRITER, LECTURER, AND SOCIAL JUSTICE ACTIVIST

•

I am thankful for a lawn that needs mowing, windows that need cleaning, and gutters that need fixing because it means I have a home. . . . I am thankful for the piles of laundry and ironing because it means my loved ones are nearby.

–NANCIE J. CARMODY • 20TH/21ST-CENTURY WRITER

If a few lustful and erotic reveries make the housework go by "as if in a dream," why not?

–NANCY FRIDAY (1933–) • AMERICAN FEMINIST WRITER

Housework can't kill you, but why take a chance?

–PHYLLIS DILLER (1917–) • AMERICAN COMEDIAN

If your house is really a mess and a stranger comes to the door greet him with, "Who could have done this? We have no enemies!"

–PHYLLIS DILLER (1917–) • AMERICAN COMEDIAN

At worst, a house unkept cannot be so distressing as a life unlived.

–ROSE MACAULAY (1881–1958) • ENGLISH NOVELIST AND ESSAYIST

Caring for others is accomplished by a dazzling array of skills in an endless variety of circumstances. As well as cooking, shopping, cleaning, laundering, planting, tending, harvesting for others, women comfort and guide, nurse and teach, arrange and advise, discipline and encourage, fight for and pacify. Taxing and exhausting under any circumstances, this service work, this emotional housework, is done both outside and inside the home.

–SELMA JAMES (1930–)
AMERICAN WRITER, FEMINIST ACTIVIST, AND FOUNDER OF THE INTERNATIONAL WAGES FOR HOUSEWORK CAMPAIGN

I am a marvelous housekeeper. Every time I leave a man I keep his house.

–ZSA ZSA GABOR (1917–) • HUNGARIAN-AMERICAN ACTOR AND SOCIALITE

REPETITION

Housework is a treadmill from futility to oblivion with stop-offs at tedium and counter-productivity.

–ERMA BOMBECK (1927–1996) • AMERICAN HUMORIST

I hate housework. You make the beds, you wash the dishes, and six months later you have to start all over again.

–JOAN RIVERS (1933–) • AMERICAN COMEDIAN AND TELEVISION HOST

Few tasks are more like the torture of Sisyphus than housework, with its endless repetition: The clean becomes soiled, the soiled is made clean, over and over, day after day.

–SIMONE DE BEAUVOIR (1908–1986) • FRENCH WRITER AND PHILOSOPHER

TASKS

The best time for planning a book is while you're doing the dishes.

–AGATHA CHRISTIE (1890–1976) • ENGLISH MYSTERY WRITER

Nature abhors a vacuum. And so do I.

–ANNE GIBBONS (1950–)
AMERICAN CARTOONIST AND ILLUSTRATOR

My idea of superwoman is someone who scrubs her own floors.

–BETTE MIDLER (1945–) • AMERICAN ACTOR AND SINGER

My second favorite household chore is ironing. My first being hitting my head on the top bunk bed until I faint.

–ERMA BOMBECK (1927–1996) • AMERICAN HUMORIST

You can't get spoiled if you do your own ironing.

–MERYL STREEP (1949–) • AMERICAN ACTOR

I'm 18 years behind in my ironing. There's no use doing it now, it doesn't fit anybody I know.

–PHYLLIS DILLER (1917–) • AMERICAN COMEDIAN

AND KIDS

A sparkling house is a fine thing if the children aren't robbed of their luster in keeping it that way.

–MARCELENE COX • 20TH-CENTURY AMERICAN WRITER

•

Cleaning your house while your kids are still growing is like shoveling the walk before it stops snowing.

–PHYLLIS DILLER (1917–) • AMERICAN COMEDIAN

•

AND MEN

How do you know if it's time to wash the dishes and clean your house? Look inside your pants. If you find a penis in there, it's not time.

–JO BRAND (1957–) • ENGLISH COMEDIAN

•

Don't cook. Don't clean. No man will ever make love to a woman because she waxed the linoleum—"My God, the floor's immaculate. Lie down, you hot bitch."

–JOAN RIVERS (1933–) • AMERICAN COMEDIAN AND TELEVISION HOST

•

A man would prefer to come home to an unmade bed and a happy woman than to a neatly made bed and an angry woman.

–MARLENE DIETRICH (1901–1992) • GERMAN-BORN ACTOR AND SINGER

•

The scorn men express for a male who does housework is exceeded only by their aversion to a woman who doesn't.

–PENNY KOME • 20TH/21ST-CENTURY CANADIAN WRITER AND EDITOR

"HUMAN NATURE"

Don't think of all the misery, but of all the beauty that still remains. In spite of everything, I still believe that people are really good at heart.

–ANNE FRANK (1929–1945) • GERMAN-JEWISH DIARIST

Man: Who is he? Too bad to be the work of God; too good for the work of chance!

–DORIS LESSING (1919–) • ENGLISH WRITER

Do we really know anybody? Who does not wear one face to hide another?

–FRANCES MARION (1888–1973)
AMERICAN JOURNALIST AND SCREENWRITER

What we call human nature in actuality is human habit.

–JEWEL (1974–) • AMERICAN SINGER-SONGWRITER

The fast pace of our lives makes it difficult for us to find grace in the present moment, and when the simple gifts at our fingertips cease to nourish us, we have a tendency to crave the sensational.

–MACRINA WIEDERKEHR • 20TH/21ST-CENTURY AMERICAN WRITER AND BENEDICTINE MONASTIC

Everyone has an invisible sign hanging from their neck saying, "Make me feel important." Never forget this message when working with people.

–MARY KAY ASH (1918–2001) • AMERICAN COSMETICS ENTREPRENEUR

I've learned that people will forget what you said, people will forget what you did, but people will never forget how you made them feel.

–MAYA ANGELOU (1928–) • AFRICAN-AMERICAN POET, MEMOIRIST, AND CIVIL RIGHTS ACTIVIST

There are so many things that we wish we had done yesterday, so few that we feel like doing today.

—MIGNON MCLAUGHLIN (1913-1983)
AMERICAN JOURNALIST AND WRITER

•

At the bottom of the heart of every human being, from earliest infancy until the tomb, there is something that goes on indomitably expecting, in the teeth of all experience of crimes committed, suffered, and witnessed, that good and not evil will be done to him.

—SIMONE WEIL (1909-1943) • FRENCH SOCIAL PHILOSOPHER AND ACTIVIST

•

Fortune does not change men, it unmasks them.

—SUZANNE NECKER (1739-1794) • FRENCH WRITER

•

"*HUMOR*"

See Laughter

•

"*HUSBANDS*"

See also Marriage

•

An archaeologist is the best husband a woman can have; the older she gets the more interested he is in her.

—AGATHA CHRISTIE (1890-1976) • ENGLISH MYSTERY WRITER

•

The best way to get most husbands to do something is to suggest that perhaps they're too old to do it.

—ANNE BANCROFT (1931-2005) • AMERICAN ACTOR

When people ask me how [my sister and I have] lived past 100, I say "Honey, we were never married. We never had husbands to worry us to death."

–BESSIE DELANY (1891-1995) • AFRICAN-AMERICAN DENTIST AND MEMOIRIST

•

A husband is what's left of the lover after the nerve has been extracted.

–HELEN ROWLAND (1875-1950) • AMERICAN JOURNALIST AND HUMORIST

•

Before marriage, a man will lay down his life for you; after marriage he won't even lay down his newspaper.

–HELEN ROWLAND (1875-1950) • AMERICAN JOURNALIST AND HUMORIST

•

I once was so poor I didn't know where my next husband was coming from.

–MAE WEST (1893-1980) • AMERICAN ACTOR, WRITER, AND SEX SYMBOL

•

When a husband brings his wife flowers for no reason, there's a reason.

–MARIAN JORDAN (AS MOLLY MCGEE) (1896-1961) • AMERICAN ENTERTAINER

•

A man should kiss his wife's navel every day.

–NELL KIMBALL (1854-1934)
AMERICAN BROTHEL AND CASINO OWNER

•

I should have suspected my husband was lazy. On our wedding day, his mother told me: "I'm not losing a son; I'm gaining a couch."

–PHYLLIS DILLER (1917-) • AMERICAN COMEDIAN

•

Husbands are like fires. They go out if unattended.

–ZSA ZSA GABOR (1917-)
HUNGARIAN-AMERICAN ACTOR AND SOCIALITE

I

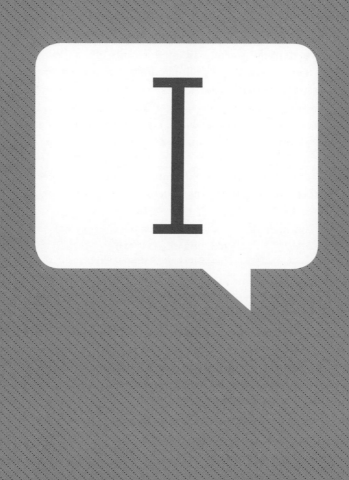

"IDEALISM"

See also Activism, Social Reform

Most reform movements in our country have been cursed by a lunatic fringe and have mingled sound ideas for social progress with utopian nonsense.

—AGNES E. MEYER (1887–1970) • AMERICAN JOURNALIST AND SOCIAL WORKER

I see the world gradually being turned into a wilderness. I hear the ever approaching thunder, which will destroy us too. I can feel the sufferings of millions and yet, if I look up into the heavens, I think that it will all come right, that this cruelty too will end, and that peace and tranquility will return again.

—ANNE FRANK (1929–1945) • GERMAN-JEWISH DIARIST

The sixties were characterized by a heady belief in instantaneous solutions.

—AUDRE LORDE (1934–1992) • AFRICAN-AMERICAN FEMINIST WRITER AND ACTIVIST

Idealism, that gaudy coloring matter of passion, fades when it is brought beneath the trenchant white light of knowledge. Ideals, like mountains, are best at a distance.

—ELLEN GLASGOW (1873–1945) • AMERICAN WRITER

Idealists . . . foolish enough to throw caution to the winds . . . have advanced mankind and enriched the world.

—EMMA GOLDMAN (1869–1940) • RUSSIAN ANARCHIST AND FEMINIST

Perhaps women have always been in closer contact with reality than men: It would seem to be the just recompense for being deprived of idealism.

—GERMAINE GREER (1939–) • AUSTRALIAN-BORN WRITER AND SOCIAL CRITIC

We come to think of an idealist as one who seeks to realize what is not in fact realizable. But, it is necessary to insist, to have ideals is not the same as to have impracticable ideals, however often it may be the case that our ideals are impracticable.

–L. SUSAN STEBBING (1802–1838) • ENGLISH WRITER AND POET

"IDENTITY"

See also Diversity, Race/Racism

Long ago I understood that it wasn't merely my being a woman that was preventing my being welcomed into the world of what I long thought of as my peers. It was that I had succeeded in an undertaking few men have even attempted: I have become myself.

–ALICE KOLLER • 20TH/21ST-CENTURY AMERICAN WRITER

What we earnestly aspire to be, that in some sense we are.

–ANNA JAMESON (1794–1860) • IRISH-ENGLISH WRITER

I am aware of myself as a four-hundred-year-old woman, born in the captivity of a colonial, pre-industrial oral culture and living now as a contemporary New Yorker.

–BHARATI MUKHERJEE (1940–) • INDIAN-AMERICAN WRITER AND PROFESSOR

A strong sense of identity gives man an idea he can do no wrong; too little accomplishes the same.

–DJUNA BARNES (1892–1982) • AMERICAN WRITER AND ARTIST

And you, are you so forgetful of your past, is there no echo in your soul of your poets' songs, your dreamers' dreams, your rebels' calls?

–EMMA GOLDMAN (1869–1940) • RUSSIAN ANARCHIST AND FEMINIST

I am because my little dog knows me.

–GERTRUDE STEIN (1874–1946) • AMERICAN POET

•

Like many immigrant offspring I felt intense pressure to be two things, loyal to the old world and fluent in the new, approved of on either side of the hyphen.

–JHUMPA LAHIRI (1967–) • INDIAN-AMERICAN WRITER

•

I could not figure out what was my village.

–MAXINE HONG KINGSTON (1940–)
CHINESE-AMERICAN WRITER

•

We really are 15 countries, and it's really remarkable that each of us thinks we represent the real America. The Midwesterner in Kansas, the Black American in Durham—both are certain they are the real American.

–MAYA ANGELOU (1928–) • AFRICAN-AMERICAN POET, MEMOIRIST, AND CIVIL RIGHTS ACTIVIST

•

To speak as black, female, and a commercial lawyer has rendered me simultaneously universal, trendy, and marginal.

–PATRICIA J. WILLIAMS (1951–) • AFRICAN-AMERICAN LAW CRITIC AND RACE THEORIST

•

I was raised to sense what someone else wanted me to be and to be that kind of person. It took me a long time not to judge myself through someone else's eyes.

–SALLY FIELD (1946–) • AMERICAN FILM AND TELEVISION ACTOR

•

"IMAGINATION"

•

Imagination makes cowards of us all.

–CRISTINA GARCIA (1958–)
CUBAN-BORN AMERICAN WRITER

To imagine the unimaginable is the highest use of the imagination.

–CYNTHIA OZICK (1928–) • AMERICAN NOVELIST, ESSAYIST, AND POET

Affliction is more apt to suffocate the imagination than to stimulate it.

–DENISE LEVERTOV (1923–1997) • ENGLISH-BORN AMERICAN POET

My imagination longs to dash ahead and plan developments; but I have noticed that when things happen in one's imaginings, they never happen in one's life, so I am curbing myself.

–DODIE SMITH (1896–1990) • ENGLISH NOVELIST AND PLAYWRIGHT

Imagination has always had powers of resurrection that no science can match.

–INGRID BENGIS (1944–) • AMERICAN-BORN RUSSIAN WRITER

The key to life is imagination. If you don't have that, no matter what you have, it's meaningless. If you do have imagination . . . you can make a feast of straw.

–JANE STANTON HITCHCOCK • 20TH/21ST-CENTURY AMERICAN WRITER

Those who have been required to memorize the world as it is will never create the world as it might be.

–JUDITH GROCH (1929–) • AMERICAN WRITER

O thou, the leader of the mental train.

–PHILLIS WHEATLEY (CA. 1753–1784)
AFRICAN-AMERICAN POET AND FREED SLAVE

The moon develops the imagination, as chemicals develop photographic images.

–SHEILA BALLANTYNE (1936–) • AMERICAN WRITER

My imagination makes me human and makes me a fool;
it gives me all the world and exiles me from it.

–URSULA K. LE GUIN (1929-) • AMERICAN WRITER

•

"INDIVIDUALITY"

•

My theory is that everyone, at one time or another, has been at the fringe of society in some way: an outcast in high school, a stranger in a foreign country, the best at something, the worst at something, the one who's different. Being an outsider is the one thing we all have in common.

–ALICE HOFFMAN (1952-) • AMERICAN WRITER

•

The tendency of organization is to kill out the spirit which gave it birth. Organizations do not protect the sacredness of the individual; their tendency is to sink the individual in the mass, to sacrifice his rights, and to immolate him on the altar of some fancied good.

–ANGELINA GRIMKÉ (1805-1879) • AMERICAN ABOLITIONIST AND REFORMER

•

If a life could have a theme song—and I believe every worthwhile one has—mine is a religion, an obsession, a mania or all of these expressed in one word—individualism. I was born with that obsession, and I've never seen and do not know now a cause more worthy, more misunderstood, more seemingly hopeless, and tragically needed.

–AYN RAND (1905-1982) • RUSSIAN-AMERICAN WRITER AND PHILOSOPHER

•

I am not eccentric. It's just that I am more alive than most people. I am an unpopular electric eel set in a pond of goldfish.

–EDITH SITWELL (1887-1964) • ENGLISH POET AND CRITIC

Always be a first-rate version of yourself, instead of a second-rate version of somebody else.

–JUDY GARLAND (1922–1969) • AMERICAN ACTOR AND SINGER

She was becoming herself and daily casting aside that fictitious self which we assume like a garment with which to appear before the world.

–KATE CHOPIN (1850–1904) • AMERICAN WRITER

I cannot and will not cut my conscience to fit this year's fashions.

–LILLIAN HELLMAN (1905–1984) • AMERICAN PLAYWRIGHT

Prove to yourself that you can do it. Prove that you were always who you thought you were, not who they said you had to be.

–RACHEL SNYDER • 20TH/21ST-CENTURY WRITER

About all you can do in life is be who you are. Some people will love you for you. Most will love you for what you can do for them, and some won't like you at all.

–RITA MAE BROWN (1944–) • AMERICAN WRITER AND ACTIVIST

"INSPIRATION"

I could never tell where inspiration begins and impulse leaves off. I suppose the answer is in the outcome. If your hunch proves a good one, you were inspired; if it proves bad, you are guilty of yielding to thoughtless impulse.

–BERYL MARKHAM (1902–1986) • ENGLISH-BORN KENYAN PILOT AND WRITER

The source of continuing aliveness was to find your passion and pursue it, with whole heart and single mind.

–GAIL SHEEHY (1937–) • AMERICAN SOCIAL CRITIC

A deadline is negative inspiration. Still, it's better than no inspiration at all.

–RITA MAE BROWN (1944–) • AMERICAN WRITER AND ACTIVIST

•

We can do no great things; only small things with great love.

–MOTHER TERESA (1910–1997)
ALBANIAN CATHOLIC NUN; WINNER OF NOBEL PEACE PRIZE

•

The most beautiful thing in the world is, precisely, the conjunction of learning and inspiration.

–WANDA LANDOWSKA (1879–1959) • POLISH HARPSICHORDIST

•

"INTELLIGENCE"

•

The people I'm furious with are the women's liberationists. They keep getting up on soapboxes and proclaiming women are brighter than men. That's true, but it should be kept quiet or it ruins the whole racket.

–ANITA LOOS (1889–1981) • AMERICAN SCREENWRITER, NOVELIST, AND ESSAYIST

•

You can never imagine what it is to have a man's force of genius in you, and yet to suffer the slavery of being a girl. To have a pattern cut out. . . . A woman's heart must be of such a size and no larger, else it must be pressed small, like Chinese feet; her happiness is to be made as cakes are, by a fixed receipt.

–GEORGE ELIOT (MARY ANN EVANS) (1819–1880) • ENGLISH WRITER

•

It takes a lot of time to be a genius. You have to sit around so much doing nothing, really doing nothing.

–GERTRUDE STEIN (1874–1946) • AMERICAN POET

•

Most beautiful but dumb girls think they are smart and get away with it, because other people, on the whole, aren't much smarter.

–LOUISE BROOKS (1906–1985) • AMERICAN ACTOR

The naked intelligence is an extraordinarily inaccurate instrument.

—MADELEINE L'ENGLE (1918-) • AMERICAN WRITER

•

We're intellectual opposites. I'm intellectual, and you're opposite.

—MAE WEST (1893-1980) • AMERICAN ACTOR, WRITER, AND SEX SYMBOL

•

Intelligence always had a pornographic influence on me.

—MAYA ANGELOU (1928-)
AFRICAN-AMERICAN POET, MEMOIRIST, AND CIVIL RIGHTS ACTIVIST

•

Men who don't like girls with brains don't like girls.

—MIGNON MCLAUGHLIN (1913-1983)
AMERICAN JOURNALIST AND WRITER

•

COMMON SENSE

Common sense is perhaps the most equally divided, but surely the most underemployed, talent in the world.

—CHRISTIANE COLLANGE (1930-) • FRENCH EDITOR AND WRITER

•

Everybody gets so much information all day long that they lose their common sense.

—GERTRUDE STEIN (1874-1946) • AMERICAN POET

•

Common sense is seeing things as they are and doing things as they ought to be.

—HARRIET BEECHER STOWE (1811-1896) • AMERICAN ABOLITIONIST

"INTUITION"

Follow your instincts . . . but you need to have all the information. To go on your instincts without being fully informed is, to me, the definition of folly.

—DEBORAH NORVILLE (1958-) • AMERICAN TELEVISION HOST AND NEWS ANCHOR

Heed the still, small voice that so seldom
leads us wrong, and never into folly.

—MADAME DU DEFFAND (1697-1780)
FRENCH HOSTESS AND INTELLECTUAL

Intuition is a spiritual faculty and does not explain, but simply points the way.

—FLORENCE SCOVEL SHINN (1871-1940) • AMERICAN ILLUSTRATOR AND INSPIRATIONAL WRITER

Instinct is the nose of the mind.

—MADAME DE GIRARDIN (1904-1955)
FRENCH WRITER

I don't believe in intuition. When you get sudden flashes of perception, it is just the brain working faster than usual. But you've been getting ready to know it for a long time, and when it comes, you feel you've known it always.

—KATHERINE ANNE PORTER (1890-1980) • AMERICAN WRITER

Intuition is a suspension of logic due to impatience.

—RITA MAE BROWN (1944-) • AMERICAN WRITER AND ACTIVIST

But still, the other voice, the intuitive, returns, like
grass forcing its way through concrete.

—SUSAN GRIFFIN • 20TH/21ST-CENTURY AMERICAN WRITER AND POET

J

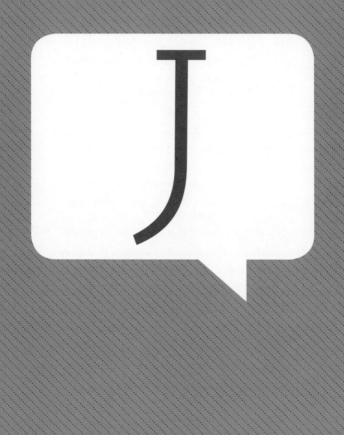

"JEALOUSY"

Jealousy, the old worm that bites.

–APHRA BEHN (1640–1689)
ENGLISH PLAYWRIGHT, POET, NOVELIST, AND SPY

To jealousy, nothing is more frightful than laughter.

–FRANÇOISE SAGAN (1935–2004)
FRENCH NOVELIST AND PLAYWRIGHT

To cure jealousy is to see it for what it is, a dissatisfaction with self.

–JOAN DIDION (1934–) • AMERICAN WRITER

Jealousy is the grave of affection.

–MARY BAKER EDDY (1821–1910)
AMERICAN WRITER AND FOUNDER OF CHRISTIAN SCIENTIST CHURCH

Jealousy is not born of love! It is a child of selfishness and distrust.

–MOURNING DOVE (1888–1936) • NATIVE AMERICAN WRITER

The knives of jealousy are honed on details.

–RUTH RENDELL (1930–) • ENGLISH WRITER

Transform jealousy to admiration, and what you
admire will become part of your life.

–YOKO ONO (1933–)
JAPANESE-BORN AMERICAN MUSICIAN, ARTIST, AND PEACE ACTIVIST

"JEWELRY"

Don't ever wear artistic jewelry; it wrecks a woman's reputation.

–COLETTE (1873-1954) • FRENCH WRITER

These gems have life in them: Their colors
speak, say what words fail of.

–GEORGE ELIOT (MARY ANN EVANS) (1819-1880)
ENGLISH WRITER

Jewelry takes people's minds off your wrinkles.

–SONJA HENIE (1912-1969)
NORWEGIAN FIGURE SKATER AND ACTOR

DIAMONDS

I really think that American gentlemen are the best after all, because kissing your hand may make you feel very very good but a diamond and sapphire bracelet lasts forever.

–ANITA LOOS (1889-1981)
AMERICAN SCREENWRITER, NOVELIST, AND ESSAYIST

Ah, the feeling that you get holding a diamond in your hand! . . . It's like holding a bit of the moon.

–ANNA MAGNANI (1918-1973) • ITALIAN ACTOR

Big girls need big diamonds.

–ELIZABETH TAYLOR (1932-)
ENGLISH-BORN AMERICAN ACTOR

Diamonds are forever, my youth is not.

—JILL ST. JOHN (1940–) • AMERICAN ACTOR

I have always felt a gift diamond shines so much better than one you buy for yourself.

—MAE WEST (1893–1980)
AMERICAN ACTOR, WRITER, AND SEX SYMBOL

"JOURNALS"

See Diaries/Journals

K

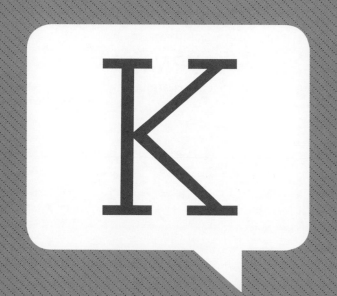

"KINDNESS"

No kind action ever stops with itself. One kind action leads to another. Good example is followed. A single act of kindness throws out roots in all directions, and the roots spring up and make new trees. The greatest work that kindness does to others is that it makes them kind themselves.

–AMELIA EARHART (1897–1937)
PIONEERING AMERICAN AVIATOR; FIRST PERSON TO FLY SOLO ACROSS PACIFIC

When somebody's nice to you, don't take advantage of it. You don't ride a free horse to death.

–BESSIE & SADIE DELANY (1891–1995; 1889–1999)
AFRICAN-AMERICAN CO-MEMOIRISTS

Guard well within yourself that treasure, kindness. Know how to give without hesitation, how to lose without regret, how to acquire without meanness.

–GEORGE SAND (AMANDINE-AURORE-LUCIE DUPIN, BARONNE DUDEVANT) (1804–1876)
FRENCH WRITER AND FEMINIST

Being considerate of others will take your children further in life than any college degree.

–MARIAN WRIGHT EDELMAN (1939–)
AFRICAN-AMERICAN FOUNDER OF THE CHILDREN'S DEFENSE FUND

If you stop to be kind, you must swerve often from your path.

–MARY WEBB (1881–1927) • ENGLISH WRITER

Don't be yourself—be someone a little nicer.

–MIGNON MCLAUGHLIN (1913–1983)
AMERICAN JOURNALIST AND WRITER

I prefer to make mistakes in kindness than work miracles in unkindness.

—MOTHER TERESA (1910–1997) • ALBANIAN CATHOLIC NUN; WINNER OF NOBEL PEACE PRIZE

•

"*KISSING*"

•

I married the first man I ever kissed. When I tell this to my children, they just about throw up.

—BARBARA BUSH (1925–) • FIRST LADY OF THE UNITED STATES

•

Nobody wants to kiss when they are hungry.

—DOROTHY DIX (ELIZABETH MERIWETHER GILMER) (1870–1951)
AMERICAN JOURNALIST AND ADVICE COLUMNIST

•

Kisses, even to the air, are beautiful.

—DREW BARRYMORE (1975–)
AMERICAN ACTOR AND PRODUCER

•

A kiss is a lovely trick designed by nature to stop speech when words become superfluous.

—INGRID BERGMAN (1915–1982) • SWEDISH ACTOR

•

Ruby wasn't particular whom she kissed. In fact she led a regular mouth-to-mouth existence.

—LILLIAN DAY (1893–1991) • ENGLISH WRITER

•

A kiss can be a comma, a question mark, or an exclamation point. That's the basic spelling that every woman ought to know.

—MISTINGUETT (1875–1956) • FRENCH ACTOR AND SINGER

They say that a good cook can ignite sparks by the way he kisses. The way I see, just because a guy can turn on the stove doesn't necessarily make him a good cook.

–STEFANIE POWERS (1942-) • AMERICAN ACTOR

Kiss me and you will see how important I am.

–SYLVIA PLATH (1932-1963)
AMERICAN POET AND PROSE WRITER

"*KNOWLEDGE*"

See also Learning

I am never afraid of what I know.

–ANNA SEWELL (1820-1878)
ENGLISH WRITER

We do not want our world to perish. But in our quest for knowledge, century by century, we have placed all our trust in a cold, impartial intellect which only brings us nearer to destruction.

–DORA RUSSELL (1894-1986) • ENGLISH FEMINIST AND SOCIAL REFORMER

Knowledge is power, if you know it about the right person.

–ETHEL WATTS MUMFORD (1878-1940) • AMERICAN WRITER AND HUMORIST

Knowingness is sexy. The opposite of sexy is naivete.

–FRAN LEBOWITZ (1950-) • AMERICAN HUMORIST

Knowledge alters what we seek as well as what we find.

–FREDA ADLER (1934-) • AMERICAN PROFESSOR OF CRIMINAL JUSTICE

And of course, men know best about everything,
except what women know better.

–GEORGE ELIOT (MARY ANN EVANS) (1819-1880)
ENGLISH WRITER

•

As long as one keeps searching, the answers come.

–JOAN BAEZ (1941-) • AMERICAN FOLK SINGER AND ACTIVIST

•

It's what you learn after you know it all that counts.

–JUDITH KELMAN (1945-) • AMERICAN WRITER

•

There comes a time when we aren't allowed not to know.

–JUDITH VIORST (1931-) • AMERICAN POET AND JOURNALIST

•

If you have knowledge, let others light their candles in it.

–MARGARET FULLER (1810-1850)
AMERICAN WRITER, EDITOR, INTELLECTUAL, AND FEMINIST

•

We have a hunger of the mind which asks for knowledge
of all around us, and the more we gain, the more is our desire;
the more we see, the more we are capable of seeing.

–MARIA MITCHELL (1818-1889) • AMERICAN ASTRONOMER

•

We are not what we know but what we are willing to learn.

–MARY CATHERINE BATESON (1939-)
AMERICAN WRITER AND CULTURAL ANTHROPOLOGIST

•

True knowledge consists in knowing things, not words.

–LADY MARY WORTLEY MONTAGU (1689-1762)
ENGLISH POET, EPISTOLARY WRITER, AND SMALLPOX VACCINE ADVOCATE

But there is no neutrality. There is only greater or less awareness of one's bias.

–PHYLLIS ROSE

20TH/21ST-CENTURY AMERICAN ESSAYIST AND BIOGRAPHER

If we would have new knowledge, we must get a whole world of new questions.

–SUSANNE K. LANGER (1895-1985)

AMERICAN PHILOSOPHER OF ART

WISDOM

To acquire knowledge, one must study; but to acquire wisdom, one must observe.

–MARILYN VOS SAVANT (1946-)

AMERICAN COLUMNIST, HOLDER OF GUINNESS WORLD RECORD FOR HIGHEST IQ

People are never so near playing the fool as when they think themselves wise.

–LADY MARY WORTLEY MONTAGU (1689-1762)

ENGLISH POET, EPISTOLARY WRITER, AND SMALLPOX VACCINE ADVOCATE

If facts are the seeds that later produce knowledge and wisdom, then the emotions and the impressions of the senses are the fertile soil in which the seeds must grow.

–RACHEL CARSON (1907-1964)

AMERICAN ZOOLOGIST AND MARINE BIOLOGIST

L

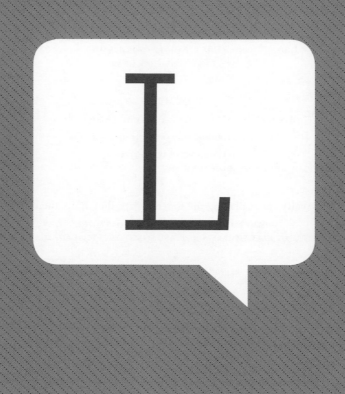

"LANGUAGE"

Language is not neutral. It is not merely a vehicle which carries ideas. It is itself a shaper of ideas.

–DALE SPENDER (1943–) • AUSTRALIAN SOCIOLINGUIST AND TECHNOLOGY THEORIST

Language helps form the limits of our reality.

–DALE SPENDER (1943–)
AUSTRALIAN SOCIOLINGUIST AND TECHNOLOGY THEORIST

I personally think we developed language because of our deep inner need to complain.

–JANE WAGNER (1935–)
AMERICAN PLAYWRIGHT AND COMEDY WRITER

All really great lovers are articulate, and verbal seduction is the surest road to actual seduction.

–MARYA MANNES (1904–1990) • AMERICAN COLUMNIST AND CRITIC

Language exerts hidden power, like the moon on the tides.

–RITA MAE BROWN (1944–) • AMERICAN WRITER AND ACTIVIST

WORDS

I believe that words can help us move or keep us paralyzed, and that our choices of language and verbal tone have something—a great deal—to do with how we live our lives and whom we end up speaking with and hearing; and that we can deflect words by trivialization, of course, but also by ritualized respect, or we can let them enter our souls and mix with the juices of our minds.

–ADRIENNE RICH (1929–) • AMERICAN POET, THEORIST, AND FEMINIST

Words are a lens to focus one's mind.

—AYN RAND (1905-1982)
RUSSIAN-AMERICAN WRITER AND PHILOSOPHER

•

The meaning of a word—to me—is not as exact as the meaning of a color. Colors and shapes make a more definite statement than words.

—GEORGIA O'KEEFFE (1887-1986) • AMERICAN ARTIST

•

These words dropped into my childish mind as if you should accidentally drop a ring into a deep well. I did not think of them much at the time, but there came a day in my life when the ring was fished up out of the well, good as new.

—HARRIET BEECHER STOWE (1811-1896) • AMERICAN ABOLITIONIST

•

Handle them carefully, for words have more power than atom bombs.

—PEARL STRACHAN HURD • 20TH-CENTURY POET AND WRITER

•

We have needed to define ourselves by reclaiming the words that define us. They have used language as weapons. When we open ourselves to what they say and how they say it, our narrow prejudices evaporate, and we are nourished and armed.

—SELMA JAMES (1930-) • AMERICAN WRITER, FEMINIST ACTIVIST, AND FOUNDER OF THE INTERNATIONAL WAGES FOR HOUSEWORK CAMPAIGN

•

My words now must be as slow, as new, as single, as tentative as the steps I took going down the path away from the house, between the dark-branching tall dancers motionless against the winter shining.

—URSULA K. LE GUIN (1929-) • AMERICAN WRITER

"LAUGHTER"

Humor distorts nothing, and only false gods are laughed off their pedestals.

–AGNES REPPLIER (1855–1950) • AMERICAN ESSAYIST

Laughter springs from the lawless part of our nature.

–AGNES REPPLIER (1855–1950) • AMERICAN ESSAYIST

Laughter is by definition healthy.

–DORIS LESSING (1919–) • ENGLISH WRITER

You grow up the day you have your first real laugh at yourself.

–ETHEL BARRYMORE (1879–1959) • AMERICAN ACTOR

One can never speak enough of the virtues, the dangers, the power of shared laughter.

–FRANÇOISE SAGAN (1935–2004) • FRENCH NOVELIST AND PLAYWRIGHT

Those who don't know how to weep with their whole heart don't know how to laugh either.

–GOLDA MEIR (1898–1978) • RUSSIAN-BORN FIRST FEMALE PRIME MINISTER OF ISRAEL

A good time for laughing is when you can.

–JESSAMYN WEST (1902–1984) • AMERICAN WRITER

I laugh a lot. It burns lots of calories.

–JESSICA SIMPSON (1980–)
AMERICAN POP SINGER AND ACTOR

A good laugh overcomes more difficulties and dissipates more dark clouds than any other one thing.

–LAURA INGALLS WILDER (1867–1957) • AMERICAN PIONEER AND WRITER

A laugh is a smile that bursts.

–MARY H. WALDRIP
20TH-CENTURY AMERICAN JOURNALIST

He who laughs, lasts.

–MARY PETTIBONE POOLE
20TH-CENTURY AMERICAN WRITER

I love myself when I am laughing. And then again when I am looking mean and impressive.

–ZORA NEALE HURSTON (1891–1960)
AFRICAN-AMERICAN FOLKLORIST AND WRITER

"*LEADERSHIP*"

The art of leadership is one which the wicked, as a rule, learn more quickly than the virtuous.

–AGNES E. MEYER (1887–1970) • AMERICAN JOURNALIST AND SOCIAL WORKER

Authority without wisdom is like a heavy axe without an edge, fitter to bruise than polish.

–ANNE BRADSTREET (1612–1672) • FIRST POET PUBLISHED IN AMERICA

Ninety percent of leadership is the ability to communicate something people want.

–DIANNE FEINSTEIN (1933–)
AMERICAN POLITICIAN, FIRST FEMALE MAYOR OF SAN FRANCISCO

The leadership instinct you are born with is the backbone. You develop the funny bone and the wishbone that go with it.

—ELAINE AGATHER • 20TH/21ST-CENTURY AMERICAN CEO

•

I have always thought that what is needed is the development of people who are interested not in being leaders as much as in developing leadership in others.

—ELLA J. BAKER (193-1986) • AFRICAN-AMERICAN CIVIL RIGHTS ACTIVIST

•

The only safe ship in a storm is leadership.

—FAYE WATTLETON (1943-)
AMERICAN FEMINIST AND REPRODUCTIVE RIGHTS ACTIVIST

•

It is high time that we had lights that are not incendiary torches.

—GEORGE SAND (AMANDINE-AURORE-LUCIE DUPIN, BARONNE DUDEVANT) (1804-1876)
FRENCH WRITER AND FEMINIST

•

A leader who doesn't hesitate before he sends his nation into battle is not fit to be a leader.

—GOLDA MEIR (1898-1978)
RUSSIAN-BORN FIRST FEMALE PRIME MINISTER OF ISRAEL

•

You manage things, you lead people. We went overboard on management and forgot about leadership. It might help if we ran the MBAs out of Washington.

—GRACE MURRAY HOPPER (1906-1992)
PIONEERING COMPUTER SCIENTIST AND REAR ADMIRAL IN THE U.S. NAVY

•

I suppose that leadership at one time meant muscle; but today it means getting along with people.

—INDIRA GANDHI (1917-1984) • PRIME MINISTER OF INDIA

You take people as far as they will go, not as far as you would like them to go.

–JEANNETTE RANKIN (1880–1973)
AMERICAN, FIRST WOMAN ELECTED TO THE U.S. HOUSE OF REPRESENTATIVES AND THE FIRST FEMALE MEMBER OF CONGRESS

•

Leadership should be born out of the understanding of the needs of those who would be affected by it.

–MARIAN ANDERSON (1897–1993) • AFRICAN-AMERICAN CONTRALTO

•

The speed of the leader is the speed of the gang.

–MARY KAY ASH (1918–2001) • AMERICAN COSMETICS ENTREPRENEUR

•

We don't fall in line with people who don't respect us and who we don't believe have our best interests at heart. We are willing to follow leaders, but only to the extent that we believe they call on our best, not our worst.

–RACHEL MADDOW (1973–) • AMERICAN POLITICAL COMMENTATOR

•

"LEARNING"

See also Education, Knowledge

•

Learning is not attained by chance. It must be sought for with ardor and attended to with diligence.

–ABIGAIL ADAMS (1744–1818) • FIRST LADY OF THE UNITED STATES

•

You can learn new things at any time in your life if you're willing to be a beginner. If you actually learn to like being a beginner, the whole world opens up to you.

–BARBARA SHER • 20TH/21ST-CENTURY AMERICAN WRITER AND SPEAKER

•

We should live and learn; but by the time we've learned, it's too late to live.

–CAROLYN WELLS (1869–1942) • AMERICAN WRITER

That is what learning is. You suddenly understand something you've understood all your life, but in a new way.

–DORIS LESSING (1919–) • ENGLISH WRITER

I am learning all the time. The tombstone will be my diploma.

–EARTHA KITT (1927–) • AFRICAN-AMERICAN AND CHEROKEE SINGER AND ACTOR

Learn from the mistakes of others. You can't live long enough to make them all yourself.

–ELEANOR ROOSEVELT (1884–1962)
AMERICAN POLITICAL LEADER AND FIRST LADY

It is best to learn as we go, not go as we have learned.

–LESLIE JEANNE SAHLER • 20TH-CENTURY FRENCH NOVELIST AND PLAYWRIGHT

Life is my college. May I graduate well, and earn some honors!

–LOUISA MAY ALCOTT (1832–1888) • AMERICAN WRITER

I've learned the most from other people. Buy yourself a brain picker—ask a lot of questions.

–TARA VANDERVEER • 20TH/21ST-CENTURY AMERICAN BASKETBALL COACH

"LEISURE"

Holidays are enticing only for the first week or so. After that, it is no longer such a novelty to rise late and have little to do.

–MARGARET LAURENCE (1926–1987) • CANADIAN WRITER

Leisure and the cultivation of human capacities are inextricably interdependent.

–MARGARET MEAD (1901–1978) • AMERICAN CULTURAL ANTHROPOLOGIST

People who know how to employ themselves always find leisure moments, while those who do nothing are forever in a hurry.

–JEANNE-MARIE ROLAND (1754–1793) • FRENCH WRITER AND REVOLUTIONARY

There is no pleasure in having nothing to do; the fun is in having lots to do and not doing it.

–MARY WILSON LITTLE • 19TH-CENTURY AMERICAN WRITER

Millions long for immortality who don't know what to do on a rainy afternoon.

–SUSAN ERTZ (1894–1985) • ENGLISH WRITER

"LESBIANS"

See also Sexual Orientation

I love doing lesbian love scenes. Before I did my lesbian scenes in *Gia*, I talked to actresses who said love scenes are easier with another woman than a man. *Bound's* Gina Gershon and Jennifer Tilly said they'd lie there and discuss the sale at Barney's between takes.

–ANGELINA JOLIE (1975–) • AMERICAN ACTOR

I will be quiet, be still, and know that it is God who put the love for women in my heart.

–BRIGITTE M. ROBERTS • 20TH/21ST-CENTURY AMERICAN WRITER AND SOCIAL WORKER

Our very strength as lesbians lies in the fact that we are outside of patriarchy; our existence challenges its life.

–CHARLOTTE BUNCH (1944–) • AMERICAN WOMEN'S AND HUMAN RIGHTS ACTIVIST

Of course it is extremely difficult to like oneself in a culture which thinks you are a disease.

–CHRYSTOS (1946–) • NATIVE AMERICAN ARTIST, POET, AND ACTIVIST

My mom blames California for me being a lesbian. "Everything was fine until you moved out there." "That's right, Mom, we have mandatory lesbianism in West Hollywood. The Gay Patrol busted me, and I was given seven business days to add a significant amount of flannel to my wardrobe."

—COLEY SOHN • 20TH/21ST-CENTURY AMERICAN ACTOR

I am not, I repeat, NOT a lesbian—even though I'd like to be one when I grow up.

—DAWN FRENCH (1957–) • ENGLISH COMEDIAN

That word, "lesbian," sounds like a disease. And straight men know because they're sure that they're the cure.

—DENISE MCCANLES • 20TH/21ST-CENTURY AMERICAN COMEDIAN

If I see one more like willy-nilly straight girl running around with her long fingernails and high heel shoes trying to be gay. . . . Not to say that there aren't lesbians that are that way, but it's frustrating when that's all you see on film.

—JILL BENNETT • 20TH/21ST-CENTURY AMERICAN ACTOR

All women are lesbians except those who don't know it.

—JILL JOHNSTON (1929–) • AMERICAN FEMINIST WRITER

Our black lesbian or bisexual sisters are sisters without cause or exception and deserve the same honor and respect that we all deserve. When we place ourselves in a position of judgment, then we turn ourselves into oppressors.

—JULIA A. BOYD • 20TH/21ST-CENTURY AFRICAN-AMERICAN PSYCHOTHERAPIST

Dealing with being a lesbian—and part of that is by being politically activist—has caused me to have a less carefree adolescence. But I don't think that's a bad thing. It has its rewards.

—KARINA LUBOFF (1974–) • AMERICAN GAY/LESBIAN RIGHTS ACTIVIST

I think coming out helped a lot for me personally, because living in honesty and living open, and in truth, is an amazing feeling and I highly recommend it for anyone. No matter what you're hiding, let it go.

K.D. LANG (1961-) • CANADIAN SINGER AND SONGWRITER

•

[On if she were still a lesbian:] Are you still the alternative?

–MARTINA NAVRATILOVA (1956-) • CZECH-AMERICAN TENNIS PLAYER

•

I resent like hell that I was maybe 18 before I ever heard the "L" word. It would have made all the difference for me had I grown up knowing that the reason I didn't fit in was because they hadn't told me there were more categories to fit into.

–MICHELLE SHOCKED (1962-) • AMERICAN SINGER-SONGWRITER AND POLITICAL ACTIVIST

•

A lesbian who does not reinvent the world is a lesbian in the process of disappearing.

–NICOLE BROSSARD (1873-1951)
CANADIAN JOURNALIST AND SUFFRAGIST

•

I became a lesbian out of devout Christian charity. All those women out there are praying for a man, and I gave them my share.

–RITA MAE BROWN (1944-) • AMERICAN WRITER AND ACTIVIST

•

You will one day be so proud of all your children, don't impede their progress now by pretending that being gay is a crime or a disease or a "rebellious act." It isn't. It's just like being born with red hair or dimples. They are what they are.

–ROSALEEN DICKSON (1921-) • CANADIAN WRITER

•

If male homosexuals are called "gay," then female homosexuals should be called "ecstatic."

–SHELLY ROBERTS • 20TH/21ST-CENTURY AMERICAN COLUMNIST

"LIFE"

I like living. I have sometimes been wildly, despairingly, acutely miserable, racked with sorrow, but through it all I still know quite certainly that just to be alive is a grand thing.

—AGATHA CHRISTIE (1890–1976) • ENGLISH MYSTERY WRITER

The moment one knows how, one begins to die a little. Living is a form of not being sure, of not knowing what next or how. . . . One leaps in the dark!

—AGNES DE MILLE (1905–1993) • AMERICAN DANCER AND CHOREOGRAPHER

There is not one big cosmic meaning for all, there is only the meaning we each give to our own life. . . . To seek a total unity is wrong. To give as much meaning to one's life as possible is right to me.

—ANAÏS NIN (1903–1977) • FRENCH WRITER AND DIARIST

Life is a process of becoming, a combination of states we have to go through. Where people fail is that they wish to elect a state and remain in it. This is a kind of death.

—ANAÏS NIN (1903–1977) • FRENCH WRITER AND DIARIST

The dedicated life is the life worth living. You must give with your whole heart.

—ANNIE DILLARD (1945–) • AMERICAN WRITER AND POET

How we spend our days is, of course, how we spend our lives.

—ANNIE DILLARD (1945–) • AMERICAN WRITER AND POET

For centuries, the battle of morality was fought between those who claimed that your life belongs to God and those who claimed that it belongs to your neighbors—between those who preached that the good is self-sacrifice for the sake of ghosts in heaven and those who preached that the good is self-sacrifice for the sake of incompetents on earth. And no one came to say that your life belongs to you and that the good is to live it.

—AYN RAND (1905-1982) • RUSSIAN-AMERICAN WRITER AND PHILOSOPHER

Your passion is your true power. The more you discover and express your passion for life, the more irresistible you will become to others.

—BARBARA DE ANGELIS
20TH/21ST-CENTURY AMERICAN WRITER AND PERSONAL GROWTH SPEAKER

Why does a person even get up in the morning? You have breakfast, you floss your teeth so you'll have healthy gums in your old age, and then you get in your car and drive down I-10 and die. Life is so stupid I can't stand it.

—BARBARA KINGSOLVER (1955-) • AMERICAN WRITER

Reality marred this happy picture.

—BARBARA TUCHMAN (1912-1989)
AMERICAN HISTORIAN AND WRITER

I don't want life to imitate art. I want life to be art.

—CARRIE FISHER (1956-) • AMERICAN ACTOR AND WRITER

Life is a verb, not a noun.

—CHARLOTTE PERKINS GILMAN (1860-1935)
AMERICAN WRITER AND SOCIAL CRITIC

What a wonderful life I've had! I only wish I'd realized it sooner.

—COLETTE (1873-1954) • FRENCH WRITER

I would rather die a meaningful death than to live a meaningless life.

–CORAZON AQUINO (1933-) • PRESIDENT OF THE PHILIPPINES; FIRST FEMALE PRESIDENT IN ASIA

Love the moment, and the energy of that moment will spread beyond all boundaries.

–CORITA KENT (1918-1986) • AMERICAN ARTIST

Ducking for apples—change one letter and it's the story of my life.

–DOROTHY PARKER (1893-1967) • AMERICAN WRITER AND CRITIC

Life is the only real counselor. Wisdom unfiltered through personal experience does not become a part of the moral tissue.

–EDITH WHARTON (1862-1937) • AMERICAN WRITER

I could not, at any age, be content to take my place by the fireside and simply look on. Life was meant to be lived. Curiosity must be kept alive. One must never, for whatever reason, turn his back on life.

–ELEANOR ROOSEVELT (1884-1962) • AMERICAN POLITICAL LEADER AND FIRST LADY

If the sight of the blue skies fills you with joy, if a blade of grass springing up in the fields has the power to move you, if the simple things of nature have a message that you understand, rejoice, for your soul is alive; and then aspire to learn that other truth, that the least of what you receive can be divided. To help, to continually help and share, that is the sum of all knowledge; that is the meaning of art.

–ELEONORA DUSE (1858-1924) • ITALIAN ACTOR

You must learn day by day, year by year, to broaden your horizon. The more things you love, the more you are interested in, the more you enjoy, the more you are indignant about, the more you have left when anything happens.

–ETHEL BARRYMORE (1879-1959) • AMERICAN ACTOR

The game of life is a game of boomerangs. Our thoughts, deeds, and words return to us sooner or later with astounding accuracy.

–FLORENCE SCOVEL SHINN (1871–1940) • AMERICAN ILLUSTRATOR AND INSPIRATIONAL WRITER

•

I wanted a perfect ending. Now I've learned, the hard way, that some poems don't rhyme, and some stories don't have a clear beginning, middle, and end. Life is about not knowing, having to change, taking the moment and making the best of it without knowing what's going to happen next.

–GILDA RADNER (1946–1989) • AMERICAN COMEDIAN

•

I will stay in the fray, in the revel of ideas and risk; learning, failing, wooing, grieving, trusting, working, reposing—in this sin of language and lips.

–GILLIAN ROSE (1947–1995) • ENGLISH PHILOSOPHER

•

Don't be afraid your life will end; be afraid that it will never begin.

–GRACE HANSEN (1913–1985) • AMERICAN DANCE DIRECTOR

•

Life is like a game of poker: If you don't put any in the pot, there won't be any to take out.

–JACKIE "MOMS" MABLEY (LORETTA MARY AIKEN) (1894–1975)
AFRICAN-AMERICAN COMEDIAN

•

We must remember the past, define the future, and challenge the present—wherever and however we can. It will take the rest of our lives even to begin. But then, what else have we to do?

–JANE O'REILLY • 20TH/21ST-CENTURY AMERICAN WRITER AND MEMOIRIST

•

So I, with eager voice and news-flushed face, cry to those caught in comas, stupors, sleeping: Come, everything is running, flying, leaping, hurtling through time! And we are in this race.

–JESSICA POWERS (1905–1988) • AMERICAN POET

You don't get to choose how you're going to die, or when. You can only decide how you're going to live now.

–JOAN BAEZ (1941–) • AMERICAN FOLK SINGER AND ACTIVIST

•

Life itself is the proper binge.

–JULIA CHILD (1912–2004)
AMERICAN CHEF AND TELEVISION PERSONALITY

•

I think, this is why a woman makes things up: because when she dies, all those lives she never got to are all going down with her. All those possibilities will just sit there like a bunch of schoolkids with their hand raised and uncalled on—each knowing, really knowing, the answer.

–LORRIE MOORE (1957–) • AMERICAN WRITER

•

Have regular hours for work and play; make each day both useful and pleasant, and prove that you understand the worth of time by employing it well. Then youth will be delightful, old age will bring few regrets, and life will become a beautiful success.

–LOUISA MAY ALCOTT (1832–1888) • AMERICAN WRITER

•

Never get so fascinated by the extraordinary that you forget the ordinary.

–MAGDALEN NABB (1947–) • ENGLISH-BORN ITALIAN WRITER

•

I have always had a dread of becoming a passenger in life.

–MARGARETH II, QUEEN OF DENMARK (1940–)
QUEEN REGNANT AND HEAD OF STATE OF DENMARK

•

Life is the first gift, love is the second, and understanding the third.

–MARGE PIERCY (1936–) • AMERICAN POET, WRITER, AND SOCIAL ACTIVIST

Study as if you were going to live forever;
live as if you were going to die tomorrow.

–MARIA MITCHELL (1818–1889)
AMERICAN ASTRONOMER

•

Of any stopping place in life, it is good to ask whether it will be a good place from which to go on as well as a good place to remain.

–MARY CATHERINE BATESON (1939–)
AMERICAN WRITER AND CULTURAL ANTHROPOLOGIST

•

Life is a mystery as deep as ever death can be.

–MARY MAPES DODGE (1831–1905)
AMERICAN CHILDREN'S WRITER AND EDITOR

•

It was the best year and a half of my life. Nothing happened.

–MAXINE HONG KINGSTON (1940–) • CHINESE-AMERICAN WRITER

•

This is my life. It is my one time to be me. I want to experience every good thing.

–MAYA ANGELOU (1928–) • AFRICAN-AMERICAN POET, MEMOIRIST, AND CIVIL RIGHTS ACTIVIST

•

The more you praise and celebrate your life, the more there is in life to celebrate.

–OPRAH WINFREY (1954–) • AFRICAN-AMERICAN TELEVISION HOST AND MAGAZINE PUBLISHER

•

I do not want to live in paradise; this world is enough,
so broken and so full of promise.

–PAM DURBAN (1947–) • AMERICAN WRITER

•

Life is a banquet, and most poor suckers are starving.

–ROSALIND RUSSELL (1907–1976) • AMERICAN STAGE AND FILM ACTOR

•

Imagination and fiction make up more than three-quarters of our real life.

–SIMONE WEIL (1909–1943) • FRENCH SOCIAL PHILOSOPHER AND ACTIVIST

Sooner or later we all discover that the important moments in life are not the advertised ones, not the birthdays, the graduations, the weddings, not the great goals achieved. The real milestones are less prepossessing. They come to the door of memory unannounced, stray dogs that amble in, sniff around a bit, and simply never leave. Our lives are measured by these.

–SUSAN B. ANTHONY (1820-1906) • AMERICAN SUFFRAGIST AND NEWSPAPER PUBLISHER

What we seek we do not find—that would be too trim and tidy for so reckless and opulent a thing as life. It is something else we find.

–SUSAN GLASPELL (1882-1948) • AMERICAN NOVELIST AND PLAYWRIGHT

There ought . . . to be a ritual for being born twice—
patched, retreaded, and approved for the road.

–SYLVIA PLATH (1932-1963) • AMERICAN POET AND PROSE WRITER

I have come to the conclusion, after many years of sometimes sad experience, that you cannot come to any conclusion at all.

–VITA SACKVILLE-WEST (1892-1962) • ENGLISH POET AND WRITER

I shall not die of a cold. I shall die of having lived.

–WILLA CATHER (1873-1947) • AMERICAN WRITER

While I am still below the allotted span of time, and notwithstanding, I feel that I have lived. I have had the joy and pain of strong friendships. I have served and been served. I have made enemies of which I am not ashamed. I have been faithless, and then I have been faithful until the blood ran down into my shoes. I have loved unselfishly with all the ardor of a strong heart, and I have hated with all the power of my soul. What waits for me in the future? I do not know. I can't even imagine, and I am glad for that. But already, I have touched the four corners of the horizon, for from hard searching it seems to me that tears and laughter, love and hate make up the sum of life.

–ZORA NEALE HURSTON (1891-1960) • AFRICAN-AMERICAN FOLKLORIST AND WRITER

DIFFICULTY

Not only is life a bitch, but it is always having puppies.

—ADRIENNE GUSOFF
20TH/21ST-CENTURY AMERICAN FREELANCE WRITER AND CREATIVE CONSULTANT

•

What do we live for, if it is not to make life less difficult for each other?

—GEORGE ELIOT (MARY ANN EVANS) (1819-1880) • ENGLISH WRITER

•

I used to believe that anything was better than nothing.
Now I know that sometimes nothing is better.

—GLENDA JACKSON (1936-) • ENGLISH ACTOR AND POLITICIAN

•

I have always thought it would be a blessing if each person could be blind and deaf for a few days during his early adult life. Darkness would make him appreciate sight; silence would teach him the joys of sound.

—HELEN KELLER (1880-1968) • AMERICAN WRITER AND ACTIVIST

•

Life is hard. After all, it kills you.

—KATHARINE HEPBURN (1907-2003)
AMERICAN ACTOR

•

I had grown up into a person who had lost one kind of faith—that people are whole and undivided—and found another: that this universe of broken and divided beings is the only world we have in which to live as best we can. What is wasteful is to live as if it were otherwise.

—PAM DURBAN (1947-) • AMERICAN WRITER

•

Birds sing after a storm; why shouldn't people feel as
free to delight in whatever remains to them?

—ROSE KENNEDY (1890-1995)
AMERICAN; MOTHER OF JOHN F. KENNEDY

Life is a hard battle anyway, and if we laugh and sing a little as we fight the good fight of freedom, it makes it all go easier.

–SOJOURNER TRUTH (1797–1883) • AFRICAN-AMERICAN ABOLITIONIST

The beauty of the world which is so soon to perish, has two edges, one of laughter, one of anguish, cutting the heart asunder.

–VIRGINIA WOOLF (1882–1941) • ENGLISH NOVELIST, ESSAYIST, AND CRITIC

"LINGERIE"

Brevity is the soul of lingerie.

–DOROTHY PARKER (1893–1967)
AMERICAN WRITER AND CRITIC

I'm superstitious . . . but not like wear-the-same-underwear-for-two-weeks superstitious.

–KATE HUDSON (1979–) • AMERICAN ACTOR

A lady is one who never shows her underwear unintentionally.

–LILLIAN DAY (1893–1991) • ENGLISH WRITER

The older you get, the higher you wear your underwear. Like rings on a tree. Eighty, ninety years old, your breasts are inside them. When you die, they just pull them up over your head.

–MARGARET SMITH • 20TH/21ST-CENTURY AMERICAN COMEDIAN

Before we can leave our parents, they stuff our heads like the suitcases which they jam-pack with homemade underwear.

–MAXINE HONG KINGSTON (1940–) • CHINESE-AMERICAN WRITER

If God wanted us to be naked, why did he invent sexy lingerie?

—SHANNON DOHERTY (1971–) • AMERICAN ACTOR

•

BRA

I was the first woman to burn my bra—it took the fire department four days to put it out.

—DOLLY PARTON (1946–)
AMERICAN COUNTRY SINGER AND ENTERTAINER

•

Every four weeks I go up a bra size. . . . it's worth being pregnant just for the breasts.

—NATASHA HAMILTON (1982–) • ENGLISH SINGER

•

CORSET

Happiness is the sublime moment when you get out of your corsets at night.

—JOYCE GRENFELL (1910–1979)
ENGLISH FILM AND TELEVISION ACTOR, COMEDIAN, AND SINGER-SONGWRITER

•

For five minutes, it's fantastic—you have this tiny waist and fantastic cleavage, but oxygen deprivation is a big problem.

—KEIRA KNIGHTLEY (1985–) • ENGLISH ACTOR

•

GIRDLE

You have to have the kind of body that doesn't need a girdle in order to get to pose in one.

—CAROLYN KENMORE
20TH/21ST-CENTURY AMERICAN WRITER AND MODEL

•

"LITERATURE"

See also Reading, Stories, Writing

Literature is an instrument of a culture, not a summary of it.

–CYNTHIA OZICK (1928-) • AMERICAN NOVELIST, ESSAYIST, AND POET

Men have been in charge of according value to literature, and . . . they have found the contributions of their own sex immeasurably superior.

–DALE SPENDER (1943-) • AUSTRALIAN SOCIOLINGUIST AND TECHNOLOGY THEORIST

Literature is the lie that tells the truth.

–DOROTHY ALLISON (1949-)
AMERICAN POET AND PROSE WRITER

Remarks are not literature.

–GERTRUDE STEIN (1874-1946)
AMERICAN POET

The test of literature is, I suppose, whether we ourselves live more intensely for the reading of it.

–ELIZABETH DREW (1887-1965)
ENGLISH-BORN AMERICAN WRITER AND CRITIC

What is commonly called literary history is actually a record of choices. Which writers have survived their time and which have not depends upon who noticed them and chose to record the notice.

–LOUISE BERNIKOW • 20TH/21ST-CENTURY AMERICAN WRITER

I believe all literature started as gossip.

–RITA MAE BROWN (1944-)
AMERICAN WRITER AND ACTIVIST

Perversity is the muse of modern literature.

–SUSAN SONTAG (1933-2004)
AMERICAN ESSAYIST, NOVELIST, INTELLECTUAL, AND ACTIVIST

Literature is the record of our discontent.

—VIRGINIA WOOLF (1882–1941)
ENGLISH NOVELIST, ESSAYIST, AND CRITIC

•

"LONELINESS"

See also Solitude

•

It is better to be alone than to wish you were.

—ANN LANDERS (ESTHER PAULINE FRIEDMAN) (1918–2002)
AMERICAN ADVICE COLUMNIST

•

Ever notice that Soup for One is eight aisles away from Party Mix?

—ELAYNE BOOSLER (1952–) • AMERICAN COMEDIAN

•

Loneliness is never more cruel than when it is felt in close propinquity with someone who has ceased to communicate.

—GERMAINE GREER (1939–) • AUSTRALIAN-BORN WRITER AND SOCIAL CRITIC

•

Domestic bliss . . . is outweighed by the pleasures of female friendship and a gregarious independence, worth the risk of loneliness.

—HERMIONE LEE (1948–) • ENGLISH CRITIC AND BIOGRAPHER

•

I've always had a huge fear of dying or becoming ill. The thing I'm most afraid of, though, is being alone, which I think a lot of performers fear. It's why we seek the limelight—so we're not alone, we're adored. . . . The fear of being alone drives my life.

—JENNIFER LOPEZ (1969–) • AMERICAN ACTOR, DANCER, AND POP/LATIN SINGER

•

Loneliness is the universal problem of rich people.

—JOAN COLLINS (1933–) • ENGLISH ACTOR AND WRITER

Who hasn't slept in an empty bed sometimes, longing for the embrace of another person on the achingly short trip to the grave?

–LEONORE FLEISCHER (1933-) • AMERICAN WRITER

The thing that makes you exceptional, if you are at all, is inevitably that which must also make you lonely.

–LORRAINE HANSBERRY (1930-1965) • AFRICAN-AMERICAN PLAYWRIGHT AND PAINTER

It is better to be lonely than to wish to be alone.

–MARGARET DELAND (1857-1945) • AMERICAN WRITER AND POET

Loneliness is the most terrible poverty.

–MOTHER TERESA (1910-1997)
ALBANIAN CATHOLIC NUN; WINNER OF NOBEL PEACE PRIZE

"LOVE"

See also Relationships

But surely for everything you love you have to pay some price.

–AGATHA CHRISTIE (1890-1976) • ENGLISH MYSTERY WRITER

There is no reciprocity. Men love women, women love children, children love hamsters.

–ALICE THOMAS ELLIS (1932-2005)
ENGLISH WRITER AND EDITOR

I have learned not to worry about love, but to honor its coming with all my heart.

–ALICE WALKER (1944-) • AFRICAN-AMERICAN WRITER AND POET

Anxiety is love's greatest killer. It makes others feel as you might when a drowning man holds on to you. You want to save him, but you know he will strangle you with his panic.

–ANAÏS NIN (1903–1977) • FRENCH WRITER AND DIARIST

•

If love means that one person absorbs the other, then no real relationship exists any more. Love evaporates; there is nothing left to love. The integrity of self is gone.

–ANN OAKLEY (1944–) • ENGLISH FEMINIST, SOCIOLOGIST, AND WRITER

•

To love deeply in one direction makes us more loving in all others.

–ANNE-SOPHIE SWETCHINE (1782–1857) • RUSSIAN-FRENCH WRITER

•

Love's greatest gift is its ability to make everything it touches sacred.

–BARBARA DE ANGELIS

20TH/21ST-CENTURY AMERICAN WRITER AND PERSONAL GROWTH SPEAKER

•

I knew what my job was: It was to go out and meet the people and love them.

–PRINCESS DIANA (1961–1997) • PRINCESS OF WALES, FIRST WIFE OF CHARLES, PRINCE OF WALES

•

Everyone admits that love is wonderful and necessary, yet no one agrees on just what it is.

–DIANE ACKERMAN (1956–) • AMERICAN POET AND NATURALIST

•

If we could raise one generation with unconditional love, there would be no Hitlers. We need to teach the next generation of children from Day One that they are responsible for their lives. Mankind's greatest gift, also its greatest curse, is that we have free choice. We can make our choices built from love or from fear.

–ELISABETH KÜBLER-ROSS (1926–2004)

SWISS PSYCHIATRIST, SPECIALIST ON GRIEVING AND DEATH

Do you want me to tell you something really subversive? Love is everything it's cracked up to be. That's why people are so cynical about it. It really is worth fighting for, being brave for, risking everything for. And the trouble is, if you don't risk everything, you risk even more.

–ERICA JONG (1942-) • AMERICAN WRITER

•

For her life, any life, she had to believe, was nothing but the continuity of its love.

–EUDORA WELTY (1899-2001) • AMERICAN WRITER

•

Come and stand in my heart, whoever you are, and a whole river would cover your feet and rise higher and take your knees in whirlpools, and draw you down to itself, your whole body, your heart too.

–EUDORA WELTY (1899-2001) • AMERICAN WRITER

•

I like not only to be loved, but to be told I am loved.

–GEORGE ELIOT (MARY ANN EVANS) (1819-1880)
ENGLISH WRITER

•

There is only one happiness in life, to love and be loved.

–GEORGE SAND (AMANDINE-AURORE-LUCIE DUPIN, BARONNE DUDEVANT) (1804-1876)
FRENCH WRITER AND FEMINIST

•

The best and most beautiful things in the world cannot be seen or even touched—they must be felt with the heart.

–HELEN KELLER (1880-1968) • AMERICAN WRITER AND ACTIVIST

•

Happiness comes more from loving than being loved; and often when our affection seems wounded it is only our vanity bleeding. To love, and to be hurt often, and to love again—this is the brave and happy life.

–J. E. BUCKROSE (ANNIE EDITH JAMESON) (1868-1931) • ENGLISH WRITER

Put your hand in the water to reach for a sea urchin or a seashell, and the thing you desired never quite lies where you had lined it up to be. The same is true of love. In prospect or in contemplation, love is where it seems to be. Reach in to lift it out and your hand misses. The water is deeper than you had gauged. You reach farther, your whole body straining, and then there is nothing for it but to slide in—deeper, much deeper than you had gauged—and still the thing eludes you.

–JEANETTE WINTERSON (1959–) • ENGLISH WRITER

Love is like a violin. The music may stop now and then, but the strings remain forever.

–JUNE MASTERS BACHER
20TH/21ST-CENTURY AMERICAN WRITER OF HISTORICAL ROMANCES

Love is like a brick. You can build a house, or you can sink a dead body.

–LADY GAGA (1986–) • AMERICAN POP SINGER AND CELEBRITY

There is always something left to love. And if you ain't learned that, you ain't learned nothing.

–LORRAINE HANSBERRY (1930–1965)
AFRICAN-AMERICAN PLAYWRIGHT AND PAINTER

Love is the big booming beat which covers up the noise of hate.

–MARGARET CHO (1968–) • KOREAN-AMERICAN COMEDIAN AND ACTOR

The pain of love is the pain of being alive. It's a perpetual wound.

–MAUREEN DUFFY (1933–) • ENGLISH POET, WRITER, AND ACTIVIST

In the arithmetic of love, one plus one equals everything, and two minus one equals nothing.

–MIGNON MCLAUGHLIN (1913–1983) • AMERICAN JOURNALIST AND WRITER

We love because it is the only true adventure.

–NIKKI GIOVANNI (1943–) • AMERICAN POET AND WRITER

•

Love never dies of starvation, but often of indigestion.

–NINON DE LENCLOS (1620–1705) • FRENCH COURTESAN

•

The sweetest joy, the wildest woe is love.

–PEARL BAILEY (1918–1990) • AMERICAN SINGER AND ACTOR

•

Love is the emblem of eternity; it confounds all notions of time; effaces all memory of beginning, all fear of an end.

–MADAME DE STAËL (1766–1817)
SWISS-BORN FRENCH WRITER AND SOCIETY FIGURE

•

If you judge people, you have no time to love them.

–MOTHER TERESA (1910–1997)
ALBANIAN CATHOLIC NUN; WINNER OF NOBEL PEACE PRIZE

•

I have found the paradox that if I love until it hurts, then there is no hurt, but only more love.

–MOTHER TERESA (1910–1997)
ALBANIAN CATHOLIC NUN; WINNER OF NOBEL PEACE PRIZE

•

Love doesn't just sit there like a stone; it has to be made, like bread, remade all the time, made new.

–URSULA K. LE GUIN (1929–) • AMERICAN WRITER

•

Where there is great love there are always miracles.

–WILLA CATHER (1873–1947) • AMERICAN WRITER

•

Nobody has ever measured, even poets, how much a heart can hold.

–ZELDA FITZGERALD (1900–1948) • AMERICAN WRITER AND SOCIETY FIGURE

Love makes your soul crawl out from its hiding place.

–ZORA NEALE HURSTON (1891–1960)
AFRICAN-AMERICAN FOLKLORIST AND WRITER

ROMANTIC

Love ceases to be a pleasure when it ceases to be a secret.

–APHRA BEHN (1640–1689) • ENGLISH PLAYWRIGHT, POET, NOVELIST, AND SPY

Free love is sometimes love but never freedom.

–ELIZABETH BIBESCO (1897–1945) • ENGLISH WRITER

Whatever our souls are made of, his and mine are the same.

–EMILY BRONTË (1818–1848) • ENGLISH WRITER

Love is a game that two can play and both win.

–EVA GABOR (1919–1995)
HUNGARIAN-BORN AMERICAN ACTOR

Every little girl knows about love. It is only her capacity to suffer because of it that increases.

–FRANÇOISE SAGAN (1935–2004)
FRENCH NOVELIST AND PLAYWRIGHT

Falling in love consists merely in uncorking the imagination and bottling the common sense.

–HELEN ROWLAND (1875–1950) • AMERICAN JOURNALIST AND HUMORIST

Love, with very young people, is a heartless business. We drink at that age from thirst, or to get drunk; it is only later in life that we occupy ourselves with the individuality of our wine.

–ISAK DINESEN (KAREN BLIXEN) (1885–1962) • DANISH WRITER AND AUTOBIOGRAPHER

Love, they say, enslaves and passion is a demon and many have been lost for love. I know this is true, but I know too that without love we grope the tunnels of our lives and never see the sun. When I fell in love it was as though I looked into a mirror for the first time and saw myself. I lifted my hand in wonderment and felt my cheeks, my neck. This was me.

–JEANETTE WINTERSON (1959–) • ENGLISH WRITER

Love is a fire. But whether it is going to warm your heart or burn down your house, you can never tell.

–JOAN CRAWFORD (1905–1977) • AMERICAN ACTOR

Love is much nicer to be in than an automobile accident, a tight girdle, a higher tax bracket, or a holding pattern over Philadelphia.

–JUDITH VIORST (1931–) • AMERICAN POET AND JOURNALIST

Ruin hath taught me thus to ruminate, that time will come and take my love away.

–KATHERINE ANNE PORTER (1890–1980) • AMERICAN WRITER

If only one could tell true love from false love as one can tell mushrooms from toadstools.

–KATHERINE MANSFIELD (1888–1923) • NEW ZEALAND WRITER

If it is your time, love will track you down like a cruise missile.

–LYNDA BARRY (1956–) • AMERICAN CARTOONIST

Are we not like two volumes of one book?

–MARCELINE DESBORDES-VALMORE (1786–1859)
FRENCH POET

We don't believe in rheumatism and true love until after the first attack.

–MARIE VON EBNER-ESCHENBACH (1830–1916) • AUSTRIAN WRITER

When you're in love you never really know whether your elation comes from the qualities of the one you love, or if it attributes them to her; whether the light which surrounds her like a halo comes from you, from her, or from the meeting of your sparks.

–NATALIE CLIFFORD BARNEY (1876–1972)
AMERICAN POET, MEMOIRIST, AND SOCIAL REBEL

Anyone can be passionate, but it takes real lovers to be silly.

–ROSE FRANKEN (1896–1988)
AMERICAN SCREENWRITER, PLAYWRIGHT, AND WRITER

Rachel says that love is like a big black piano being pushed off the top of a three-story building, and you're waiting on the bottom to catch it. But Lourdes says it's not that way at all. It's like a top, like all the colors in the world are spinning so fast they're not colors anymore and all that's left is a white hum.

–SANDRA CISNEROS (1954–) • MEXICAN-AMERICAN WRITER AND POET

No one worth possessing can be quite possessed.

–SARA TEASDALE (1884–1933) • AMERICAN LYRICAL POET

[Some] people really expect the passion of love to fill and gratify every need of life, whereas nature only intended that it should meet one of many demands. They insist on making it stand for all the emotional pleasures of life and art; expecting an individual and self-limited passion to yield infinite variety, pleasure, and distraction, and to contribute to their lives what the arts and the pleasurable exercise of the intellect gives to less limited and less intense idealists.

–WILLA CATHER (1873–1947) • AMERICAN WRITER

"LUCK"

People always call it luck when you've acted more sensibly than they have.

–ANNE TYLER (1941–) • AMERICAN WRITER

Luck? Sure. But only after long practice and only with the ability to think under pressure.

–BABE DIDRIKSON ZAHARIAS (1914–1956) • AMERICAN GOLFER

You just don't luck into things as much as you'd like to think you do. You build step by step, whether it's friendships or opportunities.

–BARBARA BUSH (1925–) • FIRST LADY OF THE UNITED STATES

When I was fifteen, I had lucky underwear. When that failed, I had a lucky hairdo, then a lucky race number, even lucky race days. After fifteen years, I've found the secret to success is simple. It's hard work.

–MARGARET GROOS • 20TH/21ST-CENTURY AMERICAN MARATHON RUNNER

Luck enters into every contingency. You are a fool if you forget it—and a greater fool if you count upon it.

–PHYLLIS BOTTOME (1884–1963) • ENGLISH WRITER

I've just sort of gone with the flow, and I ended up here. Crazy. I'm not going to start planning anything; my life is way better than anybody could have planned it.

–RACHAEL RAY (1968–) • AMERICAN CHEF AND TV HOST

It is so difficult not to become vain about one's own good luck.

–SIMONE DE BEAUVOIR (1908–1986) • FRENCH WRITER AND PHILOSOPHER

M

"MAKEUP"

Makeup is such a weird concept. I'll wake up in the morning and look in the mirror. "Gee, I really don't look so good. Maybe if my eyelids were blue, I'd be more attractive."

—CATHY LADMAN • 20TH/21ST-CENTURY AMERICAN COMEDIAN AND ACTOR

Who needs it? You muck a few stables, gallop ten or twelve horses, and if that doesn't put color in your cheeks, nothing will.

—DIANE CRUMP • 20TH/21ST-CENTURY AMERICAN, FIRST FEMALE JOCKEY IN THE KENTUCKY DERBY

I can't stand makeup commercials. "Do you need a lipstick that keeps your lips kissable?" No. I need a lipstick that gets me equal pay for equal work. How about eye shadow that makes me stop thinking I'm too fat?

—HEIDI JOYCE • 20TH/21ST-CENTURY AMERICAN COMEDIAN

I don't have time every day to put on makeup. I need that time to clean my rifle.

—HENRIETTE MANTEL • 20TH/21ST-CENTURY AMERICAN ACTOR

Taking joy in life is a woman's best cosmetic.

—ROSALIND RUSSELL (1907–1976)
AMERICAN STAGE AND FILM ACTOR

All the American women had purple noses and gray lips and their faces were chalk white from terrible powder. I recognized that the United States could be my life's work.

—HELENA RUBINSTEIN (1870–1965) • POLISH-BORN COSMETICS ENTREPRENEUR

There's no better makeup than self-confidence.

—SHAKIRA (1977–) • COLUMBIAN POP SINGER AND SONGWRITER

"MANNERS"

Do not speak of repulsive matters at table.

–AMY VANDERBILT (1908-1974)
AMERICAN ETIQUETTE EXPERT

To do exactly as your neighbors do is the only sensible rule.

–EMILY POST (1873-1960) • AMERICAN ETIQUETTE EXPERT

Manners are a sensitive awareness of the feelings of others. If you have that awareness, you have good manners, no matter what fork you use.

–EMILY POST (1873-1960) • AMERICAN ETIQUETTE EXPERT

Man is the only animal that learns by being hypocritical. He pretends to be polite and then, eventually, he becomes polite.

–JEAN KERR (1923-2003) • AMERICAN PLAYWRIGHT AND HUMORIST

Being considerate of others will take your children further in life than any college degree.

–MARIAN WRIGHT EDELMAN (1939-)
AFRICAN-AMERICAN FOUNDER OF THE CHILDREN'S DEFENSE FUND

Politeness is half good manners and half good lying.

–MARY WILSON LITTLE • 19TH-CENTURY AMERICAN WRITER

Tact is after all a kind of mind reading.

–SARAH ORNE JEWETT (1849-1909)
AMERICAN WRITER

"MARRIAGE"

See also Husbands

All married couples should learn the art of battle as they should learn the art of making love. Good battle is objective and honest, never vicious or cruel. Good battle is healthy and constructive, and brings to a marriage the principle of equal partnership.

—ANN LANDERS (ESTHER PAULINE FRIEDMAN) (1918-2002) • AMERICAN ADVICE COLUMNIST

A simple enough pleasure, surely, to have breakfast alone with one's husband, but how seldom married people in the midst of life achieve it.

—ANNE MORROW LINDBERGH (1906-2001) • AMERICAN WRITER AND PIONEERING AVIATOR

A woman asking "Am I good? Am I satisfied?" is extremely selfish. The less women fuss about themselves, the less they talk to other women, the more they try to please their husbands, the happier the marriage is going to be.

BARBARA CARTLAND (1901-2000) • ENGLISH ROMANCE NOVELIST

It is easier to live through someone else than to become complete yourself.

—BETTY FRIEDAN (1921-2006)
AMERICAN FEMINIST, WRITER AND COFOUNDER OF NATIONAL ORGANIZATION FOR WOMEN

Marriage is a matter of give and take, but so far I haven't been able to find anybody who'll take what I have to give.

—CASS DALEY (1915-1975) • AMERICAN ACTOR

The trouble with some women is they get all excited about nothing—and then they marry him.

—CHER (1946-) • AMERICAN SINGER, ACTOR, AND POP ICON

There is nothing like a good dose of another woman
to make a man appreciate his wife.

–CLARE BOOTHE LUCE (1903–1987)
AMERICAN PLAYWRIGHT, JOURNALIST, AND POLITICIAN

•

The weaker partner in a marriage is the one who loves the most.

–ELEONORA DUSE (1858–1924) • ITALIAN ACTOR

•

Marriage has no guarantees. If that's what you're
looking for, go live with a car battery.

–ERMA BOMBECK (1927–1996) • AMERICAN HUMORIST

•

A wedding is just like a funeral except that you get to smell your own flowers.

–GRACE HANSEN (1913–1985) • AMERICAN DANCE DIRECTOR

•

When a girl marries, she exchanges the attentions of all the other
men of her acquaintance for the inattention of just one.

–HELEN ROWLAND (1875–1950) • AMERICAN JOURNALIST AND HUMORIST

•

When you see what some women marry, you realize how
they must hate to work for a living.

–HELEN ROWLAND (1875–1950) • AMERICAN JOURNALIST AND HUMORIST

•

Any intelligent woman who reads the marriage contract,
and then goes into it, deserves all the consequences.

–ISADORA DUNCAN (1877–1927) • AMERICAN MODERN DANCER

•

Marriage, for a woman at least, hampers the two things that
made life to me glorious—friendship and learning.

–JANE HARRISON (1850–1928)
ENGLISH CLASSICS SCHOLAR, LINGUIST, AND FEMINIST

Sexiness wears thin after a while and beauty fades, but to be married to a man who makes you laugh every day, ah, now that's a real treat.

–JOANNE WOODWARD (1930–) • AMERICAN ACTOR

No matter how love-sick a woman is, she shouldn't take the first pill that comes along.

–JOYCE BROTHERS (1928–)
AMERICAN PSYCHOLOGIST AND COLUMNIST

One advantage of marriage it seems to me is that when you fall out of love with him or he falls out of love with you it keeps you together until maybe you fall in again.

–JUDITH VIORST (1931–) • AMERICAN POET AND JOURNALIST

There are so many responsible, nice, kind guys out there. Why marry a fixer-upper?

–LAURA SCHLESSINGER (1947–) • AMERICAN CULTURAL COMMENTATOR

There is a species of trouble women long for and sigh after and regret once they get it, like a too expensive dress that cannot be returned. That trouble is marriage.

–LOUISE ERDRICH (1954–) • NATIVE AMERICAN WRITER AND POET

Marriage is a great institution, but I'm not ready for an institution.

–MAE WEST (1893–1980) • AMERICAN ACTOR, WRITER, AND SEX SYMBOL

I've married a few people I shouldn't have, but haven't we all?

–MAMIE VAN DOREN (1931–) • AMERICAN ACTOR

If you think marriage is going to be perfect, you're probably still at your reception.

–MARTHA BOLTON
20TH/21ST-CENTURY AMERICAN COMEDY AND CHRISTIAN WRITER

•

If your husband expects you to laugh, do so; if he expects you to cry, don't; if you don't know what he expects, what are you doing married?

–MIGNON MCLAUGHLIN (1913–1983) • AMERICAN JOURNALIST AND WRITER

•

I married beneath me—all women do.

–LADY NANCY ASTOR (1879–1964)
FIRST FEMALE TO TAKE A SEAT IN BRITISH HOUSE OF COMMONS

•

A good marriage is one which allows for change and growth in the individuals and in the way they express their love.

–PEARL S. BUCK (1892–1973)
FIRST FEMALE AMERICAN WINNER OF THE NOBEL PRIZE IN LITERATURE

•

A bachelor is a guy who never made the same mistake once.

–PHYLLIS DILLER (1917–) • AMERICAN COMEDIAN

•

In a successful marriage, there is no such thing as one's way. There is only the way of both, only the bumpy, dusty, difficult, but always mutual path!

–PHYLLIS MCGINLEY (1905–1978)
AMERICAN POET, ESSAYIST, AND WRITER

•

One marries many times at many levels within a marriage. If you have more marriages than you have divorces within the marriage, you're lucky . . .

–RUBY DEE (1924–)
AFRICAN-AMERICAN ACTOR AND CIVIL RIGHTS ACTIVIST

Whenever you want to marry someone, go have lunch with his ex-wife.

–SHELLEY WINTERS (1920–2006) • AMERICAN ACTOR

•

All marriages are happy. It's trying to live together afterward that causes all the problems.

–SHELLEY WINTERS (1920–2006) • AMERICAN ACTOR

•

In fact there will be only one winner out of thousands in the lottery of marriage. The present epoch invites, even compels women to work, but it flashes before their eyes paradises of idleness and delight: It exalts the winners far above those who remain tied down to earth.

–SIMONE DE BEAUVOIR (1908–1986) • FRENCH WRITER AND PHILOSOPHER

•

Chains do not hold a marriage together. It is threads, hundreds of tiny threads which sew people together through the years. That is what makes a marriage last—more than passion or even sex.

–SIMONE SIGNORET (1921–1985) • FRENCH ACTOR

•

I feel sure that no girl would go to the altar if she knew all.

–QUEEN VICTORIA (1819–1901) • QUEEN OF ENGLAND

•

A girl can't analyze marriage, and a woman dare not.

–LADY UNA TROUBRIDGE (1887–1963)
ENGLISH WRITER, SINGER, AND SCULPTOR

•

Marriage is a lottery in which men stake their liberty and women their happiness.

–VIRGINIE DE RIEUX • 16TH-CENTURY FRENCH WRITER

•

A girl must marry for love and keep on marrying until she finds it.

–ZSA ZSA GABOR (1917–) • HUNGARIAN-AMERICAN ACTRESS AND SOCIALITE

A man in love is incomplete until he is married. Then he's finished.

–ZSA ZSA GABOR (1917–) • HUNGARIAN-AMERICAN ACTRESS AND SOCIALITE

AND MONEY

I'd marry again if I found a man who had 15 million dollars, would sign over half to me, and guarantee that he'd be dead within a year.

–BETTE DAVIS (1908–1989) • AMERICAN ACTOR

I've had an exciting time. I married for love and got a little money along with it.

–ROSE KENNEDY (1890–1995) • AMERICAN; MOTHER OF JOHN F. KENNEDY

SAME-SEX

If you wanna marry Joe Millionaire, go ahead. If you're a celebrity and you wanna marry your high school sweetheart for 55 hours, go right ahead. If you're J-Lo and you wanna marry 18 people, for six days each, hey! Go right on ahead! But if you happen to be reasonably minded and have fallen in love and wanna marry your soul mate and make a life of it, and you just so happen to be the same sex, then NO! How dare you!

–PINK (1979–) • AMERICAN POP SINGER AND SONGWRITER

WEDDINGS

In olden times sacrifices were made at the altar—a custom which is still continued.

–HELEN ROWLAND (1875–1950) • AMERICAN JOURNALIST AND HUMORIST

Our wedding plans please everybody as if we were fertilizing the earth and creating social luck.

–MARGE PIERCY (1936–) • AMERICAN POET, NOVELIST, AND SOCIAL ACTIVIST

A wedding isn't for the bride and groom, it's for the family and friends. The B. and G. are just props, silly stick figures with no more significance than the pink and white candy figures on the top of the cake.

–SUSAN CHEEVER • 20TH/21ST-CENTURY AMERICAN NOVELIST AND BIOGRAPHER

"MATERIALISM"

Why are we so blind? That which we improve, we have; that which we hoard, is not for ourselves.

–DOROTHÉE DELUZY (1747–1830) • FRENCH ACTOR

The luxuries of the few were becoming the necessities of the many.

–FLORA THOMPSON (1876–1947) • ENGLISH NOVELIST

If you think of yourself as the woman in the Cartier watch and the Hermès scarf, a house fire will destroy not only your possessions but your self.

–LINDA HENLEY • 20TH-CENTURY AMERICAN WRITER

A commercial society urges its citizens to be responsible for things, but not for people. It is the unquestioned assumption of a mercantile culture that things need and deserve attention, but that people can take care of themselves.

–MARGARET HALSEY (1910–1997) • AMERICAN WRITER

False values begin with the worship of things.

–SUSAN SONTAG (1933–2004)
AMERICAN ESSAYIST, NOVELIST, INTELLECTUAL, AND ACTIVIST

"MEDIA"

We are given in our newspapers and on TV and radio exactly what we, the public, insist on having, and this very frequently is mediocre information and mediocre entertainment.

—ELEANOR ROOSEVELT (1884-1962) • AMERICAN POLITICAL LEADER AND FIRST LADY

It is hard to tell which is worst; the wide diffusion of things that are not true, or the suppression of things that are true.

—HARRIET MARTINEAU (1802-1876) • ENGLISH JOURNALIST AND SOCIAL REFORMER

From talk radio to insult radio wasn't really that much of a leap.

—LEONORE FLEISCHER (1933-) • AMERICAN WRITER

The more people are reached by mass communications, the less they communicate with each other.

—MARYA MANNES (1904-1990) • AMERICAN COLUMNIST AND CRITIC

You should always believe what you read in the newspapers, for that makes them more interesting.

—ROSE MACAULAY (1881-1958) • ENGLISH NOVELIST AND ESSAYIST

Industrial societies turn their citizens into image junkies; it is the most irresistible form of mental pollution. Poignant longings for beauty, for an end to probing below the surface, for a redemption and celebration of the body of the world. Ultimately, having an experience becomes identical with taking a photograph of it.

—SUSAN SONTAG (1933-2004) • AMERICAN ESSAYIST, NOVELIST, INTELLECTUAL, AND ACTIVIST

The truth is not wonderful enough to suit the newspapers; so they enlarge upon it, and invent ridiculous embellishments.

–ANNE SULLIVAN (1866–1936) • AMERICAN EDUCATOR OF THE BLIND AND DEAF

•

Journalism is the ability to meet the challenge of filling space.

–REBECCA WEST (1892–1983) • ANGLO-IRISH FEMINIST AND WRITER

•

Channeling the news under intense pressure requires finely tuned skills, as worthy of respect as shoe-leather reporting. Speed of response. Fluency. Stamina. An ability to synthesize large quantities of scattered information under great pressure.

–TINA BROWN (1953–)
ENGLISH-BORN AMERICAN MAGAZINE EDITOR, COLUMNIST, AND TALK-SHOW HOST

•

"MEMORY"

•

Every journey into the past is complicated by delusions, false memories, and false namings of real events.

–ADRIENNE RICH (1929–) • AMERICAN POET, THEORIST, AND FEMINIST

•

Memory is more indelible than ink.

–ANITA LOOS (1889–1981)
AMERICAN SCREENWRITER, NOVELIST, AND ESSAYIST

•

As a life's work, I would remember everything—everything, against loss. I would go through life like a plankton net.

–ANNIE DILLARD (1945–) • AMERICAN WRITER AND POET

•

Memory is a complicated thing, a relative to truth, but not its twin.

–BARBARA KINGSOLVER (1955–) • AMERICAN NOVELIST

A childhood is what anyone wants to remember of it.

–CAROL SHIELDS (1935-2003) • AMERICAN-BORN CANADIAN NOVELIST

What we remember from childhood we remember forever—
permanent ghosts, stamped, inked, imprinted, eternally seen.

–CYNTHIA OZICK (1928-) • AMERICAN NOVELIST, ESSAYIST, AND POET

I'm always fascinated by the way memory diffuses fact.

–DIANE SAWYER (1945-) • AMERICAN TELEVISION JOURNALIST AND NEWS ANCHOR

A happy childhood can't be cured. Mine'll hang around
my neck like a rainbow, that's all, instead of a noose.

–HORTENSE CALISHER (1911-) • AMERICAN NOVELIST

We forget all too soon the things we thought we could never forget.

–JOAN DIDION (1934-) • AMERICAN WRITER

I have short-term memory loss, though I like to think
of it as presidential eligibility.

–PAULA POUNDSTONE (1959-) • AMERICAN COMEDIAN

Life began for me when I ceased to admire and began to remember.

–WILLA CATHER (1873-1947) • AMERICAN NOVELIST

Some memories are realities, and are better than
anything that can ever happen again.

–WILLA CATHER (1873-1947) • AMERICAN NOVELIST

I don't remember anybody's name. How do you
think the "dahling" thing got started?

–ZSA ZSA GABOR (1917-)
HUNGARIAN-AMERICAN ACTRESS AND SOCIALITE

"MEN"

Any woman who thinks the way to a man's heart is through his stomach is aiming about ten inches too high.

–ADRIENNE GUSOFF
20TH/21ST-CENTURY AMERICAN FREELANCE WRITER AND CREATIVE CONSULTANT

There are always women who will take men on their own terms. If I were a man I wouldn't bother to change while there are women like that around.

–ANN OAKLEY (1944-) • ENGLISH FEMINIST, SOCIOLOGIST, AND NOVELIST

Men are not the enemy, but the fellow victims. The real enemy is women's denigration of themselves.

–BETTY FRIEDAN (1921-2006)
AMERICAN FEMINIST, WRITER, AND COFOUNDER OF NATIONAL ORGANIZATION FOR WOMEN

A man's home may seem to be his castle on the outside; inside it is more often his nursery.

–CLARE BOOTHE LUCE (1903-1987)
AMERICAN PLAYWRIGHT, JOURNALIST, AND POLITICIAN

Men are very funny. If I had one of those dangly things stuffed down the front of my pants, I'd sit at home all day laughing at myself!

–DAWN FRENCH (1957-) • ENGLISH COMEDIAN

I require three things in a man. He must be handsome, ruthless, and stupid.

–DOROTHY PARKER (1893-1967) • AMERICAN WRITER AND CRITIC

A man is so in the way in the house.

–ELIZABETH GASKELL (1810-1865)
ENGLISH WRITER

A woman needs a man like a fish needs a bicycle.

–IRINA DUNN • 20TH/21ST-CENTURY AUSTRALIAN WRITER AND POLITICIAN

•

Several men I can think of are as capable, as smart, as funny, as compassionate, and as confused—as remarkable you might say—as most women.

–JANE HOWARD (1935-1996) • AMERICAN JOURNALIST AND WRITER

•

Men are those creatures with two legs and eight hands.

–JAYNE MANSFIELD (1933-1967) • AMERICAN ACTOR

•

Some women choose to follow men, and some women choose to follow their dreams. If you're wondering which way to go, remember that your career will never wake up and tell you that it doesn't love you anymore.

–LADY GAGA (1986-) • AMERICAN POP SINGER AND CELEBRITY

•

Men are very easy: You treat them well, and they behave right. You don't treat them well, and they don't behave right.

–LAURA SCHLESSINGER (1947-) • AMERICAN CULTURAL COMMENTATOR

•

The first time you buy a house you see how pretty the paint is and buy it. The second time you look to see if the basement has termites. It's the same with men.

–LUPE VELEZ (1908-1944) • MEXICAN ACTOR

•

It's not the men in my life that count, it's the life in my men.

–MAE WEST (1893-1980) • AMERICAN ACTRESS, WRITER, AND SEX SYMBOL

•

The only thing worse than a man you can't control is a man you can.

–MARGO KAUFMAN (1954-2000) • AMERICAN SCREENWRITER

With men, as with women, the main struggle is between vanity and comfort; but with men, comfort often wins.

–MIGNON MCLAUGHLIN (1913–1983)
AMERICAN JOURNALIST AND WRITER

•

Beware of men who cry. It's true that men who cry are sensitive and in touch with feelings, but the only feelings they tend to be sensitive to and in touch with are their own.

–NORA EPHRON (1941–)
AMERICAN FILM DIRECTOR, PRODUCER, SCREENWRITER, AND NOVELIST

•

Don't accept rides from strange men—and remember that all men are as strange as hell.

–ROBIN MORGAN (1941–)
AMERICAN POET, WRITER, AND RADICAL FEMINIST ACTIVIST

•

Men can read maps better than women. 'Cause only the male mind could conceive of one inch equaling a hundred miles.

–ROSEANNE BARR (1952–) • AMERICAN COMEDIAN

•

Men define intelligence, men define usefulness, men tell us what is beautiful, men even tell us what is womanly.

–SALLY KEMPTON (1943–) • AMERICAN MEDITATION TEACHER

•

No man can be held throughout the day by what happens throughout the night.

–SALLY STANFORD (1904–1982)
AMERICAN BROTHEL OWNER

•

I keep waiting to meet a man who has more balls than I do.

–SALMA HAYEK (1966–) • MEXICAN ACTOR

I like a man who can be a real friend, has a good sense of humor, a good pair of shoes, and a healthy gold card.

–VICTORIA BECKHAM (1974–) • ENGLISH SINGER

"*MENSTRUATION*"

A period is just the beginning of a lifelong sentence.

–CATHY CRIMMINS
20TH/21ST-CENTURY AMERICAN HUMOR WRITER AND MEMOIRIST

What would happen . . . if suddenly, magically, men could menstruate and women could not?

–GLORIA STEINEM (1934–)
AMERICAN FEMINIST AND COFOUNDER OF *MS.* MAGAZINE

MENOPAUSE

Rock and menopause do not mix.

–STEVIE NICKS (1948–)
AMERICAN SINGER AND SONGWRITER

PREMENSTRUAL SYNDROME

I thought I had PMS, but my doctor said, "I've got good news and bad news. The good news is, you don't have PMS. The bad news is, you're a bitch."

–RHONDA BATES • 20TH/21ST-CENTURY AMERICAN COMEDIAN

Women complain about premenstrual syndrome, but I think of it as the only time of the month when I can be myself.

–ROSEANNE BARR (1952–) • AMERICAN COMEDIAN

I needed a pint of Ben & Jerry's Super Fudge Chunk and box of tampons. Pretty much if you're shopping for one, you're shopping for the other. The cashier checked me out and asked, "Paper or plastic?" I said, "Oh, I don't want a bag. I just want to walk down the street with these things out in front of me, and watch people get out of my way."

—SABRINA MATTHEWS • 20TH/21ST-CENTURY AMERICAN COMEDIAN

"MENTAL HEALTH"

Volumes are now written and spoken about the effect of the mind upon the body. Much of it is true. But I wish a little more was thought of the effect of the body on the mind.

—FLORENCE NIGHTINGALE (1820–1910) • ENGLISH NURSE AND MEDICAL REFORMER

Neurosis is no worse than a bad cold; you ache all over, and it's made you a mess, but you won't die from it.

—MIGNON MCLAUGHLIN (1913–1983) • AMERICAN JOURNALIST AND WRITER

I always made a point of telling the doctors I was sane, and asking to be released, but the more I endeavored to assure them of my sanity, the more they doubted it.

—NELLIE BLY (ELIZABETH JANE COCHRAN) (1864–1922)
AMERICAN INVESTIGATIVE JOURNALIST

You can always trust the information given to you by people who are crazy; they have an access to truth not available through regular channels.

—SHEILA BALLANTYNE (1936–) • AMERICAN WRITER

Sanity is a cozy lie.

—SUSAN SONTAG (1933–2004)
AMERICAN ESSAYIST, NOVELIST, INTELLECTUAL, AND ACTIVIST

Lunatics are similar to designated hitters. Often an entire family is crazy, but since an entire family can't go into the hospital, one person is designated as crazy and goes inside.

—SUSANNA KAYSEN (1948–) • AMERICAN WRITER

"MISTAKES"

We are not perfect, but we are stronger and wiser than the sum of our errors.

—AUDRE LORDE (1934–1992) • AFRICAN-AMERICAN FEMINIST WRITER AND ACTIVIST

Who thinks it just to be judged by a single error?

—BERYL MARKHAM (1902–1986)
ENGLISH-BORN KENYAN PILOT AND WRITER

A blunder at the right moment is better than cleverness at the wrong time.

—CAROLYN WELLS (1869–1942) • AMERICAN WRITER

Dwell not on the past. Use it to illustrate a point, then leave it behind. Nothing really matters except what you do now in this instant of time. From this moment onwards you can be an entirely different person, filled with love and understanding, ready with an outstretched hand, uplifted and positive in every thought and deed.

—EILEEN CADDY (1917–)
ENGLISH SPIRITUAL WRITER AND COFOUNDER OF THE FINDHORN FOUNDATION

And certainly, the mistakes that we male and female mortals make when we have our own way might fairly raise some wonder that we are so fond of it.

—GEORGE ELIOT (MARY ANN EVANS) (1819–1880) • ENGLISH WRITER

I make mistakes; I'll be the second to admit it.

—JEAN KERR (1923–2003) • AMERICAN PLAYWRIGHT AND HUMORIST

A mistake is simply another way of doing things.

–KATHARINE GRAHAM (1917–2001)
AMERICAN NEWSPAPER PUBLISHER

People who are always making allowances for themselves soon go bankrupt.

–MARY PETTIBONE POOLE • 20TH-CENTURY AMERICAN WRITER

Every great mistake has a halfway moment, a split second when it can be recalled and perhaps remedied.

–PEARL S. BUCK (1892–1973)
FIRST FEMALE AMERICAN WINNER OF THE NOBEL PRIZE IN LITERATURE

If we plant a flower or a shrub and water it daily it will grow so tall that in time we shall need a spade and a hoe to uproot it. It is just so, I think, when we commit a fault, however small, each day, and do not cure ourselves of it.

–ST. TERESA OF AVILA (1515–1582) • SPANISH MYSTIC; ROMAN CATHOLIC REFORMER

If I had my life to live again, I'd make the same mistakes, only sooner.

–TALLULAH BANKHEAD (1902–1968) • AMERICAN ACTOR

"MONEY"

Every time you spend money, you're casting a vote for the kind of world you want.

–ANNA LAPPÉ
20TH/21ST-CENTURY AMERICAN WRITER, SPEAKER, AND ACTIVIST

So they went ahead and plugged their smelly paradise—"God's Own Country" they called it in their brochures—because they knew, those clever Hotel People, that smelliness, like other people's poverty, was merely a question of getting used to. A question of discipline. Of Rigor and Air-Conditioning.

–ARUNDHATI ROY (1961-) • INDIAN NOVELIST AND ACTIVIST

Wealth is the product of man's capacity to think.

–AYN RAND (1905-1982) • RUSSIAN-AMERICAN NOVELIST AND PHILOSOPHER

The price of indulging yourself in your youth in the things you cannot afford is poverty and dependence in your old age.

–DOROTHY DIX (ELIZABETH MERIWETHER GILMER) (1870-1951)
AMERICAN JOURNALIST AND ADVICE COLUMNIST

I'd like to have money. And I'd like to be a good writer. These two can come together, and I hope they will, but if that's too adorable, I'd rather have money.

–DOROTHY PARKER (1893-1967) • AMERICAN WRITER AND CRITIC

A private railroad car is not an acquired taste. One takes to it immediately.

–ELEANOR ROBSON BELMONT (1878-1979) • ENGLISH-BORN ACTRESS

When you consider the incomes of professional sports figures compared with anyone else—it's clear that Americans overvalue trivia.

–ESTELLE RAMEY (1917-2006) • AMERICAN PROFESSOR OF BIOPHYSICS AND PHYSIOLOGY

I do want to get rich, but I never want to do what there is to do to get rich.

–GERTRUDE STEIN (1874-1946) • AMERICAN POET

The shortest period of time lies between the minute you put some money away for a rainy day and the unexpected arrival of rain.

–JANE BRYANT QUINN (1939-) • AMERICAN JOURNALIST

We owe something to extravagance, for thrift and adventure seldom go hand in hand.

–JENNIE JEROME CHURCHILL (1854–1921)
ANGLO-AMERICAN SOCIETY FIGURE AND MOTHER OF WINSTON CHURCHILL

•

Women and girls have to own a part of the system—stocks, bonds, a business—if we aren't going to be owned by it.

–JOLINE GODFREY
20TH/21ST-CENTURY AMERICAN WRITER, SPEAKER, AND COLUMNIST ON FINANCIAL LITERACY

•

To me, love, spirituality, and life are all the same thing. To me they're all about honoring the circle, and they're just different ways of defining the same understanding. Our society as a whole, because we have placed our love for money above our love for life, has devalued the sacred and devalued love.

–JULIA BUTTERFLY HILL (1974–) • AMERICAN ENVIRONMENTAL ACTIVIST

•

The easiest way for your children to learn about money is for you not to have any.

–KATHARINE WHITEHORN (1926–)
ENGLISH JOURNALIST, WRITER, AND COLUMNIST

•

I won't get out of bed for less than $10,000 a day.

–LINDA EVANGELISTA (1965–) • CANADIAN SUPERMODEL

•

Women don't have to shout for their rights or their empowerment when they are able to be economically independent; then these come automatically.

–LUCIA QUACHEY
20TH/21ST-CENTURY GHANAIAN; PRESIDENT OF
AFRICAN FEDERATION OF WOMEN ENTREPRENEURS

The flour-merchant, the house-builder, and the postman charge us no less on account of our sex; but when we endeavor to earn money to pay all these, then, indeed, we find the difference.

–LUCY STONE (1818-1893) • AMERICAN SUFFRAGIST

•

Virtue has its own reward, but no box office.

–MAE WEST (1893-1980)
AMERICAN ACTRESS, WRITER, AND SEX SYMBOL

•

It is easy to be independent when you've got money. But to be independent when you haven't got a thing—that's the Lord's test.

–MAHALIA JACKSON (1911-1972) • AFRICAN-AMERICAN GOSPEL SINGER

•

No one would remember the Good Samaritan if he'd only had good intentions—he had money, too.

–MARGARET THATCHER (1925-) • FIRST FEMALE BRITISH PRIME MINISTER

•

There can be no liberty unless there is economic liberty.

–MARGARET THATCHER (1925-) • FIRST FEMALE BRITISH PRIME MINISTER

•

Where there is money, there is fighting.

–MARIAN ANDERSON (1897-1993)
AFRICAN-AMERICAN CONTRALTO

•

People who think money can do anything may very well be suspected of doing anything for money.

–MARY PETTIBONE POOLE • 20TH-CENTURY AMERICAN WRITER

•

Having money is rather like being a blonde. It is more fun but not vital.

–MARY QUANT (1934-) • ENGLISH FASHION DESIGNER

A superfluity of wealth, and a train of domestic slaves, naturally banish a sense of general liberty, and nourish the seeds of that kind of independence that usually terminates in aristocracy.

–MERCY WARREN (1728–1814) • AMERICAN REVOLUTIONARY AND WRITER

•

I want my children to have all the things I couldn't afford. Then I want to move in with them.

–PHYLLIS DILLER (1917–) • AMERICAN COMEDIAN

•

The most popular labor saving device is still money.

–PHYLLIS GEORGE (1949–) • AMERICAN BUSINESSWOMAN AND BEAUTY QUEEN

•

Money isn't everything—but it ranks right up there with oxygen.

–RITA DAVENPORT

20TH/21ST-CENTURY AMERICAN SEMINAR LEADER, HUMORIST, AND WRITER

•

I've been rich and I've been poor. Rich is better.

–SOPHIE TUCKER (1884–1966)

RUSSIAN-BORN SINGER AND COMEDIAN

•

It is remarkable . . . what a change of temper a fixed income will bring about.

–VIRGINIA WOOLF (1882–1941)

ENGLISH NOVELIST, ESSAYIST, AND CRITIC

•

Money dignifies what is frivolous if unpaid for.

–VIRGINIA WOOLF (1882–1941)

ENGLISH NOVELIST, ESSAYIST, AND CRITIC

POVERTY

I am weary seeing our laboring classes so wretchedly housed, fed, and clothed, while thousands of dollars are wasted every year over unsightly statues. If these great men must have outdoor memorials, let them be in the form of handsome blocks of buildings for the poor.

–ELIZABETH CADY STANTON (1815-1902) • AMERICAN SUFFRAGIST, WRITER, AND THEOLOGIAN

•

Most women are one man away from welfare.

–GLORIA STEINEM (1934-)

AMERICAN FEMINIST AND COFOUNDER OF *MS.* MAGAZINE

•

Poor people are allowed the same dreams as everyone else.

–KIMI GRAY (1945-2000) • AFRICAN-AMERICAN HOUSING RIGHTS ACTIVIST

•

The incognito of lower class employment is an effective cloak for any dagger one might wish to hide.

–MARGARET CHO (1968-)

KOREAN-AMERICAN COMEDIAN AND ACTOR

•

If they want to hang me, let them. And on the scaffold I will shout "Freedom for the working class!"

–MOTHER JONES (1837-1930)

AMERICAN LABOR AND COMMUNITY ORGANIZER AND ACTIVIST

•

I didn't dream about fame. I dreamed about getting my kid more than one pair of shoes, or how to make $165 worth of groceries last all month.

–WHOOPI GOLDBERG (1955-) • AMERICAN COMEDIAN AND ACTOR

There is something about poverty that smells like death. Dead dreams dropping off the heart like leaves in dry season and rotting around the feet; impulses smothered too long in the fetid air of underground caves. The soul lives in sickly air. People can be slaveships in shoes.

–ZORA NEALE HURSTON (1891-1960) • AFRICAN-AMERICAN FOLKLORIST AND WRITER

"MOTHERS"

Why do grandparents and grandchildren get along so well? They have the same enemy: the mother.

–CLAUDETTE COLBERT (1903-1996) • FRENCH-AMERICAN ACTOR

A mother is not a person to lean on but a person to make leaning unnecessary.

–DOROTHY CANFIELD FISHER (1879-1958)
AMERICAN EDUCATIONAL REFORMER, SOCIAL ACTIVIST, AND WRITER

The art of never making a mistake is crucial to motherhood. To be effective and to gain the respect she needs to function, a mother must have her children believe she has never engaged in sex, never made a bad decision, never caused her own mother a moment's anxiety, and was never a child.

–ERMA BOMBECK (1927-1996) • AMERICAN HUMORIST

Mothers are the most instinctive philosophers.

–HARRIET BEECHER STOWE (1811-1896) • AMERICAN ABOLITIONIST

The only thing that seems eternal and natural in motherhood is ambivalence.

–JANE LAZARRE (1943-) • AMERICAN NOVELIST AND MEMOIRIST

Any mother could perform the jobs of several air-traffic controllers with ease.

–LISA ALTHER (1944-) • AMERICAN WRITER

A vacation frequently means that the family goes away for a rest, accompanied by a mother who sees that the others get it.

–MARCELENE COX • 20TH-CENTURY AMERICAN WRITER

•

There was never a great man who had not a great mother.

–OLIVE SCHREINER (1855–1920) • SOUTH AFRICAN WRITER, SOCIALIST, AND FEMINIST

•

Biology is the least of what makes someone a mother.

–OPRAH WINFREY (1954–)
AFRICAN-AMERICAN TELEVISION HOST AND MAGAZINE PUBLISHER

•

But a woman does not find out who she'll be or what life will be like until she has a child. And for most women, having a child is like having all the windows in your house painted shut forever.

–PATRICIA HENLEY (1947–) • AMERICAN WRITER

•

My mom said she learned how to swim when someone took her out in the lake and threw her off the boat. I said, "Mom, they weren't trying to teach you how to swim."

–PAULA POUNDSTONE (1959–) • AMERICAN COMEDIAN

•

What's the difference between a pitbull and a hockey mom? Lipstick.

–SARAH PALIN (1964–) • AMERICAN POLITICIAN AND CELEBRITY

•

"*MOTIVATION*"

•

I don't think necessity is the mother of invention. Invention, in my opinion, arises directly from idleness, possibly also from laziness—to save oneself trouble.

–AGATHA CHRISTIE (1890–1976) • ENGLISH MYSTERY WRITER

The future belongs to those who believe in the beauty of their dreams.

–ELEANOR ROOSEVELT (1884–1962) • AMERICAN POLITICAL LEADER AND FIRST LADY

•

To live for a principle, for the triumph of some reform by which all mankind are to be lifted up—to be wedded to an idea—may be, after all, the holiest and happiest of marriages.

–ELIZABETH CADY STANTON (1815–1902)
AMERICAN SUFFRAGIST, WRITER, AND THEOLOGIAN

•

Just don't give up trying to do what you really want to do. Where there is love and inspiration, I don't think you can go wrong.

–ELLA FITZGERALD (1917–1996) • AMERICAN JAZZ SINGER

•

I used to be driven, but I pulled over.

–HEIDI JOYCE
20TH/21ST-CENTURY AMERICAN COMEDIAN

•

If you don't know what your passion is, realize that one reason for your existence on earth is to find it.

–OPRAH WINFREY (1954–)
AFRICAN-AMERICAN TELEVISION HOST AND MAGAZINE PUBLISHER

•

I shall wrassle me up a future or die trying. . . . I am going after things.

–ZORA NEALE HURSTON (1891–1960) • AFRICAN-AMERICAN FOLKLORIST AND WRITER

•

"MUSIC"

•

The truest expression of a people is in its dances and its music. . . . Bodies never lie.

–AGNES DE MILLE (1905–1993) • AMERICAN DANCER AND CHOREOGRAPHER

Music melts all the separate parts of our bodies together.

–ANAÏS NIN (1903–1977) • FRENCH WRITER AND DIARIST

•

Music has been my playmate, my lover, and my crying towel.

–BUFFY SAINTE-MARIE (1941–)
CANADIAN NATIVE AMERICAN SONGWRITER AND EDUCATOR

•

God had to create disco music so that I could be born and be successful.

–DONNA SUMMER (1948–) • AMERICAN DISCO SINGER

•

I wish the government would put a tax on pianos for the incompetent.

–EDITH SITWELL (1887–1964) • ENGLISH POET AND CRITIC

•

Some people say I cannot sing, but no one can say I didn't sing.

–FLORENCE FOSTER JENKINS (1868–1944)
AMERICAN SOPRANO

•

There is no feeling, except the extremes of fear and grief, that does not find relief in music.

–GEORGE ELIOT (MARY ANN EVANS) (1819–1880) • ENGLISH WRITER

•

Going to the opera, like getting drunk, is a sin that carries its own punishment with it.

–HANNAH MORE (1745–1833)
ENGLISH PLAYWRIGHT, RELIGIOUS WRITER, AND PHILANTHROPIST

•

Ah, music. A magic beyond all we do here!

–J. K. ROWLING (1965–) • ENGLISH WRITER

It seems to me that those songs that have been any good, I have nothing much to do with the writing of them. The words have just crawled down my sleeve and come out on the page.

–JOAN BAEZ (1941–) • AMERICAN FOLK SINGER AND ACTIVIST

An artist, in giving a concert, should not demand an entrance fee but should ask the public to pay, just before leaving, as much as they like. From the sum he would be able to judge what the world thinks of him—and we would have fewer mediocre concerts.

–KIT COLEMAN (1864–1915) • IRISH-CANADIAN JOURNALIST

I worry that the person who thought up Muzak may be thinking up something else.

–LILY TOMLIN (1939–) • AMERICAN COMEDIAN AND ACTOR

A lot of people are singing about how screwed up the world is, and I don't think that everybody wants to hear about that all the time.

–MARIAH CAREY (1970–) • AMERICAN POP AND R&B SINGER AND SONGWRITER

Music was my refuge. I could crawl into the space between the notes and curl my back to loneliness.

–MAYA ANGELOU (1928–) • AFRICAN-AMERICAN POET, MEMOIRIST, AND CIVIL RIGHTS ACTIVIST

It had never occurred to me before that music and thinking are so much alike. In fact you could say music is another way of thinking, or maybe thinking is another kind of music.

–URSULA K. LE GUIN (1929–) • AMERICAN WRITER

All my concerts had no sounds in them; they were completely silent. People had to make up their own music in their minds!

–YOKO ONO (1933–) • JAPANESE-BORN AMERICAN MUSICIAN, ARTIST, AND PEACE ACTIVIST

N

"NATURE"

In nature, nothing is perfect and everything is perfect. Trees can be contorted, bent in weird ways, and they're still beautiful.

—ALICE WALKER (1944–) • AFRICAN-AMERICAN WRITER AND POET

The best remedy for those who are afraid, lonely, or unhappy is to go outside, somewhere where they can be quiet, alone with the heavens, nature, and God. Because only then does one feel that all is as it should be and that God wishes to see people happy, amidst the simple beauty of nature.

—ANNE FRANK (1929–1945) • GERMAN-JEWISH DIARIST

After all, I don't see why I am always asking for private, individual, selfish miracles when every year there are miracles like white dogwood.

—ANNE MORROW LINDBERGH (1906–2001) • AMERICAN WRITER AND PIONEERING AVIATOR

Nature is just enough; but men and women must comprehend and accept her suggestions.

—ANTOINETTE BROWN BLACKWELL (1825–1921)
AMERICAN SUFFRAGIST, MINISTER, AND WRITER

Every year, back comes spring, with nasty little birds yapping their fool heads off and the ground all mucked up with plants.

—DOROTHY PARKER (1893–1967) • AMERICAN WRITER AND CRITIC

Nature is, by and large, to be found out of doors, a location where, it cannot be argued, there are never enough comfortable chairs.

—FRAN LEBOWITZ (1950–) • AMERICAN HUMORIST

Man is a complex being who makes deserts bloom and lakes die.

—GLADYS BRONWYN STERN (1890–1973) • ENGLISH WRITER

Once you have heard the lark, known the swish of feet through hill-top grass and smelt the earth made ready for the seed, you are never again going to be fully happy about the cities and towns that man carries like a crippling weight upon his back.

–GWYN THOMAS (1913–1981) • WELSH WRITER

I don't believe in evil, I believe only in horror. In nature there is no evil, only an abundance of horror: the plagues and the blights and the ants and the maggots.

–ISAK DINESEN (KAREN BLIXEN) (1885–1962) • DANISH WRITER AND AUTOBIOGRAPHER

A man has every season while a woman only has the right to spring.

–JANE FONDA (1937–) • AMERICAN ACTRESS, FITNESS CELEBRITY, AND POLITICAL ACTIVIST

Of all the language sources, the loss of nature seems the saddest. A thousand times a day, nature—in the most ordinary of places—has something to tell or show us; something it wants us to touch, smell, or feel; something it wants all of us, not just the overtly artistic, to express.

–JOYCE MCGREEVY • 20TH/21ST-CENTURY AMERICAN WRITER AND GARDENER

For every person who has ever lived there has come, at last, a spring he will never see. Glory then in the springs that are yours.

–PAM BROWN • 20TH-CENTURY AUSTRALIAN POET

I am comforted by life's stability, by earth's unchangeableness. What has seemed new and frightening assumes its place in the unfolding of knowledge. It is good to know our universe. What is new is only new to us.

–PEARL S. BUCK (1892–1973)
FIRST FEMALE AMERICAN WINNER OF THE NOBEL PRIZE IN LITERATURE

Man's attitude toward nature is today critically important simply because we have now acquired a fateful power to alter and destroy nature. But man is a part of nature and his war against nature is inevitably a war against himself.

—RACHEL CARSON (1907–1964) • AMERICAN ZOOLOGIST AND MARINE BIOLOGIST

•

It is a wholesome and necessary thing for us to turn again to the earth and in the contemplation of her beauties to know of wonder and humility.

—RACHEL CARSON (1907–1964) • AMERICAN ZOOLOGIST AND MARINE BIOLOGIST

•

We need to find God, and he cannot be found in noise and restlessness. God is the friend of silence. See how nature—trees, flowers, grass—grows in silence; see the stars, the moon and the sun, how they move in silence. . . . We need silence to be able to touch souls.

—MOTHER TERESA (1910–1997) • ALBANIAN CATHOLIC NUN; WINNER OF NOBEL PEACE PRIZE

•

Landscape shapes culture.

TERRY TEMPEST WILLIAMS
20TH/21ST-CENTURY AMERICAN ESSAYIST AND NATURALIST

•

Birth, life, and death—each took place on the hidden side of a leaf.

—TONI MORRISON (1931–) • NOBEL PRIZE–WINNING AFRICAN-AMERICAN NOVELIST

•

WATER

The voice of the sea speaks to the soul.

—KATE CHOPIN (1850–1904) • AMERICAN WRITER

•

For all at last returns to the sea—to Oceanus, the ocean river, like the everflowing stream of time, the beginning and the end.

—RACHEL CARSON (1907–1964) • AMERICAN ZOOLOGIST AND MARINE BIOLOGIST

All water has a perfect memory and is forever trying to get back to where it was.

–TONI MORRISON (1931–) • NOBEL PRIZE–WINNING AFRICAN-AMERICAN NOVELIST

"NORMALCY"

To discover what normal means, you have to surf a tide of weirdness.

–CHARLOTTE RAMPLING (1946–) • ENGLISH ACTOR

A normal human being . . . does not exist.

–KAREN HORNEY (1885–1952)
GERMAN NEO-FREUDIAN PSYCHOANALYST

The truly fearless think of themselves as normal.

–MARGARET ATWOOD (1939–)
CANADIAN POET, NOVELIST, CRITIC, AND ACTIVIST

Normal day, let me be aware of the treasure you are. Let me learn from you, love you, savor you, bless you before you depart. Let me not pass you by in quest of some rare and perfect tomorrow.

–MARY JEAN IRION (1922–) • AMERICAN POET AND WRITER

If society ever achieves a higher standard of what consitutes normality, it will have been the neurotic who led the way.

–NANCY HALE (1933–) • AMERICAN FEMINIST WRITER

As we do at such times, I turned on my automatic pilot and went through the motions of normalcy on the outside, so that I could concentrate all my powers on surviving the near-mortal wound on the inside.

–SONIA JOHNSON (1936–) • AMERICAN WRITER AND FEMINIST ACTIVIST

Normal is in the eye of the beholder.

–WHOOPI GOLDBERG (1955-)
AMERICAN COMEDIAN AND ACTOR

"NUDITY"

Nudity is who people are at the most interesting point of the evening, when they take off their protective layer, when no one is watching.

–BRIDGET FONDA (1964-) • AMERICAN ACTOR

I come from a country where you don't wear clothes most of the year. Nudity is the most natural state. I was born nude, and I hope to be buried nude.

–ELLE MACPHERSON (1963-) • AUSTRALIAN SUPERMODEL AND ACTOR

Unfortunately it is true that the more flesh you show, the further up the ladder you go.

–JERRY HALL (1956-) • AMERICAN MODEL AND ACTOR

I wouldn't do nudity in films. . . . To act with my clothes on is a performance; to act with my clothes off is a documentary.

–JULIA ROBERTS (1967-) • AMERICAN ACTOR

I think on-stage nudity is disgusting, shameful, and damaging to all things American. But if I were 22 with a great body, it would be artistic, tasteful, patriotic, and a progressive religious experience.

–SHELLEY WINTERS (1920-2006) • AMERICAN ACTOR

O

"OTHERS' OPINIONS"

I would much rather have regrets about not doing what people said than regretting not doing what my heart led me to and wondering what life had been like if I'd just been myself.

—BRITTANY RENÉE (1986-) • ENGLISH WRITER AND DANCER

Let me listen to me and not to them.

—GERTRUDE STEIN (1874-1946) • AMERICAN POET

I have no regrets. I wouldn't have lived my life the way I did if I was going to worry about what people were going to say.

—INGRID BERGMAN (1915-1982) • SWEDISH ACTOR

You are not in business to be popular.

—KIRSTIE ALLEY (1951-) • AMERICAN ACTOR

If you just set out to be liked, you would be prepared to compromise on anything at any time, and you would achieve nothing.

—MARGARET THATCHER (1925-) • FIRST FEMALE BRITISH PRIME MINISTER

We are so vain that we even care for the opinions of those we don't care for.

—MARIE VON EBNER-ESCHENBACH (1830-1916) • AUSTRIAN WRITER

Literature is strewn with the wreckage of those who have minded beyond reason the opinion of others.

—VIRGINIA WOOLF (1882-1941) • ENGLISH NOVELIST, ESSAYIST, AND CRITIC

P

"PAINTING"

Sometimes I could quit paint and take to charring. It must be fine to clean perfectly, to shine and polish and know that it could not be done better. In painting that never occurs.

–EMILY CARR (1871–1945) • CANADIAN ARTIST AND WRITER

They thought I was Surrealist, but I wasn't. I never painted dreams. I painted my own reality.

–FRIDA KAHLO (1907–1954) • MEXICAN PAINTER

If I hadn't started painting, I would have raised chickens.

–GRANDMA MOSES (1860–1961) • AMERICAN FOLK ARTIST

You take a painting, you have a white, virginal piece of canvas that is the world of purity, and then you put your imagery on it, and you try to bring it back to the original purity.

–LOUISE NEVELSON (1899–1988) • RUSSIAN-BORN AMERICAN SCULPTOR AND PRINTMAKER

"PARENTING"

Parents can only give good advice or put them on the right paths, but the final forming of a person's character lies in their own hands.

–ANNE FRANK (1929–1945) • GERMAN-JEWISH DIARIST

It kills you to see them grow up. But I guess it would kill you quicker if they didn't.

–BARBARA KINGSOLVER (1955–) • AMERICAN WRITER

If you have never been hated by your child you have never been a parent.

–BETTE DAVIS (1908–1989) • AMERICAN ACTOR

•

Strange new problems are being reported in the growing generations of children whose mothers were always there, driving them around, helping them with their homework: an inability to endure pain or discipline, or pursue any self-sustained goal of any sort—a devastating boredom with life.

–BETTY FRIEDAN (1921–2006)
AMERICAN FEMINIST, WRITER, AND COFOUNDER OF NATIONAL ORGANIZATION FOR WOMEN

•

The best way to keep children home is to make the home atmosphere pleasant—and let the air out of the tires.

–DOROTHY PARKER (1893–1967) • AMERICAN WRITER AND CRITIC

•

The central struggle of parenthood is to let our hopes for our children outweigh our fears.

–ELLEN GOODMAN (1941–) • AMERICAN JOURNALIST

•

A father is always making his baby into a little woman. And when she is a woman he turns her back again.

–ENID BAGNOLD (1889–1981) • ENGLISH WRITER

•

Ask your child what he wants for dinner only if he's buying.

–FRAN LEBOWITZ (1950–) • AMERICAN HUMORIST

•

Although there are many trial marriages . . . there is no such thing as a trial child.

–GAIL SHEEHY (1937–) • AMERICAN SOCIAL CRITIC

•

We've begun to raise daughters more like sons . . . but few have the courage to raise our sons more like our daughters.

–GLORIA STEINEM (1934–) • AMERICAN FEMINIST AND COFOUNDER OF *MS.* MAGAZINE

Adorable children are considered to be the general property of the human race. Rude children belong to their mother.

–JUDITH "MISS MANNERS" MARTIN (1938–)
AMERICAN ETIQUETTE EXPERT

A food is not necessarily essential just because your child hates it.

–KATHARINE WHITEHORN (1926–) • ENGLISH JOURNALIST, WRITER, AND COLUMNIST

You see much more of your children once they leave home.

–LUCILLE BALL (1911–1989) • AMERICAN COMIC ACTOR

Two important things to teach a child: to do and to do without.

–MARCELENE COX • 20TH-CENTURY AMERICAN WRITER

Never help a child with a task at which he feels he can succeed.

–MARIA MONTESSORI (1870–1952)
ITALIAN EDUCATIONAL INNOVATOR, SCIENTIST, AND PHILOSOPHER

It is the responsibility of every adult . . . to make sure that children hear what we have learned from the lessons of life and to hear over and over that we love them and that they are not alone.

–MARIAN WRIGHT EDELMAN (1939–)
AFRICAN-AMERICAN FOUNDER OF THE CHILDREN'S DEFENSE FUND

Like all parents, my husband and I just do the best we can, and hold our breath, and hope we've set aside enough money to pay for our kids' therapy.

–MICHELLE PFEIFFER (1958–) • AMERICAN ACTOR

Loving a child doesn't mean giving in to all his whims; to love him is to bring out the best in him, to teach him to love what is difficult.

–NADIA BOULANGER (1887–1979) • FRENCH COMPOSER, CONDUCTOR, AND MUSIC PROFESSOR

It would seem that something which means poverty, disorder, and violence every single day should be avoided entirely, but the desire to beget children is a natural urge.

–PHYLLIS DILLER (1917–) • AMERICAN COMEDIAN

•

If a child is to keep alive his inborn sense of wonder, he needs the companionship of at least one adult who can share it, rediscovering with him the joy, excitement, and mystery of the world we live in.

–RACHEL CARSON (1907–1964) • AMERICAN ZOOLOGIST AND MARINE BIOLOGIST

•

Whenever I held my newborn baby in my arms, I used to think that what I said and did to him could have an influence not only on him but on all whom he met, not only for a day or a month or a year, but for all eternity—a very challenging and exciting thought for a mother.

–ROSE KENNEDY (1890–1995) • AMERICAN; MOTHER OF JOHN F. KENNEDY

•

When my husband comes home, if the kids are still alive, I figure I've done my job.

–ROSEANNE BARR (1952–) • AMERICAN COMEDIAN

•

Home is the place where boys and girls first learn how to limit their wishes, abide by rules, and consider the rights and needs of others.

–SIDONIE MATSNER GRUENBERG (1881–1974)
AUSTRIAN-BORN DIRECTOR OF CHILD STUDY ASSOCIATION

•

When you are a mother, you are never really alone in your thoughts. A mother always has to think twice, once for herself and once for her child.

–SOPHIA LOREN (1934–) • ITALIAN ACTOR

That's the thing about independently minded children. You bring them up teaching them to question authority, and you forget that the very first authority they question is you.

–SUSAN SARANDON (1946-) • AMERICAN ACTOR AND POLITICAL ACTIVIST

If your kids are giving you a headache, follow the directions on the aspirin bottle, especially the part that says "keep away from children."

–SUSAN SAVANNAH • 20TH/21ST-CENTURY AMERICAN HUMORIST

Two parents can't raise a child any more than one. You need a whole community—everybody—to raise a child.

–TONI MORRISON (1931-) • NOBEL PRIZE-WINNING AFRICAN-AMERICAN NOVELIST

"PEACE"

It's odd how those who dismiss the peace movement as utopian don't hesitate to proffer the most absurdly dreamy reasons for going to war: to stamp out terrorism, install democracy, eliminate fascism, and most entertainingly, to "rid the world of evil-doers."

–ARUNDHATI ROY (1961-) • INDIAN NOVELIST AND ACTIVIST

Peace, development, and justice are all connected to each other. We cannot talk about economic development without talking about peace. How can we expect economic development in a battlefield?

–AUNG SAN SUU KYI (1945-) • BURMESE OPPOSITION LEADER AND NOBEL LAUREATE

For it isn't enough to talk about peace. One must believe in it. And it isn't enough to believe in it. One must work for it.

–ELEANOR ROOSEVELT (1884-1962) • AMERICAN POLITICAL LEADER AND FIRST LADY

You don't have to have fought in a war to love peace.

–GERALDINE FERRARO (1935–)
AMERICAN POLITICIAN AND NOMINEE FOR U.S. VICE PRESIDENT

•

I do not want the peace which passeth understanding, I want the understanding which bringeth peace.

–HELEN KELLER (1880–1968) • AMERICAN WRITER AND ACTIVIST

•

You cannot shake hands with a clenched fist.

–INDIRA GANDHI (1917–1984) • PRIME MINISTER OF INDIA

•

I believe in both my right and my responsibility to work to create a world that doesn't glorify violence and war, but where we seek different solutions to our common problems. I believe that these days, daring to voice your opinion, daring to find out information from a variety of sources, can be an act of courage.

–JODY WILLIAMS (1950–)
AMERICAN NOBEL PEACE PRIZE RECIPIENT AND ACTIVIST

•

Establishing lasting peace is the work of education; all politics can do is keep us out of war.

–MARIA MONTESSORI (1870–1952)
ITALIAN EDUCATIONAL INNOVATOR, SCIENTIST, AND PHILOSOPHER

•

If we have no peace, it is because we have forgotten that we belong to each other.

–MOTHER TERESA (1910–1997)
ALBANIAN CATHOLIC NUN; WINNER OF NOBEL PEACE PRIZE

•

America must be a light to the world, not just a missile.

–NANCY PELOSI (1940–) • US SPEAKER OF THE HOUSE

Recognizing that sustainable development, democracy, and peace are indivisible is an idea whose time has come.

—WANGARI MAATHAI (1940–)
KENYAN ENVIRONMENTALIST, FOUNDER OF THE GREEN BELT MOVEMENT, AND WINNER OF THE NOBEL PEACE PRIZE

"PEOPLE"

A hundred years from now? All new people.

—ANNE LAMOTT (1954–)
AMERICAN NOVELIST AND MEMOIRIST

If people are informed, they will do the right thing. It's when they are not informed that they become hostages to prejudice.

—CHARLAYNE HUNTER-GAULT (1942–)
AFRICAN-AMERICAN JOURNALIST AND CNN BUREAU CHIEF

I do not want people to be agreeable, as it saves me the trouble of liking them.

—JANE AUSTEN (1775–1817) • ENGLISH WRITER

There are some people who leave impressions not so lasting as the imprint of an oar upon the water.

—KATE CHOPIN (1850–1904) • AMERICAN WRITER

The people and circumstances around me do not make me what I am, they reveal who I am.

—LAURA SCHLESSINGER (1947–)
AMERICAN CULTURAL COMMENTATOR

"PERFECTION"

When things are perfect, that's when you need to worry most.

–DREW BARRYMORE (1975–) • AMERICAN ACTRESS AND PRODUCER

Striving for excellence motivates you; striving for perfection is demoralizing.

–HARRIET BRAIKER (1948–2004) • AMERICAN PSYCHOLOGIST AND WRITER

Perfectionism is not a quest for the best. It is a pursuit of the worst in ourselves, the part that tells us that nothing we do will ever be good enough—that we should try harder.

–JULIA CAMERON • 20TH/21ST-CENTURY AMERICAN WRITER

Practice is a means of inviting the perfection desired.

–MARTHA GRAHAM (1894–1991)
AMERICAN DANCER AND CHOREOGRAPHER

"PERSEVERANCE"

There are no shortcuts to any place worth going.

–BEVERLY SILLS (1929–)
AMERICAN OPERA SINGER AND OPERA MANAGER

Champions keep playing until they get it right.

–BILLIE JEAN KING (1943–) • AMERICAN TENNIS PLAYER

Be patient. It may take 30 years, but sooner or later they'll listen to you, and in the meantime, keep kicking ass.

–FLORYNCE KENNEDY (1916–2000)
AFRICAN-AMERICAN LAWYER AND ACTIVIST

If someone asked you, "Can you swim a mile?" you'd say, "Nah." But if you found yourself dumped out at sea, you'd swim the mile. You'd make it.

–GERTRUDE BOYLE (1923–)
AMERICAN ENTREPRENEUR AND CHAIR OF COLUMBIA SPORTSWEAR

I refused to take no for an answer.

–BESSIE COLEMAN (1892–1926)
FIRST AFRICAN-AMERICAN WOMAN TO BECOME AN AIRPLANE PILOT

When you get into a tight place, and everything goes against you, till it seems as though you could not hold on a moment longer, never give up then—for that is just the place and time that the tide will turn.

–HARRIET BEECHER STOWE (1811–1896) • AMERICAN ABOLITIONIST

Defeat is simply a signal to press onward.

–HELEN KELLER (1880–1968)
AMERICAN WRITER AND ACTIVIST

I've got a woman's ability to stick to a job and get on with it when everyone else walks off and leaves it.

–MARGARET THATCHER (1925–)
FIRST FEMALE BRITISH PRIME MINISTER

You may have to fight a battle more than once to win it.

–MARGARET THATCHER (1925–)
FIRST FEMALE BRITISH PRIME MINISTER

This is rather different from the receptions I used to get 50 years ago. They threw things at me then—but they were not roses.

–SUSAN B. ANTHONY (1820–1906)
AMERICAN SUFFRAGIST AND NEWSPAPER PUBLISHER

"PETS"

See Animals, Cats, Dogs, Horses

"PLASTIC SURGERY"

Everyone should have enough money to get plastic surgery.

—BEVERLY JOHNSON (1952–) • AFRICAN-AMERICAN SUPERMODEL

I don't have a problem with someone having plastic surgery, but I think it's crazy for everyone to have the same body.

—EVA GREEN (1980–) • FRENCH ACTRESS AND COMPOSER

I wish I had a twin, so I could know what I'd look like without plastic surgery.

—JOAN RIVERS (1933–)
AMERICAN COMEDIAN AND TELEVISION HOST

Plastic surgery and breast implants are fine for people who want that, if it makes them feel better about who they are. But it makes these people, actors especially, fantasy figures for a fantasy world. Acting is about being real—being honest.

—KATE WINSLET (1975–) • ENGLISH ACTOR

If anybody says their facelift doesn't hurt, they're lying. It was like I'd spent the night with an ax murderer.

—SHARON OSBOURNE (1952–)
ENGLISH MUSIC PROMOTER AND TELEVISION PERSONALITY

Researchers reported that they developed a "self-healing" plastic that repairs itself if cracked. The plastic will change the way airplanes are built and medicine is practiced. In a related story, Joan Rivers will never die.

—TINA FEY (1970–) • AMERICAN WRITER, COMEDIAN, AND ACTOR

"POLITICS"

I've learned in my years as a journalist that when a politician says, "That's ridiculous," you're probably on the right track.

—AMY GOODMAN (1957–)
AMERICAN BROADCAST JOURNALIST

We have done almost everything in pairs since Noah, except govern. And the world has suffered for it.

—BELLA ABZUG (1920–1998)
AMERICAN FEMINIST AND POLITICIAN

Basically, I have no place in organized politics. By coming to the British Parliament, I've allowed the people to sacrifice me at the top and let go the more effective job I should be doing at the bottom.

—BERNADETTE DEVLIN (1947–) • IRISH POLITICIAN AND ACTIVIST

Years ago fairy tales all began with "Once upon a time . . ."; now we know they all begin with "If I am elected. . . ."

—CAROLYN WARNER
20TH/21ST-CENTURY AMERICAN PROFESSOR OF POLITICAL SCIENCE AND GLOBAL STUDIES

The argument of the broken pane of glass is the most valuable argument in modern politics.

—EMMELINE PANKHURST (1858–1928) • ENGLISH SUFFRAGIST AND FEMINIST

If the ass is protecting the system, ass-kicking should be undertaken, regardless of the sex, ethnicity, or charm of the ass involved.

—FLORYNCE KENNEDY (1916–2000) • AFRICAN-AMERICAN LAWYER AND ACTIVIST

•

Nail polish or false eyelashes isn't politics. If you have good politics, what you wear is irrelevant. I don't take dictation from the pig-o-cratic style setters who say I should dress like a middle-aged colored lady. My politics don't depend on whether my tits are in or out of a bra.

—FLORYNCE KENNEDY (1916–2000) • AFRICAN-AMERICAN LAWYER AND ACTIVIST

•

Our democracy is but a name. We vote? What does that mean? It means that we choose between two bodies of real, though not avowed, autocrats. We choose between Tweedledum and Tweedledee.

—HELEN KELLER (1880–1968) • AMERICAN WRITER AND ACTIVIST

•

There is no such thing as being nonpolitical. Just by making a decision to stay out of politics you are making the decision to allow others to shape politics and exert power over you. And if you are alienated from the current political system, then just by staying out of it you do nothing to change it, you simply entrench it.

—JANET KIRNER (1938–) • AUSTRALIAN POLITICIAN

•

You are interested in the kitchen of the world—you want to find out what is cooking, who has a finger in the pie, and who will burn his finger.

—QUEEN JULIANA (1909–2004) • QUEEN OF THE NETHERLANDS

•

Ninety-eight percent of the adults in this country are decent, hard working, honest Americans. It's the other lousy two percent that get all the publicity. But then, we elected them.

—LILY TOMLIN (1939–) • AMERICAN COMEDIAN AND ACTOR

Politics has less to do with where you live than where your heart is.

–MARGARET CHO (1968–) • KOREAN-AMERICAN COMEDIAN AND ACTOR

In politics if you want anything said, ask a man.
If you want anything done, ask a woman.

–MARGARET THATCHER (1925–)
FIRST FEMALE BRITISH PRIME MINISTER

The reason there are so few female politicians is that it is too much trouble to put makeup on two faces.

–MAUREEN MURPHY (1952–) • AMERICAN POLITICIAN

Everybody's for democracy in principle. It's only in practice that the thing gives rise to stiff objections.

–MEG GREENFIELD (1930–1999) • AMERICAN POLITICAL JOURNALIST

The mistake a lot of politicians make is in forgetting they've been appointed and thinking they've been anointed.

–MILDRED WEBSTER PEPPER (1904–1979) • AMERICAN HUMANITARIAN AND REFORMER

I was cooking breakfast this morning for my kids, and I thought, "He's [Ronald Reagan] just like a Teflon frying pan: Nothing sticks to him."

–PAT SCHROEDER (1940–) • AMERICAN POLITICIAN

There is this idea that you can stay home and make the world better for your family—well, you can make it a whole lot better for a lot more people if you get out and do something about public policy.

–PAT SCHROEDER (1940–) • AMERICAN POLITICIAN

The advance planning and sense stimuli employed to capture a $10 million cigarette or soap market are nothing compared to the brainwashing and propaganda blitzes used to ensure control of the largest cash market in the world: the Executive Branch of the United States government.

–PHYLLIS SCHLAFLY (1924–) • AMERICAN WRITER AND CONSERVATIVE POLITICAL ACTIVIST

It's useless to hold a person to anything he says while he's in love, drunk, or running for office.

–SHIRLEY MACLAINE (1934–) • AMERICAN ACTOR AND WRITER

"PORNOGRAPHY"

Erotica is simply high-class pornography; better produced, better conceived, better executed, better packaged, designed for a better class of consumer.

–ANDREA DWORKIN (1946–2005) • AMERICAN RADICAL FEMINIST

Pornographers are the enemies of women only because our contemporary ideology of pornography does not encompass the possibility of change, as if we were the slaves of history and not its makers. Pornography is a satire on human pretensions.

–ANGELA CARTER (1940–1992) • ENGLISH WRITER AND JOURNALIST

Pornography is literature designed to be read with one hand.

–ANGELA LAMBERT (1940–) • ENGLISH JOURNALIST, ART CRITIC, AND WRITER

Those Romans who perpetrated the rape of the Sabines, for example, did not work themselves up for the deed by screening *Debbie Does Dallas*, and the monkish types who burned a million or so witches in the Middle Ages had almost certainly not come across *Boobs and Buns* or related periodicals.

–BARBARA EHRENREICH (1941–) • AMERICAN ESSAYIST AND SOCIAL CRITIC

If pornographers can hook adolescents when their hormones are raging, they know they'll have an ongoing consumer base for life.

–DONNA RICE (1958–) • AMERICAN MODEL AND ANTI-CHILD-PORNOGRAPHY ACTIVIST

•

My reaction to porn films is as follows: After the first ten minutes, I want to go home and screw. After the first twenty minutes, I never want to screw again as long as I live.

–ERICA JONG (1942–) • AMERICAN WRITER

•

The difference between pornography and erotica is lighting.

–GLORIA LEONARD (1940–)
AMERICAN EROTIC ACTRESS AND MAGAZINE PUBLISHER

•

A woman reading *Playboy* feels a little like a Jew reading a Nazi manual.

–GLORIA STEINEM (1934–) • AMERICAN FEMINIST AND COFOUNDER OF *MS.* MAGAZINE

•

Erotica is using a feather; pornography is using the whole chicken.

–ISABEL ALLENDE (1942–) • CHILEAN-AMERICAN WRITER

•

I would like to see all people who read pornography or have anything to do with it put in a mental hospital for observation so we could find out what we have done to them.

–LINDA LOVELACE (1949-2002) • AMERICAN PORNOGRAPHIC ACTOR

•

Pornography is pornography: what is there to see? Movies are attempting to destroy something that's supposed to be the most beautiful thing a man and a woman can have by making it cheap and common. It's what you don't see that's attractive.

–NANCY REAGAN (1921–) • FIRST LADY OF THE UNITED STATES

Pornography exists for the lonesome, the ugly,
the fearful—it's made for the losers.

–RITA MAE BROWN (1944–)
AMERICAN NOVELIST AND ACTIVIST

•

What pornographic literature does is precisely to drive a wedge between one's existence as a full human being and one's existence as a sexual being—while in ordinary life a healthy person is one who prevents such a gap from opening up.

–SUSAN SONTAG (1933–2004) • AMERICAN ESSAYIST, NOVELIST, INTELLECTUAL, AND ACTIVIST

•

The pornography of violence of course far exceeds, in volume and general acceptance, sexual pornography, in this Puritan land of ours. Exploiting the apocalypse, selling the holocaust, is a pornography. For the ultimate selling job on ultimate violence one must read those works of fiction issued by our government as manuals of civil defense, in which you learn that there's nothing to be afraid of if you've stockpiled lots of dried fruit.

–URSULA K. LE GUIN (1929–) • AMERICAN WRITER

•

"POWER"

•

Do not put such unlimited power into the hands of the husbands.
Remember all men would be tyrants if they could.

–ABIGAIL ADAMS (1744–1818) • FIRST LADY OF THE UNITED STATES

•

Beware of trying to accomplish anything by force.

–SISTER ANGELA MERICI (1474–1540)
ITALIAN FOUNDER OF URSULINE NUNS

I shall be an autocrat, that's my trade; and
the good Lord will forgive me, that's his.

–CATHERINE THE GREAT (1729–1796)
RUSSIAN EMPRESS

•

Openly questioning the way the world works and challenging the power of the powerful is not an activity customarily rewarded.

–DALE SPENDER (1943–)
AUSTRALIAN SOCIOLINGUIST AND TECHNOLOGY THEORIST

•

This world is run by people who know how to do things. They know how things work. They are equipped. Up there, there's a layer of people who run everything. But we—we're just peasants. We don't understand what's going on, and we can't do anything.

–DORIS LESSING (1919–) • ENGLISH WRITER

•

Power is the ability not to have to please.

–ELIZABETH JANEWAY (1913–2005)
AMERICAN NOVELIST AND CRITIC

•

Women are the only exploited group in history
to have been idealized into powerlessness.

–ERICA JONG (1942–) • AMERICAN WRITER

•

In short, the characteristics of the powerful, whatever they may be, are thought to be better than the characteristics of the powerless—and logic has nothing to do with it.

–GLORIA STEINEM (1934–) • AMERICAN FEMINIST AND COFOUNDER OF *MS.* MAGAZINE

Women will not become more empowered merely because we want them to be, but through legislative changes, increased information, and redirection of resources. It would be fatal to overlook this issue.

–GRO HARLEM BRUNDTLAND (1939–)
NORWEGIAN DIPLOMAT, PHYSICIAN, AND INTERNATIONAL LEADER

•

Power . . . is not an end in itself, but is an instrument that must be used toward an end.

–JEANE KIRKPATRICK (1926–)
AMERICAN POLITICAL SCIENTIST, FIRST FEMALE U.S. AMBASSADOR TO THE UNITED NATIONS

•

Justice is a concept. Muscle is the reality.

–LINDA BLANDFORD
20TH/21ST-CENTURY ENGLISH JOURNALIST

•

I do not wish [women] to have power over men, but over themselves.

–MARY WOLLSTONECRAFT (1759–1797) • ENGLISH WRITER

•

Unless you choose to do great things with it, it makes no difference how much you are rewarded, or how much power you have.

–OPRAH WINFREY (1954–)
AFRICAN-AMERICAN TELEVISION HOST AND MAGAZINE PUBLISHER

•

The thing women have yet to learn is nobody gives you power. You just take it.

–ROSEANNE BARR (1952–) • AMERICAN COMEDIAN

•

Scientific progress makes moral progress a necessity; for if man's power is increased, the checks that restrain him from abusing it must be strengthened.

–MADAME DE STAËL (1766–1817) • SWISS-BORN FRENCH WRITER AND FEMINIST

"PRAISE"

A pat on the back is only a few vertebrae removed from a kick in the pants, but is miles ahead in results.

–ELLA WHEELER WILCOX (1850–1919) • AMERICAN POET AND JOURNALIST

I can eat it with a spoon or with a soup ladle or anything, and I like it.

–GERTRUDE STEIN (1874–1946) • AMERICAN POET

Commending a right thing is a cheap substitute for doing it, with which we are too apt to satisfy ourselves.

–HANNAH MORE (1745–1833)
ENGLISH PLAYWRIGHT, RELIGIOUS WRITER, AND PHILANTHROPIST

Sandwich every bit of criticism between two layers of praise.

–MARY KAY ASH (1918–2001) • AMERICAN COSMETICS ENTREPRENEUR

Praise out of season, or tactlessly bestowed, can freeze the heart as much as blame.

–PEARL S. BUCK (1892–1973)
FIRST FEMALE AMERICAN WINNER OF THE NOBEL PRIZE IN LITERATURE

Praise is warming and desirable . . . what the human race lives on like bread. But praise is an earned thing. It has to be deserved like an honorary degree or a hug from a child. A compliment is manna, a free gift.

–PHYLLIS MCGINLEY (1905–1978) • AMERICAN POET, ESSAYIST, AND WRITER

"PREGNANCY"

If men were equally at risk from this condition—if they knew their bellies might swell as if they were suffering from end-stage cirrhosis, that they would have to go nearly a year without a stiff drink, a cigarette, or even an aspirin, that they would be subject to fainting spells and unable to fight their way onto commuter trains—then I am sure that pregnancy would be classified as a sexually transmitted disease and abortions would be no more controversial than emergency appendectomies.

–BARBARA EHRENREICH (1941–) • AMERICAN ESSAYIST AND SOCIAL CRITIC

When I had almost reached my term, I looked like a rat dragging a stolen egg.

–COLETTE (1873–1954) • FRENCH NOVELIST

Her child was like a load that held her down, and yet like a hand that pulled her to her feet.

–EDITH WHARTON (1862–1937) • AMERICAN WRITER

Every pregnant woman should be surrounded with every possible comfort.

–FLORA L. S. ALDRICH (1859–1921) • AMERICAN PHYSICIAN AND EDUCATOR

Now I am nothing but a veil; all my body is a veil beneath which a child sleeps.

–GABRIELA MISTRAL (LUCILA GODOY ALCAYAGA) (1899–1957)
NOBEL PRIZE–WINNING CHILEAN POET

Think of stretch marks as pregnancy service stripes.

–JOYCE ARMOR • 20TH/21ST-CENTURY AMERICAN WRITER

Now I was someone who ate like a wolf, napped like a cat, and dreamed like a madwoman.

–MARNI JACKSON • 20TH/21ST-CENTURY CANADIAN WRITER

If pregnancy were a book, they would cut the last two chapters.

–NORA EPHRON (1941–)
AMERICAN FILM DIRECTOR, PRODUCER, SCREENWRITER, AND NOVELIST

I'm beginning to have morning sickness. I'm not having a baby. I'm just sick of morning.

–PHYLLIS DILLER (1917–) • AMERICAN COMEDIAN

"PRIDE"

See also Vanity

Pride is never sinful when it is Justice.

BARBARA CHASE-RIBOUD (1939–)
AFRICAN-AMERICAN SCULPTOR AND NOVELIST

The best of all good friends is pride.

–GERTRUDE ATHERTON (1857–1948)
AMERICAN NOVELIST

Wounded vanity knows when it is mortally hurt; and limps off the field, piteous, all disguises thrown away. But pride carries its banner to the last; and fast as it is driven from one field unfurls it in another.

–HELEN HUNT JACKSON (1830–1885) • AMERICAN WRITER AND ACTIVIST

Vanity and pride are different things, though the words are often used synonymously. A person may be proud without being vain. Pride relates more to our opinion of ourselves; vanity, to what we would have others think of us.

–JANE AUSTEN (1775–1817) • ENGLISH WRITER

The intelligent man who is proud of his intelligence is like the condemned man who is proud of his large cell.

–SIMONE WEIL (1909–1943) • FRENCH SOCIAL PHILOSOPHER AND ACTIVIST

If you are discouraged it is a sign of pride, because it shows you trust in your own powers. Never bother about other people's opinions. Be humble and you will never be disturbed. Remember St. Aloysius, who said he would continue to play billiards even if he knew he was going to die. Do you play well? Sleep well? Eat well? These are duties. Nothing is small for God.

–MOTHER TERESA (1910–1997) • ALBANIAN CATHOLIC NUN; WINNER OF NOBEL PEACE PRIZE

"PRIVACY"

See also Solitude

The minute more than two people know a secret, it is no longer a secret.

–ANN LANDERS (ESTHER PAULINE FRIEDMAN) (1918–2002) • AMERICAN ADVICE COLUMNIST

The eleventh commandment—thou shalt not be found out—is the only one that is virtually impossible to keep these days.

–BERTHE HENRY BUXTON (1844–1881) • ENGLISH WRITER

I keep my own personality in a cupboard under the stairs at home so that no one else can see it or nick it.

–DAWN FRENCH (1957–) • ENGLISH COMEDIAN

The freedom of the press works in such a way that
there is not much freedom from it.

–GRACE KELLY (1929–1982)
AMERICAN ACTOR AND PRINCESS OF MONACO

The secret of having a personal life is not answering too many questions about it.

–JOAN COLLINS (1933–) • ENGLISH ACTOR AND WRITER

I've never looked through a keyhole without finding someone was looking back.

–JUDY GARLAND (1922–1969) • AMERICAN ACTOR AND SINGER

Children have no reasonable assumption of privacy while
they are minors in their parents' home.

–LAURA SCHLESSINGER (1947–) • AMERICAN CULTURAL COMMENTATOR

I restore myelf when I'm alone. A career is born in public—talent in privacy.

–MARILYN MONROE (1926–1962) • AMERICAN ACTOR AND SEX SYMBOL

Do you want to trace your family tree? Run for public office.

–PATRICIA H. VANCE (1936–) • AMERICAN POLITICIAN AND PROFESSIONAL NURSE

"PROCRASTINATION"

Procrastination is, hands down, our favorite form of self-sabotage.

–ALYCE CORNYN-SELBY • 20TH/21ST-CENTURY AMERICAN BUSINESS SPEAKER AND WRITER

One thing that's good about procrastination is that
you always have something planned for tomorrow.

–GLADYS BRONWYN STERN (1890–1973) • ENGLISH WRITER

Delay breeds fear.

–JESSAMYN WEST (1902–1984)
AMERICAN WRITER

Procrastination gives you something to look forward to.

–JOAN KONNER • 20TH/21ST-CENTURY AMERICAN JOURNALIST AND PRODUCER

That which is always within our reach, is always the last thing we take; and the chances are, that what we can do every day, we never do at all.

–L. E. LANDON (1802–1838) • ENGLISH WRITER AND POET

I . . . practiced all the arts of apology, evasion, and invisibility, to which procrastinators must sooner or later be reduced.

–MARIA EDGEWORTH (1767–1849) • IRISH NOVELIST

"*PROGRESS*"

People tend to think that life really does progress for everyone eventually, that people progress, but actually only some people progress. The rest of the people don't.

–ALICE WALKER • AFRICAN-AMERICAN AUTHOR AND POET

Things that don't get better get worse.

–ELLEN SUE STERN
20TH/21ST-CENTURY AMERICAN INSPIRATIONAL SPEAKER AND WRITER

This seems to be the law of progress in everything we do; it moves along a spiral rather than a perpendicular; we seem to be actually going out of the way, and yet it turns out that we were really moving upward all the time.

–FRANCES E. WILLARD (1839–1898)
AMERICAN SUFFRAGIST, EDUCATOR, AND TEMPERANCE REFORMER

Even the "worst blizzard of the century" accumulates one flake at a time.

–MARY KAY BLAKELY (1948–) • AMERICAN JOURNALIST

Whoever said progress was a positive thing has never been to Florida or California.

–RITA MAE BROWN (1944–) • AMERICAN NOVELIST AND ACTIVIST

Scientific progress makes moral progress a necessity; for if man's power is increased, the checks that restrain him from abusing it must be strengthened.

–MADAME DE STAËL (1766–1817) • SWISS BORN FRENCH WRITER AND SOCIETY FIGURE

"PROSTITUTION"

The whore is despised by the hypocritical world because she has made a realistic assessment of her assets and does not have to rely on fraud to make a living. In an area of human relations where fraud is regular practice between the sexes, her honesty is regarded with a mocking wonder.

–ANGELA CARTER (1940–1992) • ENGLISH WRITER AND JOURNALIST

Prostitution is not just a service industry, mopping up the overflow of male demand, which always exceeds female supply. Prostitution testifies to the amoral power struggle of sex, which religion has never been able to stop. Prostitutes, pornographers, and their patrons are marauders in the forest of archaic night.

–CAMILLE PAGLIA (1947–) • AMERICAN SOCIAL CRITIC AND PROFESSOR

These days I am still in demand—but in a different way. In my thirties I was doing doing it, in my forties I was organizing it, and now unfortunately I can only talk about it.

–CYNTHIA PAYNE (1932–) • ENGLISH MADAM AND PUBLIC SPEAKER

Aren't women prudes if they don't and prostitutes if they do?

–KATE MILLETT (1934-) • AMERICAN FEMINIST WRITER AND ACTIVIST

Punishing the prostitute promotes the rape of all women. When prostitution is a crime, the message conveyed is that women who are sexual are "bad," and therefore legitimate victims of sexual assault. Sex becomes a weapon to be used by men.

–MARGO ST. JAMES (1937-) • AMERICAN PROSTITUTES' RIGHTS ACTIVIST AND FEMINIST

The women who take husbands not out of love but out of greed, to get their bills paid, to get a fine house and clothes and jewels; the women who marry to get out of a tiresome job, or to get away from disagreeable relatives, or to avoid being called an old maid—these are whores in everything but name. The only difference between them and my girls is that my girls gave a man his money's worth.

–POLLY ADLER (1900-1962) • AMERICAN MADAM

There's a Book that says we're all sinners, and I at least chose a sin that's made quite a few people happier than they were before they met me, a sin that's left me with very little time to consider other extremely popular moral misdemeanors, like usury, intolerance, bearing false tales, extortion, racial bigotry, and the casting of that first stone.

–SALLY STANFORD (1904-1982) • AMERICAN MADAM AND SAUSALITO, CA, MAYOR

I've made so many movies playing a hooker that they don't pay me in the regular way any more. They leave it on the dresser.

–SHIRLEY MACLAINE (1934-) • AMERICAN ACTOR AND WRITER

I am white and middle-class and ambitious, and I have no trouble identifying with either the call girl or the street hustler, and I can explain why in one sentence: I've been working to support myself for 15 years, and I've had more offers to sell my body for money than I have had to be an executive.

–SUSAN BROWNMILLER (1935–) • AMERICAN RADICAL FEMINIST, JOURNALIST, AND ACTIVIST

Nothing could be more grotesquely unjust than a code of morals, reinforced by laws, which relieves men from responsibility for irregular sexual acts, and for the same acts drives women to abortion, infanticide, prostitution, and self-destruction.

–SUZANNE LA FOLLETTE (1893–1983) • AMERICAN JOURNALIST

A call girl is simply someone who hates poverty more than she hates sin.

–SYDNEY BIDDLE BARROWS (1952–) • AMERICAN MADAM, KNOWN AS THE "MAYFLOWER MADAM"

Actually, if my business was legitimate, I would deduct a substantial percentage for depreciation of my body.

–XAVIERA HOLLANDER (1943–) • DUTCH WRITER AND FORMER CALL GIRL/MADAM

Q

"QUOTATIONS"

The point of quotations is that one can use another's words to be insulting.

–AMANDA CROSS (CAROLYN HEILBRUN) (1926–2003) • AMERICAN ACADEMIC AND FEMINIST WRITER

I always have a quotation for everything—it saves original thinking.

–DOROTHY SAYERS (1893–1957) • ENGLISH WRITER AND TRANSLATOR

In spite of his practical ability, some of his experience had petrified into maxims and quotations.

–GEORGE ELIOT (MARY ANN EVANS) (1819–1880) • ENGLISH NOVELIST

I think quotes are very dangerous things.

–KATE BUSH (1958–) • ENGLISH SINGER-SONGWRITER

An apt quotation is like a lamp which flings its light over the whole sentence.

L. E. LANDON (1802–1838) • ENGLISH WRITER AND POET

When a thing has been said so well that it could not be said better, why paraphrase it? Hence my writing is, if not a cabinet of fossils, a kind of collection of flies in amber.

–MARIANNE MOORE (1887–1972) • AMERICAN MODERNIST POET

It is a joy to find thoughts one might have, beautifully expressed with much authority by someone recognizedly wiser than oneself.

–MARLENE DIETRICH (1901–1992) • GERMAN-BORN ACTRESS AND SINGER

The next best thing to being clever is being able to quote someone who is.

–MARY PETTIBONE POOLE • 20TH-CENTURY AMERICAN WRITER

R

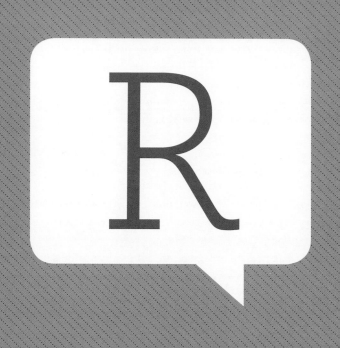

"RACE/RACISM"

See also Diversity, Identity

Those who can serve best, those who help most, those who sacrifice most, those are the people who will be loved in life and honoured in death, when all questions of color are swept away and when in a free country free citizens shall meet on equal grounds.

—ANNIE BESANT (1847-1933) • ENGLISH WRITER AND REFORMER

Anger is an appropriate reaction to racist attitudes, as is fury when the action arising from those attitudes does not change.

—AUDRE LORDE (1934-1992) • AFRICAN-AMERICAN FEMINIST WRITER AND ACTIVIST

I'm not interested in pursuing a society that uses analysis, research, and experimentation to concretize their vision of cruel destinies for those who are not bastards of the Pilgrims: a society with arrogance rising, moon in oppression, and sun in destruction.

—BARBARA CAMERON (1954-2002) • NATIVE AMERICAN ACTIVIST

Do not call for black power or green power. Call for brain power.

—BARBARA JORDAN (1936-1996) • AFRICAN-AMERICAN POLITICAN AND ATTORNEY

Most Negroes have a little black militancy swimming around in them and most white people have a little Ku Klux Klan swimming around in them. If we'd be honest with each other, we'd discover that we are all victims of the racism that is historically part of this country.

—BARBARA JORDAN (1936-1996) • AFRICAN-AMERICAN POLITICAN AND ATTORNEY

You can be up to your boobies in white satin, with gardenias in your hair and no sugar cane for miles, but you can still be working on a plantation.

–BILLIE HOLIDAY (1915–1959) • AFRICAN-AMERICAN JAZZ SINGER

•

Segregation was wrong when it was forced by white people, and I believe it is still wrong when it is requested by black people.

–CORETTA SCOTT KING (1927–2006)

AFRICAN-AMERICAN CIVIL RIGHTS ACTIVIST AND WIDOW OF DR. MARTIN LUTHER KING, JR.

•

I have not been animated in my life to fight against race and sex discrimination simply because of my own identity. That would mean that one must be South African to fight apartheid, or a poor white in Appalachia to fight poverty, or Jewish to fight anti-Semitism. And I just reject that conception of how struggles should be waged.

–ELEANOR HOLMES NORTON (1937–) • AFRICAN-AMERICAN ATTORNEY AND POLITICAN

•

Our role is to support anything positive in black life and destroy anything negative that touches it. You have no other reason for being.

–ELMA LEWIS (1921–2004)

AFRICAN-AMERICAN ARTIST, EDUCATOR, AND FOUNDER OF NATIONAL CENTER OF AFRO-AMERICAN ARTISTS

•

Let me state here and now that the black woman in America can justly be described as slave of a slave.

–FRANCES M. BEAL

20TH-CENTURY AFRICAN-AMERICAN FEMINIST AND CIVIL RIGHTS ACTIVIST

•

Black people cannot and will not become integrated into American society on any terms but those of self-determination and autonomy.

–GERDA LERNER (1920–) • AUSTRIAN-BORN AMERICAN HISTORIAN

No matter what learned scientists may say, race is, politically speaking, not the beginning of humanity but its end, not the origin of peoples but their decay, not the natural birth of man but his unnatural death.

—HANNAH ARENDT (1906–1975) • GERMAN-BORN POLITICAL PHILOSOPHER AND HISTORIAN

•

To be an Asian, to be a minority, not to see ourselves as always me the minority, the victim, you the dominant culture. It's a shift of paradigm. Once you see things differently, you gain power. All of a sudden there is enlightenment.

—JOAN CHEN (1961–) • CHINESE-AMERICAN ACTOR AND DIRECTOR

•

We can go on talking about racism and who treated whom badly, but what are you going to do about it? Are you going to wallow in that or are you going to create your own agenda?

—JUDITH JAMISON (1943–)
AFRICAN-AMERICAN MODERN DANCER AND CHOREOGRAPHER

•

I have a no-die clause in every movie. The black people can't be dying all the time.

—QUEEN LATIFAH (1970–) • AFRICAN-AMERICAN RAPPER AND ACTOR

•

Accomplishments have no color.

—LEONTYNE PRICE (1927–)
AFRICAN-AMERICAN SOPRANO

•

Negroes must concern themselves with every single means of struggle: legal, illegal, passive, active, violent, and nonviolent. . . . They must harass, debate, petition, boycott, sing hymns, pray on steps—and shoot from their windows when the racists come cruising through their communities. . . . The acceptance of our condition is the only form of extremism which discredits us before our children.

—LORRAINE HANSBERRY (1930–1965) • AFRICAN-AMERICAN PLAYWRIGHT AND PAINTER

We first crush people to the earth, and then claim the right of trampling upon them because they are prostrate.

–LYDIA MARIA CHILD (1802–1880) • AMERICAN ACTIVIST, NOVELIST, AND JOURNALIST

•

The only way not to worry about the race problem is to be doing something about it yourself. When you are, natural human vanity makes you feel that now the thing is in good hands.

–MARGARET HALSEY (1910–1997) • AMERICAN WRITER

•

Prejudice is like a hair across your cheek. You can't see it, you can't find it with your fingers, but you keep brushing at it because the feel of it is irritating.

–MARIAN ANDERSON (1897–1993) • AFRICAN-AMERICAN CONTRALTO

•

If you as parents cut corners, your children will too. If you lie, they will too. If you spend all your money on yourselves and tithe no portion of it for charities, colleges, churches, synagogues, and civic causes, your children won't either. And if parents snicker at racial and gender jokes, another generation will pass on the poison adults still have not had the courage to snuff out.

–MARIAN WRIGHT EDELMAN (1939–)
AFRICAN-AMERICAN FOUNDER OF THE CHILDREN'S DEFENSE FUND

•

We have the satisfaction of knowing that because all of us believed, we inspired, motivated, and liberated some of the most beautiful people on earth—young, gifted, and black.

–MARY ALLISON BURCH (1906–) • AFRICAN-AMERICAN ADVOCATE FOR CHILDREN

•

If our people are to fight their way up out of bondage we must arm them with the sword and the shield and the buckler of pride.

–MARY MCLEOD BETHUNE (1875–1955) • AFRICAN-AMERICAN ANTIDISCRIMINATION ACTIVIST

With more blacks and other people of color, there will be a tilt in power . . . and whites will be in the minority. It is in the best interest of white people to work harder to create better relationships with people of color so they can ensure themselves the equality that has eluded us.

—MAXINE WATERS (1938–) • AFRICAN-AMERICAN POLITICIAN

•

The realities are that . . . as a black man . . . Barack can get shot going to the gas station, you know.

—MICHELLE OBAMA (1964–)
AFRICAN-AMERICAN FIRST LADY OF THE UNITED STATES

•

I look at an ant and I see myself: a native South African, endowed by nature with a strength much greater than my size so I might cope with the weight of a racism that crushes my spirit.

—MIRIAM MAKEBA (1932–) • SOUTH AFRICAN SINGER

•

As surely as night follows day our country will fail in its democracy because of race prejudice unless we root it out. We cannot grow in strength and leadership for democracy so long as we carry deep in our being that fatal fault.

—PEARL S. BUCK (1892–1973) • FIRST FEMALE AMERICAN WINNER OF THE NOBEL PRIZE IN LITERATURE

•

We're proud of our culture and who we are. It is important to understand that your people didn't just fade out and not exist anymore. You get a little tired of hearing that you're extinct.

—QUIRINA LUNA-COSTILLAS
20TH/21ST-CENTURY NATIVE AMERICAN COFOUNDER OF THE MUTSUN LANGUAGE FOUNDATION

•

Racism is so universal in this country, so widespread and deep-seated, that it is invisible because it is so normal.

—SHIRLEY CHISHOLM (1924–2005)
EDUCATOR, WRITER, AND FIRST AFRICAN-AMERICAN WOMAN ELECTED TO U.S. CONGRESS

Contrary to today's stereotypes, racists do not always chew tobacco and drive pickup trucks with gun racks. They wear silk shirts, treat women as possessions, and talk about human rights at cocktail parties far from communities of people of color. The men in pickup trucks are just as likely to be as warm and caring as the high-minded liberals are to be racists.

–WILMA MANKILLER (1945–2010)

NATIVE AMERICAN LEADER, FIRST FEMALE PRINCIPLE CHIEF OF THE CHEROKEE NATION

•

Light came to me when I realized that I did not have to consider any racial group as a whole. God made them duck by duck and that was the only way I could see them.

–ZORA NEALE HURSTON (1891–1960) • AFRICAN-AMERICAN FOLKLORIST AND WRITER

•

"READING"

See also Literature

•

Children want to do what the grownups do. Children should learn that reading is pleasure, not just something that teachers make you do in school.

–BEVERLY CLEARY (1916–) • AMERICAN WRITER

•

The greatest gift is the passion for reading. It is cheap, it consoles, it distracts, it excites, it gives you knowledge of the world and experience of a wide kind. It is a moral illumination.

–ELIZABETH HARDWICK (1916–) • AMERICAN NOVELIST AND CRITIC

•

We live at the level of our language. Whatever we can articulate we can imagine or explore. All you have to do to educate a child is leave him alone and teach him to read. The rest is brainwashing.

–ELLEN GILCHRIST (1935–) • AMERICAN WRITER

From your parents you learn love and laughter and how to put one foot before the other. But when books are opened you discover you have wings.

–HELEN HAYES (1900–1993) • AMERICAN ACTOR

It is books that are the key to the wide world; if you can't do anything else, read all that you can.

–JANE HAMILTON • 20TH/21ST-CENTURY AMERICAN WRITER

Just the knowledge that a good book is awaiting one at the end of a long day makes that day happier.

–KATHLEEN NORRIS (1880–1966) • AMERICAN WRITER

Everyone probably thinks that I'm a raving nymphomaniac, that I have an insatiable sexual appetite, when the truth is I'd rather read a book.

–MADONNA (1958–) • AMERICAN POP SINGER AND ACTOR

The whole world opened to me when I learned to read.

–MARY MCLEOD BETHUNE (1875–1955)
AFRICAN-AMERICAN ANTIDISCRIMINATION ACTIVIST

Agatha Christie has given more pleasure in bed than any other woman.

–NANCY BANKS-SMITH • 20TH/21ST-CENTURY ENGLISH TELEVISION CRITIC

I think the diversity of authors and readers is expanding, which is wonderful, because it means the type of story being told is also expanding.

–SARAH ZETTEL (1966–) • AMERICAN WRITER

Where books are concerned, it is notoriously difficult to fix labels of merit in such a way that they do not come off.

–VIRGINIA WOOLF (1882–1941) • ENGLISH NOVELIST, ESSAYIST, AND CRITIC

LIBRARIES

One of the greatest gifts my brother and I received from my mother was her love of literature and language. With their boundless energy, libraries open the door to these worlds and so many others. I urge young and old alike to embrace all that libraries have to offer.

—CAROLINE KENNEDY (1957-)
AMERICAN, DAUGHTER OF PRESIDENT JOHN F. AND JACQUELINE KENNEDY

•

With a library you are free, not confined by temporary political climates. It is the most democratic of institutions because no one—but no one at all—can tell you what to read and when and how.

—DORIS LESSING (1919-) • ENGLISH WRITER

•

"REGRET"

•

Some things in life aren't even worth regretting. You're better off passing them like a freight train passes a hobo.

—ETHEL MERMAN (1908–1984) • AMERICAN ACTOR AND SINGER

•

I have made it a rule of my life never to regret and never to look back. Regret is an appalling waste of energy. . . . You can't build on it; it's only good for wallowing in.

—KATHERINE MANSFIELD (1888–1923) • NEW ZEALAND WRITER

•

Regrets are as personal as fingerprints.

—MARGARET CULKIN BANNING (1891–1982)
AMERICAN WRITER

•

I regret nothing, says arrogance; I will regret nothing, says inexperience.

—MARIE VON EBNER-ESCHENBACH (1830–1916) • AUSTRIAN WRITER

"If only." Those must be the two saddest words in the world.

–MERCEDES LACKEY (1950–) • AMERICAN WRITER

To weep over a folly is to double it.

–MINNA THOMAS ANTRIM (1856–1950)
AMERICAN WRITER

Never regret. If it's good, it's wonderful. If it's bad, it's experience.

–VICTORIA HOLT (ELEANOR HIBBERT) (1906–1993) • ENGLISH WRITER

"RELATIONSHIPS"

See also Love

I, with a deeper instinct, choose a man who compels my strength, who makes enormous demands on me, who does not doubt my courage or my toughness, who does not believe me naïve or innocent, who has the courage to treat me like a woman.

–ANAÏS NIN (1903–1977) • FRENCH WRITER AND DIARIST

Relationships are like a dance, with visible energy racing back and forth between partners. Some relationships are the slow, dark dance of death.

–COLETTE DOWLING (1938–) • AMERICAN PSYCHOTHERAPIST AND WRITER

Personally, I think if a woman hasn't met the right man by the age of 24 she may be lucky.

–DEBORAH KERR (1921–) • SCOTTISH-BORN ACTOR

A woman without a man cannot meet a man, any man, without thinking, even if it's for a half second, perhaps this is *the* man.

–DORIS LESSING (1919–) • ENGLISH WRITER

Absence does not make the heart grow fonder, but it sure heats up the blood.

–ELIZABETH ASHLEY (1939–) • AMERICAN ACTOR

Men and women, women and men. It will never work.

–ERICA JONG (1942–) • AMERICAN WRITER

Women are the only oppressed group in our society that lives in intimate association with their oppressors.

–EVELYN CUNNINGHAM

20TH/21ST-CENTURY AMERICAN JOURNALIST, EDITOR, AND FOUNDER OF THE COALITION OF 100 BLACK WOMEN

Different taste in jokes is a great strain on the affections.

–GEORGE ELIOT (MARY ANN EVANS) (1819–1880)

ENGLISH WRITER

"Home" is any four walls that enclose the right person.

–HELEN ROWLAND (1875–1950) • AMERICAN JOURNALIST AND HUMORIST

In nine cases out of ten, a woman had better show more affection than she feels.

–JANE AUSTEN (1775–1817)

ENGLISH WRITER

The easiest kind of relationship for me is with ten thousand people. The hardest is with one.

–JOAN BAEZ (1941–) • AMERICAN FOLK SINGER AND ACTIVIST

Opposites attract—and then aggravate.

–JOY BROWNE

20TH/21ST-CENTURY AMERICAN RADIO PSYCHOLOGIST

Sometimes I wonder if men and women really suit each other. Perhaps they should live next door and just visit now and then.

—KATHARINE HEPBURN (1907-2003) • AMERICAN ACTOR

•

If you can't handle the baggage, you'll have to get out of the baggage room.

—LAURA SCHLESSINGER (1947-) • AMERICAN CULTURAL COMMENTATOR

•

Love is a feeling, marriage is a contract, and relationships are work.

—LORI GORDON • 20TH/21ST-CENTURY AMERICAN MARRIAGE AND FAMILY THERAPIST

•

One of the oldest human needs is having someone to wonder where you are when you don't come home at night.

—MARGARET MEAD (1901-1978) • AMERICAN CULTURAL ANTHROPOLOGIST

•

There is no human litmus test for potential post-messing around weirdness, and if there were, we'd probably ignore it.

—MARIKO TAMAKI• 20TH/21ST-CENTURY CANADIAN WRITER AND PERFORMER

•

While it is perfectly okay to screw up and go home with someone who will make your life a living hell for the next two months, it totally isn't okay to turn around three months later and do it again. There, I think, you cross the boundary from having stupid sex to being a stupid person.

—MARIKO TAMAKI • 20TH/21ST-CENTURY CANADIAN WRITER AND PERFORMER

•

The only time a woman really succeeds in changing a man is when he is a baby.

—NATALIE WOOD (1938-1981) • AMERICAN FILM ACTOR

•

Be fond of the man who jests at his scars, if you like; but never believe he is being on the level with you.

—PAMELA HANSFORD JOHNSON (1912-1981)
ENGLISH POET, NOVELIST, AND SOCIAL CRITIC

The basic discovery about any people is the discovery of the relationship between its men and its women.

–PEARL S. BUCK (1892–1973)
FIRST FEMALE AMERICAN WINNER OF THE NOBEL PRIZE IN LITERATURE

•

Getting along with men isn't what's truly important. The vital knowledge is how to get along with one man.

–PHYLLIS MCGINLEY (1905–1978) • AMERICAN POET, ESSAYIST, AND WRITER

•

It takes a smart woman to fall for a good man!

–SADIE DELANY (1889–1999)
AFRICAN-AMERICAN EDUCATOR AND MEMOIRIST

•

Women might be able to fake orgasms. But men can fake whole relationships.

–SHARON STONE (1958–) • AMERICAN ACTRESS AND PRODUCER

•

Constant togetherness is fine—but only for Siamese twins.

–VICTORIA BILLINGS (1945–) • AMERICAN JOURNALIST

•

I want a man who's kind and understanding. Is that too much to ask of a millionaire?

–ZSA ZSA GABOR (1917–) • HUNGARIAN-AMERICAN ACTRESS AND SOCIALITE

•

BREAKUPS

Love never dies a natural death. It dies because we don't know how to replenish its source. It dies of blindness and errors and betrayals. It dies of illness and wounds; it dies of weariness, of withering, of tarnishing.

–ANAÏS NIN (1903–1977) • FRENCH WRITER AND DIARIST

•

Scratch a lover, and find a foe.

–DOROTHY PARKER (1893–1967)
AMERICAN WRITER AND CRITIC

The best remedy for a bruised heart is not, as so many people seem to think, repose upon a manly bosom. Much more efficacious are honest work, physical activity, and sudden acquisition of wealth.

–DOROTHY SAYERS (1893–1957) • ENGLISH WRITER AND TRANSLATOR

Falling out of love is very enlightening. For a short while you see the world with new eyes.

–IRIS MURDOCH (1919–1999) • IRISH-BORN ENGLISH NOVELIST

I was never one to patiently pick up broken fragments and glue them together again and tell myself that the mended whole was as good as new. What is broken is broken—and I'd rather remember it as it was at its best than mend it and see the broken places as long as I lived.

–MARGARET MITCHELL (1900–1949) • AMERICAN NOVELIST

"RELIGION"

I think it pisses God off if you walk by the color purple in a field somewhere and don't notice it. . . . People think pleasing God is all God care about. But any fool living in the world can see it always trying to please us back.

–ALICE WALKER (1944–) • AFRICAN-AMERICAN WRITER AND POET

We are commanded to love God with all our minds, as well as with all our hearts, and we commit a great sin if we forbid or prevent that cultivation of the mind in others which would enable them to perform this duty.

–ANGELINA GRIMKÉ (1805–1879) • AMERICAN ABOLITIONIST AND REFORMER

There is no religion without love, and people may talk as much as they like about their religion, but if it does not teach them to be good and kind to man and beast, it is all a sham.

–ANNA SEWELL (1820–1878) • ENGLISH WRITER

Our current obsession with creativity is the result of our continued striving for immortality in an era when most people no longer believe in an afterlife.

–ARIANNA HUFFINGTON (1950–) • AMERICAN COLUMNIST

Every dictator uses religion as a prop to keep himself in power.

–BENAZIR BHUTTO (1953–) • PRIME MINISTER OF PAKISTAN

The dramatic action that we need to create a way of life on Earth that really works will be taken not through personal, social, or political action, but through spiritual action.

–BROOKE MEDICINE EAGLE (BROOKE EDWARDS)
20TH/21ST-CENTURY NATIVE AMERICAN SPIRITUALIST AND SINGER

All religions are the same: Religion is basically guilt, with different holidays.

–CATHY LADMAN • 20TH/21ST-CENTURY AMERICAN COMEDIAN AND ACTOR

The goal of feminist spirituality has never been the simple substitution of Yahweh-with-a-skirt. Rather, it seeks, in all its diversity, to revitalize relational, body-honoring, cosmologically grounded spiritual possibilities for women and all others.

–CHARLENE SPRETNAK
20TH/21ST-CENTURY AMERICAN ACADEMIC IN FEMINIST SPIRITUALITY AND SOCIAL JUSTICE

[Nelson Mandela] was telling me he doesn't think he'll get into heaven. I'm thinking, "Are you kidding me? If you're not going to heaven then I am screwed."

–CHARLIZE THERON (1975–) • SOUTH AFRICAN MODEL AND ACTOR

God has more important things to worry about than who I sleep with.

–CYNDI LAUPER (1953–) • AMERICAN SINGER

A simple grateful thought turned heavenward is the most perfect prayer.

–DORIS LESSING (1919–) • ENGLISH WRITER

God's gifts put man's best dreams to shame.

—ELIZABETH BARRETT BROWNING (1806–1861) • ENGLISH POET

Seeing that the religious superstitions of women perpetuate their bondage more than all other adverse influences, I feel impelled to reiterate my demands for justice, liberty, and equality in the Church as well as the State.

—ELIZABETH CADY STANTON (1815–1902) • AMERICAN SUFFRAGIST, WRITER, AND THEOLOGIAN

They say that God is everywhere, and yet we always think of Him as somewhat of a recluse.

—EMILY DICKINSON (1830–1886) • AMERICAN POET

In spite of the way many people are turning away from God, not for other gods, but for no god; in spite of the mess we are making of this beautiful Planet Earth which God has given us, God still loves the world.

—EVA BURROWS (1929–) • AUSTRALIAN; LEADER OF SALVATION ARMY

I used to lie between cool, clean sheets at night after I'd had a bath, after I had washed my hair and scrubbed my knuckles and fingernails and teeth. Then I could lie quite still in the dark with my face to the window with the trees in it, and talk to God.

—FRANCES FARMER (1914–1970) • AMERICAN ACTOR

God is love, but get it in writing.

—GYPSY ROSE LEE (1914–1970)
AMERICAN BURLESQUE DANCER AND ACTOR

It is wonderful how much time good people spend fighting the devil. If they would only expend the same amount of energy loving their fellow men, the devil would die in his own tracks of ennui.

—HELEN KELLER (1880–1968) • AMERICAN WRITER AND ACTIVIST

When we talk to God, we're praying. When God talks to us, we're schizophrenic.

–JANE WAGNER (1935–) • AMERICAN PLAYWRIGHT AND COMEDY WRITER

If there be anywhere on earth a lover of God who is always kept safe from falling, I know nothing of it, for it was not shown me. But this was shown: that whether in falling or in rising we are always kept in the same precious love.

–JULIAN OF NORWICH (1342–CA. 1416) • ENGLISH MYSTIC

There are some forms of religion that are bad; just as there's bad cooking or bad art or bad sex, you have bad religion too.

–KAREN ARMSTRONG (1944–) • ENGLISH RELIGIOUS SCHOLAR

When you consider that God could have commanded anything he wanted—anything!—the Ten [Commandments] have got to rank as one of the great missed moral opportunities of all time. How different history would have been had he clearly and unmistakably forbidden war, tyranny, taking over other people's countries, slavery, exploitation of workers, cruelty to children, wife-beating, stoning, treating women—or anyone—as chattel or inferior beings.

–KATHA POLLITT (1949–) • AMERICAN FEMINIST WRITER AND CULTURAL CRITIC

Why do born-again people so often make you wish they'd never been born the first time?

–KATHARINE WHITEHORN (1926–) • ENGLISH JOURNALIST, WRITER, AND COLUMNIST

You remind me that the Apostle Paul told women to be silent in church. I would remind you of the word of this same apostle that in Christ there is no longer male nor female.

–KATHERINE ZELL (CA. 1497–1562) • GERMAN HYMNIST, REFORMER, AND WRITER

Spirituality comes from questioning everything but at the same time accepting everything.

K.D. LANG (1961–) • CANADIAN SINGER AND SONGWRITER

God's been going deaf. Since the Old Testament, God's been deafening up on us.

–LOUISE ERDRICH (1954-) • NATIVE AMERICAN WRITER AND POET

•

The divorce of our so-called spiritual life from our daily activities is a fatal dualism.

–M. P. FOLLETT (1868-1933)• AMERICAN SOCIOLOGIST

•

An Atheist knows that heaven is something for which we should work now—here on earth—for all men together to enjoy. An Atheist thinks that he can get no help through prayer but that he must find in himself the inner conviction and strength to meet life, to grapple with it, to subdue and enjoy it. An Atheist thinks that only in a knowledge of himself and a knowledge of his fellow man can he find the understanding that will help to a life of fulfillment. Therefore, he seeks to know himself and his fellow man rather than to know a god.

–MADALYN MURRAY O'HAIR (1919-1995)
AMERICAN ATHEIST ACTIVIST FOR SEPARATION OF CHURCH AND STATE

•

It is an open question whether any behavior based on fear of eternal punishment can be regarded as ethical or should be regarded as merely cowardly.

–MARGARET MEAD (1901-1978) • AMERICAN CULTURAL ANTHROPOLOGIST

•

I would rather walk with God in the dark than go alone in the light.

–MARY GARDINER BRAINARD (1837-1905) • AMERICAN POET

•

It is this belief in a power larger than myself and other than myself which allows me to venture into the unknown and even the unknowable.

–MAYA ANGELOU (1928-) • AFRICAN-AMERICAN POET, MEMOIRIST, AND CIVIL RIGHTS ACTIVIST

•

It's better to have a rich soul than to be rich.

–OLGA KORBUT (1955-)
BELARUSIAN GYMNAST, WINNER OF FOUR OLYMPIC GOLD MEDALS

It isn't until you come to a spiritual understanding of who you are—not necessarily a religious feeling, but deep down, the spirit within—that you can begin to take control.

–OPRAH WINFREY (1954-) • AFRICAN-AMERICAN TELEVISION HOST AND MAGAZINE PUBLISHER

Spiritual and religious traditions, when shaped by feminine principle, affirm the cyclical phases of our lives and the wisdom each phase brings, the sacredness of our bodies and the body of the Earth.

–PATRICE WYNNE • 20TH/21ST-CENTURY AMERICAN SPIRITUAL WRITER

People see God every day, they just don't recognize him.

–PEARL BAILEY (1918-1990) • AMERICAN SINGER AND ACTOR

I feel no need for any other faith than my faith in the kindness of human beings. I am so absorbed in the wonder of earth and the life upon it that I cannot think of heaven and angels.

–PEARL S. BUCK (1892-1973) • FIRST FEMALE AMERICAN WINNER OF THE NOBEL PRIZE IN LITERATURE

Religion without humanity is a poor human stuff.

–SOJOURNER TRUTH (1797-1883)
AFRICAN-AMERICAN ABOLITIONIST

I distrust those people who know so well what God wants them to do because I notice it always coincides with their own desires.

–SUSAN B. ANTHONY (1820-1906)
AMERICAN SUFFRAGIST AND NEWSPAPER PUBLISHER

A large part of the popularity and persuasiveness of psychology comes from its being a sublimated spiritualism: a secular, ostensibly scientific way of affirming the primacy of "spirit" over matter.

–SUSAN SONTAG (1933-2004)
AMERICAN ESSAYIST, NOVELIST, INTELLECTUAL, AND ACTIVIST

We must free ourselves to be filled by God. Even God cannot fill what is full.

–MOTHER TERESA (1910–1997) • ALBANIAN CATHOLIC NUN; WINNER OF NOBEL PEACE PRIZE

"REPRODUCTIVE RIGHTS"

See also Sex (Education)

If women cannot plan their pregnancies, they can plan little else in their own lives.

–ALICE S. ROSSI • 20TH/21ST-CENTURY AMERICAN SOCIOLOGIST

Hand in hand with reproductive rights, obviously, is the need for medically accurate sex education, family planning, and access to birth control. And if we were truly a civilized country, these things would be available in all languages, for people of all socioeconomic classes. Then, women wouldn't have unwanted pregnancies to terminate.

–ASHLEY JUDD (1968–) • AMERICAN ACTOR

Biological possibility and desire are not the same thing as biological need. Women have child-bearing equipment. To choose not to use the equipment is no more blocking what is instinctive than it is for a man who, muscles or no, chooses not to be a weight lifter.

–BETTY ROLLIN (1936–) • AMERICAN NEWS CORRESPONDENT AND WRITER

The freedom that women were supposed to have found in the sixties largely boiled down to easy contraception and abortion; things to make life easier for men, in fact.

–JULIE BURCHILL (1959–) • ENGLISH JOURNALIST AND COLUMNIST

No woman can call herself free who does not own and control her own body. No woman can call herself free until she can choose whether she will or will not be a mother.

–MARGARET SANGER (1879–1966) • AMERICAN BIRTH CONTROL ACTIVIST

Once again, I remind [legislators] that a woman's reproductive organs are not big enough to accommodate both ideology and gynecology.

–SALLY KALSON • 20TH/21ST-CENTURY AMERICAN COLUMNIST

ABORTION

The product, abortion, is skillfully marketed and sold to the woman at the crisis time in her life. She buys the product, finds it defective, and wants to return it for a refund. But, it's too late.

–CAROL EVERETT • 20TH/21ST-CENTURY AMERICAN ANTI-ABORTION SPOKESWOMAN

Pro-choice supporters are often heard using the cool language of the courts and the vocabulary of rights. Americans who are deeply ambivalent about abortion often miss the sound of caring.

–ELLEN GOODMAN (1941–) • AMERICAN JOURNALIST

If we can't preserve the privacy of our right to procreate, I can't imagine what rights we will be able to protect.

–FAYE WATTLETON (1943–) • AMERICAN FEMINIST AND REPRODUCTIVE RIGHTS ACTIVIST

If men could become pregnant, abortion would be a sacrament.

–FLORYNCE KENNEDY (1916–2000) • AFRICAN-AMERICAN LAWYER AND ACTIVIST

Republicans are against abortion until their daughters need one, Democrats are for abortion until their daughter wants one.

–GRACE MCGARVIE • 20TH/21ST-CENTURY AMERICAN EDUCATOR AND WRITER

I have met thousands and thousands of pro-choice men and women. I have never met anyone who is pro-abortion. Being pro-choice is not being pro-abortion. Being pro-choice is trusting the individual to make the right decision for herself and her family, and not entrusting that decision to anyone wearing the authority of government in any regard.

–HILLARY RODHAM CLINTON (1947–) • AMERICAN POLITICIAN AND FIRST LADY

No woman has an abortion for fun.

–JOAN SMITH (1953–)
ENGLISH NOVELIST, JOURNALIST, AND HUMAN RIGHTS ACTIVIST

[Abortion opponents] love little babies as long as they are in somebody else's uterus.

–JOYCELYN ELDERS (1933–) • FIRST AFRICAN-AMERICAN U.S. SURGEON GENERAL

There is no society in the world, and never has been or will be, in which having a baby you don't want is just some little blip in your life. . . . Women will never be equal to men in the workplace, or out of it either, if they have to go through life with this huge liability that can fall on their head at any moment. They will always be victims, always leading the lesser life, always dependent on the goodwill of men, for money, for marriage, for a box of Pampers.

–KATHA POLLITT (1949–) • AMERICAN FEMINIST WRITER AND CULTURAL CRITIC

The emphasis must be not on the right to abortion but on the right to privacy and reproductive control.

–RUTH BADER GINSBERG (1933–) • U.S. SUPREME COURT JUSTICE

The greatest destroyer of peace is abortion because if a mother can kill her own child, what is left for me to kill you and you to kill me? There is nothing between.

–MOTHER TERESA (1910–1997) • ALBANIAN CATHOLIC NUN; WINNER OF NOBEL PEACE PRIZE

CONTRACEPTION

You have to keep taking [the pill] every day, regardless of what's going on in your love life. It's nice, during those two-year lulls, to have a daily reminder. "I sleep alone, but it's time for my loser pill." Can you imagine if men had to wear a condom for 30 days just in case they might need it? "It's day 28, but somebody might call."

–CAROLINE RHEA (1964–) • CANADIAN-BORN COMEDIAN, ACTRESS, AND TV HOST

I'm not on the pill, but I label my Tic Tacs with the days of the week. Makes me feel like I'm in a relationship.

–CATHY LADMA • 20TH/21ST-CENTURY AMERICAN COMEDIAN AND ACTOR

The greatest of all contraceptives is affluence.

–INDIRA GANDHI (1917–1984) • PRIME MINISTER OF INDIA

Japanese women are refusing to take birth control pills, opting to leave contraception up to men. Do you know what they call women who leave birth control up to men? Mothers.

–JENNIFER VALLY • 20TH/21ST-CENTURY AMERICAN COMEDIAN

The most effective birth control is a toddler with the croup and diaper rash.

–KATE ZANNONI • 20TH/21ST-CENTURY AMERICAN COMEDIAN

I rely on my personality for birth control.

–LIZ WINSTON • 20TH/21ST-CENTURY AMERICAN COMEDIAN

When mom found my diaphragm, I told her it was a bathing cap for my cat.

–LIZZ WINSTEAD (1961–) • AMERICAN COMEDIAN AND COMEDY WRITER

I resolved that women should have knowledge of contraception. They have every right to know about their own bodies. I would strike out—I would scream from the housetops. I would tell the world what was going on in the lives of these poor women. I would be heard. No matter what it should cost. I would be heard.

—MARGARET SANGER (1879-1966) • AMERICAN BIRTH CONTROL ACTIVIST

Birth control is the means by which woman attains basic freedom.

—MARGARET SANGER (1879-1966) • AMERICAN BIRTH CONTROL ACTIVIST

The best contraceptive is the word no—repeated frequently.

—MARGARET SMITH • 20TH/21ST-CENTURY AMERICAN COMEDIAN

There's a new medical crisis. Doctors are reporting that many men are having allergic reactions to latex condoms. They say they cause severe swelling. So what's the problem?

—PHYLLIS DILLER (1917-) • AMERICAN COMEDIAN

"RESEARCH"

The way to do research is to attack the facts at the point of greatest astonishment.

—CELIA GREEN (1935-) • ENGLISH PHILOSOPHER AND PSYCHOLOGIST

To be sure, nothing is more important to the integrity of the universities . . . than a rigorously enforced divorce from war-oriented research and all connected enterprises.

—HANNAH ARENDT (1906-1975) • GERMAN-BORN POLITICAL PHILOSOPHER AND HISTORIAN

Research is a passion with me; it drives me; it is my relentless master.

—MARGARET MORSE NICE (1883-1974) • AMERICAN ORNITHOLOGIST

I most carefully confined myself to facts and arranged those facts on as thin a line of connecting opinion as possible.

–MARY H. KINGSLEY (1862–1900) • ENGLISH TRAVELER AND ETHNOGRAPHER

Research is formalized curiosity. It is poking and prying with a purpose.

–ZORA NEALE HURSTON (1891–1960) • AFRICAN-AMERICAN FOLKLORIST AND WRITER

"REVENGE"

People who fight fire with fire usually end up with ashes.

–ABIGAIL VAN BUREN (PAULINE PHILLIPS) (1918–)
AMERICAN ADVICE COLUMNIST, ORIGINATOR OF "DEAR ABBY"

Something of vengeance I had tasted for the first time; as aromatic wine it seemed, on swallowing, warm and racy: Its afterflavor, metallic and corroding, gave me a sensation as if I had been poisoned.

–CHARLOTTE BRONTË (1816–1855) • ENGLISH NOVELIST

No more tears now; I will think about revenge.

–MARY, QUEEN OF SCOTS (1542–1587) • QUEEN OF SCOTLAND

Revenge leads to an empty fullness, like eating dirt.

–MIGNON MCLAUGHLIN (1913–1983)
AMERICAN JOURNALIST AND WRITER

How many are the pains of those who hunger for revenge! . . . They have killed themselves even before they kill their enemies.

–ST. CATHERINE OF SIENA (1347–1380) • ITALIAN MYSTIC

In history it's never a tooth for a tooth, but a thousand, a hundred thousand for one.

–SYBILLE BEDFORD (1911-2006)
GERMAN-BORN ENGLISH NOVELIST AND JOURNALIST

"RISK"

Adventure is worthwhile in itself.

–AMELIA EARHART (1897-1937)
PIONEERING AMERICAN AVIATOR; FIRST PERSON TO FLY SOLO ACROSS PACIFIC

All good fortune is a gift of the gods, and . . . you don't win the favor of the ancient gods by being good, but by being bold.

–ANITA BROOKNER (1928-) • ENGLISH NOVELIST AND ART HISTORIAN

I could never tell if it was Opportunity or the Wolf knocking.

–ANNE ELLIS (1875-1938) • AMERICAN PIONEER

You may be disappointed if you fail, but you are doomed if you don't try.

–BEVERLY SILLS (1929-) • AMERICAN OPERA SINGER AND OPERA MANAGER

Be bold. If you're going to make an error, make a doozy, and don't be afraid to hit the ball.

–BILLIE JEAN KING (1943-) • AMERICAN TENNIS PLAYER

Look twice before you leap.

–CHARLOTTE BRONTË (1816-1855)
ENGLISH WRITER

There's something liberating about not pretending.
Dare to embarrass yourself. Risk.

–DREW BARRYMORE (1975–) • AMERICAN ACTOR AND PRODUCER

•

It's better to be a lion for a day than a sheep all your life.

–SISTER ELIZABETH KENNY (1880–1952)
AUSTRALIAN BUSH NURSE AND PIONEER IN THE TREATMENT OF POLIO

•

Take your life in your own hands and what happens?
A terrible thing: no one to blame.

–ERICA JONG (1942–) • AMERICAN WRITER

•

All serious daring starts from within.

–EUDORA WELTY (1899–2001) • AMERICAN WRITER

•

The only real risk is the risk of thinking too small.

–FRANCES MOORE LAPPÉ
20TH/21ST-CENTURY NUTRITIONIST, ECOLOGIST, AND ACTIVIST

•

If you risk nothing, then you risk everything.

–GEENA DAVIS (1956–) • AMERICAN ACTOR

•

There have been women in the past far more daring than we would need to be now, who ventured all and gained a little, but survived after all.

–GERMAINE GREER (1939–) • AUSTRALIAN-BORN WRITER AND SOCIAL CRITIC

•

A ship in port is safe, but that's not what ships are
built for. Sail out to sea and do new things.

–GRACE MURRAY HOPPER (1906–1992)
PIONEERING COMPUTER SCIENTIST AND U.S. NAVY REAR ADMIRAL

Avoiding danger is no safer in the long run than outright exposure. The fearful are caught as often as the bold.

–HELEN KELLER (1880–1968) • AMERICAN WRITER AND ACTIVIST

•

You have to pick the places you don't walk away from.

–JOAN DIDION (1934–) • AMERICAN WRITER

•

Leap, and the net will appear.

–JULIA CAMERON
20TH/21ST-CENTURY AMERICAN WRITER

•

If you're never scared or embarrassed or hurt, it means you never take any chances.

–JULIA SOREL (ROSALYN DREXLER) (1926–) • AMERICAN WRITER

•

Risk! . . . Do the hardest thing on earth for you.

–KATHERINE MANSFIELD (1888–1923) • NEW ZEALAND WRITER

•

It's better to be boldly decisive and risk being wrong than to agonize at length and be right too late.

–MARILYN MOATS KENNEDY
20TH/21ST-CENTURY AMERICAN CAREER CONSULTANT

•

The universe will reward you for taking risks on its behalf.

–SHAKTI GAWAIN (1948–) • AMERICAN WRITER ON PERSONAL DEVELOPMENT

•

Security is not the meaning of my life. Great opportunities are worth the risk.

–SHIRLEY HUFSTEDLER (1925–) • U.S. SECRETARY OF EDUCATION

Contentment is the positive side of resignation. It has its appeal but it's no good wearing an overcoat and furry slippers and heavy gloves when what the body really wants is to be naked.

—JEANETTE WINTERSON (1959-) • ENGLISH WRITER

All adventures, especially into new territory, are scary.

—SALLY RIDE (1951-) • FIRST AMERICAN WOMAN TO REACH OUTER SPACE

"ROLE MODELS"

External success has to do with people who may see me as a model, or an example, or a representative. As much as I may dislike or want to reject that responsibility, this is something that comes with public success. It's important to give others a sense of hope that it is possible and you can come from really different places in the world and find your own place in the world.

—AMY TAN (1952-) • ASIAN-AMERICAN NOVELIST

Strong role models and unconditional love can heal even the most emotionally impoverished person, and that goes for adults as well as youngsters.

—ANN LANDERS (ESTHER PAULINE FRIEDMAN) (1918-2002) • AMERICAN ADVICE COLUMNIST

If . . . you can't be a good example, then you'll just have to be a horrible warning.

—CATHERINE AIRD (KINN HAMILTON MCINTOSH) (1930-) • ENGLISH WRITER

Because of [Amelia Earhart], we had more women available to fly in the 1940s to help us get through World War II. And because of these women, women of my generation are able to look back and say, "Hey, they did it. They even flew military airplanes; we can do it, too."

—EILEEN COLLINS (1956-) • AMERICAN ASTRONAUT, FIRST FEMALE SPACE SHUTTLE COMMANDER

My daughter just thinks that all moms fly the space shuttle.

–EILEEN COLLINS (1956-)
AMERICAN ASTRONAUT, FIRST FEMALE SPACE SHUTTLE COMMANDER

•

I never dreamed of filmmaking when I was little. At that time I wanted to be in the secretarial pool, typing away and having fun like the women I saw on TV and in the movies.

–JULIE DASH (1952-) • AFRICAN-AMERICAN FILMMAKER

•

I didn't mean to be a role model. I just speak my truth. I guess speaking from your heart really creates a huge impact, and if I can encourage people to do that, then I would love to be a role model. If I could encourage people to use their voices loudly, then that's my reward.

–MARGARET CHO (1968-) • KOREAN-AMERICAN COMEDIAN AND ACTOR

•

How important it is for us to recognize and celebrate our heroes and she-roes!

–MAYA ANGELOU (1928-) • AFRICAN-AMERICAN POET, MEMOIRIST, AND CIVIL RIGHTS ACTIVIST

•

I am where I am because of the bridges that I crossed. Sojourner Truth was a bridge. Harriet Tubman was a bridge. Ida B. Wells was a bridge. Madame C. J. Walker was a bridge. Fannie Lou Hamer was a bridge.

–OPRAH WINFREY (1954-) • AFRICAN-AMERICAN TELEVISION HOST AND MAGAZINE PUBLISHER

•

I grew up never seeing myself on-screen, and it's really important to me to give people who look like me a chance to see themselves. I want to see myself as the hero of any story. I want to see myself save the world from the bomb.

–SANDRA OH (1971-) • CANADIAN ACTRESS

•

To me, big breasts, hot pants, and a gun in your hand aren't what makes a heroine.

–SIGOURNEY WEAVER (1949-) • AMERICAN ACTOR

S

"SACRIFICE"

I would step in the way of a bullet if it were aimed at my husband. It is not self-sacrifice to die protecting that which you value: If the value is great enough, you do not care to exist without it. This applies to any alleged sacrifice for those one loves.

–AYN RAND (1905-1982) • RUSSIAN-AMERICAN WRITER AND PHILOSOPHER

Some people are capable of making great sacrifices, but few are capable of concealing how much the effort has cost them.

–COUNTESS OF BLESSINGTON (LADY MARGUERITE BLESSINGTON) (1789-1849)
IRISH-BORN ENGLISH WRITER AND LITERARY SALON HOST

Taking somebody's sacrifices is like taking counterfeit money. You're only the poorer.

–DOROTHY CANFIELD FISHER (1879-1958)
AMERICAN EDUCATIONAL REFORMER, SOCIAL ACTIVIST, AND WRITER

Women do not have to sacrifice personhood if they are mothers. They do not have to sacrifice motherhood in order to be persons. Liberation was meant to expand women's opportunities, not to limit them.

–ELAINE HEFFNER • 20TH/21ST-CENTURY AMERICAN PSYCHOTHERAPIST AND PARENT EDUCATOR

Self-development is a higher duty than self-sacrifice.

–ELIZABETH CADY STANTON (1815-1902)
AMERICAN SUFFRAGIST, WRITER, AND THEOLOGIAN

I never know why self-sacrifice is noble. Why is it better to sacrifice oneself than someone else?

–IVY COMPTON-BURNETT (1884-1969) • ENGLISH WRITER

"SCIENCE"

I'm not afraid of facts; I welcome facts but a congeries of facts is not equivalent to an idea. This is the essential fallacy of the so-called scientific mind. People who mistake facts for ideas are incomplete thinkers; they are gossips.

–CYNTHIA OZICK (1928-) • AMERICAN NOVELIST, ESSAYIST, AND POET

To know the history of science is to recognize the mortality of any claim to universal truth.

–EVELYN FOX KELLER • 20TH/21ST-CENTURY AMERICAN PHYSICIST

If you do something once, people will call it an accident. If you do it twice, they call it a coincidence. But do it a third time, and you've just proven a natural law.

–GRACE MURRAY HOPPER (1906-1992)
PIONEERING COMPUTER SCIENTIST AND U.S. NAVY REAR ADMIRAL

If we are going to teach "creation science" as an alternative to evolution, then we should also teach the stork theory as an alternative to biological reproduction.

–JUDITH HAYES • 20TH/21ST-CENTURY AMERICAN WRITER

[Science] has challenged the super-eminence of religion; it has turned all philosophy out of door except that which clings to its skirts; it has thrown contempt on all learning that does not depend on it; and it has bribed the skeptics by giving us immense material comforts.

–KATHERINE FULLERTON GEROULD (1879-1944) • AMERICAN TEACHER AND WRITER

Science is not neutral in its judgments, nor dispassionate, nor detached.

–KIM CHERNIN (1940-) • AMERICAN WRITER AND PSYCHOANALYST

We especially need imagination in science. It is not all mathematics, nor all logic, but it is somewhat beauty and poetry.

–MARIA MITCHELL (1818–1889) • AMERICAN ASTRONOMER

A scientist in his laboratory is not only a technician: He is also a child placed before natural phenomena which impress him like a fairy tale.

–MARIE CURIE (1867–1934)
POLISH-FRENCH CHEMIST AND RADIOLOGY PIONEER; FIRST TWO-TIME NOBEL LAUREATE

Women have been more systematically excluded from doing serious science than from performing any other social activity except, perhaps, frontline warfare.

–SANDRA HARDING • 20TH/21ST-CENTURY AMERICAN FEMINIST PHILOSOPHER OF SCIENCE

The true definition of science is the study of the beauty of the world.

–SIMONE WEIL (1909–1943) • FRENCH SOCIAL PHILOSOPHER AND ACTIVIST

Science—like art, religion, political theory, or psychoanalysis—is work that holds out the promise of philosophic understanding, excites in us the belief that we can "make sense of it all."

–VIVAN GORNICK (1938–) • AMERICAN FEMINIST WRITER AND CRITIC

"SECURITY"

Only in growth, reform, and change, paradoxically enough, is true security to be found.

–ANNE MORROW LINDBERGH (1906–2001)
AMERICAN WRITER AND PIONEERING AVIATOR

To multiply the harbors does not reduce the sea.

–EMILY DICKINSON (1830–1886) • AMERICAN POET

There is no such thing as security. There never has been.

–GERMAINE GREER (1939–) • AUSTRALIAN-BORN WRITER AND SOCIAL CRITIC

No matter how big or soft or warm your bed is, you still have to get out of it.

–GRACE SLICK (1939–) • AMERICAN ROCK SINGER

Security is mostly superstition; it does not exist in nature nor do the children of men as a whole experience it. Avoiding danger is no safer in the long run than outright exposure. To keep our faces towards change and behave as free spirits in the presence of fate is strength undefeatable.

–HELEN KELLER (1880–1968) • AMERICAN WRITER AND ACTIVIST

Insisting on perfect safety is for people who don't have the balls to live in the real world.

–MARY SHAFER
20TH/21ST-CENTURY AMERICAN, CHIEF ENGINEER OF NASA DRYDEN FLIGHT RESEARCH CENTER

Women have got to make the world safe for men since men have made it so darned unsafe for women.

–LADY NANCY ASTOR (1879–1964)
FIRST FEMALE TO TAKE A SEAT IN BRITISH HOUSE OF COMMONS

"SELF-ACCEPTANCE"

I used to think I liked myself but then I realized I was just using me to get to someone else.

–DANA EAGLE • 20TH/21ST-CENTURY AMERICAN COMEDIAN

Self-esteem isn't everything; it's just that there's nothing without it.

–GLORIA STEINEM (1934–) • AMERICAN FEMINIST AND COFOUNDER OF *MS.* MAGAZINE

When any man likes me I never am surprised, for I think how should he help it? When any man does not like me, I think him a blockhead.

–HESTER LYNCH PIOZZI (1741–1821) • ENGLISH DIARIST

Delusions of grandeur make me feel a lot better about myself.

–JANE WAGNER (1935–) • AMERICAN PLAYWRIGHT AND COMEDY WRITER

All men seek esteem; the best by lifting themselves, which is hard to do, the rest by shoving others down, which is much easier.

–MARY RENAULT (1905–1983) • ENGLISH WRITER

To say something nice about themselves—this is the hardest thing in the world for people to do. They'd rather take their clothes off.

–NANCY FRIDAY (1933–) • AMERICAN FEMINIST WRITER

Women who set a low value on themselves make life hard for all women.

–NELLIE MCCLUNG (1873–1951) • CANADIAN JOURNALIST AND SUFFRAGIST

I'm five-feet-four, but I always feel six-foot-one, tall and strong.

–YVETTE MIMIEUX (1941–) • AMERICAN ACTOR

"*SELF-KNOWLEDGE*"

Figuring out who you are is the whole point of the human experience.

–ANNA QUINDLEN (1953–) • AMERICAN JOURNALIST AND WRITER

You can live a lifetime and, at the end of it, know more about other people than you know about yourself.

–BERYL MARKHAM (1902–1986)
ENGLISH-BORN KENYAN PILOT AND WRITER

The things we hate about ourselves aren't more real
than things we like about ourselves.

–ELLEN GOODMAN (1941–) • AMERICAN JOURNALIST

•

The secret of the world is this: The world is entirely circular, and you will go round and round endlessly, never finding what you want, unless you have found what you really want inside yourself. When you follow a star you know you will never reach that star; rather it will guide you to where you want to go. It's a reference point, not an end in itself, even though you seem to be following it. So it is with the world. It will only ever lead you back to yourself. The end of all your exploring will be to cease from exploration and know the place for the first time.

–JEANETTE WINTERSON (1959–) • ENGLISH WRITER

•

We are well advised to keep on nodding terms with the people we used to be, whether we find them attractive company or not. Otherwise they turn up unannounced and surprise us, come hammering on the mind's door at 4 a.m. of a bad night and demand to know who is going to make amends.

–JOAN DIDION (1934–) • AMERICAN WRITER

•

I began to have an idea of my life, not as the slow shaping of achievement to fit my preconceived purposes, but as the gradual discovery and growth of a purpose which I did not know.

–JOANNA FIELD (MARION BLACKETT MILNER) (1900–1998)
ENGLISH PSYCHOTHERAPIST AND DIARIST

•

It's where we go, and what we do when we get there, that tells us who we are.

–JOYCE CAROL OATES (1938–) • AMERICAN WRITER

•

It's a sad day when you find out that it's not accident or time
or fortune but just yourself that kept things from you.

–LILLIAN HELLMAN (1905–1984) • AMERICAN PLAYWRIGHT

Whenever I dwell for any length of time on my own shortcomings, they gradually begin to seem mild, harmless, rather engaging little things, not at all like the staring defects in other people's characters.

–MARGARET HALSEY (1910–1997) • AMERICAN WRITER

There's a period of life when we swallow a knowledge of ourselves and it becomes either good or sour inside.

–PEARL BAILEY (1918–1990) • AMERICAN SINGER AND ACTOR

When I thought about who we are as Indian women, I had to take a good look at myself. . . . I was reminded about how life, to me, is a neverending learning process, a journey of discovering ourselves, what we are capable of and what we are not, what we hold in the endless sea of our soul. . . . Who are you?

–ROXANNE SWENTZELL • 20TH/21ST-CENTURY NATIVE AMERICAN SCULPTOR

If we go down into ourselves we find that we possess exactly what we desire.

–SIMONE WEIL (1909–1943) • FRENCH SOCIAL PHILOSOPHER AND ACTIVIST

Each has his past shut in him like the leaves of a book known to him by his heart, and his friends can only read the title.

–VIRGINIA WOOLF (1882–1941) • ENGLISH NOVELIST, ESSAYIST, AND CRITIC

"SELF-RELIANCE"

Never do anything yourself that others can do for you.

–AGATHA CHRISTIE (1890–1976) • ENGLISH WRITER

I was trained by my husband. He said, "If you want a thing done—go. If not—send." I belong to that group of people who move the piano themselves.

–ELEANOR ROBSON BELMONT (1878–1979) • ENGLISH-BORN ACTRESS

The externals are simply so many props; everything we need is within us.

–ETTY HILLESUM (1914–1943) • DUTCH-BORN JEWISH DIARIST

You're all you've got.

–JANIS JOPLIN (1943–1970)
AMERICAN ROCK SINGER

In this life you have to be your own hero. By this I mean you have to win whatever it is that matters to you by your own strength and in your own way.

–JEANETTE WINTERSON (1959–) • ENGLISH WRITER

We're all in this alone.

–LILY TOMLIN (1939–)
AMERICAN COMEDIAN AND ACTOR

How can a rational being be ennobled by anything that is not obtained by its own exertions?

–MARY WOLLSTONECRAFT (1759–1797) • ENGLISH WRITER

"SELF-RESPECT"

Yes, folks today have . . . got this idea that self-respect means "I am a terrific person. I am wonderful. Me, me, me." That's not self-respect; that's vanity.

–BESSIE DELANY (1891–1995) • AFRICAN-AMERICAN DENTIST AND MEMOIRIST

In my day, we didn't have self-esteem, we had self-respect, and no more of it than we had earned.

–JANE HADDAM • 20TH/21ST-CENTURY AMERICAN MYSTERY NOVELIST

To have that sense of one's intrinsic worth which constitutes self-respect is potentially to have everything: the ability to discriminate, to love, and to remain indifferent. To lack it is to be locked within oneself, paradoxically incapable of either love or indifference.

–JOAN DIDION (1934-) • AMERICAN WRITER

The minute you settle for less than you deserve, you get even less than you settled for.

–MAUREEN DOWD (1952-) • AMERICAN COLUMNIST AND WRITER

When asked, most folks will gladly tell us about ourselves, who we are, what we're feeling, and where we should be heading. And if we don't honor ourselves by listening to our lives, we'll believe them.

–SUSAN L. TAYLOR • 20TH/21ST-CENTURY AFRICAN-AMERICAN JOURNALIST AND EDITOR

"SEX"

Sex is God's joke on human beings.

–BETTE DAVIS (1908-1989) • AMERICAN ACTOR

If God was a woman she would have made sperm taste like chocolate.

–CARRIE P. SNOW • 20TH/21ST-CENTURY AMERICAN COMEDIAN

I know it does make people happy, but to me it is just like having a cup of tea.

–CYNTHIA PAYNE (1932-) • ENGLISH MADAM AND PUBLIC SPEAKER

If all the girls who attended the Yale prom were laid end to end, I wouldn't be a bit surprised.

–DOROTHY PARKER (1893-1967) • AMERICAN WRITER AND CRITIC

As far as I can see, from Sharon Stone's love scene in *Basic Instinct*, they molded her body out of tough Plasticine. She was shagging Michael Douglas like a donkey, and not an inch moved. If that had been me, there would have been things flying around hitting me in the eye.

—EMMA THOMPSON (1959-) • ENGLISH ACTOR AND SCREENWRITER

•

Acting is not very hard. The most important things are to be able to laugh and cry: If I have to cry, I think of my sex life. And if I have to laugh, well, I think of my sex life.

—GLENDA JACKSON (1936-) • ENGLISH ACTOR AND POLITICIAN

•

Whatever else can be said about sex, it cannot be called a dignified performance.

—HELEN LAWRENSON (1904-1982)
AMERICAN WRITER AND EDITOR

•

For women the best aphrodisiacs are words. The G-spot is in the ears. He who looks for it below there is wasting his time.

—ISABEL ALLENDE (1942-) • CHILEAN-AMERICAN WRITER

•

On-screen love is so technical. The whole time you're doing it, they're telling you, "OK, tilt your head to the left. Put his hand under your right breast." Meanwhile, you're thinking about the candy bar you're going to grab when it's all over. It's as passionate as picking your toes.

—JESSICA CAUFFIEL (1976-) • AMERICAN ACTOR AND SINGER

•

Being a woman in the pop world, sexuality is half poison and half liberation.

—LADY GAGA (1986-) • AMERICAN POP SINGER AND CELEBRITY

•

To me, "sexual freedom" means freedom from having to have sex.

—LILY TOMLIN (1939-) • AMERICAN COMEDIAN AND ACTOR

Forget about the mind. The clitoris is a terrible thing to waste.

–LISA KOGAN • 20TH/21ST-CENTURY AMERICAN JOURNALIST

•

Sex is emotion in motion.

–MAE WEST (1893–1980)
AMERICAN ACTOR, WRITER, AND SEX SYMBOL

•

Those S&M people, they are bossy.

–MARGARET CHO (1968–)
KOREAN-AMERICAN COMEDIAN AND ACTOR

•

It is not sex that gives the pleasure, but the lover.

–MARGE PIERCY (1936–) • AMERICAN POET, NOVELIST, AND SOCIAL ACTIVIST

•

My body ached for experience, and I allowed my loins to take over when social decisions were being made.

–MARIKO TAMAKI • 20TH/21ST-CENTURY CANADIAN WRITER AND PERFORMER

•

Sex. In America an obsession. In other parts of the world a fact.

–MARLENE DIETRICH (1901–1992) • GERMAN-BORN ACTOR AND SINGER

•

One should never be sexually involved with anyone one genuinely cares for. A sexual relationship guarantees a loss.

–MARY GORDON (1949–) • AMERICAN WRITER

•

You mustn't force sex to do the work of love or love to do the work of sex.

–MARY MCCARTHY (1912–1989) • AMERICAN WRITER AND CRITIC

•

It doesn't make any difference what you do in the bedroom as long as you don't do it in the street and frighten the horses.

–MRS. PATRICK CAMPBELL (1865–1940) • ENGLISH ACTOR

By elevating the loss of virginity while stereotyping the state of being a virgin, we tell girls that what boys do with them is more significant to their maturing than what they themselves choose to do.

–NAOMI WOLF (1962–) • AMERICAN WRITER AND FEMINIST

•

The resistance of a woman is not always proof of her virtue but more frequently of her experience.

–NINON DE LENCLOS (1620–1705) • FRENCH COURTESAN

•

Women are like ovens. We need five to fifteen minutes to heat up.

–SANDRA BULLOCK (1964–) • AMERICAN FILM ACTOR

•

How love the limb-loosener sweeps me away . . .

–SAPPHO (CA. 630 BCE) • ANCIENT GREEK LYRIC POET

•

I'm suggesting we call sex something else, and it should include everything from kissing to sitting close together.

–SHERE HITE (1942–) • AMERICAN SEX EDUCATOR AND FEMINIST

•

Sex is hardly ever just about sex.

–SHIRLEY MACLAINE (1934–)
AMERICAN ACTOR AND WRITER

•

AIDS obliges people to think of sex as having, possibly, the direst consequences: suicide. Or murder.

–SUSAN SONTAG (1933–2004)
AMERICAN ESSAYIST, NOVELIST, INTELLECTUAL, AND ACTIVIST

•

I'm as pure as the driven slush.

–TALULLAH BANKHEAD (1902–1968)
AMERICAN ACTOR

In America you can get away with murder, but not with sex.

–XAVIERA HOLLANDER (1943–)
DUTCH WRITER AND FORMER CALL GIRL/MADAM

•

I know nothing about sex, because I was always married.

–ZSA ZSA GABOR (1917–)
HUNGARIAN-AMERICAN ACTRESS AND SOCIALITE

•

APPEAL

Sex appeal is 50 percent what you've got and 50 percent what people think you've got.

–SOPHIA LOREN (1934–) • ITALIAN ACTOR

•

I dress sexily—but not in an obvious way. Sexy in a virginal way.

–VICTORIA BECKHAM (1974–) • ENGLISH SINGER

•

EDUCATION

See also Reproductive Rights

•

Conservatives say teaching sex education in the public schools will promote promiscuity. With our education system? If we promote promiscuity the same way we promote math or science, they've got nothing to worry about.

–BEVERLY MICKINS
20TH/21ST-CENTURY AFRICAN-AMERICAN ACTOR AND COMEDIAN

•

We want better reasons for having children than not knowing how to prevent them.

–DORA RUSSELL (1894–1986)
ENGLISH FEMINIST AND SOCIAL REFORMER

It is bad enough that people are dying of AIDS, but no one should die of ignorance.

–ELIZABETH TAYLOR (1932–) • ENGLISH-BORN AMERICAN ACTOR

Most mothers think that to keep young people away from lovemaking, it is enough never to mention it in front of them.

–MARIE MADELEINE DE LA FAYETTE (1634–1693) • FRENCH WRITER

I was raised in a small town. It was so small that our school taught driver's education and sex education in the same car.

–MARY SUE TERRY • 20TH/21ST-CENTURY AMERICAN POLITICIAN

AND MEN

Guys would sleep with a bicycle if it had the right color lip gloss on. They have no shame. They're like bull elks in a field.

–TORI AMOS (1963–) • AMERICAN PIANIST AND SINGER-SONGWRITER

We have reason to believe that man first walked upright to free his hands for masturbation.

–LILY TOMLIN (1939–) • AMERICAN COMEDIAN AND ACTOR

A man will teach his wife what is needed to arouse his desires. And there is no reason for a woman to know any more than what her husband is prepared to teach her. If she gets married knowing far too much about what she wants and doesn't want then she will be ready to find fault with her husband.

–BARBARA CARTLAND (1901–2000) • ENGLISH WRITER

Men in power always seem to get involved in sex scandals, but women don't even have a word for "male bimbo." Except maybe "Senator."

–ELAYNE BOOSLER (1952–) • AMERICAN COMEDIAN

"SEXUAL ORIENTATION"

See also Lesbians

Sometimes I think if there was a third sex men wouldn't get so much as a glance from me.

—AMANDA VAIL • 20TH/21ST-CENTURY AMERICAN ART CRITIC

Honestly, I like everything. Boyish girls, girlish boys, the thick, the thin. Which is a problem when I'm walking down the street.

—ANGELINA JOLIE (1975–) • AMERICAN ACTOR

Heterosexuality is not normal, it's just common.

—DOROTHY PARKER (1893–1967) • AMERICAN WRITER AND CRITIC

The queer are the mirror reflecting the heterosexual tribe's fear: being different, being other and therefore lesser, therefore subhuman, inhuman, nonhuman.

—GLORIA ANZALDÚA (1942–2004) • CHICANA FEMINIST AND CULTURAL THEORIST

Pronouns make it hard to keep our sexual orientation a secret when our coworkers ask us about our weekend. "I had a great time with . . . them." Great! Now they don't think you're queer—just a big slut!

—JUDY CARTER

20TH/21ST-CENTURY AMERICAN HUMORIST, MOTIVATIONAL SPEAKER, AND COMEDY COACH

The next time someone asks you, "Hey, howdja get to be a homosexual anyway?" tell them, "Homosexuals are chosen first on talent, then interview . . . then the swimsuit and evening gown competition pretty much gets rid of the rest of them."

—KAREN WILLIAMS • 20TH/21ST-CENTURY AFRICAN-AMERICAN COMEDIAN AND EDUCATOR

The Bible contains six admonishments to homosexuals and 362 admonishments to heterosexuals. That doesn't mean that God doesn't love heterosexuals. It's just that they need more supervision.

–LYNN LAVNER • 20TH/21ST-CENTURY AMERICAN COMEDIAN AND MUSICIAN

•

It is so true that a woman may be in love with a woman, and a man with a man. It is pleasant to be sure of it, because it is undoubtedly the same love that we shall feel when we are angels.

–MARGARET FULLER (1810–1850) • AMERICAN WRITER, EDITOR, INTELLECTUAL, AND FEMINIST

•

Labels are for filing. Labels are for clothing. Labels are not for people.

–MARTINA NAVRATILOVA (1956–) • CZECH-AMERICAN TENNIS PLAYER

•

The single best thing about coming out of the closet is that nobody can insult you by telling you what you've just told them.

–RACHEL MADDOW (1973–) • AMERICAN POLITICAL COMMENTATOR

•

If homosexuality is a disease, let's all call in queer to work. "Hello, can't work today, still queer."

–ROBIN TYLER

20TH/21ST-CENTURY CANADIAN-BORN COMEDIAN, SINGER, AND GLBT ACTIVIST

•

If Michelangelo had been straight, the Sistine Chapel would have been wallpapered.

–ROBIN TYLER

20TH/21ST-CENTURY CANADIAN-BORN COMEDIAN, SINGER, AND GLBT ACTIVIST

•

My only regret in life is that none of my children are gay.

–SHARON OSBOURNE (1952–)

ENGLISH MUSIC PROMOTER AND TELEVISION PERSONALITY

In itself, homosexuality is as limiting as heterosexuality:
The ideal should be to be capable of loving a woman or a man; either, a human being, without feeling fear, restraint, or obligation.

—SIMONE DE BEAUVOIR (1908–1986) • FRENCH WRITER AND PHILOSOPHER

Love is love. . . . Gender is merely spare parts.

—WENDY WASSERSTEIN (1950–2006)
AMERICAN FEMINIST PLAYWRIGHT

BISEXUALITY

Homosexuality was invented by a straight world dealing with its own bisexuality.

—KATE MILLETT (1934–) • AMERICAN FEMINIST WRITER AND ACTIVIST

The time has come, I think, when we must recognize bisexuality as a normal form of human behavior.

—MARGARET MEAD (1901–1978) • AMERICAN CULTURAL ANTHROPOLOGIST

"SHOES"

If the shoe fits, it's too expensive.

—ADRIENNE GUSOFF
20TH/21ST-CENTURY AMERICAN FREELANCE WRITER AND CREATIVE CONSULTANT

A man hasn't got a corner on virtue just because his shoes are shined.

—ANNE PETRY (1908–1997) • AFRICAN-AMERICAN WRITER

Creativity often consists of merely turning up what is already there. Did you know that right and left shoes were thought up only a little more than a century ago?

—BERNICE FITZ-GIBBON (1894–1982) • AMERICAN ADVERTISING PIONEER

I did not have three thousand pairs of shoes, I had 1,060.

–IMELDA MARCOS (1929–) • FIRST LADY OF THE PHILIPPINES

Between saying and doing, many a pair of shoes is worn out.

–IRIS MURDOCH (1919–1999) • IRISH-BORN ENGLISH NOVELIST

Englishwomen's shoes look as if they had been made by someone who had often heard shoes described, but had never seen any.

–MARGARET HALSEY (1910–1997) • AMERICAN WRITER

All God's children need traveling shoes.

–MAYA ANGELOU (1928–)
AFRICAN-AMERICAN POET, MEMOIRIST, AND CIVIL RIGHTS ACTIVIST

What becomes of the broken-hearted? They buy shoes.

–MIMI POND • 20TH/21ST-CENTURY AMERICAN WRITER, CARTOONIST, AND ILLUSTRATOR

I still have my feet on the ground, I just wear better shoes.

–OPRAH WINFREY (1954–)
AFRICAN-AMERICAN TELEVISION HOST AND MAGAZINE PUBLISHER

HIGH HEELS

Yet if a woman never lets herself go, how will she ever know how far she might have got? If she never takes off her high-heeled shoes, how will she ever know how far she could walk or how fast she could run?

–GERMAINE GREER (1939–) • AUSTRALIAN-BORN WRITER AND SOCIAL CRITIC

I don't know who invented the high heel, but all men owe him a lot.

–MARILYN MONROE (1926–1962) • AMERICAN ACTOR AND SEX SYMBOL

If high heels were so wonderful, men would be wearing them.

–SUE GRAFTON (1940–) • AMERICAN WRITER

"SHOPPING"

Shopping is better than sex. If you're not satisfied after shopping you can make an exchange for something you really like.

–ADRIENNE GUSOFF
20TH/21ST-CENTURY AMERICAN FREELANCE WRITER AND CREATIVE CONSULTANT

I was street smart, but unfortunately the street was Rodeo Drive.

–CARRIE FISHER (1956–) • AMERICAN ACTRESS AND NOVELIST

If men liked shopping, they'd call it research.

–CYNTHIA NELMS (1942–1995) • AMERICAN MUSICIAN AND SINGER

Shopping is a woman thing. It's a contact sport like football. Women enjoy the scrimmage, the noisy crowds, the danger of being trampled to death, and the ecstasy of the purchase.

–ERMA BOMBECK (1927–1996) • AMERICAN HUMORIST

Win or lose, we go shopping after the election.

–IMELDA MARCOS (1929–) • FIRST LADY OF THE PHILIPPINES

The quickest way to know a woman is to go shopping with her.

–MARCELENE COX • 20TH-CENTURY AMERICAN WRITER

Buying is a profound pleasure.

–SIMONE DE BEAUVOIR (1908–1986)
FRENCH WRITER AND PHILOSOPHER

I always say shopping is cheaper than a psychiatrist.

–TAMMY FAYE BAKKER (1942–)
AMERICAN CHRISTIAN SINGER AND TELEVISION PERSONALITY

SALES

I take Him shopping with me. I say, OK, Jesus, help me find a bargain.

—TAMMY FAYE BAKKER (1942-)
AMERICAN CHRISTIAN SINGER AND TELEVISION PERSONALITY

"*SILENCE*"

Lying is done with words and also with silence.

—ADRIENNE RICH (1929-)
AMERICAN POET, THEORIST, AND FEMINIST

In the midst of putative peace, a writer can, like I did, be unfortunate enough to stumble on a silent war. The trouble is that once you see it, you can't unsee it. And once you've seen it, keeping quiet, saying nothing, becomes as political an act as speaking out.

—ARUNDHATI ROY (1961-) • INDIAN NOVELIST AND ACTIVIST

My silences have not protected me. Your silence will not protect you.

—AUDRE LORDE (1934-1992)
AFRICAN-AMERICAN FEMINIST WRITER AND ACTIVIST

Silence gives consent.

—MRS. E. D. E. N. SOUTHWORTH (1819-1899)
AMERICAN WRITER

There is no need to go to India or anywhere else to find peace. You will find that deep place of silence right in your room, your garden, or even your bathtub.

—ELISABETH KÜBLER-ROSS (1926-2004)
SWISS PSYCHIATRIST, SPECIALIST ON GRIEVING AND DEATH

Silence can be as different as sounds.

—ELIZABETH BOWEN (1899-1973)
ANGLO-IRISH WRITER

•

They tell us sometimes that if we had only kept quiet, all these desirable things would have come about of themselves. I am reminded of the Greek clown who, having seen an archer bring down a flying bird, remarked, sagely: "You might have saved your arrow, for the bird would anyway have been killed by the fall."

—ELIZABETH CADY STANTON (1815-1902)
AMERICAN SUFFRAGIST, WRITER, AND THEOLOGIAN

•

Speech is often barren; but silence also does not necessarily brood over a full nest.

—GEORGE ELIOT (MARY ANN EVANS) (1819-1880)
ENGLISH WRITER

•

Oblivion has been noticed as the offspring of silence.

—HANNAH MORE (1745-1833)
ENGLISH PLAYWRIGHT, RELIGIOUS WRITER, AND PHILANTHROPIST

•

Silence afflicts too many women's lives—the silence that keeps women from expressing themselves freely, from being full participants even in the lives of their own families.

—HILLARY RODHAM CLINTON (1947-) • AMERICAN POLITICIAN AND FIRST LADY

•

A small silence came between us, as precise as a picture hanging on the wall.

—JEAN STAFFORD (1915-1979) • AMERICAN WRITER

In silence you hear who you are becoming. You create yourself.

–JEWEL (1974–) • AMERICAN SINGER-SONGWRITER

I work out of silence, because silence makes up for my actual lack of working space. Silence substitutes for actual space, for psychological distance, for a sense of privacy and intactness. In this sense silence is absolutely necessary.

–RADKA DONNELL • 20TH/21ST-CENTURY AMERICAN QUILT ARTIST

Silence is peopled with voices.

–SOR JUANA INES DE LA CRUZ (1648–1695)
MEXICAN SCHOLAR, NUN, AND WRITER

Silence is the only genius a fool has.

–ZORA NEALE HURSTON (1891–1960)
AFRICAN-AMERICAN FOLKLORIST AND WRITER

"SIN"

Of two evils choose the prettier.

–CAROLYN WELLS (1869–1942)
AMERICAN WRITER

Women keep a special corner of their hearts for sins they have never committed.

–CORNELIA OTIS SKINNER (1899–1979) • AMERICAN WRITER AND ACTOR

There is only one real sin, and that is to persuade oneself that the second-best is anything but the second-best.

–DORIS LESSING (1919–) • ENGLISH WRITER

The only sin passion can commit is to be joyless.

–DOROTHY SAYERS (1893–1957)
ENGLISH WRITER AND TRANSLATOR

Original thought is like original sin: Both happened before you were born to people you could not have possibly met.

–FRAN LEBOWITZ (1950–) • AMERICAN HUMORIST

•

To err is human, but it feels divine.

–MAE WEST (1893–1980)
AMERICAN ACTOR, WRITER, AND SEX SYMBOL

•

When women go wrong, men go right after them.

–MAE WEST (1893–1980)
AMERICAN ACTRESS, WRITER, AND SEX SYMBOL

•

Many are saved from sin by being so inept at it.

–MIGNON MCLAUGHLIN (1913–1983)
AMERICAN JOURNALIST AND WRITER

•

A homely face and no figure have aided many women heavenward.

–MINNA THOMAS ANTRIM (1856–1950) • AMERICAN WRITER

•

The wages of sin are death, but by the time taxes are taken out, it's just sort of a tired feeling.

–PAULA POUNDSTONE (1959–) • AMERICAN COMEDIAN

•

All sins are attempts to fill voids.

–SIMONE WEIL (1909–1943)
FRENCH SOCIAL PHILOSOPHER AND ACTIVIST

•

"SINGLEHOOD"

Being an old maid is like death by drowning, a really delightful sensation after you cease to struggle.

–EDNA FERBER (1885-1968) • AMERICAN WRITER

I've never been married, but I tell people I'm divorced so they won't think something's wrong with me.

–ELAYNE BOOSLER (1952-) • AMERICAN COMEDIAN

I think, therefore I'm single.

–LIZZ WINSTEAD (1961-)
AMERICAN COMEDIAN AND COMEDY WRITER

I'm single because I was born that way.

–MAE WEST (1893-1980)
AMERICAN ACTRESS, WRITER, AND SEX SYMBOL

I figure the only time I really need a man is about once a month, when it's time to flip my mattress.

–PAMELA YAGER
20TH/21ST-CENTURY AMERICAN COMEDIAN AND BACHELORETTE PARTY PRODUCER

There are a lot of great things about not being married. But one of the worst things is no one believes that.

–STEPHANIE BRUSH
20TH/21ST-CENTURY AMERICAN WRITER, SINGER, AND ACTOR

"SISTERS"

See Family

"SLEEP"

No day is so bad it can't be fixed with a nap.

–CARRIE P. SNOW • 20TH/21ST-CENTURY AMERICAN COMEDIAN

A ruffled mind makes a restless pillow.

–CHARLOTTE BRONTË (1816–1855) • ENGLISH WRITER

Most people do not consider dawn to be an attractive experience—unless they are still up.

–ELLEN GOODMAN (1941–) • AMERICAN JOURNALIST

Go Away—I'm Asleep. [her epitaph]

–JOAN HACKETT (1934–1983) • AMERICAN ACTOR

Surely it's better to sleep late in the morning only when it's a rare privilege, not an everyday occurrence.

–LAUREN BACALL (1924–) • AMERICAN MODEL AND ACTOR

For eight years, I was sleeping with the president. If that doesn't give you special access, I don't know what does.

–NANCY REAGAN (1921–) • FIRST LADY OF THE UNITED STATES

There is always time for a nap.

–SUZY BECKER
20TH/21ST-CENTURY AMERICAN WRITER AND ILLUSTRATOR

When action grows unprofitable, gather information; when information grows unprofitable, sleep.

–URSULA K. LE GUIN (1929–) • AMERICAN WRITER

"SMOKING"

I want all hellions to quit puffing that hell fume in God's clean air.

–CARRIE NATION (1846–1911) • AMERICAN TEMPERANCE ACTIVIST

The same people who tell us that smoking doesn't cause cancer are now telling us that advertising cigarettes doesn't cause smoking.

–ELLEN GOODMAN (1941–) • AMERICAN JOURNALIST

There are some circles in America where it seems to be more socially acceptable to carry a handgun than a packet of cigarettes.

–KATHARINE WHITEHORN (1926–) • ENGLISH JOURNALIST, WRITER, AND COLUMNIST

They threaten me with lung cancer, and still I smoke and smoke. If they'd only threaten me with hard work, I might stop.

–MIGNON MCLAUGHLIN (1913–1983) • AMERICAN JOURNALIST AND WRITER

I quit smoking. I feel better. I smell better. And it's safer to drink from old beer cans lying around the house.

–ROSEANNE BARR (1952–) • AMERICAN COMEDIAN

I gave up smoking four years, two weeks, and five days ago. But who misses it?

–SANDRA SCOPPETTONE (1936–) • AMERICAN WRITER

"SOCIAL REFORM"

The master's tools will never dismantle the master's house.

–AUDRE LORDE (1934-1992) • AFRICAN-AMERICAN FEMINIST WRITER AND ACTIVIST

Thinking about profound social change, conservatives always expect disaster, while revolutionaries confidently anticipate utopia. Both are wrong.

–CAROLYN HEILBRUN (1926-2003) • AMERICAN ACADEMIC AND FEMINIST WRITER

Myth, legend, and ritual . . . function to maintain a status quo. That makes them singularly bad in coping with change, indeed counterproductive, for change is the enemy of myth.

–ELIZABETH JANEWAY (1913-2005) • AMERICAN WRITER AND CRITIC

All reformations seem formidable before they are attempted.

–HANNAH MORE (1745-1833)
ENGLISH PLAYWRIGHT, RELIGIOUS WRITER, AND PHILANTHROPIST

Use what is dominant in a culture to change it quickly.

–JENNY HOLZER (1950-) • AMERICAN CONCEPTUAL ARTIST

Reform is born of need, not pity. No vital movement of the people has worked down, for good or evil; fermented, instead, carried up the heaving, cloggy mass.

–REBECCA HARDING DAVIS (1831-1919) • AMERICAN WRITER AND JOURNALIST

To be successful a person must attempt but one reform. By urging two, both are injured, as the average mind can grasp and assimilate but one idea at a time.

–SUSAN B. ANTHONY (1820-1906) • AMERICAN SUFFRAGIST AND NEWSPAPER PUBLISHER

"SOCIETY"

To understand how any society functions you must understand the relationship between the men and the women.

—ANGELA DAVIS (1944-) • AMERICAN SOCIAL JUSTICE ACTIVIST

Women are the real architects of society.

—HARRIET BEECHER STOWE (1811-1896)
AMERICAN ABOLITIONIST

Social life and murder have a lot in common. Both are a process of elimination.

—JANE STANTON HITCHCOCK • 20TH/21ST-CENTURY AMERICAN WRITER

Miss Manners refuses to allow society to seek its own level. Having peered through her lorgnette into the abyss, she can guess how low that level will be.

—JUDITH "MISS MANNERS" MARTIN (1938-) • AMERICAN ETIQUETTE EXPERT

There are people who eat the earth and eat all the people on it like in the Bible with the locusts. And other people who stand around and watch them eat it.

—LILLIAN HELLMAN (1905-1984) • AMERICAN PLAYWRIGHT

We want a society where people are free to make choices, to make mistakes, to be generous and compassionate. This is what we mean by a moral society; not a society where the state is responsible for everything, and no one is responsible for the state.

—MARGARET THATCHER (1925-) • FIRST FEMALE BRITISH PRIME MINISTER

The person and the society are yoked, like mind and body. Arguing which is more important is like debating whether oxygen or hydrogen is the more essential property of water.

—MARILYN FERGUSON (1938-) • AMERICAN SOCIAL PHILOSOPHER

Society, that first of blessings, brings with it evils death only can cure.

–SOPHIA LEE (1750–1824) • ENGLISH NOVELIST AND PLAYWRIGHT

"SOLITUDE"

See also Loneliness, Privacy

Being solitary is being alone well. . . . Luxuriously immersed in doings of your own choice, aware of the fullness of your own presence rather than the absence of others.

–ALICE KOLLER • 20TH/21ST-CENTURY AMERICAN WRITER

I'm the kind of woman that likes to enjoy herself in peace.

–ALICE WALKER (1944–) • AFRICAN-AMERICAN WRITER AND POET

I feel we are all islands in a common sea.

–ANNE MORROW LINDBERGH (1906–2001)
AMERICAN WRITER AND PIONEERING AVIATOR

Fond as we are of our loved ones, there comes at times during their absence an unexplained peace.

–ANNE SHAW (1921–) • AMERICAN WRITER

Make one's center of life inside one's self, not selfishly or excludingly, but with a kind of unassailable serenity.

–EDITH WHARTON (1862–1937) • AMERICAN WRITER

What a lovely surprise to discover how unlonely being alone can be.

–ELLEN BURSTYN (1932–) • AMERICAN ACTOR

Solitude is un-American.

—ERICA JONG (1942–)
AMERICAN WRITER

•

When they are alone they want to be with others, and when they are with others they want to be alone. After all, human beings are like that.

—GERTRUDE STEIN (1874–1946) • AMERICAN POET

•

I like being on my own better than I like anything else, but I can't give up love. Maybe it's the tension between longing and aloneness that I need. My own funicular railway, holding in balance the two things most likely to destroy me.

—JEANETTE WINTERSON (1959–) • ENGLISH WRITER

•

If any individual lives too much in relations, so that he becomes a stranger to the resources of his own nature, he falls after a while into a distraction, or imbecility, from which he can only be cured by a time of isolation, which gives the renovating fountains time to rise up.

—MARGARET FULLER (1810–1850) • AMERICAN WRITER, EDITOR, INTELLECTUAL, AND FEMINIST

•

The great omission in American life is solitude.

—MARYA MANNES (1904–1990)
AMERICAN COLUMNIST AND CRITIC

•

Solitude is the salt of personhood. It brings out the authentic flavor of every experience.

—MAY SARTON (1912–1995)
BELGIAN-BORN AMERICAN POET, NOVELIST, AND MEMOIRIST

The person who tries to live alone will not succeed as a human being. His heart withers if it does not answer another heart. His mind shrinks away if he hears only the echoes of his own thoughts and finds no other inspiration.

—PEARL S. BUCK (1892–1973)
FIRST FEMALE AMERICAN WINNER OF THE NOBEL PRIZE IN LITERATURE

•

There is a privacy about it which no other season gives you. . . . In spring, summer, and fall people sort of have an open season on each other; only in the winter, in the country, can you have longer, quiet stretches when you can savor belonging to yourself.

—RUTH STOUT • 20TH/21ST-CENTURY AMERICAN WRITER AND GARDENER

•

"SPEAKING OUT"

•

'Tis woman's strongest vindication for speaking that the world needs to hear her voice. It would be subversive of every human interest that the cry of one-half the human family be stifled. . . . The world has had to limp along with the wobbling gait and one-sided hesitancy of a man with one eye.

—ANNA JULIA COOPER (1858–1964) • AFRICAN-AMERICAN FEMINIST AND EDUCATOR

•

If I waited to be right before I spoke, I would be sending little cryptic messages on the Ouija board, complaints from the other side.

—AUDRE LORDE (1934–1992) • AFRICAN-AMERICAN FEMINIST WRITER AND ACTIVIST

•

I really feel that if what I have to say is wrong, then there will be some woman who will stand up and say Audre Lorde was in error. But my words will be there, something for her to bounce off, something to incite thought, activity.

—AUDRE LORDE (1934–1992) • AFRICAN-AMERICAN FEMINIST WRITER AND ACTIVIST

Women have been trained to speak softly and carry a lipstick. Those days are over.

—BELLA ABZUG (1920–1998) • AMERICAN FEMINIST AND POLITICIAN

I'm just saying what I think, and if what I think happens to have some mature clarity, cool.

—FIONA APPLE (1977–) • AMERICAN SINGER-SONGWRITER

I succeeded by saying what everyone else is thinking.

—JOAN RIVERS (1933–) • AMERICAN COMEDIAN AND TELEVISION HOST

Powerlessness and silence go together. We . . . should use our privileged positions not as a shelter from the world's reality, but as a platform from which to speak. A voice is a gift. It should be cherished and used.

—MARGARET ATWOOD (1939–) • CANADIAN POET, NOVELIST, CRITIC, AND ACTIVIST

Be careful what you say. It comes true.

—MAXINE HONG KINGSTON (1940–)
CHINESE-AMERICAN WRITER

I have never had a vote, and I have raised hell all over this country. You don't need a vote to raise hell! You need convictions and a voice!

—MOTHER JONES (1837–1930) • AMERICAN LABOR AND COMMUNITY ORGANIZER AND ACTIVIST

I saw what could be done with words, for I had a vision of a new world as I talked.

—NELLIE MCCLUNG (1873–1951) • CANADIAN JOURNALIST AND SUFFRAGIST

"SPORTS"

The formula for success is simple: practice and concentration then more practice and more concentration.

–BABE DIDRIKSON ZAHARIAS (1914–1956) • AMERICAN GOLFER

It's not enough just to swing at the ball. You've got to loosen your girdle and let 'er fly.

–BABE DIDRIKSON ZAHARIAS (1914–1956) • AMERICAN GOLFER

I realized from a very early age that God gave me a gift, and that gift was to run, and I wanted to use it to the best of my ability.

–BETTY CUTHBERT (1938–) • AUSTRALIAN ATHLETE AND OLYMPIC CHAMPION

I use sports as a vehicle for learning: Just about everything you want to know is there.

–COLLEEN CANNON • 20TH/21ST-CENTURY AMERICAN TRIATHLETE

Marathon swimming is the most difficult physical, intellectual, and emotional battleground I have encountered. And each time I win, each time I touch the other shore, I feel worthy of any other challenge life has to offer.

–DIANA NYAD (1949–) • AMERICAN LONG-DISTANCE SWIMMER

Being a woman is of special interest only to aspiring male transsexuals. To actual women, it is simply a good excuse not to play football.

–FRAN LEBOWITZ (1950–) • AMERICAN HUMORIST

If you see a tennis player who looks as if he is working hard, then that means he isn't very good.

–HELEN MOODY (1905–1998) • AMERICAN OLYMPIC CHAMPION TENNIS PLAYER

Baseball is more than a game. It's like life played out on a field.

–JULIANA HATFIELD (1967–) • AMERICAN GUITARIST, SINGER, AND SONGWRITER

When I was first running marathons, we were sailing on a flat earth. We were afraid we'd get big legs, grow mustaches, not get boyfriends, not be able to have babies. Women thought that something would happen to them, that they'd break down or turn into men, something shadowy, when they were only limited by their own society's sense of limitations.

–KATHRINE SWITZER (1947–)
AMERICAN RUNNER, FIRST WOMAN TO OFFICIALLY RUN IN THE BOSTON MARATHON

I didn't have the same fitness or ability as the other girls, so I had to beat them with my mind.

–MARTINA HINGIS (1980–) • CZECH-BORN TENNIS PLAYER

I am building a fire, and every day I train, I add more fuel. At just the right moment, I light the match.

–MIA HAMM (1972–) • AMERICAN SOCCER PLAYER

The reason women don't play football is because 11 of them would never wear the same outfit in public.

–PHYLLIS DILLER (1917–) • AMERICAN COMEDIAN

With sports, you get the results back right away. With life, it's not always so black-and-white.

–REBECCA TWIG • 20TH/21ST-CENTURY AMERICAN CYCLIST

"STORIES"

See also Literature, Writing

The divine art is the story.

–ISAK DINESEN (KAREN BLIXEN) (1885–1962)
DANISH WRITER AND AUTOBIOGRAPHER

•

All sorrows can be borne if you put them into a story or tell a story about them.

–ISAK DINESEN (KAREN BLIXEN) (1885–1962) • DANISH WRITER AND AUTOBIOGRAPHER

•

Of course that is not the whole story, but that is the way with stories; we make them what we will. It's a way of explaining the universe while leaving the universe unexplained, it's a way of keeping it all alive, not boxing it into time.

–JEANETTE WINTERSON (1959–) • ENGLISH NOVELIST

•

We tell ourselves stories in order to live.

–JOAN DIDION (1934–) • AMERICAN WRITER

•

Those who don't get there first, before the books and poems and television shows, had stories no one ever really heard.

–LORRIE MOORE (1957–) • AMERICAN WRITER

•

We are the hero of our own story.

–MARY MCCARTHY (1912–1989)
AMERICAN WRITER AND CRITIC

•

The difference between mad people and sane people . . . is that sane people have variety when they talk-story. Mad people have only one story that they talk over and over.

–MAXINE HONG KINGSTON (1940–) • CHINESE-AMERICAN WRITER

•

The universe is made of stories, not of atoms.

–MURIEL RUKEYSER (1913–1980)
AMERICAN POET AND POLITICAL ACTIVIST

A lie hides the truth; a story tries to find it.

–PAULA FOX (1923–) • AMERICAN WRITER

In every outthrust headland, in every curving beach, in every grain of sand there is the story of the earth.

–RACHEL CARSON (1907–1964) • AMERICAN ZOOLOGIST AND MARINE BIOLOGIST

Story is a sacred visualization, a way of echoing experience.

–TERRY TEMPEST WILLIAMS
20TH/21ST-CENTURY AMERICAN ESSAYIST AND NATURALIST

There are only two or three human stories, and they go on repeating themselves as fiercely as if they had never happened before.

–WILLA CATHER (1873–1947) • AMERICAN WRITER

There is no agony like bearing an untold story inside you.

–ZORA NEALE HURSTON (1891–1960)
AFRICAN-AMERICAN FOLKLORIST AND WRITER

"STRENGTH"

Like water, be gentle and strong. Be gentle enough to follow the natural paths of the earth, and strong enough to rise up and reshape the world.

–BRENDA PETERSON • 20TH/21ST-CENTURY AMERICAN NOVELIST AND ESSAYIST

Never grow a wishbone, daughter, where a backbone ought to be.

–CLEMENTINE PADDLEFORD (1898–1967) • AMERICAN JOURNALIST

It is better to die on your feet than to live on your knees.

–DELORES IBARRURI (1895–1989)
SPANISH REVOLUTIONARY AND COMMUNIST LEADER

With the new day comes new strength and new thoughts.

–ELEANOR ROOSEVELT (1884–1962)
AMERICAN POLITICAL LEADER AND FIRST LADY

•

Life more often teaches us how to perfect our weaknesses than how to develop our strengths.

–ELIZABETH BIBESCO (1897–1945) • ENGLISH WRITER

•

It's a tough world out there, and women can't afford to be weenies.

–LAURA SCHLESSINGER (1947–) • AMERICAN CULTURAL COMMENTATOR

•

I have learned to love that which is meant to harm me, so that I can stand in the way of those who are less strong. I can take the bullets for those who aren't able to.

–MARGARET CHO (1968–) • KOREAN-AMERICAN COMEDIAN AND ACTOR

•

Women are never stronger than when they arm themselves with their weakness.

–MARIE DE VICHY-CHAMROND, MARQUISE DU DEFFAND (1697–1780)
FRENCH HOSTESS AND ARTS PATRON

•

I love to see a young girl go out and grab the world by the lapels. Life's a bitch. You've got to go out and kick ass.

–MAYA ANGELOU (1928–)
AFRICAN-AMERICAN POET, MEMOIRIST, AND CIVIL RIGHTS ACTIVIST

•

Our strength is often composed of the weakness we're damned if we're going to show.

–MIGNON MCLAUGHLIN (1913–1983) • AMERICAN JOURNALIST AND WRITER

•

Those who contemplate the beauty of the earth find reserves of strength that will endure as long as life lasts.

–RACHEL CARSON (1907–1964) • AMERICAN ZOOLOGIST AND MARINE BIOLOGIST

It is easy to imagine yourself sovereign when you are alone, to think yourself strong when you carefully avoid taking up any burden.

–SIMONE DE BEAUVOIR (1908–1986) • FRENCH WRITER AND PHILOSOPHER

Be faithful in small things because it is in them that your strength lies.

–MOTHER TERESA (1910–1997) • ALBANIAN CATHOLIC NUN; WINNER OF NOBEL PEACE PRIZE

"STRESS"

Keep your sense of humor. There's enough stress in the rest of your life to let bad shots ruin a game you're supposed to enjoy.

–AMY ALCOTT (1956–) • AMERICAN GOLFER

Sometimes the most important thing in a whole day is the rest we take between two deep breaths.

–ETTY HILLESUM (1914–1943) • DUTCH-BORN JEWISH DIARIST

More important, you have to stay happy and positive or the stress will kill you—but at least it will make you skinny!

–JOELY FISHER (1967–) • AMERICAN ACTOR

For fast-acting relief, try slowing down.

–LILY TOMLIN (1939–) • AMERICAN COMEDIAN AND ACTOR

Stress is an important dragon to slay—or at least tame—in your life.

–MARILU HENNER (1952–) • AMERICAN ACTOR

Stress is basically a disconnection from the earth, a forgetting of the breath. Stress is an ignorant state. It believes that everything is an emergency. Nothing is that important.

–NATALIE GOLDBERG (1948–) • AMERICAN WRITER, ARTIST, AND TEACHER

It has long been my belief that in times of great stress, such as a four-day vacation, the thin veneer of family wears off almost at once, and we are revealed in our true personalities.

–SHIRLEY JACKSON (1919–1965) • AMERICAN WRITER

There must be quite a few things that a hot bath won't cure, but I don't know many of them.

–SYLVIA PLATH (1932–1963) • AMERICAN POET AND PROSE WRITER

"STRIPPERS"

People always ask me, did I ever learn anything when I was a stripper? Yeah, I did. One man plus two beers equals 20 dollars.

–ANNA NICOLE SMITH (1967–2007) • AMERICAN EXOTIC DANCER, MODEL, AND ACTOR

I think all old folk's homes should have striptease. If I ran one I'd have a striptease every week.

–CYNTHIA PAYNE (1932–) • ENGLISH MADAM AND PUBLIC SPEAKER

There's a bit of a stripper in every woman.

–MELANIE GRIFFITH (1957–) • AMERICAN ACTOR

"SUCCESS"

If you want a place in the sun, you've got to put up with a few blisters.

–ABIGAIL VAN BUREN (PAULINE PHILLIPS) (1918–)
AMERICAN ADVICE COLUMNIST, ORIGINATOR OF "DEAR ABBY"

My personal recipe for success is: Do what you love and don't look at the clock.

–ANN LANDERS (ESTHER PAULINE FRIEDMAN) (1918–2002) • AMERICAN ADVICE COLUMNIST

•

The worst part of success is to try to find someone who is happy for you.

–BETTE MIDLER (1945–) • AMERICAN ACTOR AND SINGER

•

Being number one isn't everything to me, but for those few hours on the court it's way ahead of whatever's in second place.

–BILLIE JEAN KING (1943–) • AMERICAN TENNIS PLAYER

•

If you can react the same way to winning and losing, that's a big accomplishment. That quality is important because it stays with you the rest of your life, and there's going to be a life after tennis that's a lot longer than your tennis life.

–CHRIS EVERT LLOYD (1954–) • AMERICAN TENNIS PLAYER

•

I think the measure of your success to a certain extent will be the amount of things written about you that aren't true.

–CYBILL SHEPHERD (1950–) • AMERICAN ACTOR, SINGER, AND FASHION MODEL

•

Turn up your radio. Watch lots of telly and eat loads of choc. Feel guilty. Stay up all night. Learn everything in six hours that has taken you two years to compile. That's how I did it.

–DAWN FRENCH (1957–) • ENGLISH COMEDIAN

•

Instead of thinking about where you are, think about where you want to be. It takes 20 years of hard work to become an overnight success.

–DIANA RANKIN • 20TH/21ST-CENTURY AMERICAN WRITER, POET, STORYTELLER, AND PUBLIC SPEAKER

•

Winning may not be everything, but losing has little to recommend it.

–DIANNE FEINSTEIN (1933–) • AMERICAN POLITICIAN, FIRST FEMALE MAYOR OF SAN FRANCISCO

It's a little depressing to become number one because
the only place you can go from there is down.

–DORIS DAY (1924–) • AMERICAN SINGER, ACTOR, AND ANIMAL RIGHTS ACTIVIST

•

Act as if it were impossible to fail.

–DOROTHEA BRANDE (1893–1948)
AMERICAN WRITER AND EDITOR

•

It had long since come to my attention that people of accomplishment rarely sat back and let things happen to them. They went out and happened to things.

–ELINOR SMITH (1911–)
RECORD-BREAKING AMERICAN AVIATOR; WORLD'S YOUNGEST LICENSED PILOT

•

Success didn't spoil me; I've always been insufferable.

–FRAN LEBOWITZ (1950–) • AMERICAN HUMORIST

•

You can stand tall without standing on someone. You can be a victor without having victims.

–HARRIET WOODS (1927–) • AMERICAN POLITICIAN AND ACTIVIST

•

This is the day of instant genius. Everybody starts at the top, and then has the problem of staying there. Lasting accomplishment, however, is still achieved through a long, slow climb and self-discipline.

–HELEN HAYES (1900–1993) • AMERICAN ACTOR

•

Will and energy sometimes prove greater than either genius or talent or temperament.

–ISADORA DUNCAN (1877–1927) • AMERICAN MODERN DANCER

•

The trouble with the rat race is that even if you win, you're still a rat.

–LILY TOMLIN (1939–) • AMERICAN COMEDIAN AND ACTOR

She's the kind of girl who climbed the ladder of success, wrong by wrong.

–MAE WEST (1893–1980) • AMERICAN ACTRESS, WRITER, AND SEX SYMBOL

Success does not implant bad characteristics in people. It merely steps up the growth rate of the bad characteristics they already had.

–MARGARET HALSEY (1910–1997) • AMERICAN WRITER

People think that at the top there isn't much room. They tend to think of it as an Everest. My message is that there is tons of room at the top.

–MARGARET THATCHER (1925–) • FIRST FEMALE BRITISH PRIME MINISTER

Success is having a flair for the thing that you are doing; [while] knowing that is not enough, that you have got to have hard work and a sense of purpose.

–MARGARET THATCHER (1925–) • FIRST FEMALE BRITISH PRIME MINISTER

You can have unbelievable intelligence, you can have connections, you can have opportunities fall out of the sky. But in the end, hard work is the true, enduring characteristic of successful people.

–MARSHA EVANS • 20TH/21ST-CENTURY AMERICAN EXECUTIVE AND FORMER NAVAL OFFICER

Whoever said, "It's not whether you win or lose that counts," probably lost.

–MARTINA NAVRATILOVA (1956–) • CZECH-AMERICAN TENNIS PLAYER

Success doesn't come to you. You go to it.

–MARVA COLLINS

20TH/21ST-CENTURY AFRICAN-AMERICAN EDUCATIONAL REFORMER

The penalty of success is to be bored by people who used to snub you.

–LADY NANCY ASTOR (1879–1964)

FIRST FEMALE TO TAKE A SEAT IN BRITISH HOUSE OF COMMONS

What material success does is provide you with the ability to concentrate on other things that really matter. And that is being able to make a difference, not only in your own life, but in other people's lives.

—OPRAH WINFREY (1954-) • AFRICAN-AMERICAN TELEVISION HOST AND MAGAZINE PUBLISHER

Success is a public affair. Failure is a private funeral.

—ROSALIND RUSSELL (1907-1976) • AMERICAN ACTOR

Success will win you false friends and true enemies—succeed anyway.

—MOTHER TERESA (1910-1997) • ALBANIAN CATHOLIC NUN; WINNER OF NOBEL PEACE PRIZE

Integrity is so perishable in the summer months of success.

—VANESSA REDGRAVE (1937-) • ENGLISH ACTOR

"SUFFERING"

If we had no winter, the spring would not be so pleasant; if we did not sometimes taste of adversity, prosperity would not be so welcome.

—ANNE BRADSTREET (1612-1672) • FIRST POET PUBLISHED IN AMERICA

I do not believe that sheer suffering teaches. If suffering alone taught, all the world would be wise, since everyone suffers. To suffering must be added mourning, understanding, patience, love, openness, and the willingness to remain vulnerable.

—ANNE MORROW LINDBERGH (1906-2001) • AMERICAN WRITER AND PIONEERING AVIATOR

It's not that I don't suffer, it's that I know the unimportance of suffering, I know that pain is to be fought and thrown aside, not to be accepted as part of one's soul and as a permanent scar across one's view of existence.

—AYN RAND (1905-1982) • RUSSIAN-AMERICAN NOVELIST AND PHILOSOPHER

When the Japanese mend broken objects, they aggrandize the damage by filling the cracks with gold. They believe that when something's suffered damage and has a history it becomes more beautiful.

–BARBARA BLOOM (1951–) • AMERICAN ARTIST

•

This wasn't just plain terrible, this was fancy terrible. This was terrible with raisins in it.

–DOROTHY PARKER (1893–1967) • AMERICAN WRITER AND CRITIC

•

If you're going to go through hell . . . I suggest you come back learning something.

–DREW BARRYMORE (1975–) • AMERICAN ACTOR AND PRODUCER

•

People are like stained-glass windows. They sparkle and shine when the sun is out, but when the darkness sets in, their true beauty is revealed only if there is a light from within.

–ELISABETH KÜBLER-ROSS (1926–2004)
SWISS PSYCHIATRIST, SPECIALIST ON GRIEVING AND DEATH

•

Remember, we all stumble, every one of us. That's why it's a comfort to go hand in hand.

–EMILY KIMBROUGH (1899–1989) • AMERICAN EDITOR AND WRITER

•

Life does not accommodate you, it shatters you. It is meant to, and couldn't do it better: Every seed destroys its container or else there would be no fruition.

–FLORIDA SCOTT-MAXWELL (1883–1979)
AMERICAN SUFFRAGIST AND PSYCHOLOGIST

•

Although the world is full of suffering, it is full also of the overcoming of it.

–HELEN KELLER (1880–1968) • AMERICAN WRITER AND ACTIVIST

The cure for anything is salt water: sweat, tears, or the sea.

–ISAK DINESEN (KAREN BLIXEN) (1885–1962)
DANISH WRITER AND AUTOBIOGRAPHER

•

Difficult times have helped me to understand better than before how infinitely rich and beautiful life is in every way, and that so many things that one goes worrying about are of no importance whatsoever.

–ISAK DINESEN (KAREN BLIXEN) (1885–1962) • DANISH WRITER AND AUTOBIOGRAPHER

•

Well, you've got to take the bitter with the better.

–JANE ACE (1900–1974) • AMERICAN RADIO PERSONALITY

•

When you are unhappy, is there anything more maddening than to be told that you should be contented with your lot?

–KATHLEEN NORRIS (1880–1966) • AMERICAN WRITER

•

If you are willing to take the punishment, you are halfway through the battle.

–LILLIAN HELLMAN (1905–1984) • AMERICAN PLAYWRIGHT

•

If you're going to be able to look back on something and laugh about it, you might as well laugh about it now.

–MARIE OSMOND (1959–) • AMERICAN ENTERTAINER

•

You can't be brave if you've only had wonderful things happen to you.

–MARY TYLER MOORE (1936–) • AMERICAN ACTOR AND COMEDIAN

•

There are two ways of meeting difficulties. You alter the difficulties or you alter yourself to meet them.

–PHYLLIS BOTTOME (1884–1963) • ENGLISH WRITER

•

There are some things you learn best in calm, and some in storm.

–WILLA CATHER (1873–1947) • AMERICAN WRITER

"SUFFRAGE"

The vote means nothing to women. We should be armed.

–EDNA O'BRIEN (1930–) • IRISH WRITER

I want to say to you who think women cannot succeed, we have brought the government of England to this position, that it has to face this alternative: Either women are to be killed or women are to have the vote.

–EMMELINE PANKHURST (1858–1928) • ENGLISH SUFFRAGIST AND FEMINIST

Perhaps some day men will raise a tablet reading in letters of gold: "All honor to women, the first disenfranchised class in history who, unaided by any political party, won enfranchisement by its own effort . . . and achieved the victory without the shedding of a drop of human blood. All honor to women of the world!"

–HARRIOT STANTON BLATCH (1856–1940)
AMERICAN SUFFRAGIST AND SOCIAL REFORMER

We are told it will be of no use for us to ask this measure of justice—that the ballot be given to the women of our new possessions upon the same terms as to the men—because we shall not get it. It is not our business whether we are going to get it; our business is to make the demand. . . . Ask for the whole loaf and take what you can get.

–SUSAN B. ANTHONY (1820–1906) • AMERICAN SUFFRAGIST AND NEWSPAPER PUBLISHER

"SUICIDE"

We cannot blot out one page of our lives, but we can throw the book in the fire.

–GEORGE SAND (AMANDINE-AURORE-LUCIE DUPIN, BARONNE DUDEVANT) (1804–1876)
FRENCH WRITER AND FEMINIST

In New York City, one suicide in ten is attributed to a lack of storage space.

–JUDITH STONE • 20TH/21ST-CENTURY AMERICAN WRITER

People commit suicide for only one reason—to escape torment.

–LI ANG (1952-) • TAIWANESE FEMINIST WRITER

The right to choose death when life no longer holds meaning is not only the next liberation but the last human right.

–MARYA MANNES (1904-1990) • AMERICAN COLUMNIST AND CRITIC

"SWIMSUITS"

People shop for a bathing suit with more care than they do a husband or wife. The rules are the same. Look for something you'll feel comfortable wearing. Allow for room to grow.

–ERMA BOMBECK (1927-1996) • AMERICAN HUMORIST

BIKINIS

I was once cast in a stage play as a lesbian in a black bikini opposite a lesbian in a white bikini; I was the baddie in the black bikini.

–FELICITY KENDAL (1946-) • ENGLISH ACTOR

There's a side of my personality that goes completely against the East Coast educated person and wants to be a pinup girl in garages across America. . . . there's a side that wants to wear the pink angora bikini!

–MIRA SORVINO (1967-) • AMERICAN ACTOR

This bikini made me a success.

–URSULA ANDRESS (1936-)
SWISS ACTOR, FIRST "BOND GIRL"

T

"TALENT"

Everyone has talent. What is rare is the courage to follow the talent to the dark place where it leads.

—ERICA JONG (1942-) • AMERICAN WRITER

Gift, like genius, I often think, only means an infinite capacity for taking pains.

—JANE ELLICE HOPKINS (1836-1904) • ENGLISH SOCIAL REFORMER

Talent isn't genius, and no amount of energy can make it so.

—LOUISA MAY ALCOTT (1832-1888) • AMERICAN WRITER

Any talent that we are born with eventually surfaces as a need.

—MARSHA SINETAR
20TH/21ST-CENTURY AMERICAN ORGANIZATIONAL PSYCHOLOGIST AND SPEAKER

Timing and arrogance are decisive factors in the successful use of talent.

—MARYA MANNES (1904-1990) • AMERICAN COLUMNIST AND CRITIC

I believe talent is like electricity. We don't understand electricity. We use it. You can plug into it and light up a lamp, keep a heart pump going, light a cathedral, or you can electrocute a person with it. Electricity will do all that. It makes no judgment. I think talent is like that. I believe every person is born with talent.

—MAYA ANGELOU (1928-) • AFRICAN-AMERICAN POET, MEMOIRIST, AND CIVIL RIGHTS ACTIVIST

Getting ahead in a difficult profession requires avid faith in yourself. That is why some people with mediocre talent, but with great inner drive, go so much further than people with vastly superior talent.

—SOPHIA LOREN (1934-) • ITALIAN ACTOR

"TAXES"

Is there a phrase in the English language more fraught with menace than *a tax audit*?

–ERICA JONG (1942–) • AMERICAN WRITER

Only the little people pay taxes.

–LEONA HELMSLEY [ATTRIBUTED] (1920–2007)
AMERICAN HOTEL AND REAL ESTATE INVESTOR

Philosophy teaches a man that he can't take it with him; taxes teach him he can't leave it behind either.

–MIGNON MCLAUGHLIN (1913–1983) • AMERICAN JOURNALIST AND WRITER

I am thankful for the taxes I pay because it means that I'm employed.

–NANCIE J. CARMODY • 20TH/21ST-CENTURY WRITER

Why does a slight tax increase cost you two hundred dollars and a substantial tax cut save you 30 cents?

–PEG BRACKEN (1918–) • AMERICAN WRITER

"TEACHERS"

There are many teachers who could ruin you. Before you know it you could be a pale copy of this teacher or that teacher. You have to evolve on your own.

–BERENICE ABBOTT (1898–1991) • AMERICAN PHOTOGRAPHER

The task of the excellent teacher is to stimulate "apparently ordinary" people to unusual effort. The tough problem is not in identifying winners: It is in making winners out of ordinary people.

–K. PATRICIA CROSS • 20TH/21ST-CENTURY AMERICAN EDUCATOR AND UNIVERSITY ADMINISTRATOR

•

I like a teacher who gives you something to take home to think about besides homework.

–LILY TOMLIN (1939-) • AMERICAN COMEDIAN AND ACTOR

•

The most extraordinary thing about a really good teacher is that he or she transcends accepted educational methods. Such methods are designed to help average teachers approximate the performance of good teachers.

–MARGARET MEAD (1901-1978) • AMERICAN CULTURAL ANTHROPOLOGIST

•

That is the difference between good teachers and great teachers: Good teachers make the best of a pupil's means; great teachers foresee a pupil's ends.

–MARIA CALLAS (1923-1977) • GREEK SOPRANO

•

The greatest sign of success for a teacher . . . is to be able to say, "The children are now working as if I did not exist."

–MARIA MONTESSORI (1870-1952)
ITALIAN EDUCATIONAL INNOVATOR, SCIENTIST, AND PHILOSOPHER

•

For every one of us that succeeds, it's because there's somebody there to show you the way out. The light doesn't always necessarily have to be in your family; for me it was teachers and school.

–OPRAH WINFREY (1954-) • AFRICAN-AMERICAN TELEVISION HOST AND MAGAZINE PUBLISHER

•

A master can tell you what he expects of you. A teacher, though, awakens your own expectations.

–PATRICIA NEAL (1926-) • AMERICAN ACTOR

I'm bilingual. I speak English and I speak educationese.

–SHIRLEY HUFSTEDLER (1925-) • U.S. SECRETARY OF EDUCATION

Culture is an instrument wielded by teachers to manufacture teachers, who, in their turn, will manufacture still more teachers.

–SIMONE WEIL (1909-1943) • FRENCH SOCIAL PHILOSOPHER AND ACTIVIST

A toy company is releasing Teacher Barbie. Apparently, it's like Malibu Barbie, only she can't afford the Corvette.

–STEPHANIE MILLER (1961-) • AMERICAN PROGRESSIVE RADIO HOST

Great teachers transcend ideology.

–SUZANNE FIELDS
20TH/21ST-CENTURY AMERICAN COLUMNIST AND SOCIAL CRITIC

"TEACHING"

See also Education

The test of a good teacher is not how many questions he can ask his pupils that they will answer readily, but how many questions he inspires them to ask him which he finds it hard to answer.

–ALICE WELLINGTON ROLLINS (1847-1897) • AMERICAN WRITER

Teaching was the hardest work I had ever done, and it remains the hardest work I have done to date.

–ANN RICHARDS (1933-2006) • AMERICAN POLITICIAN AND GOVERNOR OF TEXAS

I am teaching. . . . It's kind of like having a love affair with a rhinoceros.

–ANNE SEXTON (1928-1974) • AMERICAN POET

My heart is singing for joy this morning. A miracle has happened! The light of understanding has shone upon my little pupil's mind, and behold, all things are changed.

–ANNE SULLIVAN (1866–1936) • AMERICAN EDUCATOR OF THE BLIND AND DEAF

•

Children require guidance and sympathy far more than instruction.

–ANNE SULLIVAN (1866–1936) • AMERICAN EDUCATOR OF THE BLIND AND DEAF

•

I cannot join the space program and restart my life as an astronaut, but this opportunity to connect my abilities as an educator with my interests in history and space is a unique opportunity to fulfill my early fantasies.

–CHRISTA MCAULIFFE (1948–1986)

FIRST AMERICAN TEACHER IN SPACE; DIED IN SPACE SHUTTLE *CHALLENGER* EXPLOSION

•

Teaching is the greatest act of optimism.

–COLLEEN WILCOX

20TH/21ST-CENTURY AMERICAN EDUCATOR AND ADMINISTRATOR

•

If I were asked to enumerate ten educational stupidities, the giving of grades would head the list. . . . If I can't give a child a better reason for studying than a grade on a report card, I ought to lock my desk and go home and stay there.

–DOROTHY DE ZOUCHE • 20TH-CENTURY AMERICAN EDUCATOR

•

Housework is a breeze. Cooking is a pleasant diversion. Putting up a retaining wall is a lark. But teaching is like climbing a mountain.

–FAWN M. BRODIE (1915–1981) • AMERICAN BIOGRAPHER

•

Good teaching is one-fourth preparation and three-fourths theater.

–GAIL GODWIN (1937–) • AMERICAN WRITER

Theories and goals of education don't matter a whit if you do not consider your students to be human beings.

–LOU ANN WALKER (1952–)
AMERICAN CONSULTANT, SIGN LANGUAGE INTERPRETER, WRITER, AND EDITOR

•

Teaching consists of equal parts perspiration, inspiration, and resignation.

–SUSAN OHANIAN • 20TH/21ST-CENTURY AMERICAN PUBLIC SCHOOL TEACHER AND WRITER

•

A teacher's day is one-half bureaucracy, one-half crisis, one-half monotony, and one-eightieth epiphany. Never mind the arithmetic.

–SUSAN OHANIAN • 20TH/21ST-CENTURY AMERICAN PUBLIC SCHOOL TEACHER AND WRITER

•

True expertise is the most potent form of authority.

–VICTORIA BOND (1945–) • AMERICAN COMPOSER AND CONDUCTOR

•

The first duty of a lecturer: to hand you after an hour's discourse a nugget of pure truth to wrap up between the pages of your notebooks, and keep on the mantlepiece forever.

–VIRGINIA WOOLF (1882–1941) • ENGLISH NOVELIST, ESSAYIST, AND CRITIC

•

"TECHNOLOGY"

•

For a list of all the ways technology has failed to improve the quality of life, please press "3."

–ALICE KAHN • 20TH/21ST-CENTURY AMERICAN WRITER AND NURSE PRACTITIONER

•

Even if smog were a risk to human life, we must remember that life in nature, without technology, is wholesale death.

–AYN RAND (1905–1982) • RUSSIAN-AMERICAN WRITER AND PHILOSOPHER

Life was simple before World War II. After that, we had systems.

–GRACE MURRAY HOPPER (1906-1992)
PIONEERING COMPUTER SCIENTIST AND U.S. NAVY REAR ADMIRAL

Films have a certain place in a certain time period. Technology is forever.

–HEDY LAMARR (1913-2000) • AUSTRIAN-BORN ACTOR AND INVENTOR

Technology evolves so much faster than wisdom.

–JENNIFER STONE (1933-)
AMERICAN JOURNALIST AND COMMENTATOR

Once upon a time we were just plain people. But that was before we began having relationships with mechanical systems. Get involved with a machine and sooner or later you are reduced to a factor.

–ELLEN GOODMAN (1941-) • AMERICAN JOURNALIST

There might be new technology, but technological progress itself was nothing new—and over the years it had not destroyed jobs, but created them.

–MARGARET THATCHER (1925-) • FIRST FEMALE BRITISH PRIME MINISTER

It is difficult not to wonder whether that combination of elements which produces a machine for labor does not create also a soul of sorts, a dull resentful metallic will, which can rebel at times.

–PEARL S. BUCK (1892-1973)
FIRST FEMALE AMERICAN WINNER OF THE NOBEL PRIZE IN LITERATURE

"TEETH"

Beastly things, teeth. Give us trouble from the cradle to the grave.

–AGATHA CHRISTIE (1890-1976) • ENGLISH WRITER

I don't have false teeth. Do you think I'd buy teeth like these?

—CAROL BURNETT (1933-) • AMERICAN COMEDIAN

•

The first thing I do in the morning is brush my teeth and sharpen my tongue.

—DOROTHY PARKER (1893-1967) • AMERICAN WRITER AND CRITIC

•

"*TELEPHONE*"

•

By inventing the telephone we've damaged the chances of telepathy.

—DOROTHY M. RICHARDSON (1873-1957) • ENGLISH WRITER

•

The telephone is a good way to talk to people without having to offer them a drink.

—FRAN LEBOWITZ (1950-) • AMERICAN HUMORIST

•

It is not rude to turn off your telephone by switching it on to an answering machine, which is cheaper and less disruptive than ripping it out of the wall. Those who are offended because they cannot always get through when they seek, at their own convenience, to barge in on people are suffering from a rude expectation.

—JUDITH "MISS MANNERS" MARTIN (1938-)
AMERICAN ETIQUETTE EXPERT

•

Hi, this is Sylvia. I'm not at home right now, so when you hear the beep . . . hang up.

—NICOLE HOLLANDER
20TH/21ST-CENTURY AMERICAN ARTIST AND CREATOR OF COMIC "SYLVIA"

"TELEVISION"

I'm always amazed that people will actually choose to sit in front of the television and just be savaged by stuff that belittles their intelligence.

—ALICE WALKER (1944-) • AFRICAN-AMERICAN WRITER AND POET

Art may imitate life, but life imitates TV.

—ANI DIFRANCO (1970-)
AMERICAN FEMINIST SINGER, GUITARIST, AND SONGWRITER

Television has proved that people will look at anything rather than each other.

—ANN LANDERS (ESTHER PAULINE FRIEDMAN) (1918-2002) • AMERICAN ADVICE COLUMNIST

Today, watching television often means fighting, violence, and foul language—and that's just deciding who gets to hold the remote control.

—DONNA GEPHART • 20TH/21ST-CENTURY AMERICAN FREELANCE WRITER

There are days when any electrical appliance in the house, including the vacuum cleaner, seems to offer more entertainment possibilities than the TV set.

—HARRIET VAN HORNE (1920-) • AMERICAN COLUMNIST AND CRITIC

There is a young and impressionable mind out there that is hungry for information. It has latched on to an electronic tube as its main source of nourishment.

—JOAN GANZ COONEY (1929-) • AMERICAN BUSINESSWOMAN AND TELEVISION PRODUCER

If you read a lot of books you are considered well read. But if you watch a lot of TV, you're not considered well viewed.

—LILY TOMLIN (1939-) • AMERICAN COMEDIAN AND ACTOR

Art is moral passion married to entertainment.
Moral passion without entertainment is propaganda, and
entertainment without moral passion is television.

–RITA MAE BROWN (1944–) • AMERICAN NOVELIST AND ACTIVIST

•

I honestly don't understand the big fuss made over nudity and sex in films. It's silly. On TV, the children can watch people murdering each other, which is a very unnatural thing, but they can't watch two people in the very natural process of making love. Now, really, that doesn't make any sense, does it?

–SHARON TATE (1943–1969) • AMERICAN ACTOR

•

"*TEMPTATION*"

•

To tempt and be tempted is much the same thing.

–CATHERINE THE GREAT (1729–1796) • RUSSIAN EMPRESS

•

I generally avoid temptation unless I can't resist it.

–MAE WEST (1893–1980) • AMERICAN ACTOR, WRITER, AND SEX SYMBOL

•

It's not easy being quiet and good, it's like hanging on to the edge of a bridge when you've already fallen over; you don't seem to be moving, just dangling there, and yet it is taking all your strength.

–MARGARET ATWOOD (1939–) • CANADIAN POET, NOVELIST, CRITIC, AND ACTIVIST

•

I believe in practicing prudence at least once every two or three years.

–MOLLY IVINS (1944–2007) • AMERICAN JOURNALIST AND POLITICAL COMMENTATOR

•

Lead me not into temptation; I can find the way myself.

–RITA MAE BROWN (1944–) • AMERICAN WRITER AND ACTIVIST

"THANKSGIVING"

See Holidays

"THERAPY"

The trouble with therapy is that it makes life go backward.

–ANNE SEXTON (1928–1974) • AMERICAN POET

A garden is the best alternative therapy.

–GERMAINE GREER (1939–)
AUSTRALIAN-BORN WRITER AND SOCIAL CRITIC

Fortunately, psychoanalysis is not the only way to resolve inner conflicts. Life itself remains a very effective therapist.

–KAREN HORNEY (1885–1952) • GERMAN NEO-FREUDIAN PSYCHOANALYST

Going into therapy doesn't guarantee poop on toast.

–LAURA SCHLESSINGER (1947–) • AMERICAN CULTURAL COMMENTATOR

Men, as a general rule, shy away from therapy because there is no obvious way to keep score.

–MERRILL MARKOE • 20TH/21ST-CENTURY AMERICAN COMEDIAN AND COMEDY WRITER

Sometimes sweat is the best form of therapy.

–SAMANTHA DUNN
20TH/21ST-CENTURY AMERICAN JOURNALIST AND WRITER

When you feel really lousy, puppy therapy is indicated.

–SARA PARETSKY (1947–) • AMERICAN WRITER

"THINKING"

He does not need opium. He has the gift of reverie.

—ANAÏS NIN (1903–1977) • FRENCH WRITER AND DIARIST

Think wrongly, if you please, but in all cases think for yourself.

—DORIS LESSING (1919–) • ENGLISH WRITER

Cease trying to work everything out with your minds. It will get you nowhere. Live by intuition and inspiration and let your whole life be Revelation.

—EILEEN CADDY (1917–)
ENGLISH SPIRITUAL WRITER AND COFOUNDER OF THE FINDHORN FOUNDATION

How do most people live without any thoughts. There are many people in the world. . . . How do they live. How do they get strength to put on their clothes in the morning.

—EMILY DICKINSON (1830–1886) • AMERICAN POET

The most unpardonable sin in society is independence of thought.

—EMMA GOLDMAN (1869–1940) • RUSSIAN ANARCHIST AND FEMINIST

Don't be angry with the gentleman for thinking, whatever be the cause, for I assure you he makes no common practice of offending in that way.

—FANNY BURNEY (1752–1840) • ENGLISH WRITER

The reason the All-American boy prefers beauty to brains is that the All-American boy can see better than he can think.

—FARRAH FAWCETT (1947–2009) • AMERICAN ACTOR

Nous sommes peu à penser trop, trop à penser peu. (There are a few who think too much, and many who think too little.)

–FRANÇOISE SAGAN (1935–2004) • FRENCH WRITER AND PLAYWRIGHT

There are no dangerous thoughts; thinking itself is dangerous.

–HANNAH ARENDT (1906–1975)
GERMAN-BORN POLITICAL PHILOSOPHER AND HISTORIAN

A high standard of living is usually accompanied by a low standard of thinking.

–MARYA MANNES (1904–1990) • AMERICAN COLUMNIST AND CRITIC

The mind has great advantages over the body; however the body often furnishes little treats . . . which offer the mind relief from sad thoughts.

–NINON DE LENCLOS (1620–1705) • FRENCH COURTESAN

It's hard to fight an enemy who has outposts in your head.

–SALLY KEMPTON (1943–) • AMERICAN MEDITATION TEACHER

"*TIME*"

You can't turn back the clock. But you can wind it up again.

–BONNIE PRUDDEN (1914–) • AMERICAN ROCK CLIMBER

Living the past is a dull and lonely business; looking back strains the neck muscles, causes you to bump into people not going your way.

–EDNA FERBER (1885–1968) • AMERICAN WRITER

Never think you've seen the last of anything.

–EUDORA WELTY (1899–2001) • AMERICAN WRITER

Time is a dressmaker specializing in alterations.

–FAITH BALDWIN (1893–1978) • AMERICAN WRITER

It is never too late to be what you might have been.

–GEORGE ELIOT (MARY ANN EVANS) (1819–1880) • ENGLISH WRITER

Time wounds all heels.

–JANE ACE (1900–1974)
AMERICAN RADIO PERSONALITY

There has never been an age that did not applaud the past and lament the present.

–LILLIAN EICHLER WATSON
20TH-CENTURY EDITOR, WRITER, AND LETTER-WRITING EXPERT

I've been on a calendar, but never on time.

–MARILYN MONROE (1926–1962)
AMERICAN ACTOR AND SEX SYMBOL

But to look back all the time is boring. Excitement lies in tomorrow.

–NATALIA MAKAROVA (1940–) • RUSSIAN BALLET DANCER

Our faith in the present dies out long before our faith in the future.

–RUTH BENEDICT (1887–1948) • AMERICAN ANTHROPOLOGIST

There are years that ask questions and years that answer.

–ZORA NEALE HURSTON (1891–1960)
AFRICAN-AMERICAN FOLKLORIST AND WRITER

FUTURE

The future: a consolation for those who have no other.

–COUNTESS OF BLESSINGTON (LADY MARGUERITE BLESSINGTON) (1789–1849)
IRISH-BORN ENGLISH WRITER AND LITERARY SALON HOST

•

The future is made of the same stuff as the present.

–SIMONE WEIL (1909–1943)
FRENCH SOCIAL PHILOSOPHER AND ACTIVIST

•

"TRADITION"

•

One of my favorite phobias is that girls, especially those whose tastes aren't routine, often don't get a fair break. . . . It has come down through the generations, an inheritance of age-old customs which produced the corollary that women are bred to timidity.

–AMELIA EARHART (1897–1937)
PIONEERING AMERICAN AVIATOR; FIRST PERSON TO FLY SOLO ACROSS PACIFIC

•

Conventionality is not morality. Self-righteousness is not religion. To attack the first is not to assail the last.

–CHARLOTTE BRONTË (1816–1855) • ENGLISH WRITER

•

You can't teach an old dogma new tricks.

–DOROTHY PARKER (1893–1967)
AMERICAN WRITER AND CRITIC

•

Traditions that have lost their meaning are the hardest of all to destroy.

–EDITH WHARTON (1862–1937) • AMERICAN WRITER

Traditions are the guideposts driven deep in our subconscious minds. The most powerful ones are those we can't even describe, aren't even aware of.

–ELLEN GOODMAN (1941–) • AMERICAN JOURNALIST

The heresy of one age becomes the orthodoxy of the next.

–HELEN KELLER (1880–1968) • AMERICAN WRITER AND ACTIVIST

Old-fashioned ways which no longer apply to changed conditions are a snare in which the feet of women have always become readily entangled.

–JANE ADDAMS (1860–1935) • NOBEL PRIZE–WINNING AMERICAN SOCIAL REFORMER AND HUMANITARIAN

Let us not confuse stability with stagnation.

–MARY JEAN LETENDRE (1948–)
AMERICAN EDUCATOR AND U.S. GOVERNMENT OFFICIAL

"*TRAVEL*"

A trip is what you take when you can't take any more of what you've been taking.

–ADELINE AINSWORTH • 20TH-CENTURY AMERICAN WRITER

The tourist may complain of other tourists, but he would be lost without them.

–AGNES REPPLIER (1855–1950) • AMERICAN ESSAYIST

The impulse to travel is one of the hopeful symptoms of life.

–AGNES REPPLIER (1855–1950) • AMERICAN ESSAYIST

Travelers are always discoverers, especially those who travel by air. There are no signposts in the air to show a man has passed that way before. There are no channels marked. The flier breaks each second into new uncharted seas.

–ANNE MORROW LINDBERGH (1906–2001) • AMERICAN WRITER AND PIONEERING AVIATOR

Travel, instead of broadening the mind, often merely lengthens the conversation.

—ELIZABETH DREW (1887–1965) • ENGLISH-BORN AMERICAN WRITER AND CRITIC

Through travel I first became aware of the outside world; it was through travel that I found my own introspective way into becoming a part of it.

—EUDORA WELTY (1899–2001) • AMERICAN WRITER

Traveling is the ruin of all happiness! There's no looking at a building after seeing Italy.

—FANNY BURNEY (1752–1840) • ENGLISH WRITER

To awaken quite alone in a strange town is one of the pleasantest sensations in the world.

—FREYA STARK (1893–1993) • FRENCH-BORN ENGLISH TRAVEL WRITER

I think that to get under the surface and really appreciate the beauty of any country, one has to go there poor.

—GRACE MOORE (1898–1947) • AMERICAN SOPRANO AND ACTOR

Loving life is easy when you are abroad. Where no one knows you and you hold your life in your hands all alone, you are more master of yourself than at any other time.

—HANNAH ARENDT (1906–1975) • GERMAN-BORN POLITICAL PHILOSOPHER AND HISTORIAN

When traveling with someone, take large doses of patience and tolerance with your morning coffee.

—HELEN HAYES (1900–1993) • AMERICAN ACTOR

To me travel is a triple delight: anticipation, performance, and recollection.

—ILKA CHASE (1905–1978) • AMERICAN ACTOR, WRITER, AND RADIO PERSONALITY

Surely one advantage of traveling is that, while it removes much prejudice against foreigners and their customs, it intensifies tenfold one's appreciation of the good at home.

–ISABELLA L. BIRD (1831-1904)
ENGLISH TRAVEL WRITER AND FIRST FEMALE MEMBER OF THE ROYAL GEOGRAPHIC SOCIETY

•

Almost all travel is lost on teenagers. . . . The young do not discover the world. They discover themselves, and travel only interrupts their trips to the interior.

–JESSAMYN WEST (1902-1984) • AMERICAN WRITER

•

Suffering makes you deep. Travel makes you broad. In case I get my pick, I'd rather travel.

–JUDITH VIORST (1931-) • AMERICAN POET AND JOURNALIST

•

Most passport pictures are good likenesses, and it is time we faced it.

–KATHARINE BRUSH (1901-1952) • AMERICAN WRITER AND ESSAYIST

•

Travel is as much a passion as ambition or love.

–L. E. LANDON (1802-1838) • ENGLISH WRITER AND POET

•

The trip and the story of the trip are always two different things. . . . One cannot go to a place and speak of it; one cannot both see and say, not really. One can go and upon returning make a lot of hand motions and indications with the arms. The mouth itself, working at the speed of light, at the eye's instructions, is necessarily struck still; so fast, so much to report, it hangs open and dumb as a gutted bell. All that unsayable life!

–LORRIE MOORE (1957-) • AMERICAN WRITER

•

The only aspect of our travels that is interesting to others is disaster.

–MARTHA GELLMAN • 20TH/21ST-CENTURY AMERICAN WRITER

Perhaps travel cannot prevent bigotry, but by demonstrating that all peoples cry, laugh, eat, worry, and die, it can introduce the idea that if we try and understand each other, we may even become friends.

–MAYA ANGELOU (1928-) • AFRICAN-AMERICAN POET, MEMOIRIST, AND CIVIL RIGHTS ACTIVIST

•

Certainly, travel is more than the seeing of sights; it is a change that goes on, deep and permanent, in the ideas of living.

–MIRIAM BEARD (1901-1983) • AMERICAN WRITER

•

One's travel life is basically as incommunicable as his sex life.

–PEG BRACKEN (1918-) • AMERICAN WRITER

•

This is what holidays, travels, vacations are about. It is not really rest or even leisure we chase. We strain to renew our capacity for wonder, to shock ourselves into astonishment once again.

–SHANA ALEXANDER (1925-2005) • AMERICAN JOURNALIST AND COLUMNIST

•

I am never happier than when I am alone in a foreign city; it is as if I had become invisible.

–STORM JAMESON (1891-1986) • ENGLISH WRITER AND EDITOR

•

Foreigners can't help living abroad because they were born there, but for an English person to go is ridiculous, especially now that the sun-tan lamps are so readily available.

–SUE TOWNSEND (1946-) • ENGLISH WRITER

•

I haven't been everywhere, but it's on my list.

–SUSAN SONTAG (1933-2004)
AMERICAN ESSAYIST, NOVELIST, INTELLECTUAL, AND ACTIVIST

•

Men travel faster now, but I do not know if they go to better things.

–WILLA CATHER (1873-1947) • AMERICAN WRITER

"TRUTH"

If one cannot invent a really convincing lie,
it is often better to stick to the truth.

–ANGELA THIRKELL (1890–1961) • ENGLISH WRITER

The unvarnished truth is always better than the best-dressed lie.

–ANN LANDERS (ESTHER PAULINE FRIEDMAN) (1918–2002)
AMERICAN ADVICE COLUMNIST

Nagging is the repetition of unpalatable truths.

–BARONESS EDITH SUMMERSKILL (1901–1980)
ENGLISH PHYSICIAN, FEMINIST, POLITICIAN

Keep the other person's well-being in mind when you feel
an attack of soul-purging truth coming on.

–BETTY WHITE (1922–) • AMERICAN ACTRESS

Truth is a theory that is constantly being disproved.
Only lies, it seems, go on forever.

–EARTHA KITT (1927–)
AFRICAN-AMERICAN AND CHEROKEE SINGER AND ACTOR

The woman whose behavior indicates that she will make
a scene if she is told the truth asks to be deceived.

–ELIZABETH JENKINS (1905–) • ENGLISH WRITER AND BIOGRAPHER

The truth does not change according to our ability to stomach it.

–FLANNERY O'CONNOR (1925–1964) • AMERICAN WRITER

Examine your words well, and you will see that even when you have no motive to be false, it is a very hard thing to say the exact truth, even about your own immediate feelings—much harder than to say something fine about them which is not the exact truth.

–GEORGE ELIOT (MARY ANN EVANS) (1819-1880) • ENGLISH WRITER

•

We want the facts to fit the preconceptions. When they don't, it is easier to ignore the facts than to change the preconceptions.

–JESSAMYN WEST (1902-1984) • AMERICAN WRITER

•

Truth has never been, can never be, contained in any one creed or system.

–MRS. HUMPHRY (MARY AUGUSTA ARNOLD) WARD (1851-1920) • ENGLISH WRITER

•

Truth is always exciting. Speak it, then; life is dull without it.

–PEARL S. BUCK (1892-1973)

FIRST FEMALE AMERICAN WINNER OF THE NOBEL PRIZE IN LITERATURE

•

Revolutions are notorious for allowing even nonparticipants—even women!—new scope for telling the truth since they are themselves such massive moments of truth, moments of such massive participation.

–SELMA JAMES (1930-)

AMERICAN WRITER, FEMINIST ACTIVIST, AND FOUNDER OF THE INTERNATIONAL WAGES FOR HOUSEWORK CAMPAIGN

•

If you do not tell the truth about yourself you cannot tell it about other people.

–VIRGINIA WOOLF (1882-1941) • ENGLISH NOVELIST, ESSAYIST, AND CRITIC

•

If truth is not to be found on the shelves of the British Museum, where, I asked myself, picking up a notebook and pencil, is truth?

–VIRGINIA WOOLF (1882-1941) • ENGLISH NOVELIST, ESSAYIST, AND CRITIC

V

"VANITY"

See also Pride

Is there any vanity greater than the vanity of those who believe themselves without it?

–AMANDA CROSS (CAROLYN HEILBRUN) (1926–2003)
AMERICAN ACADEMIC AND FEMINIST WRITER

Those who live on vanity must, not unreasonably, expect to die of mortification.

–ANNE ELLIS (1875–1938) • AMERICAN PIONEER

I have often wished I had time to cultivate modesty . . . but I am too busy thinking about myself.

–EDITH SITWELL (1887–1964) • ENGLISH POET AND CRITIC

The inner vanity is generally in proportion to the outer self-deprecation.

–EDITH WHARTON (1862–1937) • AMERICAN WRITER

Vanity is the quicksand of reason.

–GEORGE SAND (AMANDINE-AURORE-LUCIE DUPIN, BARONNE DUDEVANT) (1804–1876)
FRENCH WRITER AND FEMINIST

Vanity, like murder, will out.

–HANNAH COWLEY (1743–1809)
ENGLISH PLAYWRIGHT AND POET

The sin of pride may be a small or a great thing in someone's life, and hurt vanity a passing pinprick, or a self-destroying or ever murderous obsession.

–IRIS MURDOCH (1919–1999) • IRISH-BORN ENGLISH WRITER

Possibly, more people kill themselves and others out of hurt vanity than out of envy, jealousy, malice, or desire for revenge.

—IRIS MURDOCH (1919-1999) • IRISH-BORN ENGLISH WRITER

•

You have a good many little gifts and virtues, but there is no need of parading them, for conceit spoils the finest genius. There is not much danger that real talent or goodness will be overlooked long, and the great charm of all power is modesty.

—LOUISA MAY ALCOTT (1832-1888) • AMERICAN WRITER

•

"*VIOLENCE*"

•

Violence is a symptom of impotence.

—ANAÏS NIN (1903-1977) • FRENCH WRITER AND DIARIST

•

We need to end rape. We need to end incest. We need to end battery. We need to end prostitution and we need to end pornography. That means that we need to refuse to accept that these are natural phenomena that just happen because some guy is having a bad day.

—ANDREA DWORKIN (1946-2005) • AMERICAN RADICAL FEMINIST

•

Women want to be free to choose from the same range of options that men take for granted. In our quest for equal pay, equal access to education and opportunities, we have made great strides. But until women can move freely and think freely in their homes, on the streets, in the workplace without the fear of violence, there can be no real freedom.

—ANITA RODDICK (1942-) • ENGLISH ACTIVIST AND ENTREPRENEUR, FOUNDER OF THE BODY SHOP

But remember that if the struggle were to resort to violence, it will lose vision, beauty, and imagination. Most dangerous of all, it will marginalize and eventually victimize women. And a political struggle that does not have women at the heart of it, above it, below it, and within it is no struggle at all.

–ARUNDHATI ROY (1961–) • INDIAN WRITER AND ACTIVIST

All history shows that the hand that cradles the rock has ruled the world, not the hand that rocks the cradle!

–CLARE BOOTHE LUCE (1903–1987)
AMERICAN PLAYWRIGHT, JOURNALIST, AND POLITICIAN

The practice of violence, like all action, changes the world, but the most probable change is to a more violent world.

–HANNAH ARENDT (1906–1975)
GERMAN-BORN POLITICAL PHILOSOPHER AND HISTORIAN

If I die a violent death, as some fear and a few are plotting, I know that the violence will be in the thought and the action of the assassins, not in my dying.

–INDIRA GANDHI (1917–1984) • PRIME MINISTER OF INDIA

A violent act pierces the atmosphere, leaving a hole through which the cold, damp draft of its memory blows forever.

–JANE STANTON HITCHCOCK • 20TH/21ST-CENTURY AMERICAN NOVELIST

America has become numb to violence because it just drowns in it, day in and day out.

–JANET RENO (1938–) • FIRST FEMALE ATTORNEY GENERAL OF THE UNITED STATES

I get mad at the fact that, as a woman in America in the '90s, I have to worry about being attacked all the time.

–JULIANA HATFIELD (1967–) • AMERICAN GUITARIST, SINGER, AND SONGWRITER

Nonviolence doesn't always work—but violence never does.

–MADGE MICHEELS-CYRUS
20TH/21ST-CENTURY AMERICAN CIVIL RIGHTS AND PEACE ACTIVIST

•

No society that feeds its children on tales of successful violence can expect them not to believe that violence in the end is rewarded.

–MARGARET MEAD (1901–1978) • AMERICAN CULTURAL ANTHROPOLOGIST

•

Murder is part of the American motif.

–SAPPHIRE
20TH/21ST-CENTURY AFRICAN-AMERICAN WRITER AND POET

•

DOMESTIC VIOLENCE

Few people who are hit once by someone they love respond in the way they might to a singular physical assault by a stranger.

–BELL HOOKS (1952–) • AFRICAN-AMERICAN ACTIVIST AND THEORIST

•

Domestic violence causes far more pain than the visible marks of bruises and scars. It is devastating to be abused by someone that you love and think loves you in return.

–DIANNE FEINSTEIN (1933–) • AMERICAN POLITICIAN, FIRST FEMALE MAYOR OF SAN FRANCISCO

•

Domestic violence is the front line of the war against women.

–PEARL CLEAGE (1948–)
AFRICAN-AMERICAN NOVELIST, PLAYWRIGHT, AND PERFORMANCE ARTIST

•

RAPE

The attack between the thighs is only an extension of the bullet between the eyes.

–ALJEAN HARMETZ • 20TH/21ST-CENTURY AMERICAN JOURNALIST

•

Rape is not aggressive sexuality, it is sexualized aggression.

–AUDRE LORDE (1934–1992) • AFRICAN-AMERICAN FEMINIST WRITER AND ACTIVIST

If [rape] is a totally devastating psychological experience for a woman, then she doesn't have a proper attitude toward sex. It's this whole stupid feminist thing about how we are basically nurturing, benevolent people, and sex is a wonderful thing between two equals. With that kind of attitude, then of course rape is going to be a total violation of your entire life.

–CAMILLE PAGLIA (1947–) • AMERICAN SOCIAL CRITIC AND PROFESSOR

•

Rape is the only crime in which the victim becomes the accused.

–FREDA ADLER (1934–) • AMERICAN PROFESSOR OF CRIMINAL JUSTICE

•

Rapists perform for sexist males the same function that the Ku Klux Klan performed for racist whites; they keep women in their "place" through fear.

–JO-ANN EVANS GARDNER (1925–) • AMERICAN PSYCHOLOGIST AND FEMINIST

•

Bad judgment and carelessness are not punishable by rape.

–PEARL CLEAGE (1948–)
AFRICAN-AMERICAN NOVELIST, PLAYWRIGHT, AND PERFORMANCE ARTIST

•

Fighting back. On a multiplicity of levels, that is the activity we must engage in, together if we—women—are to redress the imbalance and rid ourselves and men of the ideology of rape.

–SUSAN BROWNMILLER (1935–) • AMERICAN RADICAL FEMINIST, JOURNALIST, AND ACTIVIST

•

Rape is a culturally fostered means of suppressing women. Legally we say we deplore it, but mythically we romanticize and perpetuate it, and privately we excuse and overlook it.

–VICTORIA BILLINGS (1945–) • AMERICAN JOURNALIST

"WAR"

One is left with the horrible feeling now that war settles nothing; that to win a war is as disastrous as to lose one.

—AGATHA CHRISTIE (1890–1976) • ENGLISH WRITER

I really do think that if, for one week, in the U.S. we saw the true face of war, we saw people's limbs sheared off, we saw kids blown apart, for one week, war would be eradicated. Instead, what we see in the U.S. media is the video war game.

—AMY GOODMAN (1957–) • AMERICAN BROADCAST JOURNALIST

The moral absolute should be: If and when, in any dispute, one side initiates the use of physical force, that side is wrong—and no consideration or discussion of the issues is necessary or appropriate.

—AYN RAND (1905–1982) • RUSSIAN-AMERICAN WRITER AND PHILOSOPHER

War is the unfolding of miscalculations.

—BARBARA TUCHMAN (1912–1989)
AMERICAN HISTORIAN AND WRITER

If you weigh well the strengths of our armies you will see that in this battle we must conquer or die. This is a woman's resolve. As for the men, they may live or be slaves.

—BOADACEIA • 1ST-CENTURY CELTIC WARRIOR QUEEN

I may be compelled to face danger, but never fear it, and while our soldiers can stand and fight, I can stand and feed and nurse them.

—CLARA BARTON (1821–1912) • FOUNDER OF THE AMERICAN RED CROSS

Patriotism assumes that our globe is divided into little spots, each one surrounded by an iron gate. Those who had the fortune of being born on some particular spot consider themselves better, nobler, grander, more intelligent than the living beings inhabiting any other spot. It is, therefore, the duty of everyone living on that chosen spot to fight, kill, and die in the attempt to impose his superiority upon all others.

–EMMA GOLDMAN (1869–1940) • RUSSIAN ANARCHIST AND FEMINIST

The militancy of men, through all the centuries, has drenched the world with blood, and for these deeds of horror and destruction men have been rewarded with monuments, with great songs and epics. The militancy of women has harmed no human life save the lives of those who fought the battle of righteousness. Time alone will reveal what reward will be allotted to women.

–EMMELINE PANKHURST (1858–1928) • ENGLISH SUFFRAGIST AND FEMINIST

Militarism . . . is the chief bulwark of capitalism. When it is that militarism is undermined, capitalism will fail.

–HELEN KELLER (1880–1968) • AMERICAN WRITER AND ACTIVIST

Strike against war, for without you no battles can be fought! Strike against manufacturing shrapnel and gas bombs and all other tools of murder! Strike against preparedness that means death and misery to millions of human beings! Be not dumb, obedient slaves in an army of destruction! Be heroes in an army of construction!

–HELEN KELLER (1880–1968) • AMERICAN WRITER AND ACTIVIST

You can no more win a war than you can win an earthquake.

–JEANNETTE RANKIN (1880–1973)
AMERICAN POLITICIAN, FIRST WOMAN ELECTED TO THE U.S. HOUSE OF REPRESENTATIVES AND THE FIRST FEMALE MEMBER OF CONGRESS

If it's natural to kill, why do men have to go into training to learn how?

–JOAN BAEZ (1941–) • AMERICAN FOLK SINGER AND ACTIVIST

•

Militarists say that to gain peace we must prepare for war.
I think we get what we prepare for.

–JODY WILLIAMS (1950–) • AMERICAN NOBEL PEACE PRIZE RECIPIENT AND ACTIVIST

•

Arise, then, women of this day! Arise all women who have hearts, whether our baptism be that of water or of tears! We will not have great questions decided by irrelevant agencies. Our sons shall not be taken from us to unlearn all that we have been able to teach them of charity, mercy, and patience.

–JULIA WARD HOWE (1819–1910) • AMERICAN POET AND PHILANTHROPIST

•

The real war is not between the West and the East. The real war is between intelligent and stupid people.

–MARJANE SATRAPI (1969–) • IRANIAN GRAPHIC NOVELIST

•

I hate those men who would send into war youth to fight and die for them; the pride and cowardice of those old men, making their wars that boys must die.

–MARY ROBERTS RINEHART (1876–1958) • AMERICAN WRITER

•

We always prefer war on our own terms to peace on someone else's.

–MIGNON MCLAUGHLIN (1913–1983) • AMERICAN JOURNALIST AND WRITER

•

When men talk about defense, they always claim to be protecting women and children, but they never ask the women and children what they think.

–PAT SCHROEDER (1940–) • AMERICAN POLITICIAN

•

I feel like I'm witnessing the systematic destruction of a people's ability to survive. It's horrifying.

–RACHEL CORRIE (1979–2003) • AMERICAN PEACE ACTIVIST

The calamity of war, wherever, whenever and upon whomever it descends, is a tragedy for the whole of humanity.

–RAISA GORBACHEV (1932-1999)
RUSSIAN POLITICAL FIGURE AND SOCIOLOGIST, WIFE OF SOVIET LEADER MIKHAIL GORBACHEV

•

Before a war, military science seems a real science, like astronomy. After a war it seems more like astrology.

–REBECCA WEST (1892-1983) • ANGLO-IRISH FEMINIST AND WRITER

•

He now understood why the army was organized as it was. It was indeed quite necessary. No rational form of organization would serve the purpose. He simply had not understood that the purpose was to enable men with machine guns to kill unarmed men and women easily and in great quantities when told to do so. Only he still could not see where courage, or manliness, or fitness entered in.

–URSULA K. LE GUIN (1929-) • AMERICAN WRITER

•

Societies and economies can be destroyed by bombs. Societies can also be destroyed by locking every aspect of life, like provision of food and water, through an economic war.

–VANDANA SHIVA (1952-) • INDIAN PHYSICIST, ECOFEMINIST, AND ACTIVIST

•

War is not women's history.

–VIRGINIA WOOLF (1882-1941)
ENGLISH NOVELIST, ESSAYIST, AND CRITIC

•

War has crossed out the day and replaced it with horror, and now horrors are unfolding instead of days.

–ZLATA FILIPOVIK (1980-) • BOSNIAN DIARIST

"WEIGHT"

See also Dieting

Gaining weight and pulling my head out of the toilet was the most political act I have ever committed.

—ABRA FORTUNE CHERNIK • 20TH/21ST-CENTURY AMERICAN FEMINIST ESSAYIST

As you get older, the pickings get slimmer, but the people don't.

—CARRIE FISHER (1956–) • AMERICAN ACTOR AND WRITER

Give me a dozen such heartbreaks, if that would help me lose a couple of pounds.

—COLETTE (1873–1954) • FRENCH WRITER

If I had been around when Rubens was painting, I would have been revered as a fabulous model. Kate Moss? Well, she would have been the paintbrush.

—DAWN FRENCH (1957–) • ENGLISH COMEDIAN

We have women in the military, but they don't put us in the front lines. They don't know if we can fight or if we can kill. I think we can. All the general has to do is walk over to the women and say, "You see the enemy over there? They say you look fat in those uniforms."

—ELAYNE BOOSLER (1952–) • AMERICAN COMEDIAN

The chief excitement in a woman's life is spotting women who are fatter than she is.

—HELEN ROWLAND (1875–1950) • AMERICAN JOURNALIST AND HUMORIST

Fat is not a moral problem. It's an oral problem.

—JANE THOMAS NOLAND • 20TH/21ST-CENTURY WRITER AND EDITOR

I have gained and lost the same ten pounds so many times over and over again my cellulite must have déjà vu.

—JANE WAGNER (1935–) • AMERICAN PLAYWRIGHT AND COMEDY WRITER

Why do people suck in their stomachs in when they weigh themselves? So they can see the scale.

—MARTA CHAVES • 20TH/21ST-CENTURY NICARAGUAN-CANADIAN COMEDIAN

The only way to lose weight is to check it as airline baggage.

—PEGGY RYAN (1924–2004) • AMERICAN DANCER AND ACTOR

It's okay to be fat. So you're fat. Just be fat and shut up about it.

—ROSEANNE BARR (1952–) • AMERICAN COMEDIAN

To all of you that have something nasty to say about me, or other women that are built like me . . . I have one thing to say to you: Kiss my fat ass.

—TYRA BANKS (1973–) • AMERICAN MODEL AND TELEVISION HOST

"WISDOM"

See Knowledge

"WOMEN"

Girls just want to have funds.

—ADRIENNE GUSOFF

20TH/21ST-CENTURY AMERICAN FREELANCE WRITER AND CREATIVE CONSULTANT

Women will not simply be mainstreamed into the polluted stream. Women are changing the stream, making it clean and green and safe for all—every gender, race, creed, sexual orientation, age, and ability.

–BELLA ABZUG (1920–1998) • AMERICAN FEMINIST AND POLITICIAN

•

The failure to realize the full possibilities of their existence has not been studied as a pathology in woman. For it is considered normal feminine adjustment, in America and in most countries of the world.

–BETTY FRIEDAN (1921–2006)
AMERICAN FEMINIST, WRITER, AND COFOUNDER OF NATIONAL ORGANIZATION FOR WOMEN

•

Women are in league with each other, a secret conspiracy of hearts and pheromones.

–CAMILLE PAGLIA (1947–) • AMERICAN SOCIAL CRITIC AND PROFESSOR

•

If I imagine myself (woman has always asked) whole, active, a self, will I not cease, in some profound way, to be a woman? The answer must be, imagine, and the old idea of womanhood be damned.

–CAROLYN HEILBRUN (1926–2003) • AMERICAN ACADEMIC AND FEMINIST WRITER

•

Women's virtue is man's greatest invention.

–CORNELIA OTIS SKINNER (1899–1979)
AMERICAN WRITER AND ACTOR

•

I'm just a person trapped inside a woman's body.

–ELAYNE BOOSLER (1952–) • AMERICAN COMEDIAN

•

I would have girls regard themselves not as adjectives but as nouns.

–ELIZABETH CADY STANTON (1815–1902) • AMERICAN SUFFRAGIST, WRITER, AND THEOLOGIAN

We haven't come a long way, we've come a short way. If we hadn't come a short way, no one would be calling us baby.

—ELIZABETH JANEWAY (1913–2005) • AMERICAN NOVELIST AND CRITIC

It's fun to be a woman. It's fun to flirt and wear makeup and have boobs.

—EVA MENDES (1974–) • AMERICAN MODEL AND ACTOR

God gave women intuition and femininity. Used properly, the combination easily jumbles the brain of any man I've ever met.

—FARRAH FAWCETT (1947–2009) • AMERICAN ACTOR

Men are irrelevant. Women are happy or unhappy, fulfilled or unfulfilled, and it has nothing to do with men.

—FAY WELDON (1931–) • ENGLISH NOVELIST, SHORT STORY WRITER, PLAYWRIGHT, AND ESSAYIST

Women have not to prove that they can be emotional, and rhapsodic, and spiritualistic; every one believes that already. They have to prove that they are capable of accurate thought, severe study, and continuous self-command.

—GEORGE ELIOT (MARY ANN EVANS) (1819–1880) • ENGLISH WRITER

Women have very little idea of how much men hate them.

—GERMAINE GREER (1939–) • AUSTRALIAN-BORN WRITER AND SOCIAL CRITIC

I'd much rather be a woman than a man. Women can cry, they can wear cute clothes, and they are the first to be rescued off of sinking ships.

—GILDA RADNER (1946–1989) • AMERICAN COMEDIAN

Some of us are becoming the men we wanted to marry.

—GLORIA STEINEM (1934–)
AMERICAN FEMINIST AND COFOUNDER OF *MS.* MAGAZINE

Women power is a formidable force.

–GRO HARLEM BRUNDTLAND (1939-)
NORWEGIAN DIPLOMAT, PHYSICIAN, AND INTERNATIONAL LEADER

•

Things are starting to be written, things that will constitute a feminine Imaginary. . . . Forms for women on the march, or as I prefer to fantasize, "in flight," so that instead of lying down, women will go forward by leaps in search of themselves.

–HÉLENÈ CIXOUS (1937-) • FRENCH FEMINIST THEORIST

•

I think it will be truly glorious when women become real people and have the whole world open to them.

–ISAK DINESEN (KAREN BLIXEN) (1885-1962)
DANISH WRITER AND AUTOBIOGRAPHER

•

Was there ever any so abused, so slandered, so railed upon, so wickedly handled undeservedly, as are we women.

–JANE ANGER
16TH-CENTURY WRITER, FIRST ENGLISH FEMALE TO PUBLISH A DEFENSE OF WOMEN (PAMPHLET)

•

Girls have got balls. They're just a little higher up that's all.

–JOAN JETT (1958-) • AMERICAN ROCK AND ROLL GUITARIST, SINGER, AND ACTOR

•

Women have been called queens for a long time, but the kingdom given them isn't worth ruling.

–LOUISA MAY ALCOTT (1832-1888) • AMERICAN NOVELIST

•

The world has never yet seen a truly great and virtuous nation because in the degradation of woman the very fountains of life are poisoned at their source.

–LUCRETIA MOTT (1793-1880)
AMERICAN QUAKER ABOLITIONIST, SOCIAL REFORMER, AND PROPONENT OF WOMEN'S RIGHTS

Smart girls know how to play tennis, piano, and dumb.

—LYNN REDGRAVE (1943–2010) • ENGLISH ACTOR

All the women I know feel a little like outlaws.

—MARILYN FRENCH (1929–2009) • AMERICAN WRITER AND FEMINIST

What women have to stand on squarely is not their ability to see the world in the way men see it, but the importance and validity of their seeing it in some other way.

—MARY AUSTIN (1868–1934) • AMERICAN WRITER

Women are like dogs really. They love like dogs, a little insistently. And they like to fetch and carry and come back wistfully after hard words, and learn rather easily to carry a basket.

—MARY ROBERTS RINEHART (1876–1958) • AMERICAN WRITER

Long before *Playboy*, woman was not the sum of her parts; her parts were her sum.

—MARYA MANNES (1904–1990) • AMERICAN COLUMNIST AND CRITIC

Women are repeatedly accused of taking things personally. I cannot see any other honest way of taking them.

—MARYA MANNES (1904–1990) • AMERICAN COLUMNIST AND CRITIC

Where there is a woman there is magic.

—NTOZAKE SHANGE (1948–)
AFRICAN-AMERICAN PLAYWRIGHT AND PERFORMANCE ARTIST

Women are not inherently passive or peaceful. We're not inherently anything but human.

—ROBIN MORGAN (1941–)
AMERICAN POET, WRITER, AND RADICAL FEMINIST ACTIVIST

Women are cursed, and men are the proof.

–ROSEANNE BARR (1952–) • AMERICAN COMEDIAN

•

To be somebody, a woman does not have to be more like a man, but has to be more of a woman.

–SALLY E. SHAYWITZ • 20TH/21ST-CENTURY AMERICAN PHYSICIAN AND PROFESSOR

•

Women were the slave class that maintained the species in order to free the other half for the business of the world.

–SHULAMITH FIRESTONE (1945–) • CANADIAN-BORN RADICAL FEMINIST

•

One is not born a woman, one becomes one.

–SIMONE DE BEAUVOIR (1908–1986)
FRENCH WRITER AND PHILOSOPHER

•

Women are all female impersonators to some degree.

–SUSAN BROWNMILLER (1935–)
AMERICAN RADICAL FEMINIST, JOURNALIST, AND ACTIVIST

•

A woman must have money and a room of her own.

–VIRGINIA WOOLF (1882–1941) • ENGLISH NOVELIST, ESSAYIST, AND CRITIC

•

Women have served all these centuries as looking-glasses possessing the magic and delicious power of reflecting the figure of man at twice its natural size.

–VIRGINIA WOOLF (1882–1941) • ENGLISH NOVELIST, ESSAYIST, AND CRITIC

•

A woman's life can really be a succession of lives, each revolving around some emotionally compelling situation or challenge, and each marked by some intense experience.

–WALLIS SIMPSON, DUCHESS OF WINDSOR (1896–1986)
AMERICAN WIFE OF PRINCE EDWARD

Woman is the nigger of the world.

–YOKO ONO (1933–)

JAPANESE-BORN AMERICAN MUSICIAN, ARTIST, AND PEACE ACTIVIST

"WOMEN'S MOVEMENT"

If particular care and attention is not paid to the ladies, we are determined to foment a rebellion, and will not hold ourselves bound by any laws in which we have no voice or representation.

–ABIGAIL ADAMS (1744–1818) • FIRST LADY OF THE UNITED STATES

If society will not admit of woman's free development, then society must be remodeled.

–ELIZABETH BLACKWELL (1821–1910)

ENGLISH-BORN FIRST WOMAN TO EARN MEDICAL DEGREE IN THE UNITED STATES

People have been writing premature obituaries on the women's movement since its beginning.

–ELLEN GOODMAN (1941–) • AMERICAN JOURNALIST

If it's a movement, I sometimes think it needs a laxative.

–FLORYNCE KENNEDY (1916–2000) • AFRICAN-AMERICAN LAWYER AND ACTIVIST

Women's Liberation is just a lot of foolishness. It's the men who are discriminated against. They can't bear children. And no one's likely to do anything about that.

–GOLDA MEIR (1898–1978) • RUSSIAN-BORN, FIRST FEMALE PRIME MINISTER OF ISRAEL

I owe nothing to Women's Lib.

–MARGARET THATCHER (1925–)

FIRST FEMALE BRITISH PRIME MINISTER

Because women's liberation is a movement of the powerless for the powerless, its attraction is not immediately clear to the powerless, who feel they need alliance with the powerful to survive.

–ROSEMARY O'GRADY • 20TH-CENTURY AUSTRALIAN WRITER

Resolved, that the women of this nation in 1876, have greater cause for discontent, rebellion, and revolution than the men of 1776.

–SUSAN B. ANTHONY (1820–1906) • AMERICAN SUFFRAGIST AND NEWSPAPER PUBLISHER

The Queen is most anxious to enlist everyone in checking this mad, wicked folly of "Women's Rights." It is a subject which makes the Queen so furious that she cannot contain herself.

–QUEEN VICTORIA (1819–1901) • QUEEN OF ENGLAND

The history of men's opposition to women's emancipation is more interesting perhaps than the story of that emancipation itself.

–VIRGINIA WOOLF (1882–1941) • ENGLISH NOVELIST, ESSAYIST, AND CRITIC

The women's movement hasn't changed my sex life. It wouldn't dare.

–ZSA ZSA GABOR (1917–) • HUNGARIAN-AMERICAN ACTRESS AND SOCIALITE

"WORK"

See also Equality

Work is a world apart from jobs. Work is the way you occupy your mind and hand and eye and whole body when they're informed by your imagination and wit, by your keenest perceptions, by your most profound reflections on everything you've read and seen and heard and been part of. You may or may not be paid to do your work.

–ALICE KOLLER • 20TH/21ST-CENTURY AMERICAN WRITER

Once you put your hand to the plow, you can't put it down until you get to the end of the row.

—ALICE PAUL (1885–1977) • AMERICAN SUFFRAGIST LEADER

•

The woman who can create her own job is the woman who will win fame and fortune.

—AMELIA EARHART (1897–1937)

PIONEERING AMERICAN AVIATOR; FIRST PERSON TO FLY SOLO ACROSS PACIFIC

•

Opportunities are usually disguised as hard work, so most people don't recognize them.

—ANN LANDERS (ESTHER PAULINE FRIEDMAN) (1918–2002)

AMERICAN ADVICE COLUMNIST

•

No one can arrive from being talented alone. God gives talent; work transforms talent into genius.

—ANNA PAVLOVA (1881–1931) • RUSSIAN BALLERINA

•

Laziness may appear attractive, but work gives satisfaction.

—ANNE FRANK (1929–1945) • GERMAN-JEWISH DIARIST

•

I don't try to work every day. I *do* work every day.

—BEATRICE WOOD (1893–1998) • AMERICAN ARTIST

•

When people go to work, they shouldn't have to leave their hearts at home.

—BETTY BENDER • 20TH/21ST-CENTURY AMERICAN PROFESSOR

•

To do the work that you are capable of doing is the mark of maturity.

—BETTY FRIEDAN (1921–2006)

AMERICAN FEMINIST, WRITER, AND COFOUNDER OF NATIONAL ORGANIZATION FOR WOMEN

Work is either fun or drudgery. It depends on your attitude. I like fun.

–COLLEEN C. BARRETT (1944–) • AMERICAN AIRLINE EXECUTIVE

For the last third of life there remains only work. It alone is always stimulating, rejuvenating, exciting, and satisfying.

–DORIS LESSING (1919–) • ENGLISH WRITER

Employment and ennui are simply incompatible.

–DOROTHÉE DELUZY (1747–1830) • FRENCH ACTOR

Normal is getting dressed in clothes that you buy for work and driving through traffic in a car that you are still paying for—in order to get to the job you need to pay for the clothes and the car, and the house you leave vacant all day so you can afford to live in it.

–ELLEN GOODMAN (1941–) • AMERICAN JOURNALIST

Women who bear children before they establish serious habits of work may never establish them at all.

–ERICA JONG (1942–) • AMERICAN WRITER

I think I'll work all my life. When you're having fun, why stop having fun?

–HELEN THOMAS (1920–) • AMERICAN JOURNALIST AND WHITE HOUSE CORRESPONDENT

I believe in hard work. It keeps the wrinkles out of the mind and the spirit.

–HELENA RUBINSTEIN (1870–1965) • POLISH-BORN COSMETICS ENTREPRENEUR

My grandfather once told me that there were two kinds of people: those who do the work and those who take the credit. He told me to try to be in the first group; there was much less competition.

–INDIRA GANDHI (1917–1984) • PRIME MINISTER OF INDIA

What you get is a living—what you give is a life.

–LILLIAN GISH (1893–1993) • AMERICAN ACTOR

Work is something you can count on, a trusted, lifelong friend who never deserts you.

–MARGARET BOURKE-WHITE (1904–1971) • AMERICAN PHOTOGRAPHER

Men for the sake of getting a living forget to live.

–MARGARET FULLER (1810–1850)
AMERICAN WRITER, EDITOR, INTELLECTUAL, AND FEMINIST

The one important thing I have learnt over the years is the difference between taking one's work seriously and taking oneself seriously. The first is imperative and the second disastrous.

–MARGOT FONTEYN (1919–1991) • ENGLISH BALLET DANCER

Do not feel entitled to anything you do not sweat or struggle for.

–MARIAN WRIGHT EDELMAN (1939–)
AFRICAN-AMERICAN FOUNDER OF THE CHILDREN'S DEFENSE FUND

I am his mistress. His work is his wife.

–MARION JAVITS
20TH/21ST-CENTURY AMERICAN, WIFE OF NEW YORK POLITICIAN JACOB JAVITS

When her last child is off to school, we don't want the talented woman wasting her time in work far below her capacity. We want her to come out running.

–MARY INGRAHAM BUNTING (1910–1998)
AMERICAN SCIENTIST, FIRST WOMAN TO SIT ON THE ATOMIC ENERGY COMMISSION

It's not so much how busy you are, but why you are busy. The bee is praised; the mosquito is swatted.

–MARY O'CONNOR (1925–1964) • AMERICAN WRITER

Work is work, and everything else is everything else.

–MONIKA FALTISS • 20TH/21ST-CENTURY AMERICAN EDITOR

What the world really needs is more love and less paperwork.

–PEARL BAILEY (1918–1990) • AMERICAN SINGER AND ACTOR

The secret of joy in work is contained in one word: excellence. To know how to do something well is to enjoy it.

–PEARL S. BUCK (1892–1973)
FIRST FEMALE AMERICAN WINNER OF THE NOBEL PRIZE IN LITERATURE

I don't wait for moods. You accomplish nothing if you do that. Your mind must know it has got to get down to earth.

–PEARL S. BUCK (1892–1973)
FIRST FEMALE AMERICAN WINNER OF THE NOBEL PRIZE IN LITERATURE

I believe you are your work. Don't trade the stuff of your life, time, for nothing more than dollars. That's a rotten bargain.

–RITA MAE BROWN (1944–) • AMERICAN WRITER AND ACTIVIST

The whole point of getting things done is knowing what to leave undone.

–STELLA READING (1894–1971)
ENGLISH FOUNDER OF GREAT BRITAIN'S WOMEN'S ROYAL VOLUNTARY SERVICE

CAREERS

When other little girls wanted to be ballet dancers, I kind of wanted to be a vampire.

–ANGELINA JOLIE (1975–) • AMERICAN ACTOR

If you find something you really love as you're growing up, look hard to see if you can make a living at it instead of giving it up for something more sensible.

–JENNIFER LAMB • 20TH/21ST-CENTURY AMERICAN STUNTWOMAN

Adults are always asking little kids what they want to be when they grow up because they're looking for ideas.

–PAULA POUNDSTONE (1959–) • AMERICAN COMEDIAN

•

The time to reach young ladies is during their first years of school. Research has shown that although children may change their minds several times about their eventual careers, the possibilities of them selecting a nontraditional role must be nurtured at an early age.

–PEGGY BATY
20TH-CENTURY AVIATION INSTRUCTOR AND ADMINISTRATOR, FOUNDER OF WOMEN IN AVIATION, INTL.

•

"WORRY"

•

It ain't no use putting up your umbrella till it rains.

–ALICE CALDWELL RICE (1870–1942)
AMERICAN HUMORIST AND CHILDREN'S WRITER

•

We all have a tendency to obscure the forest of simple joys with the trees of problems.

–CHRISTIANE COLLANGE (1930–) • FRENCH EDITOR AND WRITER

•

Worry does not empty tomorrow of its sorrow; it empties today of its strength.

–CORRIE TEN BOOM (1892–1983) • DUTCH EVANGELIST AND HOLOCAUST SURVIVOR

•

It is not good to cross the bridge before you get to it.

–JUDI DENCH (1934–) • ENGLISH STAGE AND FILM ACTOR

•

You can't start worrying about what's going to happen. You get spastic enough worrying about what's happening now.

–LAUREN BACALL (1924–) • AMERICAN MODEL AND ACTOR

Worry a little bit every day and in a lifetime you will lose a couple of years. If something is wrong, fix it if you can. But train yourself not to worry. Worry never fixes anything.

—MARY HEMINGWAY (1908–1984) • AMERICAN JOURNALIST

A request not to worry . . . is perhaps the least soothing message capable of human utterance.

—MIGNON G. EBERHART (1899–1996) • AMERICAN WRITER

Worrying is all about the illusion of control. When you worry, you are expending energy, and it feels like you are doing something.

—TAMMY CRAVIT • 20TH/21ST-CENTURY AMERICAN JOURNALIST AND NOVELIST

"WRITING"

See also Literature, Reading, Stories

What else is there to write about than love and loss?

—ALICE HOFFMAN (1952–) • AMERICAN WRITER

The role of a writer is not to say what we all can say, but what we are unable to say.

—ANAÏS NIN (1903–1977) • FRENCH WRITER AND DIARIST

You know, when you think about writing a book, you think it is overwhelming. But, actually, you break it down into tiny little tasks any moron could do.

—ANNIE DILLARD (1945–) • AMERICAN WRITER AND POET

You only learn to be a better writer by actually writing.

—DORIS LESSING (1919–) • ENGLISH WRITER

Everywhere I go I'm asked if I think the university stifles writers. My opinion is that they don't stifle enough of them. There's many a bestseller that could have been prevented by a good teacher.

–FLANNERY O'CONNOR (1925–1964) • AMERICAN WRITER

•

I shall live badly if I do not write, and I shall write badly if I do not live.

–FRANÇOISE SAGAN (1935–2004) • FRENCH NOVELIST AND PLAYWRIGHT

•

However satisfying writing is—that mix of discipline and miracle, which leaves you in control, even when what appears on the page has emerged from regions beyond your control—it is a very poor substitute indeed for the joy and the agony of loving.

–GILLIAN ROSE (1947–1995) • ENGLISH PHILOSOPHER

•

Writing is the only thing that, when I do it, I don't feel I should be doing something else.

–GLORIA STEINEM (1934–) • AMERICAN FEMINIST AND COFOUNDER OF *MS.* MAGAZINE

•

It has taken me years of struggle, hard work, and research to learn to make one simple gesture, and I know enough about the art of writing to realize that it would take as many years of concentrated effort to write one simple, beautiful sentence.

–ISADORA DUNCAN (1877–1927) • AMERICAN MODERN DANCER

•

If Shakespeare had to go on an author tour to promote *Romeo and Juliet*, he never would have written *Macbeth*.

–JOYCE BROTHERS (1928–) • AMERICAN PSYCHOLOGIST AND COLUMNIST

•

If you are a writer you locate yourself behind a wall of silence and no matter what you are doing, driving a car or walking or doing housework you can still be writing, because you have that space.

–JOYCE CAROL OATES (1938–) • AMERICAN WRITER

When you are in the middle of a story it isn't a story at all, but only a confusion; a dark roaring, a blindness, a wreckage of shattered glass and splintered wood; like a house in a whirlwind, or else a boat crushed by the icebergs or swept over the rapids, and all aboard powerless to stop it.

—MARGARET ATWOOD (1939–) • CANADIAN POET, NOVELIST, CRITIC, AND ACTIVIST

•

Writing is the thing that one can do anywhere, in a hotel bedroom, in solitary confinement, in a prison cell, a defense more final, less destructible, than the company of love.

—MARGARET DRABBLE (1939–) • ENGLISH NOVELIST, BIOGRAPHER, AND CRITIC

•

We sometimes received—and I would read—two hundred manuscripts a week. Some of them were wonderful, some were terrible; most were mediocre. It was like the gifts of the good and bad fairies.

—MARILYN HACKER (1942–) • AMERICAN POET AND EDITOR

•

The art of writing is the art of applying the seat of the pants to the seat of the chair.

—MARY HEATON VORSE (1874–1966)
AMERICAN PIONEER OF LABOR JOURNALISM, SUFFRAGIST, AND NOVELIST

•

The first four months of writing the book, my mental image is scratching with my hands through granite. My other image is pushing a train up the mountain, and it's icy, and I'm in bare feet.

—MARY HIGGINS CLARK (1927–) • AMERICAN WRITER

•

I resent people who say writers write from experience. Writers don't write from experience, though many are hesitant to admit that they don't. I want to be clear about this. If you wrote from experience, you'd get maybe one book, maybe three poems. Writers write from empathy.

—NIKKI GIOVANNI (1943–) • AMERICAN POET AND WRITER

Most young men are alarmed on hearing that a young woman writes poetry. Combined with an ill-groomed head of hair and an eccentric style of dress, such an admission is almost fatal.

–STELLA GIBBONS (1902–1989) • ENGLISH WRITER AND POET

The ability of writers to imagine what is not the self, to familiarize the strange and mystify the familiar, is the test of their power.

–TONI MORRISON (1931–) • NOBEL PRIZE–WINNING AFRICAN-AMERICAN NOVELIST

I would venture to guess that Anon, who wrote so many poems without signing them, was often a woman.

–VIRGINIA WOOLF (1882–1941) • ENGLISH NOVELIST, ESSAYIST, AND CRITIC

Novels are not about expressing yourself, they're about something beautiful, funny, clever, and organic. Self-expression? Go and ring a bell in the yard if you want to express yourself.

–ZADIE SMITH (1975–) • ENGLISH WRITER

POETRY

The poem has a social effect of some kind whether or not the poet wills it to have. It has kinetic force, it sets in motion . . . elements in the reader that would otherwise be stagnant.

–DENISE LEVERTOV (1923–1997) • ENGLISH-BORN AMERICAN POET

When I gently suggested to one student that it might benefit her to read some poetry if she planned to spend her life writing it, she told me that yes, she knew she should read more but when she encountered a really good poem it only made her depressed.

–KATHA POLLITT (1949–) • AMERICAN FEMINIST WRITER AND CULTURAL CRITIC

She had put [her poems] on the back burner,
and they had fallen behind the stove.

–LORRIE MOORE (1957–) • AMERICAN WRITER

REASONS FOR

I write entirely to find out what I'm thinking, what I'm looking at, what I see, and what it means. What I want and what I fear.

–JOAN DIDION (1934–) • AMERICAN WRITER

Writing is a cop-out. An excuse to live perpetually in fantasy land, where you can create, direct, and watch the products of your own head. Very selfish.

–MONICA DICKENS (1915–1992) • ENGLISH WRITER

I always tell people that I became a writer not because I went to school but because my mother took me to the library. I wanted to become a writer so I could see my name in the card catalog.

–SANDRA CISNEROS (1954–) • MEXICAN-AMERICAN WRITER AND POET

AND SOCIAL ISSUES

I have never felt a placard and a poem are in any way similar.

–KRISTIN HUNTER (1931–) • AFRICAN-AMERICAN WRITER

I do not think that literature is the primary instrument for social transformation, but I do think it has potency. So I work to tell the truth about people's lives; I work to celebrate struggle, to applaud the tradition of struggle in our community, to bring to center stage all those characters, just ordinary folks on the block, who've been waiting in the wings, characters we thought we had to ignore because they weren't pimp-flashy or hustler-slick or because they didn't fit easily into previously acceptable modes or stock types. I want to lift up some usable truths . . .

–TONI CADE BAMBARA (1939–1995) • AFRICAN-AMERICAN WRITER AND SOCIAL ACTIVIST

Y

"YOUTH"

See also Age

Youth condemns; maturity condones.

–AMY LOWELL (1874–1925)
AMERICAN IMAGIST POET AND CRITIC

Time misspent in youth is sometimes all the freedom one ever has.

–ANITA BROOKNER (1928–) • ENGLISH WRITER AND ART HISTORIAN

Childhood sometimes does pay a second visit to man, youth never.

–ANNA JAMESON (1794–1860) • IRISH-ENGLISH WRITER

This is a youth-oriented society, and the joke is on them because youth is a disease from which we all recover.

–DOROTHY FULDHEIM (1893–1989)
FIRST WOMAN TO ANCHOR AMERICAN TELEVISION NEWS PROGRAM

All your youth you want to have your greatness taken for granted; when you find it taken for granted, you are unnerved.

–ELIZABETH BOWEN (1899–1973) • ANGLO-IRISH NOVELIST

Youth has a quickness of apprehension, which it is very apt to mistake for an acuteness of perception.

–HANNAH MORE (1745–1833)
ENGLISH PLAYWRIGHT, RELIGIOUS WRITER, AND PHILANTHROPIST

It's disturbing at my age to look at a young woman's destructive behaviour and hear the echoes of it, of one's own destructiveness in youth.

–HELEN GARNER (1942–) • AUSTRALIAN NOVELIST, JOURNALIST, AND PLAYWRIGHT

Youth cannot know how age thinks and feels. But old men are guilty if they forget what it was to be young.

–J. K. ROWLING (1965–) • ENGLISH WRITER

There's nothing worse than the 25-year-old novelist regarding her own misspent youth. Live first!

–JUDITH KRANTZ (1928–) • AMERICAN WRITER

Youth is stranger than fiction.

–MARCELENE COX
20TH-CENTURY AMERICAN WRITER

I've never understood why people consider youth a time of freedom and joy. It's probably because they have forgotten their own.

–MARGARET ATWOOD (1939–) • CANADIAN POET, NOVELIST, CRITIC, AND ACTIVIST

My idea of hell is to be young again.

–MARGE PIERCY (1936–)
AMERICAN POET, NOVELIST, AND SOCIAL ACTIVIST

The troubles of the young are soon over; they leave no external mark. If you wound the tree in its youth the bark will quickly cover the gash; but when the tree is very old, peeling the bark off, and looking carefully, you will see the scar there still. All that is buried is not dead.

–OLIVE SCHREINER (1855–1920) • SOUTH AFRICAN WRITER, SOCIALIST, AND FEMINIST

Why, I wonder, do people who at one time or another have all been young themselves, and who ought therefore to know better, generalize so suavely and so mendaciously about the golden hours of youth—that period of life when every sorrow seems permanent, and every setback insuperable?

–VERA BRITTAIN (1893–1970) • ENGLISH WRITER, PACIFIST, AND FEMINIST